The Republic Unsettled

The Republic Unsettled

Duke University Press Durham and London 2014

Muslim French and the Contradictions of Secularism

MAYANTHI L. FERNANDO

Designed by Courtney Leigh Baker
Typeset in Quadraat by Westchester Publishing Services

Library of Congress Cataloging-in-Publication Data
Fernando, Mayanthi L.
The republic unsettled : Muslim French and the contradictions of secularism / Mayanthi
L. Fernando.
pages cm
Includes bibliographical references and index.
ISBN 978-0-8223-5734-6 (cloth : alk. paper)
ISBN 978-0-8223-5748-3 (pbk. : alk. paper)
1. Muslims—France.
2. Islam—France.
3. Secularism—France. I. Title.
DC34.5.M87F47 2014
305.6'970944—dc32014000768

Cover art: Maïmouna Guerresi, Infinity Sound 1, 2009. Sculpture in white resin, mirror,
120 × 27 × 22 cm. © Maïmouna Guerresi, courtesy Stux Gallery, New York.

Contents

Acknowledgments

I have been tremendously fortunate in writing this book, and many who were crucial to the project were entirely unpredictable gifts. In Michel-Rolph Trouillot I found an intellectual touchstone and second father. It was Rolph who pushed me to work on France, to attempt an anthropology of the West. He was—to use one of his favorite phrases—the condition of possibility for my scholarship. I am equally grateful to Saba Mahmood, whose guidance has shaped me in ways I am still discovering. Saba was, and remains, a mentor and model, her intellectual rigor consistently matched by her care for me as a scholar and a person. I owe her a debt that can never be repaid. Nawel Gafsia has become a sister. She opened all kinds of doors for my research, and her warmth and integrity always made me feel welcome. I begin the book with her name as a pseudonym in a small gesture of thanks. Monique Nadal took me under her wing and introduced me to Paris, making my two years there not just livable but thoroughly enjoyable. Nawel and Monique did more than make my research possible; they made France my home.

This project began at the University of Chicago. I would like to thank Jean Comaroff, my dissertation committee cochair, who, in a moment of characteristic generosity, took me on as an advisee after Rolph's illness. Her wisdom and determination continue to inspire me. I am indebted to the rest of my committee—Nadia Abu el-Haj, Leora Auslander, and Elizabeth Povinelli—for pushing me in directions I otherwise would not have gone.

In Yarimar Bonilla I found a lifelong friend and interlocutor. Yari has been a sister in arms and kindred spirit from the beginning, and she remains an unparalleled source of affection, laughter, and intellectual and emotional support. Jessica Greenberg, Andrea Muehlebach, and other members of the Anthropology of Europe graduate student workshop were my scholarly anchors at Chicago. The remarkable Anne Ch'ien made everything come together. Anne-Carinne Trouillot continues to make Chicago a home away from home.

This book really took shape at the Institute for Advanced Study, and I thank all the participants in the Secularism seminar there. In Princeton, New Jersey, I lived and grew in ways I never would have imagined, and three people in particular are responsible for that. Joan W. Scott has long been an inspiration. I am honored to have become an interlocutor of hers and am deeply grateful not only for her multiple careful readings of my manuscript, but also for her unparalleled generosity, kindness, and support over the last few years. Gil Anidjar turned everything inside out; his critical engagement, friendship, and care continue to sustain me. Judith Surkis proved that one can think and laugh simultaneously, and it is a pleasure to be in her intellectual and familial orbit.

The University of California, Santa Cruz, is a place like no other, and I am lucky to be surrounded here by exceptional colleagues. Lisa Rofel and Susan Harding have been the mentors all junior faculty members wish for. Lisa read my manuscript on numerous occasions, and she has guided me, supported me, and encouraged me throughout my time at Santa Cruz. Susan's insistence on challenging everything pushed me to think in new ways. I am particularly thankful to Lisa and Susan for persuading me to let my ethnography do more work in the book. I was glad to have Danilyn Rutherford as a writing partner; her unexpected insights propelled my manuscript in novel directions and helped me clarify my arguments. Mark Anderson has become a trusted friend, and I am grateful for how much he looks out for me; a better left tackle I won't find. Andrew Mathews, Anna Tsing, and Matthew Wolf-Meyer helped me to think in more rhizomatic ways. I have also been fortunate to make the Department of Feminist Studies a second home. I laugh constantly with and learn constantly from Anjali Arondekar and Gina Dent, who have looked after me in extraordinary ways. Neda Atanasoski's kindness and friendship sustained me in difficult times. I am grateful to Debbie Gould, another writing partner, for her comments on various chapters and her general camaraderie. The Center for Cultural Studies has been an invaluable site of critical engagement. Debbie Neal,

Fred Deakin, Christina Domitrovich, Courtney Hewitt, and Allyson Ramage have made everything run smoothly. I would also like to acknowledge the support I have received from all my colleagues in the Department of Anthropology and from Sheldon Kamieniecki, dean of the Division of Social Sciences. They let me follow a trajectory that likely would have been impossible at other institutions.

Beyond the redwoods of Santa Cruz, Gary Wilder has been a wonderfully generous interlocutor; his careful comments on my chapters and papers, as well as his own work, have fundamentally reshaped my thinking. Paul Silverstein and Susan Terrio provided much-needed support and guidance from the very beginning of this project, when I was still a graduate student, to its end. Other friends and colleagues have also given generously of their time, providing critique and encouragement at various points. They include Hussein Agrama, Valérie Amiraux, John Bowen, Matti Bunzl, Naomi Davidson, Lara Deeb, Nadia Fadil, Didier Fassin, Eric Fassin, Nilufer Göle, Manu Goswami, Nacira Guénif Souilamas, Steven Hause, Charles Hirschkind, Cécile Laborde, Ruth Mas, Adeline Masquelier, Russell McCutcheon, Megan Moodie, Annelies Moors, Denis Provencher, Lucinda Ramberg, Ruba Salih, Noah Salomon, Andrew Shryock, Benjamin Soares, and Winnifred Sullivan. The manuscript was completed while I was a visiting professor at Wesleyan University, and I am grateful to Jennifer Tucker, Peter Gottschalk, Mary-Jane Rubenstein, and the Feminist, Gender, and Sexual Studies Program for so generously making that opportunity possible.

Beyond the world of academe, Elizabeth Markovits, Bennett Hazlip, and Buddy made my two years in St. Louis a blast. I am happy to have finally joined my surrogate grandparents, Rhoda and Leon Litwack, in California. Clara Petit has kept me grounded. Jessica Seddon continues to teach me that contentment comes in all configurations. Michelle Pollock has picked up the pieces and made me laugh, over and over. And Dorian Bell was a kind and brilliant companion, reading chapters meticulously and encouraging me unfailingly.

My book is based primarily on twenty months of fieldwork in Paris, Rennes, and Nantes, most of it conducted between 2002 and 2004, with additional research undertaken between 2007 and 2011. All names except those of recognizable public figures are pseudonyms. In some ways that is unfortunate, because the book would not have been possible without the generosity of my interlocutors in France, all of whom I wish I could thank by name. They spoke to me candidly and forthrightly about some difficult issues. For their time, openness, and patience with my questions, I would like to thank in particular Farid Abdelkrim; Zahra Ali; the members of Jeunes Musulmans de France in Nantes, al-Houda in Rennes, and the Collectif Une École pour Tou(te)s; my *lycée* colleagues in La Courneuve, especially those on the English team; and the staff and volunteers at the Institut des Cultures d'Islam, especially Soufiane Torkmani and Véronique Rieffel. France is not just a site of fieldwork, though; it has become a home. Kadija Azougach, Youssef Boussoumah, Houria Bouteldja, Julien Clément, Wassila Djamel, Thomas Deltombe, Giuliana Fassano, Chiraz Gafsia, Samira Khattab, Hassan Mezine, Stephen Suffern, Nadia Tahhar, and Hèla Yousfi have kept me going back to Paris all these years. I use some of their names as pseudonyms in homage to their role in making Paris so energizing for me.

Ken Wissoker patiently explained to me a long time ago, when I was fresh out of graduate school, the difference between a dissertation and a book. I am thrilled to have circled back to his astute editorship. I thank the two anonymous readers for Duke University Press, who gave me such productive comments about the manuscript; my copyeditor, Jeanne Ferris; and Elizabeth Ault, Danielle Szulczewski, and the entire editorial team at Duke. I am also very grateful to Anitra Grisales for her keen eye and careful editing of the manuscript.

Finally, I would like to thank various members of my family. The first full version of the manuscript was, somehow fittingly, completed in Colombo, Sri Lanka, when I went back home after eight years away and was surrounded by much love and laughter. My cousin Shalini Dias, whom I have known all my life, made it seem like I had never left. Malsiri Dias, my aunt, remains as generous and formidable as ever. My father, Nalin Fernando, always a wittily unconventional soul, was still impossible to pin down. In Nilan Fernando, I rediscovered a big brother full of equal parts wisdom and mischief, and I treasure my memories of sitting at the dining table at 14 De Fonseka, as I did as a child, finishing this book. Hoppy knows my manuscript better than most, having lain indifferently on various printed drafts; she remains a constant source of unadulterated joy, a being of pure being. Lastly, the independence and integrity of my mother, Marina Wikramanayake Fernando, are an inspiration to me. She has always blazed her own trail, and I would like to hope that I am cut from the same cloth.

The National Science Foundation, Chateaubriand Foundation, Social Science Research Council, U.S. Fulbright Scholar Program, the University of California Hellman Fellows Program, the University of California Center for though they speak French, it is heavily accented, and they are more comfortable in Tunisian Arabic. I sense that Nawel is crying for a few reasons: the strain of more than a year of difficulties at the school, as well as the stress of watching her father humiliated by the principal. This is, of course, a family drama that any child with immigrant parents will recognize, a concatenation of racial, religious, cultural, linguistic, and class asymmetries. In France it emerges from the history of colonization and postcolonial immigration, and it suffuses the ordinary lives of Muslim French, as well as the extraordinary national drama around France's Muslim question.

The teachers at Jean Nouvel felt under siege, too. La Courneuve is home to 35,000 people of eighty different nationalities. Many of its current adult residents arrived in the 1950s and 1960s from French colonies and protectorates in North Africa, recruited as laborers to rebuild postwar France; they married and settled their wives and children in France. Other residents arrived more recently from West Africa, East and South Asia, and Eastern Europe. All of these immigrants' children populate La Courneuve's public schools, including Jean Nouvel, which has seen a massive demographic shift as the white, lower-middle- and working-class parents whose children used to attend the school have moved out of the banlieue. Once a keystone in Paris's Red Belt—the ring of working-class suburbs that were Communist Party strongholds in the first half of the twentieth century—La Courneuve now occupies a very different place in the national imaginary as one of the French Republic's "lost territories" associated with immigrant poverty, rising crime, and failing schools.[1] When I worked there, the unemployment rate was a staggering 28 percent (Sciolino 2005), more than double the national average. That figure is even higher for young people between the ages of eighteen and twenty-five.

Jean Nouvel is often called a difficult school. Classes are large, students can be unruly, and only 50 percent of its students pass the baccalauréat, the national high-school exit exam commonly known as the bac (the national average is 80 percent). And, as in the rest of France, Jean Nouvel has witnessed an Islamic revival among its students. Although still a tiny minority (twenty girls in a school of a thousand students), more girls have begun to wear the headscarf. Some wear plain black hijabs; others wear multicolored hijabs; and still others, like Nawel, wear large cotton wraps tied in a knot at the back of the neck. Before the law of March 15, 2004, some teachers allowed headscarves in their classrooms, while others did not; the school's administration generally left decisions up to individual teachers, and students usually complied, though a few pushed back.

Throughout the month of Ramadan, the cafeteria was nearly empty, since at lunchtime fasting students went home, attended the nearby mosque, or hung out in the library. Teachers complained about the listlessness of fasting students ("they're even lazier than usual," one teacher lamented), and conflicts sometimes arose when students asked for a five-minute break at sundown to end the day's fast. Many students brought dates, the traditional way to break the fast, while others purchased food from vending machines in the lobby. Some teachers allowed students to snack; others forbade what one teacher called "religious rituals in the republican school."

Most teachers found these forms of Islamic practice quite disconcerting, and a number reminded me pointedly of the Third Republic's hard-won battle against the Catholic Church to make public education secular. Many educators continue to see themselves as guardians of the republican school, which they deemed increasingly fragile for overlapping reasons. Since the 1980s various governments have followed a policy of decentralization, and proposals in 2003 to further decentralize school curricula to satisfy regional market needs angered my colleagues. Teachers also bemoaned efforts to integrate French education into a uniform European model. And they were frustrated by the lack of resources: classes often consisted of more than thirty students, some of whom spoke French as a second language. Moreover, many students, fully aware of the dearth of opportunities awaiting them as the children of poor immigrants, were not particularly inclined to work hard or respect the school's authority. The sense of fragility felt by the guardians of the republican school was exacerbated by a quirk of urban geography that put the headquarters of the Union of Islamic Organizations of France (Union des Organisations Islamiques de France, or UOIF) and its large mosque just around the corner from Jean Nouvel. This proximity unsettled a number of teachers, and rumors flew about the UOIF's role in "manipulating" and "radicalizing" Jean Nouvel's students. For many teachers, the UOIF was a wolf at the door, metonymic of an Islamic threat confronting the republican school.

This feeling of being under siege helps make sense of Nawel's treatment and the extraordinary but widespread notion, in the school and in France as a whole, that a few teenage girls in headscarves would destroy the republican school. My field notes mention my initial incomprehension after speaking with Nawel. I describe the asymmetry, beginning with the encounter between Nawel and her head teacher, and the symbolism of that physical discrepancy: a slight young woman facing a burly middle-aged man who represents not just Jean Nouvel's teachers and administrators but also the authority of the entire republican school. Yet, somehow, Nawel is the threat, the "little monster," as one teacher called her, imbued with the capacity to disrupt class, the school, and the French Republic itself.

This book attends to the disruptions caused by "little monsters" like Nawel. Since 1989, when three schoolgirls from the outer suburbs of Paris refused to remove their headscarves in class, a debate has raged about the Muslim question and France's future. That initial headscarf affair—the first of many—signaled the advent of an Islamic revival among the children of North African immigrants, evidenced by the proliferation of Islamic bookstores, civic associations, and modes of dress, all forms of public Muslim religiosity that many French find inimical to secular norms. But the headscarf affair also indexed a broader debate concerning the place of France's Muslim population[2] within the framework of laïcité (secularism), a cornerstone of the French Republic. In the last two decades, the French state has undertaken various measures to manage the Muslim presence in France; these range from exclusionary laws banning headscarves and face veils to the establishment of inclusionary bodies meant to recognize Islam and Muslims.

The trope of disruption underpins many reflections on the headscarf and the general presence of Islam in France. Consider the political philosopher Seyla Benhabib's framing: "L'affair foulard [sic] eventually came to stand for all dilemmas of French national identity in the age of globalization and multiculturalism: how to retain French traditions of laïcité, republican equality, and democratic citizenship in view of . . . the pressures of multiculturalism generated through the presence of second- and third-generation immigrants from Muslim countries on French soil" (2002, 99–100). Benhabib repeats a common narrative in which "second- and third-generation immigrants" disrupt the otherwise seamless traditions of a unified France.

This book adopts a very different notion of disruption, one in which Muslim French like Nawel unsettle taken-for-granted ideas, practices, and norms, exposing the instability and disunity, the contradictions and confusions, and the production and forceful performance—the seams—of the secular republic. It draws on Talal Asad's contention that secularity, because it forms the basis of modern life, is not easy to study directly and must be pursued "through its shadows" (2003, 16). I hold that the emerging forms of Muslim French religiosity and political praxis articulated in the shadows of the secular republic reveal a great deal about French secularism and French republicanism. The book therefore alternates between an analysis of Muslim French politics, ethics, and social life and an analysis of the French secularity that this new Muslim subjectivity reflects and refracts. I explore how Muslim French draw on both Islamic and secular-republican traditions as they fashion new modes of ethical and political engagement, reconfiguring those traditions to imagine a future for France. I also examine how the institutions, political and legal practices, and dominant discourses that comprise French secularity regulate and govern—and profoundly disrupt—Muslim life. In so doing, I trace a series of long-standing tensions and contradictions immanent to laïcité and to republican citizenship, tensions not so much generated as precipitated by the presence of Muslim French. I show how many of these tensions are nevertheless deferred and displaced onto France's Muslims, who, now responsible for the republic's own contradictions, are delegitimated as viable citizen-subjects. Moreover, by not taking the republic for granted as a coherent or stable formation, I examine how secularism and republicanism coalesce despite—or, more precisely, through—their immanent contradictions. Staged around a series of public debates, each chapter of the book focuses on a specific set of tensions that reveal both the tenuousness of secular-republican unity and the process of deferral that helps consolidate a unified, if contradictory, secular national formation.

Thus chapter 1 examines the ambiguity between racial and religious visibility and invisibility in dominant conceptions of Frenchness by analyzing the difficulty of being Muslim French when those two terms—Muslim, French—are considered incommensurable. Chapters 2 and 5 attend to the tension between universal and particular in secular-republican citizenship, the former by taking up the refusal of Muslim French to portray public religiosity as a claim to difference, and the latter by examining the crucial role that secular Muslim women play in secularism's self-narrative of universal progress. Chapter 3 considers state attempts to turn Islam into a proper religion, discrete from culture and politics; I argue that these attempts ironically destabilize the separation between religion and politics that is supposed to constitute the basis of secularism. Taking up the 2004 ban on headscarves, chapter 4 explores the tension between the imperatives of autonomy and authority that underpin the production of secular citizens. And chapter 6, which focuses on accusations of Muslim homophobia, examines the impasse between competing obligations to respect personal autonomy and to abide by moral norms that underlie secular tolerance.

In tracing these tensions through an anthropological account of contemporary France, this book takes a particular approach to history, one that attempts to hold onto both continuities and discontinuities between past and present. Without discounting the constantly evolving nature of modern French politics, law, and public discourse, I am nonetheless interested in the structuring logics of French republicanism and French secularity. Thus, when attending to the specificity of Muslim exclusion from French citizenship over the past three decades, I also revisit the tension between abstract universalism and embodied particularism that has historically been entrenched in republican citizenship. Similarly, I analyze the distinct iteration of Muslim alterity in the postcolonial present but also examine how it draws on earlier, colonial configurations of the Muslim "native." And I explore the state's new attempts to secularize Islam in relation to colonial-era projects of modernization and transformation, thereby tracing a long-standing ambivalence in French secularism between separating and interweaving religion and politics. In other words, even as I recognize and analyze the distinctiveness of contemporary laïcité and republicanism, I consider these formations as longue durée phenomena, just as I take seriously the colonial legacies of the postcolonial intersection of Islamic and secular-republican traditions.

Unsettling France

In 1989, at the height of the first headscarf affair, Minister of Education Lionel Jospin asked the Conseil d'Etat, the highest administrative court in France, to give a legal opinion. The Conseil declared that headscarves were permitted in public schools as long as they were not ostentatious, the wearer did not proselytize, and the headscarf did not disrupt the regular functioning of the school. The Conseil essentially called on school principals to judge the headscarf contextually, and over the next fourteen years, it refined its jurisprudence through a series of other decisions. By the early 2000s, however, numerous politicians and pundits were clamoring for "clarity" in schools and better protection for the principle of laïcité. In July 2003 President Jacques Chirac appointed a commission of academics, political functionaries, and education specialists to study threats to laïcité and propose solutions. In December 2003 the Stasi Commission—named after its president, Bernard Stasi—released a report that recommended, among other measures, a law banning the wearing of conspicuous religious signs (signes religieux ostensibles) in public schools. In his introductory letter to

President Chirac, Stasi affirmed that these measures "would make the principle of laïcité, the foundation of national unity, recognized and respected by all who live in our territory" (Commission de Réflexion 2004, 9).

What most irked critics of the Conseil's initial ruling was its advocacy of case-by-case adjudication, which they claimed produced only ambiguity and disunity. Gisèle Halimi, an influential feminist and lawyer, called the method "a patchwork lacking any rigor," adding that "disparate decisions . . . put our republican principles in danger in the long run" (Halimi 2003, 66). In his January 2004 report on the proposed law banning headscarves and other religious symbols, Pascal Clément, a deputy in the French parliament, referred to the Conseil's jurisprudence as "an ambiguous juridical regime" (Clément 2004, 10). For critics like Clément and Halimi, such ambiguity contravened laïcité and thus threatened the republic itself. The journalist Christophe Barbier declared the law against headscarves a necessary step to ensure the future of France. "Laïcité is no longer a principle; it is a battlefield," he wrote. The National Assembly's vote on the proposed law "will determine if the republic is closer to Waterloo or to Austerlitz" (Barbier 2004).[3]

In the months preceding the vote, members of the Stasi Commission spoke at a number of public venues; though these events were advertised as debates, any disagreement came from the audience only. In February 2004, I attended one such event at the Museum of the Art and History of Judaism in Paris. Rémy Schwartz, the commission's general secretary, began by noting that despite a diversity of opinions and philosophies among the members of the commission, all twenty-six propositions in its report had been adopted unanimously. This was not quite accurate; the historian Jean Baubérot had abstained from the commission's proposal to ban religious signs. Schwartz obliquely referenced Baubérot's abstention but deftly swept it aside, observing: "As everyone knows, an abstention is not an opposition." The disavowal of dissension occurred at a broader level as well. Polls showed that although many teachers supported the proposed law, substantial numbers of them remained opposed or ambivalent, and these national polls echoed the internal divisions I witnessed at Jean Nouvel. Moreover, the Education League—the largest federation of French educators, with over two million members—opposed the law. Nonetheless, most of the national media and the political elite continued to portray teachers as a monolithic bloc desirous of a law that would bring clarity.

At the end of the event at the Museum of the Art and History of Judaism, an audience member asked the panelists why the Stasi Commission had not called for reevaluating the status of Alsace-Moselle, a region in northeast France bordering Germany. Alsace-Moselle was annexed from France by Prussia in 1870 and was not part of the French Republic when a 1905 law separating church and state went into effect in the rest of France; though reincorporated into the republic after World War I, it continues to be ruled under a Napoleon-era Concordat system. In Alsace-Moselle, Catholicism, Calvinism, Lutheranism, and Judaism remain officially recognized religions, and religious education in one of these four is obligatory for public school students there. In addition, the French president names the archbishop of Strasbourg and the bishop of Metz—two major cities in the region—and the French state pays the salaries of clergy from the four recognized religions. Responding to the audience member's question, Schwartz declared that the people of Alsace-Moselle were strongly attached to the Concordat tradition and that it was important to respect local law. Throughout the evening, Schwartz had criticized the "patchwork" approach to the headscarf and reiterated the need for one law that would uphold laïcité and national unity. He seemed oblivious to any inconsistency in his sudden defense of local law and tradition when it came to Alsace-Moselle.

In his concluding remarks, Schwartz returned to the theme of eroding national identity, lamenting the decline of French national dignity: "What do we propose today to immigrants with regard to pride in being French? I'm not saying glorify France systematically, but we have gone from a laudatory way of thinking to permanent denigration. . . . We have to stop this self-denigration and create a certain pride in living in this country."

Schwartz was clearly worried about the future of France, and he was not alone. In 2009 the Ministry of Immigration, Integration, and National Identity initiated a Grand Debate on National Identity, comprising a website and a series of public forums around the country. The debate followed a 2007 presidential campaign in which bolstering French national identity was an important theme. Moreover, a growing list of popular nonfiction works is devoted to the greatness and longevity of the French nation, such as Max Gallo's *Fier d'être français* (Proud to be French; 2006), which traces a continuous French identity all the way back to the eighth century. One could interpret this obsessive reiteration of national identity as a postimperial condition, generated by France's decline as a world power and by immigration to the metropole from its former colonies. To focus entirely on the changes wrought by decolonization, however, concedes too much to the newness of disunion and fragmentation and seems to assume an earlier France that was more stable, cohesive, and settled. Yet that was never the case. Before the 1789 Revolution, direct contact between the central government and residents of the provinces was limited, and in southern regions like Gascony and Provence, the name France often referred simply to a small area with Paris at its center (Robb 2007, 25). Until the mid-nineteenth century, most people refused to identify with the nation, or even with their province; they belonged to a town, a suburb, a village, or a family (25). A 1794 report, written for the governing National Convention by the Abbé Henri Grégoire and called "The Necessity and Means of Exterminating Patois and Universalizing the Use of the French Language," found that more than six million French citizens did not speak the national language, and another six million were only barely conversant in it. Although French was the lingua franca of European elites, only 11 percent of the population of France used French as their first language (53). Well into the nineteenth century, French citizens held onto village and provincial loyalties and spoke languages other than French, such as Catalan, Flemish, Alsatian, Breton, Basque, Corsican, and Occitan. This linguistic multiplicity propelled the Third Republic's pedagogical mission to "turn peasants into Frenchmen" (Weber 1976). Regional identities have nonetheless remained powerful, as nationalist and devolutionist movements in Corsica, Occitania, Brittany, and the Basque country—not to mention overseas separatist movements in Guadeloupe and New Caledonia—attest.

Furthermore, though the 1958 constitution and the official seal of the republic affirm that France is one and indivisible, republican power has long operated through differential legal and political arrangements. The most obvious examples occurred in French colonies and protectorates, where the French empire functioned through a variegated legal and political system. Not only were assorted imperial outposts—including Indochina, Algeria, Senegal, Mauritius, Guadeloupe, Tahiti, French Guyana, and Pondicherry—governed differently from each other, but even within a single political unit, distinct legal regimes applied to distinct populations (Lebovics 1992; Silverstein 2004; Wilder 2005; Saada 2006). Thus in colonial Algeria, different legal systems existed for Kabyles, Arab Muslims, and Jews, a situation deemed entirely compatible with republican unity (Shepard 2006).

This composite arrangement applies to secularism as well; Schwartz affirmed it even as he lamented the disunity of France. Though laïcité is often declared to be a cornerstone of the republic, it has never been a unified or stable formation. If secular rule can be defined broadly as the determination of where to draw the line between the religious and the political (Agrama 2012), this determination has differed consistently within what wear headscarves. The teachers did not press the issue with the principal since they had let Nawel wear her hijab for more than a month. Nonetheless, her life became more difficult. One of her professors barely spoke to her. Another asked why she was hiding her beautiful hair. A third asked her to remove the headscarf in class but otherwise continued to treat her as before. Nawel found it particularly ironic that she was treated differently than her friend Sonia, who also wore a headscarf—but only outside of school, so the teachers had no idea that she too was a practicing Muslim.

Nawel ended up failing her final exams and decided to repeat her second year; when she went to register at the school, however, she was told there were no more slots. She found out a few days later from one of her professors that this was untrue, and that Jean Nouvel was actually recruiting students for its BTS program. So Nawel went to the local board of education, which called the school and found her a place. She returned to the school, without her headscarf, and registered with the principal, who was new and did not know her as the veiled problem student.

Then began the drama.

A few days after registering, Nawel was called to the principal's office. Her head teacher had complained about her reappearance to the principal, who was irate. "We didn't accept you here," he yelled, "and you don't have the right to come back. Your teacher came down to see me and he told me that he had refused you a place." Nawel, nervous but annoyed, shot back: "He doesn't have the right to reject me. You do. You had a place open, the local board of education found me that open place, and now you're required to keep me."

The principal promptly threw her out of his office. In tears, she called her father, who came at once to the school. But when they went to see the principal together, the principal began shouting at her father.

At this point in her story, Nawel begins to cry. Embarrassed, I look down at my white plastic coffee cup. Nawel keeps talking as she cries: "The principal just treated him like garbage, like he was a piece of shit." She looks up at me, still crying, and says, "Excuse me." I'm about to ask her if she wants to stop the interview, but she keeps going: "When it happens to you, you don't care. But when it happens to someone in your family, when you see your father, who has done so much for you . . ." Her voice trails off, then she continues: "I'm not someone who loses her cool easily, but that day, wow, I really insulted the principal before we finally left."

I imagine the scene. Nawel's father, a window washer, came to France as a teenager in the early 1970s from a village in Tunisia. Once in Paris, he married a woman from the same village. Neither parent has a high-school degree;

Introduction

Nawel and I sit at a Formica table in a small room next to the library at the Lycée Jean Nouvel, a public high school in a working-class immigrant suburb (*banlieue*) named La Courneuve, on the northeast perimeter of Paris. The windows in the room look out onto the school's entrance and beyond, to the looming housing projects and black asphalt that have come to define La Courneuve. Nawel is studying for a *brevet de technicien supérieure* (BTS)—akin to a two-year associate's degree—in communications. Because of her poor grades, she is repeating her final year in the program.

Nawel had been in my class the previous year, when I taught BTS students as part of my job as a language assistant at the school, but this is my first lengthy meeting with her. She is twenty years old, a wisp of a girl with wide, dark eyes set in a pale, bird-like face. Her hair is covered by a black headscarf, or hijab, that is coiled into a large knot at the back of her neck. She wears no makeup, and she is dressed in a white tunic and black trousers. I ask her to tell me about her headscarf troubles at school.

Nawel's second year of the BTS program had not gone well. She began to wear a headscarf at the beginning of the year. At first, the teachers took it for a fashion statement. When it became clear that Nawel was wearing it every day, they realized it was "the veil" (*le voile*), and some of them told her she did not have the right to wear it. This was incorrect, since the law of March 15, 2004, banning conspicuous religious signs in public schools had yet to be passed, but confusion reigned in the school about whether students could

New Racial Studies, and the Committee on Research at the University of California, Santa Cruz, all funded research for this book. The writing of it was enabled by a Woodrow Wilson Foundation Charlotte W. Newcombe fellowship, as well as an Andrew W. Mellon postdoctoral fellowship in Modeling Interdisciplinary Inquiry at Washington University in St. Louis. While I was at the Institute for Advanced Study, I benefited from a University of California President's Faculty Fellowship.

Parts of chapter 4 appeared in "Reconfiguring Freedom: Muslim Piety and the Limits of Secular Law and Public Discourse in France," in *American Ethnologist*, and in "Belief in/and the Law," in *Method & Theory in the Study of Religion*. Sections of chapter 5 also appeared as "Exceptional Citizens: Secular Muslim Women and the Politics of Difference in France," in *Social Anthropology*, and as "Save the Muslim Woman, Save the Republic: Ni Putes Ni Soumises and the Ruse of Neo-Liberal Sovereignty," in a special issue of *Modern and Contemporary France* on Maghrebi-French sexualities. I thank the publishers and journals for permitting me to reuse this material. I would also like to thank the Collective against Islamophobia in France and William Barylo for permission to use their photograph in chapter 1.

scholars often take as a singular, coherent French model of secularism. The 1905 "law of separation," imagined as the foundation of modern laïcité, was not fully applied in French Algeria until 1947 even though Algeria, unlike most other colonies, was ruled as a department of France rather than an overseas territory. Even today, eight different legal regimes organize relations between state and religion in metropolitan and overseas France. In the overseas department of French Guyana, for example, Catholicism is still regulated according to an 1828 royal ordinance, and the department pays the salaries of Catholic clergy. In Mayotte, another overseas department with a Muslim majority, local customary law continues to be applied.

This variegated secularism exists in metropolitan France as well. As noted above, Alsace-Moselle continues to be governed by the Napoleonic Concordat system, with four recognized religions subsidized and regulated by the state. The 1905 law of separation itself contains a number of confluences between the state and organized religion. It stipulates, for instance, that the state pay the salaries of clergy working in hospitals and prisons, and though it forbids state financing of new religious buildings, it allows the government to pay maintenance costs for religious edifices built before 1905. Thanks to later laws, the state also subsidizes private religious schools, most of them Catholic. The point is not that secular sovereignty entails making exceptions (cf. T. Asad 2006; Mas 2006). Rather, Algeria and Alsace-Moselle are not so much exceptions as examples, indicative of the heterogeneous arrangement of secular rule in France. The case-by-case administrative jurisprudence regarding headscarves in school was actually very much in line with the political and legal practice of French secularism.

What are the political and analytical implications of the simultaneous reproduction and disavowal of France as a fragmented legal, political, and social formation? Politically, the discrepancy between the ideological commitment to unity and the reality of a composite system poses a problem for Muslims. When Muslim French demand the kind of accommodations offered to other religious communities in France—for example, state-funded Muslim schools and a school calendar that observes Muslim holy days—they are reminded that France is a secular country where proper citizenship requires the separation of religious and political life. Thus Muslim claims to equal citizenship within the legal and political parameters of laïcité paradoxically become the basis for questioning Muslims' fitness as citizens.

But analytically, too, how does one attend to both the inchoate quality of France and the regulatory force of its legal and political apparatus? How does one study an object—the secular French Republic—that constantly posits its own unity but is in fact rife with disunity and contradiction, that is never entirely coherent but has significant effects on the subjects it regulates? In answering this question, I draw on theorists of sexuality who argue that sex and gender norms, inconsistent and unstable as they might be, nonetheless have enormous regulatory power (Foucault 1978; Butler 1993). Indeed, the historian Judith Surkis argues that "instability, rather than undermining masculinity as a regulatory political and social ideal [in nineteenth-century France], actually lent it its force" (2006, 8). The fragmentary and unsettled nature of republican secularism likewise does not diminish its power but rather enhances it through a continual process of reiteration, rearticulation, and regeneration. Precisely because it remains inchoate and fragmentary, and because tensions and contradictions suffuse its imperatives and norms, the secular formation called France must continually reconstitute itself as a cohesive entity, redrawing its boundaries and regulating its subjects. To productively analyze this process we must examine the secular republic's contradictions, on the one hand, and its effects as a regulatory political project, on the other.

Muslim French

Since the mid-1990s France, like the rest of the world, has experienced an Islamic revival, defined as the unprecedented engagement with scholarly texts and theological reasoning by Muslims not necessarily trained at traditional religious institutions (Eickelman and Piscatori 1996; Hirschkind 2006).[4] In France those involved are primarily the children and sometimes the grandchildren of immigrants from Algeria, Morocco, and Tunisia. Participants also include young people of West African descent, white and Antillean converts to Islam, and older first-generation immigrants who came to France as laborers or foreign students. As in the rest of the Middle East and North Africa, the Islamic revival in France encompasses many doctrinal trends, political sensibilities, and ritual and hermeneutical practices. Moreover, in France generational divergences add to this diversity. My analysis therefore does not apply to all participants in the Islamic revival, and certainly not to all Muslims in France. Most of my Muslim interlocutors were from the second generation[5]—the children of immigrants from the Maghreb and, to a lesser extent, sub-Saharan Africa. A few were converts. Almost all had been born in France, and all had grown up there, mostly in the blue-collar suburbs of Paris, Rennes, Nantes, and Lyon. In addition, though their parents were part of a proletarian workforce, most of my interlocutors had their *bac*, and many were studying for or already had higher degrees, often in communications, education, accounting, or social work.

The practices and sensibilities I describe are particularly relevant to those I call Muslim French: women and men committed to practicing Islam as French citizens and to practicing French citizenship as pious Muslims. Muslim French create and participate in Islamic civic associations, found and frequent Islamic bookstores, wear various forms of modest Islamic dress, run voter registration drives, and write editorials and blog posts on national issues. They also work toward reforming immigration laws, alleviating inner-city poverty, and ensuring religious freedom. Their actions and sensibilities constitute what Lara Deeb (2006) calls publicly engaged religiosity, which sets aside the distinction between public politics and private religiosity usually considered to be the grounds for secular democracy. Muslim French religious and ethical commitments are fused with their political commitments. Though many define themselves as practicing and not just believing Muslims (*musulmans pratiquants* versus *musulmans croyants*), it is not simply their adherence to ritual practices like praying, fasting, or veiling but their *public* practice of Islam that provokes secular consternation. For Muslim French, however, democratic citizenship and public religiosity are entirely compatible. Muslim French are therefore distinct from adherents of other revivalist movements like the pietist Tabligh wa Daʿwa and various rigorist Salafi groups. Tablighis and Salafis are generally indifferent to identifying as French and show little interest in civic engagement as citizens. In contrast, Muslim French understand themselves as French, staking a claim to France and its future. This entails working against their social, political, and economic marginalization, and against a dominant imaginary that continually excludes Muslims.

The republican model of citizenship ostensibly treats individuals as individuals rather than as members of a community, and it therefore requires immigrants to subsume any particular ethnic, racial, cultural, or religious attachments to a universal French national identity. Yet nonwhite immigrants and their descendants are subjected to systematic discrimination on the basis of their race, culture, and religion. Nonwhite citizens and residents suffer disproportionately high levels of unemployment (Silverstein and Tetreault 2005; Wacquant 2009) and face discrimination in the hiring process (De Rudder and Vourc'h 2006). They are disproportionately imprisoned, due in part to rampant racial profiling and differential treatment in the criminal justice system (Jobard 2005; Terrio 2009; D. Fassin 2011). Immigrant-headed households are overrepresented in public housing projects (Lepoutre 2001;

Silverstein and Tetreault 2005). The children of poor and nonwhite immigrants also disproportionately attend overcrowded, underfunded public schools (Van Zanten 2006), and the republican school, long considered the crucible for turning immigrant children into citizens, has become a site for the reproduction of inequality (Keaton 2006). As Étienne Balibar writes, nonwhite young people are "contradictorily *excluded* as 'non-citizens' [from the French Republic] . . . to which they only have limited illegitimate access, but of which they are *themselves a part, that in a way is part of themselves* and their identity" (2007, 51 [emphasis in original]). Balibar calls this predicament internal exclusion.

Aside from a growing number of commentators in France who favor a "clash of civilizations" thesis,[6] many analysts argue that the French Islamic revival is fueled by internal exclusion and the concomitant contradiction between an ideal universalist republicanism that claims not to differentiate and the reality of the social, political, and economic marginalization of citizens and residents of North African descent (Gaspard and Khosrokhavar 1995; Khosrokhavar 1997b; Cesari 1998; Auslander 2000; Bouzar 2001 and 2004; Göle 2005). This contradiction has produced, these scholars argue, a crisis of belonging among the members of the second generation who, born and educated in France, are no longer Tunisian, Moroccan, or Algerian, nor are they regarded as fully French. Turning to Islam, especially in a growing climate of social, political, and legal Islamophobia, becomes a way to affirm a communalist identity against the failed universalism of French republicanism.

Although we must acknowledge the predicament of internal exclusion, this conventional framework often treats Islam as a means for various ends: social valorization, communal identification, opposition to the state, existential comfort, and so forth. But it says little about how young people fashion themselves into pious Muslims and their resulting ethical and political subjectivities. Without disputing the fact that some revivalists begin their self-transformation in reaction to Islamophobia, turning signs of stigma into signs of prestige (Göle 2005), I wish to go further and examine in more depth my Muslim French interlocutors' engagement with theological, doctrinal, and hermeneutical debates within the Islamic tradition. Drawing on the work of Saba Mahmood (2005) and Charles Hirschkind (2006), I examine the modes of argumentation and ethical practice through which Muslim French become what they consider proper Muslims.[7] At the same time, I also attend to the specificity of the French context, asking how Muslims' status as minorities transforms the ethical and political commitments deemed essential to Islam, and how Muslim French imbrication in secular-republican epistemologies and values affects their engagement with Islamic traditions. I am interested, too, in how Muslim French, drawing on certain Islamic political orientations and hermeneutics of the self, speak back to, unsettle, challenge, and reconfigure dominant secular-republican assumptions.

The question remains of how to theorize the exclusion of Muslims from dominant conceptions of the nation without reinscribing or naturalizing that predicament; here I follow the lead of my Muslim interlocutors by taking seriously their claims to Frenchness. This means breaking with the analytic paradigm of immigration-integration that underpins many studies of Arab-Muslim life in France. That paradigm made sense in important earlier scholarship (Noiriel 1988; Weil 1991; Sayad 2004) dealing with immigrants who were not French nationals, yet some (for example, Cesari 2004; Laurence and Vaisse 2006) continue employing it to think about nonmigrants born and raised in France who experience exclusion quite differently.[8] To take Muslim French claims to Frenchness seriously, then, I engage with a different set of ideas about citizenship, pluralism, secularism, and religious and racial difference. I also propose the neologism *Muslim French*. The self-description that I heard most often from my interlocutors was *citoyen français de confession musulmane* (French citizen of Muslim faith). I translate that lengthy term as *Muslim French*, a decision I explain in more detail in chapter 1. The neologism is supposed to be linguistically awkward, just as the identity it describes does not fit easily into the conventional imagination. Recognizing Muslim French claims as those of citizens will, I hope, destabilize standard notions both of France and of Islam.

Citizenship and the Problem of Difference

Given the dominant non-Muslim majority's perception of Muslims as different and even dangerous, and given Muslims' exclusion from the national imaginary, it is unsurprising that the framework of difference grounds much of the theorizing about the Muslim question in France, and in the West more broadly. What remains notable, however, is the tendency to collapse ethno-racial, cultural, and religious lines of differentiation and subordination. Most political theorists of multiculturalism continue to use a facile notion of culture as the model for interpreting other attachments, including ethical ones. For many of these theorists, what is often called cultural membership is not defined by norms but rather by what the political philosopher Will Kymlicka calls "a shared heritage (language, history, etc.)" (1989, 168).[9] Liberal nation-states enable minority communities to flourish by allowing them to "express their cultural particularity and pride" (Kymlicka 1995, 31). A number of critics have rightly taken Kymlicka and like-minded theorists to task for their notion of cultures as hermetically sealed and unchanging (Markell 2003; Song 2007), but these critics have largely missed how this concept of culture also cannot comprehend certain forms of deep ethical or religious attachment. For Kymlicka, religious practices are expressions of membership, as if religion—or culture or ethnicity—were a club to which one publicly belonged. Kymlicka is not alone in using the language of expression to describe religiosity; many scholars regard the practice of veiling, for instance, as the expression of a sociopolitical or religious identity, signaling the wearer's membership in a particular group (Göle 1996; Khosrokhavar 1997a; Keaton 2006). This framework of religion as culture cannot conceptualize Islam as an authoritative system of norms that engenders deep ethical and moral commitments on the part of the practitioner.

If some analysts tend to collapse religion into culture, other scholars writing on the Islamic revival in France privilege race and class, treating religious identity and religious discrimination as epiphenomenal to more primary forms of belonging and exclusion. Christian Joppke, for example, maintains that "the real causes of disadvantage" for Muslims in Europe "are mainly socio-economic" (2009, 109). Similarly, Balibar argues that "religion functions as a refuge and a substitute for social recognition" in a context of pauperization and discrimination (2007, 56). Although he acknowledges that religion can play a central role in how actors see themselves, he nonetheless insists that religious discrimination is "essentially a component of a more general *racial* (or neo-racial) discrimination" and that "religion functions essentially as an index of racial identity" (56 [emphasis in original]). My point is not that "the real causes of disadvantage" are religious. Rather, it is that analysts need to consider more comprehensively the distinctive problem that public Muslim religiosity poses for the secular state. Using a framework that flattens race, religion, and culture or that considers religion epiphenomenal to race and class often leads us to misconstrue the specific nature of certain forms of public religiosity and to misunderstand both the secular republican state's exclusions and the kind of counterclaims that Islamic revivalists make.

Balibar's otherwise incisive analysis illustrates this conceptual and political problem. For him, religion organizes the private sphere and focuses "on control of the family and in particular on the relation of the sexes" (2007, 56). As a result, religion cannot be the basis for political critique or political praxis, unlike racial or class identities. This quintessentially secular interpretation of religion as private and apolitical cannot grasp the political imagination of Muslim French as anything but fundamentalism born out of socioeconomic frustration. This interpretation also takes for granted the boundary between public and private that ostensibly defines secularity but that is constantly trespassed by secular power (Surkis 2010; Agrama 2012; Fernando 2014). That is to say, it misunderstands the nature of secular rule. Balibar's belief that only religion, and not secularism too, regulates family and sexuality underscores my point that inattention to the distinctive problem of Muslim piety misdiagnoses the recent controversies and overlooks the tensions of secular government precipitated by its interpellation of Muslims. Race and/or class prove inadequate as the primary analytical lens, and in many instances a framework of religion and secularity is more productive. The latter better captures the ethical and political orientations of many Muslim French. It also attends to how Muslim French unsettle secular assumptions about the self, community, agency, authority, politics, and citizenship, and how contemporary conflicts are often symptomatic of long-standing tensions integral to secularity itself.

This does not mean that race should be ignored; after all, Muslims are increasingly perceived, both in France and elsewhere in the West, in racialized terms (Geisser 2003; Modood 2005; D. Fassin and E. Fassin 2006; Puar 2007; El-Tayeb 2011). The term *Muslims* has come to identify, pejoratively, a population of North and West African descent, whose members a few decades earlier were referred to either as immigrants and foreigners, or with terms that marked their ethnicity or national origin. The recent invocation in mainstream public and political discourse of the signifier *Muslim* signals, then, less the increasing religiosity of this population than a fusion of racial, religious, and cultural bases for alterity. Didier Fassin (2006) has written of the emergence in France of a racism without race that is evident in terminological slippages—the confusion between *immigré* (immigrant) and *d'origine immigré* (of immigrant origin), *maghrébin* (Maghrebi) and *d'origine maghrébine* (of Maghrebi origin), *musulman* (Muslim) and *maghrébin* (Maghrebi)—and in common euphemisms such as *les jeunes* (youth) and *les banlieusards* (outer-city residents), as well as in the amalgamation in public discourse and political legislation of immigration, delinquency, terrorism, and Islam. What Fassin means is that the classical biological basis of race has been culturalized;

race, religion, and culture now intertwine to construct a reified notion of radical alterity that takes the signifier Muslim (musulman).[10]

Fassin is correct, of course. But this intertwining is not new. It constitutes not an emergence so much as a reemergence, a reinstantiation of a much older process of interpellation, categorization, and differentiation. The people now (or once again) called Muslim were previously Arabs (Arabes) in the post-1974 era of economic downturn that led to the official end of labor migration, immigrant laborers (travailleurs immigrés) before that, and musulmans or natives (indigènes) in the colonial period. Race and religion have always formed a nexus. In colonial Algeria there was never a strict division between race and religion, and race referred to a community of values that were not necessarily biological but were no less intractable (Saada 2006). Algerians were Arabs were Muslims.[11] Similarly, even if the alterity of immigrant workers and Arabs was coded as ethnic, racial, or cultural, these populations' intractable Muslimness thoroughly informed that coding. Muslimness as a marker of alterity and identity was never absent before the recent Islamic revival; it was just nested within an alterity framed as primarily racial, cultural, or ethnic. Without ignoring the specific contours of the new Islamophobia (Geisser 2003; Hajjat and Mohammed 2013) that has emerged in the wake of the 1979 Iranian Revolution and the global Islamic revival, nor of the new racism to which Fassin gestures, we should nonetheless remember that contemporary designations of the Muslim as Other continue to draw on older figurations of alterity.[12]

This book examines the nexus of race and religion in France by keeping in mind both the historicity and the contemporaneity of the Muslim as Other. In tracing the continuities and discontinuities between colonial and postcolonial constructions of race and religion, I show how racialization and secularization intersect to produce contemporary forms of Muslim alterity.[13] Moreover, rather than simply take for granted that religious and racial alterity come together to construct Muslim difference, the book examines the processes, both historical and contemporary, that generate race and religion as distinct categories of rule and as fundamentally imbricated in the figure of the Muslim. It attends to the inconsistencies of racial and religious thinking—to the production of race and religion as distinct ontologies, on the one hand, and to the simultaneous isomorphism of race and religion in the figure of the Muslim, on the other hand. It also asks how racial and religious difference operates across a sexual matrix, and how particular heterosexual norms provide the grounds for distinguishing between us (French) and them (Muslims) within the overlapping narratives of secularism and republicanism.

At the same time, the construction of Muslim difference in France is not purely a process of homogenization and exclusion. Much recent scholarship on both sides of the Atlantic has focused on Muslim minorities as a problem for French national identity, presenting the matter either as a clash of civilizations (Joppke 2009) or as the illegitimate exclusion of Muslims from the republic (Geisser 2003; Keaton 2006; J. Scott 2007). What unites these otherwise divergent arguments is the notion that French national identity is secured through the exclusion of a homogeneous Muslim difference, an analytical framework that underpins wider-ranging studies of Muslim alterity in the West as well (see, for example, Puar 2007; El-Tayeb 2011). Yet modern political power does not always seek to homogenize or obliterate difference; it also "works effectively through institutionalized differences . . . disaggregating subject populations in order to better administer them" (T. Asad 1993, 264). Accordingly, liberal states govern minorities, and in the process reinforce national identity and state sovereignty, through acts not just of exclusion but of inclusion too (Markell 2003; W. Brown 2008). Exclusion is certainly a major part of the story. A wholesale focus on exclusion, though, misses the myriad political, legal, and social regulatory practices through which Muslims have been included in France as forms of commensurable difference, practices I treat in more depth in chapters 2, 3, and 5 and that signal the transformative force of republican secularism.

Secularism

Secularism, in France and elsewhere, is generally understood to entail three overlapping phenomena: the political and juridical separation of church and state; the retreat of religion to the private sphere; and the increasingly insignificant role of religion in people's daily lives. In France the significance of laïcité was long thought to lie in the separation of church and state, which guarantees the absolute neutrality of the public and political realms. Most public intellectuals focusing on laïcité laud the way the secular state, through various acts of legislation in the nineteenth century, extricated public and political life from the grip of the Catholic Church. "The essential innovation of the twentieth century," writes the renowned historian and philosopher Marcel Gauchet, "is the putting into place of a partition of the collective between a properly political sphere and a civil sphere, between a sphere of public life and a sphere of private interests" (1997, 53). Laïcité, according to Gauchet and many others (Coq 1995; Kintzler 1998; Poulat 2003; Baubérot and Milot 2011), secures the autonomy of politics from religion and that of religion from politics, institutionalizes the neutrality of the public sphere, and guarantees the freedom of individual conscience. In recent years the focus on Muslims, and their ostensible inability to separate public politics and private religiosity, has tilted the emphasis toward the privatization of religion, with laïcité presented as a cultural norm integral to national identity. Islam has been portrayed as antagonistic to laïcité and, concomitantly, as needing to be secularized—sometimes with punitive laws—so as to conform. At the same time, a few critics have distinguished this culturalist, interventionist, and often Islamophobic laïcité (which they term la laïcité nouvelle) from historical laïcité (la laïcité historique), which they see as a more neutral juridical and political arrangement that guarantees rather than constrains religious freedom (see, for example, Baubérot and Milot 2011).

I tell a different story about laïcité, one that does not make such a stark distinction between la laïcité nouvelle and la laïcité historique, and one that takes laïcité as a sustained project of governmentality that did not begin, or end, with the famous 1905 law of separation. This story is about the imbrication of religion and politics rather than their separation, about active state management rather than neutrality, and about the production and regulation of religious subjects rather than simply the guarantee of their freedom. It therefore treats recent laws against veiling (usually understood as repressive tactics) and the state's establishment of institutions like the French Council on the Muslim Religion and the Institute for the Cultures of Islam (usually understood as inclusionary gestures) as part of an array of disciplinary techniques aimed at cultivating properly religious (that is, secular) Muslim subjects.

Talal Asad (1993 and 2003) has paved the way for contemporary scholars to study secularism as a pattern of political rule, rather than a space-clearing arrangement that institutes political and legal neutrality. Secularism is a historically evolving, normative project of government that entails the administrative intervention into and transformation of what are called, retroactively, religious traditions, institutions, and sensibilities. As many scholars now argue, the notion of religion itself—understood as a set of propositions or beliefs to which the believer assents; a sphere of life separate from politics, science, or the economy; and a transhistorical and transgeographical phenomenon—is an effect of secularism (D. Scott 1999; Agrama 2012). In order to deal with religion, either to regulate it and/or to protect it, secular authorities must first identify it. Hussein Agrama contends that, as a result, "the [secular] state is always drawing a line between the religious and the secular . . . [by] promoting an abstract notion of 'religion,' defining the spaces it should inhabit, authorizing the sensibilities proper to it, and then working to discipline actual religious traditions so as to conform to this abstract notion to fit into those spaces, and to express those sensibilities" (2010, 503). This produces a tension immanent to the secular republic: the political, legal, and institutional discourses and practices that attempt to separate religion from politics, and to make Islam private, must constantly breach the very boundary that secular government attempts to establish between the two. Although many recent critical analyses of secularism, including Agrama's, have justly focused on the effects of legal transformation, especially in the colonial period, this book considers the French state's projects of reformation not only in contemporary law and politics but also in social and cultural life.

Significantly, to argue that secular rule regulates religious life is not to argue that this entails a contradiction of or deviation from secularism, as if there could be a form of secular rule that did not regulate religion and that did not imbricate the religious and the political. Nor is it to posit the existence of more or less secular states. Indeed, I hope that my analysis of *laïcité* will put to rest the notion that France, and laicism more generally, is somehow further along the separation spectrum than other models of secularism, including the United States (cf. Hurd 2008; Joppke 2009). Scholars like Janet Jakobsen and Ann Pellegrini (2004) find the American state's regulation of sexuality to be an overly religious project that contradicts secularism; they call for a truly secular state that would fully separate religion from politics and allow real religious and sexual freedom. In contrast, I regard the regulation of religion (and, incidentally, of sex), and the competing imperatives of separation and administration, as crucial to secularism's operation. Like Agrama (2012), I am interested precisely in the intractable tensions of secular rule. But I am just as interested in how these tensions are displaced onto the subjects of regulation who become targets of an impossible reformation. The tensions of secularism, I argue, are asymmetrically distributed in a constant recalibration that sustains secular rule. Muslims, seen as incapable of separating religion from politics, become the sources of contradiction, rather than secular rule itself.

Moreover, secularism is not a totalizing or monolithic project: as the example of Alsace-Moselle demonstrates, secular rule has always been variegated. Its decisions have also been haunted by contingency and instability.[14] If secular rule involves determining where to draw the line between religion and politics (T. Asad 2006; Agrama 2012), it must first define what constitutes religion, disaggregating religion from other forms of social identity and communal attachment and separating it from the spheres of politics, economy, and law. But as this book demonstrates, decisions about what constitutes religion—as opposed to race, culture, and politics—are never settled and often raise new questions and new dilemmas. Take, for instance, the 2004 law banning headscarves in French public schools. Many scholars have rightly focused on the peculiar nature of secular sovereignty, whereby legal and political authorities determine "the signs of religion's presence" (T. Asad 2006, 500). What has been less scrutinized is how the authoritative determination of the headscarf as a religious sign provoked a series of new questions about what constitutes religion, what makes a sign, and how to distinguish between religious and other forms of identity. If headscarves were religious signs, were not beards as well—and in that case, how would one tell an Islamic beard from a secular one? Hence the Ministry of Education's short-lived effort to consider the question of excessively hirsute schoolboys. Moreover, were Sikh turbans religious signs or, as many teachers at the Lycée Jean Nouvel believed, ethno-cultural ones? The Ministry of Education determined that they were religious. And what to do about the overseas department of Mayotte, where the majority of the population is Muslim, many schoolgirls cover their heads, and the law of 1905 has never been applied? There was initially some doubt about whether the 2004 law should apply in Mayotte; when the National Assembly decided that it should, the ministry nonetheless determined that headscarves in Mayotte were cultural, not religious, and that local school authorities would have more leeway than their counterparts in metropolitan France in deciding whether to enforce the law. That raised the question as to whether Muslim schoolgirls in the metropole could simply declare their headscarves cultural and continue to wear them, since the law bans religious signs, not cultural ones.

The point is that determining the signs of religion's presence is a slippery and always incomplete task. It continually raises new questions and creates the need for more decisions, undermining not so much the authority or sovereignty of the decision maker but the possibility of a final decision that will not raise new questions. Yet in many ways, it is precisely this instability, and the need for boundary-drawing decisions, that constitutes and reconstitutes secular power. As chapter 3 demonstrates, the attempt to secularize Islam by turning it into religion, distinct from culture and politics, simultaneously renders the distinction between religion and culture unstable and the separation between religion and politics untenable. Rather than undermine the project of secularization, however, the failure to disaggregate religion, culture, and politics simply generates other attempts at reform. The confusions and conflations that secularization produces continue to figure the Muslim as a subject in need of secularization. That project is never finished, which is precisely what constitutes its regulatory force.

It would be easy to view this fraught interpellation of Muslims as peculiar to France, and thus to read my arguments in a culturalist vein, as particular to French republican secularism. Americans often point out how much more tolerant U.S. secularism is than the French version, or they conversely point to laïcité as a truly separationist secularism that does not privilege Christianity the way American secularism does.[15] Other studies less invested in the positive or negative attributes of French versus American secularism have nevertheless proposed various models of secularism—secularisms in the plural rather than a singular secularism—that play out differently in different parts of the world (Hurd 2008; Jakobsen and Pellegrini 2008; Hurd and Cady 2010). Yet there exist striking convergences between secularity in France and secular formations elsewhere, including various tensions and contradictions. I am, therefore, unconvinced of the analytical purchase of pluralizing secularism, and I take my analysis of French secularity to bear on considerations of secularity more generally. I appreciate efforts to provincialize secularism's supposed universality and agree that secularity operates differently across historical time and geographical space. After all, laïcité emerges out of a particular set of historical circumstances, and France's current controversies are generated by a particular modality of Muslim difference. Nonetheless, it remains important to attend to the globalizing power of the sensibilities, forms of sociality, and political and legal arrangements that secularity entails and enacts. I am less interested in whether or not the categories and configurations of the secular are universally translatable than in the attempt to make them so. To take just one example, minority religiosities often become similarly unintelligible within the legal regimes that protect religious freedom in France and the United States, two countries with very different histories of the theological-political; this convergence indicates a shared normalizing force to secularity that an analytic of pluralization misses. We certainly must not accept secularism's claim to universality, but we do need to attend to the broad, trans-Atlantic genealogy of its formation, to the effects of its universalizing imperatives, and to the increasing hegemony of the sensibilities and political, legal, and institutional practices that make secularism a global project.

Silences and Asymmetries

Linking the epistemological, methodological, and political purchase of anthropology, Asad once observed that the traditional Geertzian approach of translating across cultures by making strange concepts familiar is "too comforting. . . . I would like to think that that kind of translation forces one to rethink some of our own traditional categories and concepts" (quoted in D. Scott 2006, 274). In a somewhat different linkage of the epistemological, methodological, and political, Michel-Rolph Trouillot (2003) distinguishes between an object of study and an object of observation. Collapsing the two, he argues, turns cultural formations into closed units outside global webs of power and history; differentiating the two, and using one's object of observation to access a broader object of study, enables anthropologists to attend to wider patterns of power relations—that is, the historical processes and global flows that produce our objects of observation in the first place. Trouillot also argues that anthropologists need to "reassess the epistemological status of the native voice, to recognize its competency so as to make the native a potential—if not a full—interlocutor" (2003, 136).

This book takes my Muslim French interlocutors seriously as sources of knowledge and as theorists (and not simply practitioners) in their own right. Conversely, I treat the conceptual arguments of secular-republican philosophers and public intellectuals as political practices, too. Though perhaps less recognizable as ethnography than the sections on Muslim French, my discussions of these intellectuals constitute an ethnography of the French public sphere, in which public discourse both reflects sociopolitical norms and contributes to their production and evolution. These figures represent, reproduce, and reconfigure a secular-republican tradition that engages and constrains Muslim French life in a range of ways.

I carried out most of my field research between 2002 and 2004 in Paris, Nantes, and Rennes, with shorter research trips to Paris between 2007 and 2011.[16] Importantly, in addition to observation and conversation, my fieldwork consisted of active involvement in some of the political associations my Muslim French interlocutors belonged to, most notably the One School for All Collective that mobilized against the 2004 ban on headscarves. I often found myself in political solidarity with a general mobilization against racism and Islamophobia, though I did not always see eye to eye with my more conservative Muslim interlocutors, especially with regard to gender and sexuality, and I was sometimes uncomfortable with their strict moralism. Yet I found that long discussions generated by these disagreements—about the ethics of polygamy, the purchase and meaning of gender equality, the practice of premarital sex, and the moral status of homosexuality—helped me understand these interlocutors' worldviews and the network of principles and concepts that underpins them. These simultaneous convergences and divergences also helped me carefully consider the possibilities, and impasses, of alliances between disparate groups, which I trace in chapters 2 and 6.

Moreover, although critics have already debunked the fantasy of objectivity in fieldwork and scholarship, of a clear distinction between inside and outside (see, for example, Clifford and Marcus 1986), it is equally important to note that active participation and subjective solidarities can open up rather than close off analysis. When I first went to the field, I imagined a more classic ethnography of Muslim French life, in which my object of observation and object of study were one. It was precisely close attention to the experiences of my Muslim French interlocutors that led me to widen my analytical lens, turning it toward the source of their often tenuous predicament—namely, the secular republic's discourses, institutions, and political and legal practices. For example, if my Muslim interlocutors insisted on their Frenchness, why were their claims dismissed? If they insisted that the headscarf was both a choice and an obligation, why was this so hard for secular law and public discourse to grasp? If Muslim French experiences remained my object of observation, republican secularism—and its contradictions, contingencies, and anxieties—emerged as my object of study. At the same time, though my book is not a classic ethnography of Muslims, neither is it a classic ethnography of France in all its diversity. It is, instead, an inquiry into dominant modes of secular-republican power.

One could argue that I might just as well have focused on the contradictions of Islam, rather than (or in addition to) those of secularism. Such critiques of Islam already abound, and they often reflect secular assumptions about ethics, politics, and the human (see, for example, Roy 1994; Schielke 2009; Bangstad 2011). In contrast, my book traces how many of the tensions in Muslim French discourse—the accentuation of Muslimness while demanding a right to indifference, the reinscription of exclusive nationalism while insisting on inclusion, the claiming of the headscarf as both a choice like any other and integral to the pious self—are produced by Muslims' embeddedness in France, and by the contradictory demands that the secular-republican state and society make on them. My analytical method here draws on Joan Scott's seminal *Only Paradoxes to Offer*, which traces how the ambiguities of republicanism have been "carried into and exposed by feminist arguments" in different historical periods (1996, 11). But my method also emerges from my ethnography: attending closely to forms of Muslim French religiosity and political praxis, including the tensions within, redirected me to the contingencies and contradictions of secularism and republicanism that Muslim French life reflects and refracts.

That method produced the book's asymmetrical structure, in which my object of study, and therefore my object of critique, remains secular-republican power. To attempt some kind of symmetry would miss the point, for my analytical focus proceeds from the situation on the ground: the secular republic interpellates subjects in asymmetrical ways, displacing the burden of its immanent contradictions onto Muslims and turning Muslims into a national problem, not vice versa. Muslim French are an object of serious consternation in France, and therefore a common object of study for French sociologists, anthropologists, and political scientists as well as a common target of governmental intervention. This book is a purposeful attempt to redirect that political and analytical attention precisely by taking it as my object of study and, ultimately, critique.

Nevertheless, we should remember the fundamentally asymmetrical structure of American anthropology (and of American power), which often turns its gaze outward to other societies without much reflection on American society itself (Trouillot 2003). Though not a comparative study, this book is written against such a paradigm. I purposely locate French secularism and French republicanism within a broad North Atlantic tradition, which accounts for my tacking back and forth between French and Anglo-American political philosophy, both contemporary and foundational. Though they may play out differently, and with different marginalized populations, the exclusions and contradictions I trace here anchor American society, too, a point American readers should not forget.

One final caveat: Muslim French are not my main object of study, but they remain an object of ethnographic observation, in a context in which there is an active political interest and investment in knowing about Muslims in France. Just as their ancestors were surveilled by a colonial apparatus that depended on a symbiotic relationship between the state and social scientists (Lorcin 1999), Muslims remain the objects of much postcolonial attention, not only for the state security service but for academics and journalists as well, a fact not lost on my interlocutors. In addition, much of the research that takes place is policy driven. That which is not concerned with delineating and rooting out so-called extremism is largely framed in terms of a series of overlapping questions: Are Muslims integrated? If not, how can they be? Is Islam compatible with democracy (or secularism or feminism)? Can Islam be French? Muslim French cannot escape the sense that they are consistently under the microscope, a problem to be solved, the objects of ethnographic, sociological, and ultimately political interest. Indeed, part of their claim to Frenchness involves a desire to be ordinary, what one of my interlocutors referred to as his "right to indifference," his right "to be forgotten."

The insistent desire for and production of knowledge about Islam are not restricted to France, of course. A quick look just at academic job listings reveals a demand for specialists of Islam, an unsurprising fact given our global context, in which maintaining Trouillot's distinction between one's object of observation and one's object of study can be difficult. Many anthropologists (myself included) see themselves as scholars working on secularism or sovereignty or the state but were hired as scholars of Islam and teach undergraduates who expect to learn about Islam and Muslims—that is, about the Savage, not the construction of the Savage slot (Trouillot 2003). As I think more about my interlocutor's demand for indifference, I often wonder whether we—whether I—should simply stop talking about Islam, given that we sit at the heart of an empire with a vested interest in knowing about Muslims. Beyond the geopolitical location of our knowledge production, there remains the more pragmatic problem that, despite our best political intentions, our work is sometimes, even often, willfully misread, misinterpreted, and misused. And beyond that is the question of intelligibility itself. As much as we try to represent the "epistemological competence" of our interlocutors (Trouillot 2003, 133), their insights—as well as ours—are not always intelligible or thinkable. The flip side of trying to make the unfamiliar familiar is that we end up making the unfamiliar even more unfamiliar, with potentially dramatic consequences.

Yet if anthropologists of Islam were simply to fall silent, we would leave the field of expertise to scholars like Bernard Lewis, Gilles Kepel, and Samuel Huntington, whose work, views, and collaboration with neocolonial governments many of us are writing in opposition to. We have to function as counterexperts; without us, there wouldn't even be damage control. So as much as I want to respect my interlocutors' right to indifference, I am not sure how to go about doing so, or even if I should try. Do I fall silent about Muslim French, undertaking a kind of ethnographic refusal?[17] Do I simply turn my ethnographic lens to the dominant West? But how could I do so without reinscribing the North Atlantic as, once again, the center of the world? Besides, other disciplines in the humanities and social sciences—political science, political theory, sociology, literature, psychology, and economics—already teach Americans and Europeans about themselves. Doesn't the provincialization of Europe (Chakrabarty 2000) require, if not an Other or an Elsewhere, then at least a someone else and a somewhere else for perspective and critique? After more than ten years of working in this field and grappling with these issues, I keep coming back to a phrase from Trouillot's infinitely provocative meditation on the culture concept that gestures to the always open future, to the pitfalls and possibilities, of our work and our words. "Once launched," wrote Trouillot, "the concepts we work with take on a life of their own. They follow trajectories that we cannot always predict or correct [and] there is no guarantee that the final meaning will be ours" (2003, 112).

FIELD NOTES I   "Vive la République Plurielle"

In January 2004 the law school at the University of Paris II hosted an event, open to the public, called "*Laïcité* in Question?" The Stasi Commission had submitted its report a month earlier; the event at the University of Paris featured Bernard Stasi and Jacqueline Costa-Lascoux, two members of the commission.

I went with two friends—Claire, a PhD student working on Egyptian legal history, and Najette, a Franco-Tunisian immigration lawyer—and we sat in the balcony section. The rest of the audience was composed largely of upper-middle-class white students from the University of Paris. About thirty minutes into the event, a young man and three women entered the room and sat down near the front. Not knowing the university, a cavernous maze of hallways and stairwells, they had got lost finding the room. All four were in their early twenties, of Maghrebi descent, and members of the Muslim Students of France (Étudiants Musulmans de France, or EMF), a satellite wing of the Union of Islamic Organizations of France. Two of the women wore brightly colored headscarves.

The moderator, a professor of law at the university, introduced Stasi, a longtime state bureaucrat. In his remarks, Stasi emphasized that the commission had heard from a wide range of social and political actors, that *laïcité* was what enabled us to live together (*vivre ensemble*), and that a law banning headscarves would not jeopardize religious liberty. He also took great pains to reiterate that the commission had not simply determined whether to ban the veil in schools, nor had its work concerned only Islam or Muslims. "The essential issue was not the veil," he said. "*Laïcité* is first of all about tolerance, not interdiction." The veil had become the central issue, Stasi claimed, because Muslims felt particularly targeted, even though the law bans all conspicuous religious signs, a point he reiterated numerous times. Stasi seemed genuinely chagrined that political and media discourse had ignored the commission's other twenty-five propositions. These included making Aïd el Kébir[1] and Yom Kippur school holidays; offering a course in Islam as one option alongside already existing courses in Catholicism, Lutheranism, and Judaism for public schools' religious education curriculum in Alsace-Moselle; and adopting a charter of *laïcité* to be recited at various occasions and prominently displayed in schools and city halls. But Stasi's disappointment with the direction of national debate was rather odd, since the occasion for the commission's convening and the bulk of its report concerned the supposed threats to *laïcité* by Muslim *communautarisme* (communalism). Moreover, the commission devoted many pages of its report to the international legality of banning the headscarf in particular.

This dissonance—or what the French disparagingly call *le double discours* (double talk)—was repeated when Costa-Lascoux spoke after Stasi. A well-known sociologist of immigration, Costa-Lascoux explained that most of the commission's members had initially been against a law banning headscarves in public schools but had changed their minds during the course of the commission's work. Costa-Lascoux put herself in that camp and said she had been persuaded after hearing about "everything that goes on in various public domains, in schools, hospitals, courts." She gave examples of female patients who refuse treatment from male doctors, of magistrates whose objectivity is questioned because their last names sound Jewish, of women in the army who refuse to take first-aid courses because touching a man in cardiac arrest—"even in order to save his life," Costa-Lascoux kept reiterating—would be impure. Particularly interesting about Costa-Lascoux's examples was that though she did not explicitly mention Islam or Muslims, these are all common instances in the ongoing public debate about Muslim communalism in immigrant *banlieues*. Costa-Lascoux added that she had also been moved to change her mind about a legal ban after hearing testimony from Muslim women. "'Protect us,' they said," according to Costa-Lascoux. The sociologist explained that people "who have traveled thousands of kilometers to live in a democratic country should be protected." At this point I wondered what the two young veiled women from the EMF were thinking, women who had not traveled thousands of kilometers to come to France but had rather been born there, women who were neatly elided from Costa-Lascoux's impassioned speech. They and other women like them had also been largely overlooked by the commission itself, which only on the very last day of its proceedings heard from any French-born women who wore the headscarf by choice, and then only at the request of Jean Baubérot, who was surprised that they were not already on the commission's list of people to consult.

After the two commission members spoke, the moderator opened the floor to questions, and in a barb directed at the four EMF students, he thanked those in the audience who had come on time. "That is what we call respect and tolerance," the professor remarked. He then specified that the first set of questions should be limited to the subject of jurisprudence concerning laïcité. A student in the audience asked if there was a juridical definition of the term; Stasi said no. Another student then inquired, mentioning the EMF by name, about the problem of student organizations with "a communalist platform," and Costa-Lascoux responded that such threats were only just the beginning. A third member of the audience observed that the root problem lay not in specific cases but in communautarisme itself, and that it concerned not only Muslims but Jews as well. Stasi agreed, noting, "communalism is contagious." At this point, Claire, who had had her hand up for a while but was not being called on by the moderator, began to shout out her question, decrying how the law banning headscarves in public schools was both neocolonialist and an attack on religious liberty. The moderator shouted her down, yelling—falsely—that the debate was only for students from Paris I and Paris II. Najette, a former student at Paris I, immediately raised her hand. Assuming that she and Claire were there together and that Najette would make a similar point, the moderator refused to call on her, noting sarcastically, "Yes, yes, we know what your question is."

After taking a few more innocuous questions, the moderator turned to Stasi and Costa-Lascoux and thanked them, declaring the event over, at which point Farah, one of the EMF students, quickly raised her hand. She was ignored. When I asked her afterward why she hadn't raised her hand earlier, she told me her question did not concern jurisprudence specifically and she had assumed the moderator would make it clear when more general questions could be asked. As everyone else stood up to leave, Soufiane, the male EMF member, pleaded with the audience and presenters to stay so that they could all, Muslim students included, discuss the proposed legislation and its effects on young Muslim women, but most of the audience paid no attention to him and began to file out. Before Stasi stepped down from the dais, he said, very loudly and earnestly, shaking his fist, "*Vive la république* [Long live the republic]!" The EMF students, who were standing near the stage, responded, "Yes, long live the republic!" One of them, named Assia, quickly added, "Long live the plural republic [*Vive la république plurielle*]!" As Stasi pushed past them, Soufiane commented, referring to Stasi's parting shot, "There they go again, as if we're not French too."

One   "The Republic Is Mine"

Farid Abdelkrim's father was born in 1918 in a small town in Algeria. He came to metropolitan France when he was twenty-five to work for the SNCF, the national railway. Like many Maghrebi immigrants, Farid's father arrived in France thanks to a coordinated effort by the French government and French industry to import manual labor from the colonies, which began in the years between the world wars and accelerated after World War II. Once in France, Farid's father married Farid's mother, also an Algerian immigrant. Born in 1967, Farid grew up in Bellevue, a low-income neighborhood in the city of Nantes. Dotted with high-rise housing projects, Bellevue is inhabited mostly by North African and West African immigrants and their French-born children.

Farid was not a particularly successful student and was encouraged to attend a vocational high school, still a common educational venue for a disproportionate number of nonwhite teenagers in France. Nor was he particularly involved in any civic associations, the bedrock of French social and political life. As a teenager, Farid, like many of his friends, had taken to vandalism, drugs, petty larceny, and car theft. Then, a few months before Farid's eighteenth birthday, his friend Radouane was shot and killed by a policeman. Radouane's death and his wake at a Muslim center led to Farid's spiritual and political awakening. Until this time, Farid had not prayed or fasted, and, as he put it, he did "a lot of things that have nothing to do with Islam." But at Radouane's wake Farid met three foreign students from North Africa who had come to pursue their graduate degrees in France. All three were practicing Muslims, and Farid was impressed by their educational success, general ambition, and spiritual commitment. They, in turn, encouraged him not only to study but also to seek a more profound engagement with the Islamic tradition. Farid soon became what he called a more practicing Muslim: he began to pray, abstain from alcohol and drugs, and alter his previous behavior in significant ways. Yet individual spiritual practice was not enough; he also wanted to do something for his community and his peers. He knew from personal experience that at this time (the late 1980s), most mosques served only first-generation immigrants: "Young people, if they came, it was to pray, but they weren't really taken into account. Friday sermons were done in Arabic, sermons during the week were done in Arabic, there was nothing for young people. So we said to ourselves, we have to find a bridge between this Islam, of which our parents are the bearers, and a generation that knows nothing of its religion." He and some friends created the Association for Change (Association pour Changer) to offer courses in Arabic, after-school tutoring, social activities, and conferences on Islam.

In the early 1990s the association invited a young man named Hassan Equioussen to speak at one of its conferences. Equioussen was already active within the influential Union of Islamic Organizations of France (Union des Organisations Islamiques de France, or UOIF), and through him Farid came to know the UOIF leaders. In 1992 he was chosen, along with Equioussen and some other young Muslim activists, to form a UOIF-affiliated youth movement called Young Muslims of France (Jeunes Musulmans de France, or JMF), with local chapters in major cities across the country. Farid became president of JMF-Nantes, then of the entire JMF, stepping down in 2000. Since then, he has published two books that combine autobiography, self-help, and political and social commentary. He also served as a member of the UOIF's executive board and tours the country as a speaker at weekend conferences hosted by mosques, Islamic bookstores, and local Muslim associations.

On April 20, 2003, Farid took the stage at Le Bourget, a convention center on the northern outskirts of Paris where, since 1983, the UOIF has held an ever-growing annual congress. In 2003 about 80,000 people attended the four-day event, which drew Muslims not only from Paris and its suburbs but also from all over France, as well as from neighboring Belgium. Attendees jostled past each other as they went from stall to stall in the crowded exhibit hall, perusing books and recorded sermons; searching for prayer mats and prayer beads; and browsing through racks of clothing, which ranged from traditional *jellabas* and *abayas* to hip-hop–style tracksuits by the American Muslim company Dawah Wear. Men and women, most of them between sixteen and forty, stood in line outside the fatwa tent, where Islamic scholars affiliated with the UOIF issued religious opinions in response to individuals' queries. Bustling vendors in the cafeteria served halal couscous, sandwiches, and french fries. Visitors from out of town slept in the sex-segregated dormitories fashioned out of former airplane hangars. As always, the congress also featured four days of panels with presentations by Muslim intellectuals, activists, and religious scholars.

Farid strode onstage dressed in a black shirt and black trousers, with a pair of black plastic glasses perched on his nose. Built like a rugby player and brimming with charisma, he immediately established a sense of familiarity with his audience, alternating between joking self-deprecation and an aggressive, sometimes haranguing, exhortation. He began his speech by invoking his dead father, who had come to France to work for the national railway—not as a conductor or a driver, Farid noted pointedly, but as a track-layer. Farid spoke eloquently and forcefully about the need for historical memory, reminding his audience: "Our parents built this country on their backs." He then turned to the present. "Stop talking to me about integration!" he thundered to wild applause. "I am here, and I am French. France is my homeland, the republic is mine [La France est mon bled, la république est la mienne]." He urged the crowd to choose the party they preferred and to vote in municipal, regional, and national elections, declaring to much applause that "we are not genetically conditioned to vote for the Left." The previous evening, Nicolas Sarkozy—then minister of the interior—had given the keynote address, and Farid suddenly asked, half jesting, half serious, "Would you vote for me if I were interior minister?" At this point, the 10,000-strong crowd roared in appreciation, and many people, most of them in their twenties and thirties, rose to give Farid a standing ovation, while older members of the UOIF looked on in consternation and tried to get the rowdy crowd to sit down. Farid ended his speech with a booming exhortation: "Engagement, engagement, engagement!"[1]

In *The Suffering of* the *Immigrant*, a seminal ethnography of immigration and exile from the late 1970s, the sociologist Abdelmalek Sayad writes eloquently of Algerian laborers who migrated to France and of the double absence they endure, being neither fully in Algeria nor fully in France. One key mode of first-generation immigrant life that Sayad recounts is what he calls politeness—that is, how the immigrant is "always anxious not to disturb [the dominant majority] because a foreign presence is always a cause for concern" (2004, 289). As a result, Sayad writes, immigrants either become as invisible as they can, or they reassure their hosts "by attenuating the distinctive signs that make them stand out" (290). "But the height of both civil and political impoliteness," he continues, "seems to be attained by those 'immigrants' who are not immigrants: the children of immigrants. . . . They are not foreigners in cultural terms, as they are integral products of this society. . . . Nor are they foreigners in national terms. . . . We therefore do not know how to regard or treat these new-style immigrants, nor do we know what to expect of them" (291).[2]

The terms Sayad uses to describe postcolonial France—invisibility and visibility, politeness and impoliteness, "immigrants" who are not immigrants—help frame this chapter and the next, which take up questions of citizenship and the management of so-called Muslim difference. Republican citizenship demands that individuals abstract their particular racial or religious identities in order to be proper, universal citizens. This distinction between particular and universal maps onto the distinction between religion and politics that undergirds secularism as a political arrangement, in which religion is privatized and religious commitments are divorced from political engagement. The distinctions between universal and particular, public and private, and politics and religion produce the Muslim question as a matter of visibility and invisibility: to be an integrated, secular citizen means abstracting one's Muslimness and rendering it invisible in the public sphere. Conversely, to embrace one's particularity in the public sphere is to threaten the civic unity and universality of the French Republic. Doing so represents a form of *communautarisme*, best glossed as communalism or neotribalism and defined as the practice of enclosing oneself in one's community and privileging particular ethnic, racial, or religious affiliations over national ones. Yet the insistence that Muslims become publicly invisible as Muslims is a ruse, for Islam has always marked colonial and postcolonial subjects of North African descent as distinctively Other, as not French.

Moreover, even though secular republican citizenship remains grounded in a distinction between universal and particular, the French Republic has been defined since its inception by its imperatives to both universalize and particularize (Wilder 2007). Hence the concurrently contractual and cultural bases of republican citizenship: though ostensibly a universalist contract between abstract citizens, the republican nation has always presumed particular ethnic, racial, religious, and kinship norms that privilege whiteness, Christianity, maleness, and heterosexuality.[3] It is precisely this tension that both demands that Muslims abstract their Muslimness in the public sphere and makes impossible any such abstraction. Taking seriously Farid's claim that "France is my homeland," in this chapter I trace the ways Muslim French refuse to remain politely invisible and how they define their Muslimness as always already French. I also examine the difficulties of inhabiting Muslim French identity when the very term *Muslim French* functions as an oxymoron for much of French society, and when being publicly and visibly Muslim renders one invisible, unviable, and unrecognizable as French. In sum, I analyze the dilemma of how to be Muslim French in a world in which Muslim means not French and French means not Muslim— that is, how to inhabit an identity that is unintelligible in the terms of dominant discourse, and how to be recognized as oneself when one is unrecognizable as what one is.

"Muslims, You Know, Are Part of French Society"

The French Islamic revival has taken form in diverse ways: the proliferation of Islamic bookstores and publishing houses, the production and circulation of books and taped lectures by European Muslim preachers and scholars, the formation of large federations like the UOIF, the increasing presence of men and women in "modest" Muslim dress, the construction of mosques both large and small, and demands on the state for the public recognition of what is often called France's second religion. Farid's personal trajectory exemplifies how local associations in particular have emerged as key sites in the formation and propagation of both piety and civic consciousness among Muslims. Although civic and civil associations have long been an integral element of French citizenship and immigrant integration into the nation, contemporary Muslim associations reflect a generational shift from ethno-racial to religious forms of identifications as well as more recent ideas about the relationship of Islam to France.

Farid came of age during a key moment in these developments. In 1981, as part of its program of decentralization and what was called the right to difference (*le droit à la différence*), the newly elected Socialist government lifted restrictions on the establishment of associations by nonnationals, spurring the social and political activism of North African immigrants and their children and culminating in what became known as the Beur movement.[4] Deploying a language of hybridity, Beur youth opted for an in-between status, claiming to be neither fully French nor fully Algerian but rather Beur (Cesari

1994; Silverstein 2004). At once civically, politically, and culturally oriented, Beurs demonstrated against racism, created local ethno-cultural and political associations to serve immigrant-origin populations, and produced music and literature that expressed Beur political subjectivity (Silverstein 2004). The Beur generation was purposefully secular, formulating its relationship to the Islamic tradition as a cultural attachment rather than a religious or ethical one. Most Beurs accepted the notions that religiosity should be a matter of private belief and that Islamic practices like fasting at Ramadan should be confined to the private sphere of the home. Consequently, the kind of visibility Beurs sought to valorize and make acceptable in the public sphere concerned their ethno-cultural difference, not their Muslimness, which was conceptualized as purely religious and therefore private. Although originally launched as a sharp critique of French racism and narrow conceptions of national identity, the Beur movement was ultimately co-opted by the Socialist Party, and a number of Beur activists have had political careers within the party. By the mid-1990s, a nascent Islamic revival among second-generation youth had replaced the Beur generation.

Although most analysts consider the Beur movement to be the major outcome of the 1981 deregulation of immigrant associations, the effect was actually more widespread. Self-consciously Islamic associations, such as the UOIF, were established by pietist and Islamist foreign students who, fleeing anti-Islamist crackdowns in Tunisia and Morocco and all-out war in Algeria, laid some of the institutional and ideological foundations for the contemporary Islamic revival in France.[5] Farid's spiritual awakening, as he put it, grew out of his interaction with pious foreign students, and his personal history parallels the broader generational shift from an ethno-cultural identity to a publicly religious one, as well as the latter's institutionalization in local associations. I differentiate between ethno-cultural and religious associations not to reinscribe the distinction between culture and religion so central to laïcité, but to underline the shift in how civic activists saw themselves and the relationship between political action and the Islamic tradition. Farid and other activists began to break down the notion of religion as a discrete form of life separate from culture and politics, and to move past the religion-politics dichotomy thought to be foundational to political action.

If the JMF grew directly out of the institutional largesse of the UOIF and remains strongly affiliated with the organization, the Union of Young Muslims (Union des Jeunes Musulmans, or UJM) has always been a more independent, and often more politically progressive, association. Founded in 1987 by a group of Franco-Maghrebi men in their early twenties living in the *banlieues* of Lyon, the UJM was one of the first second-generation associations to explicitly identify itself as Muslim instead of Maghrebi, Beur, or antiracist, and it is widely considered the prototype of second-generation Islamic associations. Although similar to Beur social welfare associations established earlier in the decade with its after-school tutoring and social activities for *banlieue* youth, the UJM's avowedly Muslim character—even featuring the word *Muslim* in its title—constituted a marked departure from the avowed secularity of those earlier associations. From its inception, the UJM organized conferences on Islam and offered courses in Arabic. Strongly allied with the Muslim Swiss intellectual Tariq Ramadan in its early years, the UJM established a publishing house, Editions Tawhid, which continues to publish numerous books on Islam, both original works in French and translations of work in Arabic. Editions Tawhid also produces and sells recordings of lectures by intellectuals like Ramadan and preachers like Equioussen. In the mid-2000s, a number of UJM activists left the association, creating other local associations and joining with activists around the country to found the national-level Collective of French Muslims (Collectif de Musulmans de France, or CMF).

Younès, a social worker of Tunisian descent in his early forties, was a founding member of the UJM and CMF who came of age in Lyon during the Beur movement. Though a decade older than Farid, Younès also lived a life of petty delinquency before turning first to Trotskyite groups and then to Islam and what he termed a respectable citizenship. He recalled how he and many of his peers felt frustrated not only by his parents' generation's seeming disregard for the linguistic and sociocultural sensibilities of youth born or raised in France, but also by the Beur generation's emphasis on ethnocultural rather than religious aspects of their identity. Though he shared the Beurs' criticism of French racism and attended some political meetings after the 1983 March for Equality and Against Racism, he "would have felt like a Martian among earthlings" if he had participated more fully: "How would I have prayed with those guys? They were always thinking about smoking hash, picking up girls, clubs, evenings out, alcohol, you know? There weren't any limits." Beyond their lack of piety, Younès was severely critical of the Beurs for what he perceived as their shame in even being associated with Islam: "Instead of going by Mohammed, they went by Momo, they distorted their identity. Fatima no longer wanted to be called Fatima but Fofo. Oh, it's true! I lived through this period, when people hid their identity . . . because it was embarrassing to be associated with something backward." Though the Beurs' active criticism of French racism certainly cannot be called polite invisibility, Younès nonetheless faulted them for attempting to render their Muslimness invisible in order to fit in.

Throughout the 1990s, local associations like the UJM and JMF were self-consciously and publicly Muslim.[6] I asked Mohammed, a member of the governing board of JMF-Nantes, why the organization had opted for the appellation *jeunes Musulmans* (young Muslims) instead of *jeunes Nantais* (young Nantians) or *jeunes Maghrébins* (young Maghrebis). He replied: "Because we are here! Muslims, you know, are part of French society, and we said to ourselves that we have to show that we aren't entirely separate as citizens but that we are part of the French landscape, that we are here [as Muslims]." Younès echoed Mohammed's explanation in stronger terms:

> After the failure of the March for Equality and Against Racism in 1983—after the failure, really, of those who wanted to play at assimilation at all costs—we realized that there was a dimension of our identity that was hidden . . . that was sometimes demonized . . . sometimes by Muslims themselves, who rejected Islam and considered Islam as something retrograde, not adapted to the West, to democracy, to modern society. But we who began to live our spirituality realized that this wasn't true, that there wasn't any incompatibility, that this was a preconception, a prejudice that the slave had appropriated from his master.

Mohammed and Younès identify a shift in associational politics that reflects and reproduces a broader shift in the second generation's self-conception: in their engagement with the Islamic tradition, young people of Maghrebi descent treat Islam as an authoritative source of disciplinary practice and reject the separation between public politics and private religion that is so central to secularism. Unlike their parents and the Beur generation, members of the JMF and UJM and like-minded Islamic revivalists refuse to attenuate, as Sayad put it, the distinctive signs that make them stand out. In fact, as Younès indicated, the project of assimilation failed largely because the signs that make this population distinctive (race, religion—in a word, Islam) cannot be erased. Rejecting even the attempt to become invisible, actively embracing a self-consciously Muslim identity, and understanding their public religiosity as entirely compatible with Frenchness, Muslim French assert their right to practice Islam in both private and public, to be piously and visibly Muslim in the public sphere. In so doing, they unsettle the notion that private religiosity can be separated from public politics and that embodied particularity can be abstracted to create a universal republican citizenship. They also reframe their relationship to France beyond the Beur ethos of hybridity, reimagining the link between Muslimness and Frenchness.

L'Autre, or le Musulman

Héla was born in the Parisian working-class suburb of Sartrouville to Tunisian parents who had come to France in the late 1960s. She and her four brothers grew up in a household that was not particularly pious, and it was only in high school that Héla began to engage more self-consciously with the Islamic tradition, reading the Quran and studying the translated work of Islamic scholars. She started to pray regularly and decided to don the hijab at age twenty, much to the chagrin of her parents. "It was catastrophic," she told me, laughing at her family's horrified reaction to her patterned headscarves. "They are part of a generation," she speculated, "that wanted above all to integrate. I don't think about France like that." What Héla meant was that she took for granted her belonging, her Frenchness, her integration. "I'm French," she said, "I vote here, I obey the law here, and once I'm done with school I'll pay my taxes here." She told me that members of the second generation are "much more vocal than their parents because they were born here, they belong here, they are French. Our parents' generation didn't dare claim their rights. The second generation, we know our rights, we're waking up, we're demanding more things than our parents ever did."

Unlike her parents, who have now retired to their family's village, Héla feels little attachment to Tunisia. But with her hijab, she also has a difficult time living in France. "The French don't like difference," she told me. "You can't wear [the headscarf] in schools, no one will hire you for jobs, and you can't wear it for work if you work in the public sector. Even in the private sector, you're not technically barred from wearing it, but you won't get hired because people are prejudiced, and the government does nothing about this kind of discrimination."

Héla should know. She is currently working toward a PhD in sociology with a focus on gender in Iran, despite the fact that she is certain she will never obtain a teaching post in France as long as she continues to wear her headscarf. After all, few people seem able to look past the scarf. In a telling example, her professor of Persian consistently referred to her in class as Madame le Voile. After returning from a year of fieldwork in Iran, Héla has tried to find temporary jobs while she writes her thesis. That has been difficult, too. In 2008 she applied for a job teaching adults computer literacy, but her prospective employers illegally asked her to remove her headscarf, and she refused; they turned her down, warning her that she would never find a job dressing as she does. Undeterred, Héla soon found a position tutoring at-risk immigrant-origin youth in another Parisian suburb. Though she started as a temporary replacement for a tutor on medical leave, she was asked to remain permanently. Unfortunately for Héla, the former tutor came to visit her old colleagues, declared it "scandalous" that a veiled woman would be in an educational role, and threatened to take the issue to the local municipal government, which has a contract with the tutoring agency. Fearing a crisis, her employers asked Héla to resign, which she did. When I noted that she had every legal right to remain and should sue her employers for discrimination and wrongful termination, Héla replied that she simply did not want to go through the hassle and expense of pursuing legal action.

There were other daily reminders that she was a figure of alterity. When we were together in public, I witnessed the stares and comments from random passersby. Conversing over lunch in central Paris, for example, we were interrupted by a server who paused in front of our table, looked at Héla, and said, "You're Muslim!" "Yes," Héla replied evenly. He laughed and went on his way, and Héla shrugged. Other encounters were more ominous, like the drunken white Frenchman who accosted her one night, shouting, "Go back to your country, you dirty whore." Or the middle-aged white woman who, at the height of the North Atlantic Treaty Organization's war against the Taliban, stopped Héla on the street and said kindly, "Don't worry, you'll soon be liberated." Héla has a theory that the frequency of street comments like these is linked to whether Islam is in the news or not, a theory supported by annual reports compiled by the Collective against Islamophobia in France (Collectif contre l'Islamophobie en France, or CCIF). Héla told me in the summer of 2009—after government-led campaigns against various forms of veiling and a corresponding rise in attacks on veiled women—that she now stands well away from the tracks in the metro, since "you never know if some crazy person is going to see your veil and push you off the platform. People have really lost their minds about it."[7] And she recounted a 2008 trip to visit her cousins in Holland, recalling how strange it was that no one commented on her appearance or insulted her in public during the week she was there. Laughing, she told me that her cousins jokingly offered to pay someone to insult her so that she would feel more at home.

The discrimination and insults that Héla experiences every day mirror wider national-level discourses and practices. A striking example of the concatenation of race, religion, nationality, immigration, and delinquency—and the way Muslim and French are consistently constructed as intractably opposed—occurred at a December 14, 2009, local town hall meeting during the Grand Debate on National Identity, inaugurated by the newly created Ministry of Immigration, Integration, and National Identity.[8] Nadine Morano, President Sarkozy's secretary of state for family and solidarity, responded to an audience member's question about whether Islam has a place within French national identity. Morano began by affirming that "one person should not be superior to another . . . so the other has to try to assimilate."[9] She then noted that "our French roots are Judeo-Christian" before acknowledging the law of 1905, which guarantees "our respect" for Protestant temples, synagogues, and now mosques. (Note the dominant, unmarked Catholic majority.) Morano went on to invoke the various "rules" for coming to France (including regularized papers ensuring that the new arrival is working and not relying on welfare) and the need to reinforce legislative measures "for those who don't respect our laws in certain neighborhoods." She added: "One must respect the other as soon as he respects the law, as soon as he respects the terms of his entry into France [contrat d'accueil, literally "welcome contract"], as long as he respects equality between men and women, as long as he doesn't accept the burqa, as long as he accepts our traditions." Referring to the hypothetical situation of "a young Muslim," Morano declared: "I want him to love France because he lives in this country, to find a job, to not speak in slang, to not wear his baseball cap backward. . . . But I believe that living together, when one is young, there is nothing more beautiful in terms of hope."

Morano's rambling eight-minute monologue reveals many of the slippages and underlying tropes in mainstream French political and media discourse about Muslims. Note, for example, how Morano seamlessly moves from a discussion of laïcité and minority religions' place in France to the legal requirements for immigration, to delinquency, then back to religion, then to French norms and traditions, then to the proverbial "young Muslim" and his inveterate social deviance. Note, too, how Morano consistently expels Islam and Muslims from France and renders them literally Other—she uses the word l'autre (the other) five times during the eight-minute speech—first in her remark about France's so-called Judeo-Christian heritage and then in her positioning of Muslims as outsiders, as foreigners and immigrants to be accepted by France only on the condition that they abide by "our laws" and accept "our traditions." Her use of the term contrat d'accueil assumes either that no Muslims can claim France as their country of citizenship or that even for those who can, their citizenship is conditional, a legal contract rather than a cultural fact. The latter assumption was made manifest in Sarkozy's 2010 threat to strip certain naturalized citizens of their citizenship for crimes like polygamy and female genital cutting, practices often associated with Muslims.

The rendering of certain Muslim practices as irredeemably foreign has characterized public discussions about veiling. Whether in debates about the headscarf in schools or more recently about the so-called burqa, veiling in its various forms is routinely analyzed through a framework of gender oppression in Iran, Algeria, and Afghanistan. The common use of the term *burqa* to refer to full face veils in media and political discourse—the more precise term is *niqab*—exemplifies French politicians' ignorance about basic categories of Muslim head covering, as well as the concerted effort to paint the practice of veiling as inherently foreign.[10] One of the most visually arresting examples of this is the cover of Chahdortt Djavann's book *Bas les voiles!* (Down with veils!). Published in 2003 at the height of the debate on headscarves in public schools, *Bas les voiles!* compares veiling to rape and describes Djavann's personal suffering as a young woman in Khomeini's Iran. It became a popular prism through which to analyze the practice of veiling in France. After its initial publication in austere pamphlet form, *Bas les voiles!* was republished in 2006 with a colorful cover depicting two Afghan women, one a young girl with her head covered by a *dupatta* (light shawl), the second a woman in a traditional blue burqa. The image enacts an astonishing semiotic collapse: an Afghan woman in burqa represents a treatise about veiling in Iran, which in turn is used to analyze the practice of veiling in France. Given the dominance of these kinds of amalgamations, it is unsurprising that Héla would be told to go back to her country and be promised liberation.

Exclusion is not only discursive, of course, though discursive practices engender and cement material and legal ones. Individuals and communities of North and West African descent suffer discrimination and institutionalized racism in housing, policing, the criminal justice system, employment, and education.[11] Though statistics broken down by race and ethnicity are difficult to come by given the French Republic's ideological stance against recognizing race, empirical field research reveals systemic racism resulting from "rules and procedures of treatment that, in their various forms, have been incorporated into the ethical and sociocultural rules in the ordinary functioning of institutions, organizations, and, more generally, society itself" (de Rudder and Vourc'h 2006, 179). To this long-standing state of affairs must be added a new mode of exclusion, what Vincent Geisser calls the new Islamophobia, "a process of stigmatization that combines an ethnic referent (Arab) and a religious referent (Muslim)" (2003, 11; see also Hajjat and Mohammed 2013). The new Islamophobia, which draws on much older tropes of Islam and Muslims, emerged after the 1979 revolution in Iran, picking up traction with the Algerian civil war, 9/11, and the ensuing global War on Terror. Often morphing into a defense of Western secularism, the new Islamophobia regards Islam as a civilizational threat. The problem with Islam, according to this discourse, is that it cannot separate religious and political life and be merely a religion—hence its supposed existential threat to the secular West.[12] Accordingly, though they may differ on whether some Muslims can eventually become French citizens or will remain irredeemably Other, most mainstream republicans on both the Right and Left agree that France must resist the so-called Islamization of its minority population to maintain its intrinsically secular national identity. As Geisser argues, the problem of the new "Arabo-Muslim menace" thus "justifies . . . defensive and punitive policies against all visible signs of Islam [islamité]" (2003, 11).

These defensive measures have taken various forms. In June 2004 the National Assembly voted to extend the conditions under which foreigners can be deported from France; they can now be expelled for "deliberately and explicitly" calling for "discrimination, hate, or violence against a specific person or a group of people," including women.[13] The law was a direct response to the case of Abdelkader Bouziane, an imam who in a local magazine interview advocated polygamy and corporal punishment for unfaithful wives. Bouziane was deported via a ministerial decree in April 2004 for his statements. Since then, numerous imams have been deported for preaching values deemed contrary to the republic's. A number of other security measures have been adopted under the aegis of fighting Islamic terrorism, including a 2005 law that increased from ten to fifteen years the period of time after naturalization during which a naturalized citizen can be stripped of French nationality. The legislation that has received the most media attention concerns veiling. In 2004 the National Assembly and Senate voted to ban conspicuous religious signs (read: headscarves) in public schools in France, and in 2009 both legislative bodies voted to ban clothing intended to hide the face (read: niqabs), stipulating a fine of €150 and/or a citizenship course as punishment for choosing to wear a niqab, and one year in prison or a fine of up to €30,000 for anyone forcing a woman to wear a niqab. Note the implications here: a French Muslim woman wearing the niqab has either been forced to do so or is not a proper citizen if she has chosen to veil herself.

Even my Muslim French interlocutors not directly affected by this legislation felt its stigmatizing effects. As the CCIF argues, many Muslims suffer extralegal forms of discrimination and violence based on hostility "to Islam as a religion and to Muslims as real or presumed bearers of this religion." This is the result, the CCIF claims, of the "ideological banalization" of antipathy toward Islam (Collectif contre l'Islamophobie en France 2005, 15).[14] The organization's yearly reports catalogue verbal and physical aggression toward individual Muslims, the vandalism of Muslim places of worship, and the profanation of Muslim graves. Remarkably, the CCIF found that much discrimination, especially against women in headscarves, comes from employees of public institutions like a school or mayor's office. In July 2004, for instance, an employee in the mayor's office in Châtenay-Malabry (in Hauts-de-Seine) refused to give a woman wearing a hijab her birth certificate unless she removed her headscarf. In March 2004 the CCIF counted ten separate instances where women in headscarves were illegally denied entry to vote in town halls across France. Other veiled women have been refused entry to their university classes, as well as to private banks, doctors' offices, and bowling alleys. And in one of the few cases that actually led to any punishment for discrimination, Horia Demiati and her family were denied entry to a private vacation home they had rented when the owner saw that Demiati and her mother wore headscarves.[15]

Keep in mind that the CCIF can only track instances of harassment and violence reported by the media or directly to the organization's hotline, and that many women (like Héla) do not press charges. Administrative, legal, or public sanction remains rare. Meanwhile, the denigration of Islam and Muslims in media and political discourse is common, and legal measures that target supposed Muslim deviancy have multiplied. All of this excludes Muslims from France both symbolically and physically, rendering them conditional French citizens, if not simply foreigners. When Muslim French like Farid and Héla stake their claims to France, then, they do so within and against a discursive and institutional context in which Muslim means not French and French means not Muslim. This long-standing incommensurability makes inhabiting Muslim French subjectivity particularly complicated.

Naming, Shaming, Reclaiming

When we spoke about the Beur generation, almost all of my interlocutors would pause, midsentence, to note their dislike of the term itself. This did not stem merely from an ideological disagreement with Beur politics. Something else was at work, although few of my interlocutors could say why the term made them uneasy. Farid came closest in one of our discussions about the paradigmatic Beur organization, SOS Racisme. "We were given names," Farid recounted, "like, for example, the word Beur. I don't like it—I'm not a Beur. I'm not a Beur because . . . you know, you look at the different stages in the formation of this word, what I call double-verlanization. First it was 'the Arabs,' then, in reverse, it's Re-beu, then Re-beu become Beur-e, you take away the last letter, and you have the inverse of an Arab, and then, finally, you realize, you are not really the inverse of an Arab, you are between the two . . . but still someone separate." Though Farid's narrative is not entirely etymologically accurate, he nevertheless expresses a clear discomfort with the act of naming as an act of recognition.

We might productively read Farid's claim that "we were given names" as a moment of Althusserian interpellation, whereby the individual is constituted as a subject in ideology by recognizing himself as the subject being hailed. To illustrate, Louis Althusser describes the act of hailing: "'Hey, you there.'" He continues: "Assuming that the theoretical scene I have imagined takes place in the street, the hailed individual will turn around. By this mere one-hundred-and-eighty-degree physical conversion, he becomes a *subject*. . . . The one hailed always recognizes that it is really him who is being hailed" (1972, 174 [emphasis in original]). Subjectivation occurs in that double moment of hailing and recognition. In Althusser's account of interpellation, it seems obvious to the subject-to-be that he should turn around, recognizing himself in the hail.

Farid's comments interrupt the seamlessness of that moment of hailing and recognition, and of subjectivation itself. Although Farid was speaking about the term Beur, I want to extend his comments to reflect on the interpellation of French like him as "Muslims." Recall, for instance, the various moments in Héla's life when she has been hailed as a Muslim—for example, when we were at lunch. Recall, too, that ordinary actors, politicians, and scholars increasingly use the term Muslim to refer to the same racial and religious population that once went under the signifier Arab and later Beur. Farid's comments evoke the difficulty of recognizing oneself and being recognized as Muslim in France—in short, of being Muslim in France. The problem for Muslim French is that they do not know whether to turn around when they are hailed as Muslim, for the Muslim being hailed and the Muslim they inhabit are not necessarily one and the same. To put it another way, when Héla is hailed as a Muslim ("You're a Muslim"), she certainly recognizes that it is she who is being hailed ("Yes"), but she also does not necessarily recognize herself in the Muslim being hailed ("Go back to your country"), in the way that Muslim has come to be defined as backward, retrograde, fundamentalist, and, ultimately, that which is not French. Unlike the Muslim being hailed, she does not need to be liberated, and she is already at home. Conversely, that disjuncture repeats itself in the uncanniness—and remember that the German *unheimliche* (Freud 1919, 219n1) literally means unhomely—of being Muslim French in France. After all, Héla feels most at home when she is being insulted, when she is unwelcome in her own home, and when Muslim French like her are asked by politicians like Morano to adhere to a welcome contract in their own home. Part of the struggle of being Muslim French entails the predicament of being doubly Muslim and uncannily French, both overdetermined as Muslim and unhomely as French.

I purposely use the term *overdetermined* to evoke another well-known moment of naming, recognition, and interpellation, when, in *Black Skin, White Masks*, Frantz Fanon describes walking by a white child and her mother in a train car:

> "Look, a Negro!" It was a passing sting. I attempted a smile. . . . "Look, a Negro!" . . . "I'm scared!" Scared! Scared! . . . I wanted to kill myself laughing, but laughter had become out of the question. I couldn't take it any longer, for I knew there were legends, stories, history, and especially the *historicity* that Jaspers had taught me. . . . I was responsible not only for my body but also for my race and my ancestors. I cast an objective gaze over myself, discovered my blackness, my ethnic features; deafened by cannibalism, backwardness, fetishism, racial stigmas, slave traders, and above all, yes, above all, the grinning *Y a bon Banania*." (Fanon 2008, 92 [emphasis in original])[16]

Fanon depicts the representational burden that certain subjects must carry, a burden fixed in and through the moments of recognition that bring them into being as subjects. The moment of recognition that Fanon describes, similar to the naming that Farid decries, "*fixes the meaning of one's self before one even has had the opportunity to live and make a self more nearly of one's own choosing*" (Holt 1995, 2 [emphasis in original]). The hailed subject is both fixed and affixed to a community and a history, responsible for her body, her race, and her ancestors. Like Fanon, Héla does not have to speak to be recognized as Muslim, nor does she have to speak afterward; the dominant public already knows what she has to say, what she really is. The discursive amalgamations and semiotic collapses I outlined earlier testify to this ontological fixing, and to the radical disindividuation of Muslims in France.

It remains entirely unsurprising, therefore, that the Stasi Commission invited only two women in headscarves to its hearings, only on the very last day, and only as an afterthought. The very act of wearing a headscarf ostensibly says everything that needs to be said; according to Stasi himself, the headscarf can have only one "objective" meaning, namely, "the alienation of women" (quoted in Gresh 2013). This reductive moment does not merely deny the polysemy of the veil as object but of the veiled subject as well. A woman in a headscarf becomes the headscarf itself; she is simply Madame le Voile and can never be more than a Muslim. How, then, to be Muslim and French, to be Muslim French, against the weight of the overdetermination that being Muslim in France entails?

"I Am Here, and I Am French"

Sayad's distinction between the politeness of new immigrants and the impoliteness of the second generation continues to resonate in contemporary France. In 2003 Minister of Education Xavier Darcos observed, in reference to two high-school girls who were refusing to remove their headscarves in class, that "what has changed in the last fifteen years is a kind of insolence on the part of third-generation immigrants from the Arab-Muslim world" (quoted in Tevanian 2007, 48). What Sayad called impoliteness and Darcos insolence is the Muslim French claim to France as their homeland—their bled—and their civic and political activism as citizens. Farid's exhortations for engagement at Le Bourget mirror the quieter declaration by Héla that "our parents didn't dare claim their rights," but "the second generation, we know our rights, we're waking up." The following sections trace some of the ways that Muslim French mobilize the sign of France to insert themselves into a symbolic and political space that otherwise excludes them.

The thunderous applause that greeted Farid's demand to "stop talking to me about integration" and his declaration that "I am here, and I am French" articulates the frustration of a generation repeatedly told to integrate. In a conversation I had with him a few days later, Farid complained: "I spend my whole life here, my education in the secular public school, and then, at age twenty-five, thirty, thirty-six, you speak to me about integration? . . . I was born here, my father worked and died here. My father was a foreigner. He wasn't welcomed. But me, I was born here."

In identifying so strongly with France, Muslim French inhabit a political subjectivity quite different from that of the Beur generation and its embrace of hybridity. It also differs from other trends in the contemporary Islamic revival, most notably the pietist Tablighi and ultraconservative Salafi[17] movements, the members of which remain largely uninterested in identifying as French Muslims or in engaging politically as French citizens. In contrast, Muslim French have made a concerted effort to Frenchify (*franciser*) the Islamic tradition, making them part of a broader subtrend of the Islamic revival that has attempted over the past decade to Gallicize Islam institutionally and exegetically (see Bowen 2009).

Franciser was a term used by Mounia and Chiraz, two sisters in their late twenties whose parents emigrated from Tunisia to Nantes in the 1960s. At the time of my fieldwork, both were active members of JMF-Nantes. The sisters had created an innovative head covering that looks less like a conventional headscarf and more like a fedora with a neck scarf attached; they sold various versions of the prototype—for summer or winter, in different prints and colors—at the yearly UOIF congress in Le Bourget. Mounia claimed it was a way "to adapt and to integrate," but Chiraz disagreed vehemently: "What am I integrating into? I'm French!" Mounia contended that Chiraz had misunderstood her point, and that although covering the head, neck, and ears remains a religious obligation for Muslim women, the precise form that covering takes can be culturally specific. French Muslim women therefore needed to Frenchify the headscarf. "We're not in Iran, we're not in Egypt, we're not in Tunisia, we're in France," Mounia said. She was not arguing that Muslims are not integrated into French society and therefore need to adapt, but rather that because Muslims like her are already French, they need to act like it and not adopt dress styles from the Middle East or the Maghreb.

Mounia's reasoning draws implicitly on one of the major interpretive trends within the modernist, reformist currents of the contemporary Islamic revival—namely, the abstraction of Islam into a site of fundamental principles and universal values, like justice, equality, and rationality, that are instantiated differently in different historical and cultural contexts. Best exemplified in Europe by Tariq Ramadan, who himself draws on a much longer interpretive tradition concerning the relationship between divine and human law (see D. Brown 1996; Messick 1996; Hallaq 2009b), this position takes the *shariʿa* as the immutable, revealed path of God and *fiqh* as its always dynamic human articulation. Ramadan, who has become the major reference for many Muslim French, writes: "The application of Islamic law and jurisprudence (*fiqh*) necessarily takes into consideration the sources [that is, the Quran and the Sunna] and the social, cultural, political, and economic context. This application is evolving and flexible (it progresses and regresses) and represents . . . the *shari'a*, at a given moment of History in a given society" (1999, 93). After underscoring the historicity of Islamic jurisprudence, Ramadan moves to a consideration of Islam in Europe, where circumstances different from those in majority-Muslim regions necessitate, he argues, new concepts and new *fiqh*.[18] Though Islam is universal—indeed, because Islam is universal—Ramadan contends that "there should be an Islam rooted in the cultural universe of Europe, just as there exists an Islam rooted in African or Asian tradition. Islam, and its Islamic references, is *one and unique*; the methods of judicial application are, however, differentiated . . . and its concretization in a given place and a given time is by nature plural" (325 [emphasis in original]). In his effort to reconceptualize Islam in Europe, Ramadan turns away from the distinction between *dar al-islam* (abode of Islam) and *dar al-harb* (abode of war), which traditionally refer to Muslim and non-Muslim spaces. That distinction usually hinges on whether or not Islamic law is propagated by governing states; Ramadan instead focuses on whether or not individual Muslims have the right to practice their faith. Arguing that they do in Europe, he redefines Europe as *dar al-shahada* (abode of testimony or witnessing).

One of the most interesting effects of Ramadan's theology is how, by making Islam the site of the universal, he locates France as the site of the particular, of culture, thus inverting the common republican paradigm in which France is universal and Islam particular (either as culture, religion, or race).[19] Being French and being Muslim are not incompatible, according to Ramadan's reasoning, because the Islamic tradition already encompasses French values claimed as universal—such as liberty, equality, and fraternity—and because, by dint of their Frenchness, Muslims already share the values claimed as particularly French. The irony, of course, is that most republicans balk at the notion that their universal values are those of Islam and therefore shared by Muslims. In other words, it is precisely when Muslim French accept the universality of many republican values that republicanism comes crashing back to the particular always contained within it.

The day-to-day effects of this interpretive gesture extend beyond sartorial reconfigurations like those of Mounia and Chiraz. A number of Muslim French advocate training and hiring imams born and raised in France, arguing that such imams better understand the specific needs of Muslim French than their foreign counterparts do. Other Muslim French activists have called for mosque sermons to be given in French, rather than or in addition to Arabic. Mourad, a young entrepreneur and member of JMF-Nantes's governing board, has actively campaigned for French-language sermons at his local mosque. "They [the Friday preachers] are speaking to French people, not to Arabs," he observed. Amira, an eighteen-year-old high-school student and Muslim activist in Rennes, echoed Mourad's emphasis on French as the lingua franca of French Islam. During one of our conversations over tea in her kitchen a few months after the 2004 UOIF congress at Le Bourget, Amira criticized what she regarded as the illegitimate use of Arabic at the congress. "Either you say that we are French and we do our conferences only in French," she argued, "or, if you bring scholars from outside, because that can be enriching, having a Malaysian or Saudi scholar, you translate. And translate well." She then told me that she had attended a seminar on the Quran organized by the UOIF. "We are all citizens of France, people who live in France," she said, "and the sheikh spoke the whole morning in Arabic, and then someone came and said, 'Okay, I don't want to lose too much time so I'm going to translate in ten minutes.'" Even though she speaks Arabic fluently, Amira rolled her eyes in frustration. "*We are in France!*" she declared, thumping on the table for emphasis. "They should speak ten minutes in Arabic and one hour in French." Given the French context, Amira felt it more appropriate that the language of common use be French. But beyond that nationalist impulse lay an epistemological one—namely, that meaningful, effective piety must be the result of active, reasoned, and conscious knowledge, so that the practicing believer fully understands the doctrinal bases and pragmatic or theological import of specific beliefs and practices. This attitude is a central feature of modernist revivalism worldwide, and in France it demands vernacularization into French.

The discourse of French citizenship grounds and inflects Muslim French attitudes toward perceived injustice, such as everyday racism, discrimination at work, and the failure of schools in immigrant *banlieues*. Many of my interlocutors—and here they were joined by members of other antiracist groups who do not explicitly identify as practicing Muslims—considered the political, social, and economic marginalization of those of Maghrebi and African descent a sign of the republic's hypocrisy and a betrayal of constitutionally guaranteed rights. During one of my visits to the JMF-Nantes headquarters, I struck up a conversation with Abdel, a bushy-haired high-school student of Algerian origin who was not a member of the JMF but participated in its activities. When I asked why, he answered: "Because I recognize myself in the organization. I am young, I am Muslim, and I am

French." He lamented the fact that he was eighteen years old and would soon be looking for a job, all the while knowing that he would not have the same opportunities as others due to his skin color, Muslim heritage, and *banlieue* address. "We are French," Abdel said, "we are citizens. And I want the same rights as every citizen." Here, discrimination is more than a form of oppression; it is a denial of rightful citizenship.

The claims that Muslim French make to Frenchness, and the concomitant grounding of those claims in the paradigm of citizenship, were strikingly displayed during a December 2003 demonstration against the then-proposed law banning headscarves in public schools. Three or four thousand demonstrators—most of them young women and many of them clad in red, white, and blue headscarves—marched from the Place de la République to the Place de la Bastille, chanting slogans and holding placards, all in French. One sign read: "School: my path. The veil: my choice. France: my right." A number of the young women held aloft their national identity cards and voter registration cards. I noticed that some of the young women at the head of the procession held faded French flags wrapped around poles in the fashion of the revolutionary period. As we approached the Bastille, a message rippled through the crowd: the few hundred men present were told to get out of the procession because the women were going "to storm the Bastille," after which a number of young women, many of them in headscarves, climbed onto the base of the gilded column that marks the site of the former prison whose storming symbolically constitutes the founding moment of the revolutionary republic. Through these various means, the women in the demonstration inscribed themselves into the French nation, presenting themselves as classical *citoyennes* adorned not only with the symbolic accoutrements of the citizen (the flag) but also with the practical tools of active citizenship (voting cards). That gesture of inscribing Muslims into the founding moment of the republic was repeated in 2012 by the CCIF for its "Nous Aussi Sommes la Nation" (We too are the nation) campaign. One of the images in a series of advertisements—which the Paris transit authority refused to display because of its "religious character" and "political demands"—reimagines Jacques-Louis David's revolution-era "Tennis Court Oath" in the present, with veiled women, Arab men in hoodies, and visibly Orthodox Jews, among other citizens, holding aloft French flags and copies of the oath (figure 1.1). The politeness that Sayad ascribed to the first generation has given way to the self-confident claiming of France as a right of citizenship and the depiction of Muslims as original *citoyens*.

FIGURE 1.1. Poster from the 2012 "Nous Aussi Sommes la Nation"
(We too are the nation) campaign of the Collectif contre l'Islamophobie en France
(CCIF). Courtesy William Barylo and CCIF.

Exclusions of the National

The gap Sayad invoked in juxtaposing first-generation politeness and second-generation impoliteness plays out in more politically insidious ways as well. In staking their claims to France as citizens, many Muslim French, even as they expand French national identity, revive the exclusivity of the national paradigm. They thus delegitimize the experiences, desires, and attachments of immigrants and foreigners who were not born in France or who are not committed to certain dominant moral and political values. Some Muslim French activists criticize the UOIF as unrepresentative of French Islam, distinguishing between Muslim French young people and the older generation of so-called *blédards*, a pejorative term roughly translated as "those from the home country." A number of my interlocutors outside the UOIF were highly critical of the organization's participation in the French Council on the Muslim Religion, established by the state as the representative body for Islam—on par with the other representative councils for Catholicism, Protestantism, and Judaism—to regulate and ameliorate the conditions of Muslim religious life.[20] Younès attributed the UOIF's aspiration for political recognition to the fact that its leaders were *blédards*, with a colonial mentality "of submission to authority." Amira told me that the UOIF represented a form of Maghrebi rather than French Islam. "It's like back in the homeland," she explained. "In fact, [UOIF leaders] act like the colonized." In response to these attacks on the UOIF as somehow not French enough, members of the UOIF and its affiliate organizations have criticized Tariq Ramadan, the intellectual leader of the UJM and CMF, for speaking out of place, since he is not French but Swiss. For example, Mourad, a member of JMF-Nantes, dismissed Ramadan as irrelevant to French Muslims. "What does he know about what's going on here on the ground?" he scoffed."He lives in Geneva." Once again, the terms of exclusion were national.

Another instance of boundary drawing in the Gallicization of Islam entails the neo-Orientalist notion that the evolution of the Islamic tradition and its adaptation to modernity will come from the West.[21] A number of Muslim French activists in both the CMF and the UOIF, for instance, speak of the presence of Muslims in Europe as an "opportunity" for Islam to escape the "malaise" of the Middle East, with its authoritarian states and stagnant *ijtihad* (independent reasoning). The dominant North Atlantic cliché of modernity versus tradition that so often distinguishes the West from Islam is thereby redeployed, with the Islam practiced by Muslim French now included in modernity. Part of the distinction between modern and traditional Islam, which operates in other locations as well (see, for example, Deeb 2006), involves the common distinction between so-called true Islam—practiced by literate, educated Muslim French—and the "cultural" or "traditional" practices of their parents. Rooted in the abstraction of Islam into an acultural universal, this distinction operates along an axis of three crucial markers that distinguish true Islam from the customary practices of the first generation. Those markers are liberty, equality, and a rationalist hermeneutics, all key republican values that seemingly mark modernity as distinct from tradition.

Consider the following outburst from Assia, a member of the Muslim Students of France, as we discussed the burgeoning Islamic revival among young people in France:

Yes, there is a return to religion, but not to the religion of our parents, not to archaic religion, not to the religion that follows North African tradition that is totally nuts and that we should get rid of. There's a return to religion through a return to the sources, the source of the

Quran. The source is not North African tradition. . . . Today, as the children of immigrants, we go to school, we develop a critical spirit, we learn how to see for ourselves, and we realize that our parents have rejected their [Islamic] origins. . . . They say: "This is what our ancestors did." Me, I don't really give a damn about the ancestors. It's not [Islamically] legal and it doesn't conform to Islamic morality.

Assia redeploys here the old anthropological categories of rural folk Islam and urban literate Islam (see, for example, Gellner 1981) by separating the so-called unlearned Islam of her barely literate parents from the learned Islam of her generation, whose religious knowledge comes largely from texts and quasi-academic conferences. For Muslim French like Assia, true spirituality emerges not from what she called ancestral knowledge—another of my informants called it hearsay—but rather from authoritative sources like the Quran, the prophetic hadiths, and the vast exegetical literature central to the Islamic tradition. Furthermore, a true Muslim must cultivate what Assia calls a critical spirit in approaching Islam. During many years of interactions with my Muslim French interlocutors, I often heard them criticize their parents for "unthinking" acquiescence to various beliefs and practices. The so-called ancestral practices that caused the most consternation were forced marriage, female circumcision, virginity tests, and the general treatment of women as doormats (soumises), all perceived as forms of gender oppression that Assia and others attributed to a "macho culture" in North Africa and the Middle East that they found inconsistent with Islamic norms.

Parents were not the only targets of criticism; Salafis were another. Céline, a thirty-year-old Muslim French convert and substitute teacher, once told me how she had attended Friday prayers at a mosque with which she was unfamiliar. She got a sinking feeling, she said, when she saw "streams of men with beards down to here [pointing to her stomach] and women in niqabs" coming to the mosque. After the sermon, she tried to talk with some of the women about Tariq Ramadan, and one of the women said: "Oh no, you mustn't read stuff like that, it's bid'a [innovation]." "Oh really?" Céline said she replied ("I was playing dumb," she told me). "Why is it bid'a?" According to Céline, the woman "couldn't really answer my question, she just kept repeating that it was bid'a." Céline's point, one that numerous Muslim French made to me, was that these women—and Salafis in general—cannot think for themselves, cannot have a reasoned debate, and have no conception of the logic behind certain Quranic and hadith-based injunctions.[22] The Muslim French critique of so-called literalist interpretations of the *Quran* and hadiths also applies to the pietist Tabligh wa Da'wa, whose members emulate the comportment of the Prophet and his wives; many Tablighi men therefore dress as the Prophet dressed, and Tablighi women tend to prefer somber colors and dark *abayas*. In emulating the Prophet, particularly conscientious members of the Tabligh use *miswak* (bark) rather than a toothbrush and sleep on a mat on the floor, practices that a number of my interlocutors derided. Mounia and Chiraz, the two sisters from Nantes, claimed that such practices were not only stupid but also useless, and that if toothbrushes and mattresses had existed in the Prophet's era, he would undoubtedly have used them. They hastened to add that these Muslims have the right to their interpretation of the sources, however backward and stupid it may be. Although Tablighis are generally held in higher regard than Salafis, who are thought to have jihadist inclinations, many Muslim French believe Tablighis practice an Islam that, as one UOIF leader put it, is "a bit simplistic."

This emphasis on reasoned interpretation over literalism, educated choices over blind submission, and true Islam over customary practice is common in other modernist revivalist circles worldwide. What remains particular to France is how these elements intertwine with a generational struggle and a highly contentious politics of immigration and citizenship. The negative perception of Islam held by much of the non-Muslim French majority forces Muslim French to carry a heavy representational burden. By underscoring their commitment to equality, liberty, and a particular form of rationalist hermeneutics, and by distinguishing their practice of Islam from the folk practices of their parents, Muslim French inscribe themselves into the French nation, and into its national qua universal values. They expand the scope of these values to include Muslims like themselves who have long been excluded from the national imaginary and thought incapable of sharing the nation's moral, political, and cultural norms. But they also redeploy the exclusionary terms of national belonging, implicitly resurrecting a distinction between citizen and foreigner based on cultural and moral norms that define who belongs to the French nation (themselves) and who does not belong (their parents, as well as other "simplistic" Muslims). In so doing, they rehearse many of the tropes that have come to define Islamic fundamentalism—literalism, terrorism, and unthinking obedience to authority—in order to tweak and redeploy the prevailing distinction between good Muslims and bad ones (Mamdani 2005). Forced marriage, female genital cutting, and virginity tests are precisely the practices that a dominant republican discourse references to mark the supposed inequality of women in the Islamic tradition, and the fundamental difference of Islam from French modernity. By rejecting these practices as barbaric, backward, and un-Islamic, Muslim French attempt to incorporate themselves and the Islam they practice—understood as Islam *tout court*, or the real, universal tradition—into the cultural and moral norms of France. But by using terms that were once the basis for their exclusion, they reinforce the link between particular moral and cultural norms and Frenchness, marking certain practices and beliefs, and the people who hold them, as inherently foreign. Even as they press for voting rights for their noncitizen parents, many also unintentionally write this older generation out of the moral and cultural nation.

We should be careful, however, to recognize that the sometimes exclusionary logic of Muslim French political subjectivity grows out of the structural position that Muslim French occupy. It is instructive here to turn to another historical case of minority subjects in France: colonial African and Antillean quasi-citizens who criticized the racism embedded in universalist republicanism while at the same time appealing to the principles of republicanism to claim political rights. In exploring this double gesture, Gary Wilder points to what Gayatri Spivak terms " 'the deconstructive predicament of the post-colonial,' who must make political claims 'from a space that one cannot not want to inhabit and yet must criticize' " (Wilder 2005, 195). In staking a claim to French citizenship, Muslim French find themselves in a similar predicament. They are critical of the narrowness of French republican citizenship, which they regard as excluding publicly Muslim postcolonial subjects like themselves, and they seek to expand notions of Frenchness by claiming their right to France as bona fide citizens. Yet in trying to expand national citizenship by claiming a place in the nation, they do so on certain normative epistemological, moral, and cultural grounds. Thus they cannot but resurrect the series of exclusions that are the basis for dominant republican notions of the French nation.[23]

"France Is My *Bled*"

Despite seemingly excluding their parents from the moral and cultural nation, however, many Muslim French also reincorporate them by refuting any stark historical, political, or cultural rupture between France and the Maghreb. Importantly, Muslim French claims to France do not imply a break with the past, or with the complicated history that binds France to Algeria (its former settler colony) and to Morocco and Tunisia (its former protectorates). Recall Farid's statement that "La France est mon *bled*," a declaration with various layers of meaning. Bled is an Arabic word that means both village and homeland. On the face of it, by declaring France to be his bled, Farid makes a strong claim to national belonging: France, rather than Algeria, is his homeland. His statement refutes an important trope of his parents' generation, who often classify yearly family summer vacations to the Maghreb as a return to the homeland (rentrer au bled). In naming France as his bled, Farid articulates the attitude of many of my French-born interlocutors who recall these vacations not as returns home but rather as voyages to the land of their parents, where they rarely feel at home. Farid's declaration marks a clear distinction between the national and cultural sensibilities of his parents' generation, whose bled is overseas, and his own generation, whose bled is France.

Even as he makes this distinction, however, Farid's deployment of the term bled Arabizes France, seamlessly configuring it as a Muslim and North African place. In fact, the term bled has entered the French lexicon, utilized by non-Maghrebi French to refer to their native village or region in France. Farid's use of the expression calls attention to how the metropolitan presence of Franco-Maghrebis like him and his parents—and the ensuing linguistic, cultural, religious, and demographic pluralism—has brought about a new France, what Assia called la république plurielle. Farid's use of bled also signals the possibility of transnational and transpolitical affiliations (Silverstein 2004) that defy conventional notions of national identity and citizenship. Even though some practicing Muslims claim little connection to the homelands of their parents, other Muslim French activists maintain a strong interest in the Maghreb, and many have dual nationality. Younès, for example, is a French and Tunisian citizen. Rather than the Beur ni-ni (neither-nor) political sensibility, Younès claims to be et-et (both-and). He maintains an active interest in Tunisian politics, returning every summer to Tunisia. Other Muslim French, even if they do not visit often or vote in Tunisian, Moroccan, or Algerian elections, closely follow politics in the Maghreb. Many Muslim French also advocate giving voting rights in French municipal elections to long-term residents—that is, their parents' generation. Despite the various differences in their attitudes toward the Maghreb, what unites Muslim French is a commitment to fundamentally expanding the boundaries of France beyond the dominant racial and religious national imaginary.

The new France imagined here is at the same time an old France, and Farid's pluralization of his bled operates in diachronic and synchronic registers. The Muslim French reconfiguration of France constitutes a distinctly postcolonial project, where *post* suggests not a spatial or temporal break but rather an ineluctable connection between colonial pasts and post-colonial presents. Muslim French ground their claim to France not only in their birth and education there but also in the facts that their grandparents fought and died in France's colonial armies during the two world wars and that their parents worked to rebuild metropolitan France in the aftermath of World War II. On the heels of his reminder that "our parents built this country on their backs," Farid pointed out to me that individuals like him were not in France by accident. "It's not like we got lost along the way," he observed, referring to France's colonization of the Maghreb and the active recruitment of Maghrebi laborers by French industry and the French state throughout the twentieth century. "People have to realize that, and France has to assume its destiny." By staking a claim to France through his ances-tors, Farid reconnects French colonial history to the nation's present and future, defying increasing attempts by the non-Muslim French majority and the French state to turn away from the Mediterranean and toward Europe.[24] Through this reconnection, he and other Muslim French seek to transform conventional notions of French history by asserting their present and their past—their ancestors, the Arabs and Berbers—as an integral part of France's national historical narrative, not just of their own particular history.

In so doing, they enact in the realm of politics the kind of reformulations that a number of historians have recently begun to theorize about as well (Balibar 2002; Blanchard, Bancel, and Lemaire 2005; Wilder 2005; Shepard 2006). Working in France and beyond, these scholars examine the relation-ship between the metropole and its colonies, implicitly asking the crucial question that Wilder articulates most clearly: "What are we to make of the fact that republican France was never not an imperial nation-state?" (2005, 3).[25] Wilder's point is that imperialism was not a detour from or failure of the republic but rather integral to it, and racialist colonial discourses and prac-tices were internal to republicanism rather than violations of it. Modern France and its colonial outposts were constituted together, with the colo-nies often serving as blueprints or staging grounds for forms of modern government aimed at transforming populations in the metropole.[26] This recent historical scholarship suggests that it remains impossible to unsu-ture France from its colonial genealogy, to think France without thinking Algeria, Morocco, Tunisia, Senegal, and so on. Or, as Étienne Balibar puts it in his provocatively titled "Algerie, France: Une ou deux nations?" (Algeria, France: one or two nations?), "The France of today was made (and without a doubt is still being made) in Algeria, with and against her" (2002, 73).

Similarly, when Farid observes that "it's not like we [Muslim French] got lost along the way," he reconnects France's past to its present and its future, undoing the taken-for-granted notion that the Muslim presence in France is a new and alien one.[27] And the historicity inscribed into Muslim French politics presupposes a futurity. France does not simply have to assume its past but also, as Farid noted, its destiny; indeed, the two are ineluctably linked. Importantly, Muslim French do not focus on France's colonial genealogy to make the republic atone for its past, as many republican critics anxiously and angrily contend (see, for example, Finkielkraut 1987; Gallo 2006), but rather to enable all French to imagine the present and the future more capaciously. And this appeal for what could be called a cosmopolitics (Mandel 2008) is both a reality check and a political manifesto, a recognition of France as it was, as it is, and as it can be.

Not incidentally, by conjuring forth a new political imagination for the future, one that emerges out of the historical and contemporary realities of France, Muslim French implicitly reverse the accusation of *communautarisme* that mainstream republican politicians and scholars consistently direct at them. Muslim French reveal republicans as having a meager grasp of history, a narrow understanding of community, and, consequently, an impoverished political imagination. As a number of scholars have noted, the republican tradition constitutes itself and its authority through a powerful sense of political and cultural continuity of French identity over time (Favell 2001; Coller 2010). A recent book titled *Fier d'être français* (Proud to be French) by the novelist and popular historian Max Gallo (2006), for example, begins with five dated epigraphs—from the *Chanson de Roland* (eleventh century), Joachim du Bellay (sixteenth century), Charles de Gaulle (1940), Marc Bloch (1940), and René Char (twentieth century)[28]—to produce a continuous notion of France stretching back a thousand years. This erases the epistemic ruptures that have taken place since then as well as the purposeful construction of modern France through various military, political, and legal operations. More specifically, the myth of continuity enables mainstream republicans to claim the republican model of citizenship not as one model among many political possibilities but as authentically French, and therefore integral to the continuation of French national identity (Favell 2001). Muslim French undo this continuity—or, to be more precise, they radically expand it to such an extent that continuity and rupture become difficult to disentangle in the colonial and postcolonial periods. They also write those excluded from an ostensibly continuous French identity back into France's history. In so doing, Muslim French disrupt the tight relation between contemporary republican politics and Frenchness, making it possible to imagine as equally French other ways of organizing the polity and other ways of practicing politics.

One major aspect of the Muslim French historicist and futurist project of reconfiguring France into a robustly cosmopolitical or plural entity—imagining politics and citizenship otherwise—entails normalizing the practice of Islam, including its public practice, as simply one more way of being French. Note the precise nature of this reconfiguration. Muslim French do not simply contend, as have a number of scholars, that one can be both French and Muslim, that practicing Islam and being a French citizen are compatible.[29] Rather, Muslim French make the more radical claim that Muslim is French.[30] Muslim French thus problematize any neat separation between public and private, politics and religion, and universal and particular, a separation that secular-republican citizenship both demands and consistently contravenes. By refusing to even attempt to make themselves invisible and by demanding why their Muslimness is subsequently read as excessively visible, as insolence or impoliteness, Muslim French reveal the particular ethno-racial, religious, and cultural attachments embedded in the republican universal and the supposedly neutral public and political sphere. But beyond merely unmasking universalist citizenship as actually particular, they make it possible to think Muslim as French, French as Muslim—to think Muslim French.

A Poverty of Imagination

I would have liked to end this chapter on a hopeful note, with Muslim French opening up the political imagination. To do so, however, would minimize the unrelenting power of a dominant discourse in France that refuses to conceive, and even seems incapable of conceiving, of Muslim as French and French as Muslim. In fact, language itself struggles to capture the nature of that emerging identity, a difficulty both indexed and embraced by the neologism that I have coined. As I noted in the introduction, the description of themselves that I heard most often in French from my interlocutors was *citoyen français de confession musulmane* (French citizen of Muslim faith), which I translate as Muslim French, using it as both a subject and an adjective to describe both a population and a political ethic. I chose the term because it does not roll easily off the tongue in English. And I avoid the more common term *French Muslims* since the structure of that term prioritizes a Muslim identity and makes the context of France a matter of happenstance.

That is not how my interlocutors understand their subject position. At the same time, language, whether French or English, presents a set of difficulties in naming, since the rules of grammar cannot countenance two nouns (Muslim and French) as one subject. Grammar demands their separation: one identity (the noun) must take precedence over the other (the qualifying adjective). Nonetheless, I hope that *Muslim French* can unsettle as much as possible this grammatical qua ontological exclusivity. I have thought about simply referring to my interlocutors as French; that is, after all, what they are. But the point, of course, is that they are also Muslim, and to continue to render that aspect of their identity invisible would elide their ethical and political commitments as well as the basis for the discrimination they suffer.

The linguistic difficulties of articulating Muslim French parallel analytical ones, demonstrating how entrenched the incommensurability between Muslim and French remains in the trans-Atlantic imagination. Most analyses of Islam in France revolve around the issues of immigration and integration and ask, essentially: Are Muslims integrated, and if not, how can they be? Even studies arguing that Muslims are better integrated than was previously assumed to be the case reinforce the trope of integration as the primary analytical and political lens through which to consider the presence of Muslims in France (see, for example, Cesari 2004; Laurence and Vaisse 2006). In addition, these studies often implicitly mark Muslims as in France but not of France, evidenced by a tendency to talk about "host societies" and "third-generation immigrants" (Cesari 2004), the latter term a downright oxymoron that reinscribes a certain population as immutably foreign. Even analysts otherwise critical of essentialist arguments nonetheless inadvertently invoke Muslims and French or Europeans as separate and discrete categories (see, for example, Göle 2005; Bowen 2006), speaking to the difficulty of imagining Muslims as fully, completely, and unqualifiedly French.

One of the most revealing examples of this conceptual impasse emerges in the work of Balibar, and I want to examine more carefully his "Algerie, France: Une ou deux nations?," mentioned above. Balibar aims to interrupt the conventional narrative of the French nation-state by arguing that France was and continues to be constituted "in Algeria, with and against her," and that the not entirely two nations are indelibly linked (2002, 78). "To speak of the relation of France to Algeria," Balibar writes, "is above all to speak of France's relation 'to herself,' to the alterity that is contained within her and that, for the most part, she denies" (78). "These are two people and two States," Balibar continues, even if they are not exactly two nations. Moreover,

Algeria is irreducibly present within France just as France is within Algeria, and, "on either side, 'the foreign body' is that much more impossible to eliminate since it is dependent not only on physical presences, but also on memory and on the very constitution of identity: each [country] is affected by an internal difference, by an essential noncontemporaneity and nonidentity with itself [*non-contemporanéité à soi*]" (81–82). Quite remarkable, given Balibar's attempt to invoke a process of coconstitution, are the binary categories of Self and Other in these passages. Balibar consistently invokes Algeria as the otherness within France, the otherness through which and against which France is constituted, and vice versa. Algeria becomes the "internal difference" that disrupts France's relation to itself. Seemingly despite his own intentions, Balibar outlines a relationship whose structure produces a preexisting self (France, *le soi*) that can never assume itself because of the fundamental alterity (Algeria, *l'alterité*) that was essential to its constitution. In attempting to write the histories of Algeria and France together, Balibar seems incapable of thinking of Algeria as anything but a form of alterity, of not France even as it produces France. In fact, the terms of his argument seem to presume that France could have achieved identity with itself—been fully itself—were it not for Algeria. One wonders, too, where to locate Muslim French within the "two peoples" (78), French and Algerian, to whom Balibar refers, given the essential alterity they constitute for each other. One encounters similar ambiguities in Balibar's writing on immigration and citizenship as well. Take, for example, his claim that "foreigners have become metics or *second-class citizens* whose residence and activities are the objects of particular surveillance" (2004, 171 [emphasis in original]). It is unclear to whom Balibar is referring here: foreigners (that is, noncitizen residents, undocumented migrants, and asylum seekers) or citizens (that is, nonforeigners)? My point in asking this question is not to reinforce a distinction between citizen and noncitizen but to underscore how that distinction is often collapsed for certain populations—not only in state practice but also in scholarly analysis—so that some citizens are classified as foreigners even when the point is to critique their treatment as second-class citizens.

The fact that these collapses and slippages occur in the writings of someone who understands his work as a critique of the dominant political imagination speaks to the intractability of conceptualizing *Muslim* as anything other than alterity and, consequently, thinking of *Muslim* and *French* as anything other than incommensurable. This common political and conceptual impasse helps to explain why Muslim French constantly foreground their

Frenchness. Their Muslimness, of course, goes without saying. After all, it is precisely their overdetermined visibility as Muslim that necessitates the insistent declarations—in public; in private; and in sartorial pronouncements like red, white, and blue headscarves—that they are equally French. This insistent repetition of Frenchness reveals the constitutive bind Muslim French find themselves in. The very act of claiming French citizenship only undermines their claim; if they were accepted as French, as full citizens, they would not have to keep asserting their citizenship. The more they assert their Frenchness, the more they reveal the precariousness of their belonging.

I close this chapter, then, where I began it, with the UOIF congress at Le Bourget in 2003, though not with Farid Abdelkrim. Instead, I turn to Nicolas Sarkozy, then minister of the interior, whose keynote address preceded Farid's rousing speech by a day. On the chilly evening of April 19, Sarkozy made a rock star's entrance, flanked by bodyguards and followed by a gaggle of reporters. He was the first major politician to speak at the UOIF congress in its twenty-year history, and the enormous hangar that served as the conference hall was filled to capacity, with people standing in the aisles and the exits; estimates by the UOIF and the press put the crowd at 10,000 people. Before Sarkozy even started to speak, the audience gave him a standing ovation, partly in response to his reputation as friendlier than most to a multiculturalist politics of recognition. This was two years before Sarkozy, responding to a wave of civil disturbances in 2005 and already preparing for the 2007 presidential elections, famously threatened to "pressure wash" "the scum" out of immigrant neighborhoods (quoted in Silverstein and Tetreault 2005).[31]

Sarkozy proclaimed his visit to be a sign of the acceptance and recognition of France's Muslim citizens, and he began his speech by noting: "It is not acceptable . . . that a citizen would not have the right to live his religion, to transmit it to his children, in a context of respect and dignity." After a rocky patch in the middle of his speech, when he was booed for demanding that Muslim women bare their heads when being photographed for national identity cards, Sarkozy slowly won back the crowd. "Muslims are full citizens just like others," he declared. "Your families, like those of all our co-citizens, have the right to live in peace," he continued, adding that hate and racism had no place in the French Republic. By this time, Sarkozy had most of the crowd back on his side, and he concluded his speech with the following statement: "The national community holds out its hand to you. It is watching you. You are from now on accountable for the image of each and every Muslim in France. Take this hand held out to you by the republic. Do not disappoint it, for the consequences would be enormous." And with that ominous warning, Sarkozy left the stage, accompanied by a standing ovation from much of the crowd, who seemed overwhelmed that they had finally been officially recognized as citizens of France.

I want to parse this moment of inclusion for the simultaneous recognition and denial of citizenship it enacts. On the one hand, Sarkozy extends citizenship to the Muslims of France, calling them full citizens and co-citizens who have the right to practice their religion, just like any other citizen, in a context of respect and dignity. On the other hand, he immediately affixes certain conditions to that practice, announcing that "Islam must be perfectly respectful of the laws of the republic" (as if that would be in any doubt) and declaring that the republic "is watching you" (to verify compliance). With these words, Sarkozy renders Muslim French citizenship conditional even as he welcomes Muslim French into the republic. In short, he outlines a *contrat d'acceuil* for those who are already at home. The precariousness of Muslim French belonging and citizenship becomes particularly evident when juxtaposing the minister's speech with Farid's remarks a day later. Recall that Farid claimed France as his *bled*, underscoring Muslims' right to France as full citizens, a right most vividly enacted by his consequent claim to Sarkozy's own job as interior minister. In many ways, Farid was implicitly responding to Sarkozy's speech and to the assumptions therein. Yet Farid's assertion of his citizenship was fundamentally undermined in advance, before he had even spoken, by the minister's parting statement. "The national community holds out its hand to you," Sarkozy proclaimed, as if the 10,000 Muslims to whom he was speaking were not already part of the national community. Farid's rejoinder to Sarkozy the next day—staking his claim to the national community without needing an invitation—seems to make Sarkozy's pronouncement meaningless, and the invitation of citizenship he extended to people who were already citizens obsolete. Still, Sarkozy's declaration highlights the tenuousness of the claims to France made by Farid and other Muslim French. To have practical political or discursive effects, their claims must be recognized by the state and by the normative majority.

In offering his addressees citizenship they already hold, Sarkozy's declaration highlights the fragility of Muslim French citizenship. His offer of inclusion also bespeaks the reinscription of power central to the process of political recognition: because claims of citizenship must be recognized in order to have any efficacious political meaning, what begins as the claiming of a right ("France: my right") is transformed into the bestowal of a conditional gift ("Take this hand held out to you by the republic. Do not disappoint it") that denies—renders incoherent—the very claims being made. In the moment of declaring that Muslim French belong to the nation, Sarkozy—whose own belonging goes without saying—only reinforces the tenuousness of Muslim French citizenship. The ambiguous inclusion that Sarkozy proffered at Le Bourget illustrates some of the pitfalls of recognition—the representational burden it inflicts, the fixing of identity it engenders, and the reinscription of power it effects—that Fanon and others describe (Povinelli 2002; Markell 2003; Fanon 2008). In a contemporary context in which the politics of recognition is, for many, the best way to adjudicate minority demands for justice and inclusion, Sarkozy's forked gesture of inclusion and exclusion forces a reevaluation of the merits of such a politics. His remarks also underscore the intractable bind of being Muslim French in a society that continually marks Muslims as not French and French as not Muslim. How, then, to imagine and practice a politics that might get Muslim French out of this bind, a politics that bypasses recognition as the solution and refuses to constrain Muslimness to a space of difference or alterity?

Two   Indifference, or the Right to Citizenship

On a chilly evening in December 2009, a group of Muslim French activists, loosely organized as United Against Islamophobia (Collectif Unis Face à l'Islamophobie, or UFI), met in a café in the Gare de Lyon, a train station in Paris. They were discussing their strategy for combating the rising tide of racism and Islamophobia following the recent government-initiated Grand Debate on National Identity. I had come with Karima, an unemployed law clerk of Moroccan descent in her late twenties who had been born and raised in Lyon. Divorced and living with her infant daughter and mother in a Parisian suburb, Karima had pursued a master's degree in legal studies and was now running a small association that defends the civil rights of Muslim women and immigrants in France. The meeting at the train station also included activists from the more established Collective Against Islamophobia in France. All of the attendees were concerned about the tenor of national political discourse, the upsurge in Islamophobic incidents, and various legislative proposals like banning the niqab in public places or retracting naturalized citizenship for those who practice polygamy.

As this legislation suggests, the debate on French national identity largely concerns Muslims in France. In his ministerial directive to departmental and police prefects outlining the goals of the debate, Interior Minister Eric Besson noted: "This debate responds . . . to the preoccupations raised by the resurgence of certain forms of *communautarisme*, of which the Burqa Affair is one illustration" (Besson 2009). Thus, safeguarding national identity often means protecting the universal French Republic and its neutral public sphere against particularist, communalist Islam. The specter of *communautarisme* hovered over the conversation between Karima and her fellow activists as they strategized about how to compel Muslims' inclusion as legitimate interlocutors in any debate about national identity. One proposal was to publicize a manifesto the activists had written against the anti-immigrant and anti-Muslim bases of the current debate. However, a few attendees wondered whether focusing on Muslim problems would mark them as narrow, even communalist. "But we're the ones being discriminated against," Karima pointed out. "We're the targets. How can we possibly not talk about Islam and Muslims?" She turned to me. "What do you think, Mayanthi?" "In my opinion," I offered cautiously, "you need to speak as citizens. You need to emphasize the fact that you're citizens of the republic, and that you're speaking to your fellow citizens." Karima nodded, but another activist remarked: "France is a profoundly racist country, and we'll always be Arabs to them."

The previous chapter considered the difficulty of being Muslim French through the framework of visibility, arguing that Muslim French are rendered hypervisible as Muslims and invisible as French. This chapter recasts the Muslim French desire for simple visibility as a claim to equal citizenship. In a conversation about SOS Racisme, the flagship association of the Beur movement, Farid Abdelkrim decried the association's famous demand for le droit à la différence (the right to difference). "Slogans like the right to difference contribute to the idea that we are still not entirely French," he explained. "We are still separate. Instead of being full citizens [*citoyens à part entière*] we are still fully separate [*citoyens entièrement à part*]." He added: "I don't want the right to difference. I want the right to *indifference*. That is to say, I don't want people to pay attention to me. I want to be forgotten."

Farid here grapples with the same dilemma that haunts the UFI: how to act as a citizen within a political arrangement premised on abstract universalism when one is consistently reduced to one's embodied, particular difference; how to speak back as the obvious target of anti-Muslim discrimination without reinforcing one's communal difference; and how to intervene as both a Muslim and a citizen when the particularity of the former contravenes the universalism of the latter. His demand for the right to indifference constitutes a novel response, one this chapter explores. Not all Muslim French use or would agree with Farid's framework of the right to indifference, and some Muslim activists understand their claims precisely as a right to difference. Nevertheless, Farid's turn of phrase reflects a rearticulation of the relationship between public piety and citizenship that a number of Muslim French have begun to undertake, in which Muslimness no longer means only alterity or difference. In examining this rearticulation, the chapter intervenes in a trans-Atlantic conversation about minorities in liberal polities and what William Connolly (2002) calls the problem of identity/difference. Drawing on the political ethic and citizenship practices of Muslim French, including the very notion of Muslim French itself, I problematize the framework of recognizing difference that increasingly governs the scholarly analysis and political adjudication of minorities' claims in France and elsewhere in the West. I ask, instead, whether one can be publicly Muslim without automatically being classified as different and whether one can be visibly but unremarkably Muslim in France—that is, a citizen, a Muslim, Muslim French.

The Dominance of Difference

Farid's demand for the right to indifference is located in the context of an evolving French politics concerning citizenship and minority difference. After various policy experiments in the 1970s regarding how to manage North African immigrants and their children in France, the 1981 electoral victory by the Socialist Party ushered in a right-to-difference era. This new paradigm was part of a larger project of economic and political decentralization that sought to embrace and preserve regional particularities. Over the next few years, the right to difference would become a politically acceptable rallying cry not only for regional movements (Giordan 1982) but for ethno-cultural immigrant movements as well, which borrowed the rhetoric of regionalist differentialism to garner political and financial support for immigrant and second-generation cultural associations (Cesari 1994; Silverstein 2004). Through various government-inspired policies and pluralist rhetoric, numerous immigrant and second-generation associations, including those of the Beur movement, articulated their right to cultural difference without seeming to threaten the integrity of the French nation, at least in the minds of Left-leaning republicans.

By the mid-1980s, however, even the Left had abandoned the right to difference. Most scholars attribute this political and rhetorical about-face to the rise of Jean-Marie Le Pen's extreme Right party, the National Front (Feldblum 1999; Favell 2001; Lebovics 2004). Drawing on nineteenth-century racialism and Catholic nationalism to posit a homogeneous and deeply Catholic idea of France, Le Pen turned the right-to-difference argument on its head, claiming that France, too, had a right to cultural purity, free from the polluting influences of its Muslim North African and West African residents. In the face of Le Pen's xenophobic redeployment of the right to difference, a remarkable consensus emerged between the mainstream Left and Right that promoted the primacy of the republican model of integration. Since then, in "the political discourse that has reigned virtually unchallenged . . . 'multiculturalism' and such related terms as 'difference,' 'communities,' and 'ethnic minorities' have been interpreted as signaling the actual or potential breakdown of French society" (Blatt 1997, 46). A number of republican commentators even blame the idea of the right to difference for the rise of the National Front.[1]

In this political context, public expressions of Muslim ritual life as well as various appeals by Muslims—for state-funded Muslim private schools, the right to wear headscarves in public schools, the incorporation of Muslim holy days into the national school calendar, and state funds to build mosques—are interpreted by many republicans as unacceptable demands to recognize and institutionalize Muslim difference. This flies in the face of the assimilationist model of integration, in which subnational differences are meant to be subsumed by the national qua universal general will (Schnapper 1994).[2] So-called identitarian movements like the Islamic revival are thought to constitute a form of *communautarisme*, understood as privileging ethnic, religious, or racial affiliations over belonging to the nation and thereby threatening the civic unity of the republic. In *La république enlisée* (The sinking republic), for example, the political philosopher Pierre-André Taguieff chastises theorists of multiculturalism—in particular, the Canadian philosopher Charles Taylor and the French sociologist Michel Wieviorka—for celebrating "a politics of difference" that contravenes "the universalist conception of national citizenship, especially that of the French tradition" (Taguieff 2005, 114, 281). Taguieff goes on to criticize the emergence of a publicly engaged Muslim religiosity as the manifestation of "a politics founded on the 'right to difference' [in which] each individual [must] maintain above all 'his difference'" (278). He argues that "in order to bring into being an 'integrated' Islam, one must rely on an integrative political structure whose founding principles generate the strong adherence of citizens and fire the imaginations of candidates for integration" (305). Taguieff's argument implies that not only are public practices of Muslim piety a politics of difference, but also that they represent an unintegrated

Islam whose practitioners are "candidates for integration" rather than citizens of the republic. Taguieff is hardly alone in making this argument. I single him out because he is a well-known public intellectual with a long presence in the French public sphere, and because he so succinctly sets forth the three intertwining narratives that dominate mainstream republican thinking about the French Islamic revival: first, that publicly pious Muslims are not fully French because they are not yet integrated; second, that their public practice of Islam constitutes a demand for the right to difference, which in turn confirms their lack of integration of French norms; and third, that public piety politicizes religious and cultural identities that should remain in the private sphere.

Republicans like Taguieff dominate public, political, and scholarly life in France. However, in the late 1990s a group of intellectuals began critiquing what they considered a repressive republicanism hostile to difference. These scholars continue to call for a more inclusive republic open to recognizing religious, cultural, racial, and sexual differences. In fact, Taguieff is correct to invoke Taylor and Wieviorka together: though inclusivists like Wieviorka generally eschew the term multiculturalism, they are nonetheless in conversation with key Anglo-American theorists of identity and recognition. Wieviorka (1997), Alain Touraine (2000 and 2005), and Farhad Khosrokhavar (1997b) depart from the traditional republican stance that identities based on cultural, ethno-racial, religious, and sexual orientations must remain private or risk destabilizing the nation. Instead, these scholars understand new identity movements as the inevitable sociohistorical product of a postindustrial age that is no longer defined by relations of production but by a different set of terms: subjectivity, identity, recognition, and alterity. The scholars interpret the Islamic revival as stemming from the contradiction between a universalist republicanism that claims not to recognize subnational difference and the reality of sociopolitical and economic discrimination based on ethno-racial and religious difference. French of Maghrebi descent take on an Islamic identity, the argument goes, for a postnational, postethnic sense of belonging in a society that otherwise rejects them. In fact, a number of scholars understand the Islamic revival as an embracing of the stigma of Muslim difference. Writing about the headscarf, Nilufer Göle contends that wearers seek to transform the veil from a "sign of 'stigma'" into a "sign of 'prestige,'" an analysis she then extends to the revival more generally: "The Islamist movement subscribes to a similar logic in seeking, through the production of religious difference and through its exacerbation via 'ostentatious' signs, to achieve a public visibility" (2005, 123).

Göle is not alone in interpreting the demand for public visibility as the iteration of Muslim difference. Though scholars like Khosrokhavar, Wieviorka, and Touraine avoid the language of the right to difference that they associate with "radical multiculturalism" (Khosrokhavar 1997b, 150), they nonetheless propose "cultural rights" (Touraine 2005, 31) and the "recognition of cultural difference" (Wieviorka 1997, 53) as the most pragmatic way forward in an increasingly multicultural, multiethnic, and multireligious France. They thereby echo the descriptive and prescriptive analysis of other, non-French political philosophers who recommend the recognition and accommodation of cultural, ethno-racial, religious, and sexual differences as the most effective form of justice (Taylor 1994; Honneth 1995; Kymlicka 1995).

Two themes inform inclusivist republicans' work. First, these writers group together nonnormative ethno-racial, religious, and sexual identities under the sign of difference, and especially of cultural differences (*différences culturelles*), interpreting any desire to practice these identities publicly as a demand for cultural rights (*droits culturels*). Second, and concurrently, they claim that these new cultural movements are apolitical and should not, unlike classical political movements, be analyzed under the rubric of citizenship.[3] Touraine, for example, defines cultural demands as "the right to one's beliefs, to one's life habits, etc." (2005, 126) and observes: "The most important thing to understand is that one cannot consider cultural rights an extension of political rights, in the sense that the latter must be accorded to all citizens, while cultural rights protect, by definition, particular populations. This is the case for Muslims, who demand the right to observe Ramadan; it is also the case for gays and lesbians, who demand the right to marry. What is at issue here is no longer the right to be like others, but the *right to be other*" (270).[4] Wieviorka similarly states that the political framework of citizenship is not useful in adjudicating questions of cultural particularity. The rubric of citizenship, he writes, does not resolve "demands that are simultaneously, at their source, identitarian and social." Such demands require the "particular recognition of cultural difference" (1997, 53).

Without reducing the assimilationist politics of republicans like Taguieff to the far more pluralist politics of Touraine and Wieviorka, I nonetheless want to highlight how both positions continue to reinscribe Islam as a sign or practice of difference in France. The two groups of public intellectuals diverge only in how they propose to manage that difference: the former group calls for assimilation, the latter for limited recognition. Wieviorka and Touraine specifically engage the domain of policy, and Touraine's work highlights the political imaginary behind the analytical lens of difference. Touraine served as a member of the Stasi Commission and has long been a major intellectual presence in academia and the French public sphere. I therefore want to parse the example of cultural rights that Touraine offers, namely the right to observe Ramadan without suffering punitive sanctions in one's professional or educational life. When Muslim French assert such a right, many of them regard it as a matter of equality: since observant Christians are already accommodated by a professional and school calendar organized around Christian holy days, observant Muslims should have an equal right to absences on Muslim holy days. Such a demand does not necessarily have to be construed as a right to Muslim difference but rather as a right to equal citizenship. According to Touraine, however, the right to observe Ramadan comprises a demand "to be other."

Underlying Touraine's politics of recognition that relegates minorities to the space of difference is the refusal to acknowledge Muslim as French and French as Muslim. Here, the distinction between French and Muslim is transposed onto the distinction between the polity (or simply "us") and difference. A seemingly inclusive politics that recognizes Muslim difference actually reproduces certain ways of being and thinking as different, as Other, leaving dominant norms and assumptions intact. In his contention that the right to celebrate Ramadan and to marry a same-sex partner are demands for the recognition of difference, Touraine—despite being open to the institutional accommodation of some of these demands—not only reproduces Muslims and queers as fundamentally Other but also reinscribes the religious and sexual majority's identity and values as the neutral norm, as not different, as "us."

By framing Muslim French demands as an assertion of otherness or difference, inclusivist republicans turn these claims into matters of culture rather than politics. As Touraine declares, whereas political rights must be accorded to all citizens, "cultural rights protect, by definition, particular populations"; cultural rights therefore cannot be considered an extension of political rights since what is at issue is not "the right to be like others, but the right to be other." Various implications follow. In the context of debates about what constitutes the nation, to be Other is not to be French, as Others are necessarily different from the French norm. Moreover, since Muslims are always already outside the norm and outside the national polity—which their status as Others confirms—their demands become particular, for they concern not the polity as a whole but rather a small subset of Others. And if this is the case, they are not truly political demands but cultural ones, not the demands of citizens concerned with claiming or extending citizenship rights but rather the demands of Others concerned with affirming their particular cultural difference. In the two examples Touraine offers—marriage rights for gays and lesbians and the right to observe Ramadan for Muslims—he does not regard these two claims as demands for the extension of existing political rights that have been unjustly denied to some citizens. Instead, he can only conceive of them as demands to be Other, and therefore as cultural demands. When Touraine blithely observes that cultural rights "always concern a particular population, almost always in the minority" (2005, 270), it never occurs to him that there may be a relation between those two observations. He does not see that a racial, religious, or sexual minority's a priori status as an excluded community, as already outside the norm, overdetermines the group's political demands for full citizenship as the so-called particular demands of a cultural minority. Furthermore, he does not see that the preexisting exclusion of minorities makes the demand for the extension of political rights of citizenship (read as cultural rights) necessary in the first place.

Inclusivist public intellectuals like Touraine and Wieviorka are certainly more open to public Muslim life than assimilationist republicans are. But they nonetheless maintain a fairly traditional idea of France that positions Muslimness as inherently different from the norm. Despite policy disagreements, then, apparently opposed political positions share the binary terms in which the Muslim question is usually posed: assimilation versus difference, political versus cultural, French versus not quite French. Whereas Touraine proposes the recognition and accommodation of Muslim difference, Taguieff decries it, but they both position Muslim as inherently different from French. Whereas Touraine finds the supposedly cultural claims of the Islamic revival to be apolitical, Taguieff finds that they illegitimately politicize the properly religious, but both affirm a distinction between the religious or cultural and the political. And, as a result, both believe the right to public Muslim piety has little to do with citizenship.

Yet the UFI manifesto written by Karima and her colleagues is an explicit political intervention, interweaving assertions of citizenship and of Muslim particularity. It stakes a claim to France by appealing to "our society," and it calls on other citizens to affirm "the right of Muslim citizens to live their faith" (Unis Face à l'Islamophobie 2010). The manifesto offers a small glimpse of how to be a Muslim and a citizen, a French citizen of Muslim faith. The following sections explore these simultaneous claims.

The bedrock of the French Islamic revival remains the local association. Hundreds of Muslim associations dot the country. Some of them are extremely local, while others are regional or national. Some of them are concerned with social and cultural activities, while others are more conventionally political. Some serve particular segments of the population, while others construe their mission more broadly. One such local association is the Nantes branch of Young Muslims of France (Jeunes Musulmans de France, or JMF). Its headquarters is on the ground floor of a run-down commercial center surrounded by public housing towers in Bellevue. Male teenagers, most of them of Maghrebi or West African descent, often mill around the concrete plaza outside, playing pickup games of soccer, riding scooters, and chatting. Inside the JMF headquarters, the linoleum floor shines and the small fridge is stocked with sodas for youth who hang out there after school and on weekends. On the wall, two signs are posted: "No insults or vulgar language" and "Please keep the center clean." JMF-Nantes, staffed by volunteers and two full-time workers whose salaries are paid by local government contracts to promote youth employment, offers after-school activities, job counseling, weekend social activities, and sports tournaments, all aimed at the underprivileged youth in the neighborhood. In 2004 the governing board of JMF-Nantes was made up of ten Muslim French in their mid-twenties to mid-thirties, many of whom had been friends since childhood.

Though the services that JMF-Nantes offers are not explicitly Islamic, a group of practicing Muslims founded and continue to run the association. Signs of Muslim religiosity abound: a bulletin board advertises conferences and seminars offered by local mosques and Muslim associations, and the bathroom is fitted with a row of hand and foot sinks for ablutions before prayer. The staff is nonetheless adamant that the services JMF-Nantes provides are for everyone, Muslim and non-Muslim alike, and although some of the local youth I spoke with who participate in JMF-Nantes activities foregrounded their Muslimness, many others did not. Still, the JMF's name—Young Muslims of France—emphasizes its Muslim identity and what one member called its Muslim ethic.

One of the youth activities I attended was a training session in business management conceived and run by Mourad, a young man of Algerian descent in his mid-twenties. Soft-spoken and attentive, Mourad was one of the few male leaders of JMF-Nantes who had never been a petty criminal as a youth, and his aberrantly spotless record was a source of much amusement to his friends and colleagues in JMF-Nantes. Four male high-school students of Moroccan, Tunisian, Algerian, and Vietnamese descent attended Mourad's workshop. The group met every Tuesday evening to plan the creation of a new brand of sneakers. The town of Nantes was underwriting the project, the goal of which, according to Mourad, was to teach the teenagers the virtues of investment, creativity, and entrepreneurship, as well as to give them professional skills that would be useful in the job market. All the young men told me that they had come because they wanted to learn competitive job skills that would get them out of Bellevue and because they were interested in sports and fashion. Mourad told me later that he had chosen the sneaker idea so as to "remain within our cultural references," by which he meant the banlieue culture of French youth, steeped in le foot (soccer), sports-oriented fashion (tracksuits, sneakers, and soccer jerseys), and American and French hip-hop and its attendant practices (break dancing and le tag, or graffiti). Mourad also told me that "in France, there is a welfare culture where people just try to get by on assistance from the state," and that this project was a way to get neighborhood youth "out of that ghetto mentality." Though many businesses in Nantes had been wary of subsidizing an association with the term Muslim in its name, Mourad had managed to garner financial backing from one bank, the Caisse d'Epargne. Normally placid and not particularly politically critical, Mourad became visibly angry about how difficult it had been to get support for his project. He declared that regardless of the municipality's discomfort with the Muslim label of his association, JMF-Nantes had a right to subsidies as a registered cultural association.

Since the conversation had turned to the Muslim label of JMF-Nantes, I asked Mourad and his workshop protégés why they had opted for that name if the association's activities were not just for Muslims. Abdel, a bushy-haired eighteen-year-old of Algerian descent, immediately retorted: "Let me ask you: Why remove it? We are young, we are Muslim, we are French." It would be easy to read Abdel's declaration, and the existence of JMF-Nantes more generally, as a demand for the recognition of Muslim difference, and that is how outsiders have read the Muslim associational movement. But Abdel's simultaneous invocation of "Muslim" and "French" and the general political ethic of JMF-Nantes suggest a very different politics at work, one that Farid alluded to in our discussion of citizenship and difference. For Farid, the recognition of difference continues to reinscribe Muslim subjects like him as outside France. Rather than a right to or recognition of difference, he and other Muslim French implicitly and explicitly claim instead a right to indifference, which they understand as a right to equal citizenship.

Attempting to reframe entirely the current debate about so-called Muslim difference, Farid insists on his right to indifference, but on terms that do not require his assimilation to majority religious, cultural, and racial norms. This is representative of a broader Muslim French political ethic, exemplified by associations like JMF-Nantes. In contrast to the politics of republican integration, Muslim French seek to publicly inhabit their non-normative identities, conventionally understood as their difference. But in contrast to a differentialist politics, they do not want their difference to be recognized as such. Consequently, Muslim French call for the indifference to difference, so that their identity is neither abstracted nor overdetermined, rendered neither invisible nor hypervisible. Muslim French demand the right to be visible but unremarkable—put simply, the right to be. The word *unremarkable* captures both the Muslim French desire to be unremarked on as well as their desire to represent an unexceptional occurrence in French public space. Houria Bouteldja, a founding member of the Natives of the Republic Party (Parti des Indigènes de la République, or PIR), put it this way in a conversation with me: "We want the right to be *ordinary* [on veut le droit d'être *banal*]." The similarity between Bouteldja's and Farid's phrases underscores how widespread this sentiment remains among French of Maghrebi and African descent, since the PIR is an antidiscrimination collective that does not position itself as explicitly Muslim, but rather represents the concerns of nonwhite subjects more generally. The desire to be ordinary propels many Muslim French to claim the public practice of Islam not as a right to difference but as an entitlement of equal citizenship. Rather than occupying the place of difference within a more tolerant and inclusive France, Muslim French argue that they are *not* different: they are French.

For those activists theorizing explicitly about the right to indifference, it takes two specific forms. The first is best exemplified by Bouteldja, who mentioned Arabs' and blacks' right to ordinariness in the middle of a conversation about homophobia among French Muslims. She was describing the PIR's decision not to work with progressive queer-rights organizations like the Pink Panthers, since the PIR's base, she claimed, would neither understand nor approve of such alliances. Bouteldja was quite frank in ascribing a casual homophobia to much of the Muslim and Maghrebi community, but she wanted to know why this homophobia was any more problematic than that of any other community, and why Muslim homophobia should constitute a citizenship deficit in a way that Catholic or Jewish (or, I would add, secular-republican) homophobia does not.[5] In asserting the right to ordinariness, Bouteldja was insisting that homophobic attitudes among Maghrebi-origin French, and criminal or delinquent acts by citizens and residents of Maghrebi descent, should not be treated any differently from forms of homophobia, criminality, or delinquency practiced by those often referred to as "autochthonous French" (*français de souche*). She was questioning, in other words, why homophobia on the part of Muslims or Franco-Maghrebis should signify a lack of Frenchness and provoke the threat of expulsion when similar attitudes among non-Muslims—including members of the governing Union for a Popular Movement—remain utterly ordinary.

The second, somewhat different, articulation of the right to indifference concerns the right to participate in French society and shape its general interest as citizens. Younès, a member of the Collective of French Muslims (Collectif de Musulmans de France, or CMF), put it in the following terms: "If one is a French citizen of Muslim faith, that means that all spaces of dialogue, of debate, of social transformation—all these spaces concern us." Bouteldja's notion of indifference leaves intact the organization of center and periphery, the latter a space of discrete communal differences. In contrast, Younès and the CMF—a national-level umbrella group of Muslim French activists who participate in or lead smaller local associations across France—seek to unsettle the very notion of difference itself, imagining the polity as crosscut by a multiplicity of differences without any essential form of nondifference (or natural majority). Younès's spatial metaphor— "all these spaces concern us"—undoes the distinctions between general and particular and between center and periphery that undergird both the republican model of integration and the differentialist politics of recognition. Younès's declaration has two connected meanings that come together in JMF-Nantes's activities. First, as he explicitly announces, Muslim French can and should intervene in French society as a whole and not only in their particular communities. Second, he argues implicitly that even when acting in their own particular community, Muslim French are always already intervening in France more broadly, since Muslim French are by definition French.

These divergent interpretations of the difference-indifference paradigm, represented by Bouteldja and Younès, reemerge in an ongoing debate among Muslim French about state-funded Muslim private schools. The debate exemplifies the various ways in which Muslim activists in France understand and approach Muslims' relationship to the broader national community of citizens, as well as Muslims' relationship to the state. The state continues to fund private religious schools—most of them Catholic—that teach the national curriculum. Only two state-funded Muslim schools exist in France, an inequality that has become particularly glaring since the 2004 law. Although Catholic and Jewish students who wish to be conspicuously religious can attend, respectively, private Catholic and Jewish schools, Muslim schools for students who wish to be conspicuously Muslim remain almost nonexistent.

To correct this inequality, a number of Muslim organizations, including the Union of Islamic Organizations of France (Union des Organisations Islamiques de France, or UOIF), have called for the establishment of more private Muslim schools that would teach the national curriculum and eventually be recognized as officially "under contract" with, and thereby funded by, the state. Thami Breze, president of the UOIF, explained to me that private Muslim schools are a matter of equal citizenship, and Muslims in France should receive the same accommodations that other religious communities receive within the legal and political framework of laïcité. Unlike many republicans, he does not regard private Muslim schools as an act of separatist communautarisme but as an act of citizenship. State-funded private Muslim schools would, according to Breze, constitute a major step toward full political equality for French Muslims through the existing framework that accommodates other religious communities.

The CMF agrees with the principle of equality undergirding Breze's position and finds it unfair that Muslims have not been extended the right of state-funded private education. However, CMF members do not advocate for the creation of Muslim private schools. They claim instead that public schools should serve all students, including conspicuously Muslim ones. They contend that public education is a right of citizenship, and that rather than creating a separate educational domain for religious Muslims, existing public schools should address the religious needs of its young Muslim French citizens, including dietary requirements, sartorial practices, and time off for religious holidays. They also argue that opening up the public school in this way would enable students to learn from each other, promoting a citizenship based on mutual respect.[6] Instead of leaving intact a political architecture in which Muslim educational equality would be achieved by creating separate Muslim educational spaces, accommodated as spaces of difference, the CMF reimagines the configuration of educational and political space itself. Not surprisingly, the CMF was at the forefront of the One School for All Collective, the major organizing force against the 2004 law that brought together various groups with differing ethical and political commitments around the singular goal of the right to public education.[7]

The distinction between the right to difference and the right to indifference is not simply a matter of semantics, then, but goes to the heart of differing political visions. Moreover, those who construe the Islamic revival as nonpolitical, or as a retreat into a communalist identity, misapprehend a major trend within the revival and misconstrue both the particular political interventions Muslim associations are making and their imbrication in a long tradition of republican citizenship. As the historians Philip Nord (1998) and Sudhir Hazareesingh (1998 and 1994) have demonstrated, since the late nineteenth century associational activities have constituted a key aspect of citizenship and participatory democracy in France. According to Nord, republican political thinkers believed that voluntary associations trained men and women in the habits of democratic citizenship, and he contends that Jewish and Protestant associational life played a formative role in developing the republicanism of the Third Republic. Hazareesingh further notes that the 1901 law enshrining the freedom of association—under which almost all Muslim French associations have been established—was considered a fundamental feature of participatory democracy (1994, 81). Muslim French associations reproduce this tradition of classical republican citizenship in two ways. First, the day-to-day activities involved in founding and running a Muslim civic association constitute citizenship in action, indirectly cultivating the sensibilities and commitments of the engaged republican citizen. And second, many Muslim French associations see themselves as explicitly pedagogical, offering services and activities that teach banlieue youth citizenly values like social solidarity and care for the environment.

Indeed, associations like the JMF, CMF, Muslim Students of France, and Union of Young Muslims (Union des Jeunes Musulmans, or UJM) frame their activities as practices of fraternity and solidarity, two foundational principles of the republic that, Muslim French argue, are being increasingly forgotten, usually to the detriment of nonwhite immigrants, the poor, and the aged. More than a few of my interlocutors brought up the death of 15,000 mostly elderly people during the 2003 heat wave in France as the shameful result of state inaction and many French people's general disregard for their fellow citizens. A few months after the heat wave, Farid invoked the image of elderly men and women left to die as their grown children and professional caregivers vacationed at the beach. He lambasted the lack of familial and social ties that had allowed such a tragedy to occur, concluding angrily: "Who are they to give us lessons in citizenship?" Farid's point was twofold. First, it alluded to the hypocrisy of a mainstream French society that constantly disparages French Muslims' supposed lack of citizenship but cannot seem to fulfill its own commitment to fraternity. And second, it asserted that Muslim French are the true practitioners of French citizenship, the ones who know what real citizenship is and who practice what others only preach.

Although civic action and social justice are integral to practicing good citizenship, they are also foundational to being a practicing Muslim. Books and lectures by Tariq Ramadan on the Islamic duty of working for the social good not surprisingly resonated greatly with many of my interlocutors. In *Être musulman européen* (Being a European Muslim), for example, Ramadan writes that "justice and equality are not only notions or intellectual categories; they are the necessary steps to an ascension to truth and goodness, to generosity, to charity and love that allows the believer to be nearer to God" (1999, 55). The true comprehension of the teachings of Islam and of their authentic application, Ramadan continues, lies not only in faith (*al-iman*), consciousness of God (*al-taqwa*), and the regular practice of worship (*al-ibadat*), but also in one's mode of life and personal morality (*al-khuluq*), which entails "generosity, love of humanity, the effort to spread justice and do good" (54). Earlier, Ramadan had reminded his readers that "the Quranic teaching is clear: to believe is to act" (49). Thus, being a proper Muslim entails not simply correct belief but also right conduct, especially toward others in the world. In the domain of social action, the universality of republican values like fraternity, equality, and solidarity meets the universality of an Islamic ethos of justice.

How different Muslim French associations interpret the call to justice and to socially engaged action differs, of course. JMF-Nantes largely restricts its work to classically civil (rather than civic) activities. In addition, Mourad told me, "JMF-Nantes refuses to align itself with any political party—it's unhealthy." Nonetheless, JMF-Nantes members distinguish their association from purely humanitarian ones. Chiraz, a member of the association's governing board, once explained that distinction. Although JMF-Nantes members feel ethically compelled to help those in less fortunate situations, she said, their goal is not simple charity but rather the cultivation of citizenship among youth. Echoing nineteenth-century republican thinkers, JMF-Nantes activists see a pedagogical function to the association's activities, which seek to instill values—care for neighbors, self-respect, personal responsibility, thrift, and concern for the natural and built environment— that are equally Islamic and citizenly.

If JMF-Nantes has chosen to focus on local social services and eschews more conventionally political or civic activities, other Muslim associations are more explicitly political and extend their activities beyond the local. For instance DiverCité, to which Younès belongs, unites Muslim French activists and members of the Green Party in Lyon. It was formed specifically to promote political consciousness and political praxis among banlieue residents, and its Muslim French members generally lean further Left than the JMF-Nantes activists. DiverCité seeks to raise awareness about local candidates for office and to develop the capacity to influence politicians by building an electoral base in the banlieues. In 2007 it initiated voter registration drives and get-out-the-vote campaigns for the presidential election. Younès also belongs to the CMF, which is particularly notable for its work with non-Muslim progressive groups, such as the One School for All Collective. The CMF also conducted an awareness-raising campaign during the 2005 French referendum on the European Constitution, publishing opinion pieces in Muslim and non-Muslim media. Along with other French progressive groups, the CMF has criticized Europeanization as a neoliberal capitalist project that exacerbates national and global inequalities. CMF members have participated in antiglobalization summits like the European Social Forum and José Bové's summer gathering at Larzac. In addition, many women in the CMF are part of the Feminists for Equality Collective, formed in 2004 by progressive Franco-French and Franco-Maghrebi feminists as a forum to consider issues pertaining to religion and gender.

Being Muslim French therefore entails multiple, sometimes conflicting political sensibilities. Despite their similar commitment to good citizenship, CMF activists criticize the ethos of self-reliance and entrepreneurship that JMF-Nantes propagates. For the CMF, JMF-Nantes justifies antisocial neoliberal politics and rationalizes the rolling back of the welfare state, which has left poor and especially immigrant-origin communities to fend for themselves. JMF-Nantes members, in turn, disparage what they call a culture of dependence cultivated by turning to the state for help. Farid and Mourad both claimed that immigrants, in particular, need to take better charge of their lives in order to improve their circumstances without relying on the goodwill of the state. Mourad also told me that he did not understand how the CMF could align itself with the Green Party given the latter's call for the legalization of drugs, which he found contrary to Islamic norms of sobriety and moderation. What these disagreements signify, nonetheless, is a robust engagement by Muslim French with regard to what good citizenship entails—an engagement that, in turn, constitutes the practice of citizenship itself, according to republican political norms. That practice of citizenship, however, remains largely unacknowledged by the mainstream press, most politicians, and many scholars.[8]

Inclusivist republicans who see the discourses and practices of Muslim French not as a form of citizenship but as a form of difference nevertheless seek to accommodate them, but others have been less generous. Regardless of Muslim French activists' clear commitment to practicing citizenship, they are routinely accused of *communautarisme*, of promoting and practicing an inward-looking, particularist identity contrary to republican citizenship.[9] Dounia Bouzar, an anthropologist who has studied Muslim associations, finds that despite their espousal of engaged citizenship, Muslim French groups like the JMF and the UJM nonetheless allow themselves "to be enclosed within Islam." She finds it paradoxical to use "Muslim values . . . in order to construct a political and citizen-oriented sense of collective belonging" (2004, 139).[10] Bouzar's contention, one shared by most republicans, is that it is fundamentally contradictory to claim both a publicly Muslim identity and French citizenship.

In criticizing Muslim French for highlighting their Muslim particularity despite the universalist demands of French citizenship, commentators like Bouzar accept the hypothetical applicability and historical veracity of an unmediated relationship between citizen and state. This leaves no room for particular interests and culminates in a universal, abstract general will, Rousseau's *volonté générale*.[11] Republican political ideology often contrasts French civic citizenship, which entails participation through institutionalized political structures like political parties and trade unions, with Anglo-American civil citizenship, which is said to emerge through relations between individuals and groups.[12] Within such a schema, civil associational life is the domain of particular interests, which, in theory, have no place in French civic citizenship. Yet civil associational life has, at least since the late nineteenth century, played a constitutive role in the construction of French civic citizenship and the enactment of participatory democracy (Hazareesingh 1998; Nord 1998).

Beyond the historical inaccuracy of the civic-civil distinction at play in defining universal French citizenship, there remains a more intractable problem for acknowledging Muslim French as citizens: the fact that the general will has never been abstract or universal. Rather, it has represented and continues to represent a set of particular, embodied identities—usually white, male, bourgeois, heterosexual, and secular or Christian—that have proclaimed themselves universal. The general will, and the supposedly universal norms and principles it claims to represent and enact, has always been associated with particular identities and interests. Hence the concurrently contractual and cultural bases of republican citizenship, conceived of as a contract between free individuals yet also grounded in particular ethnoracial, religious, and kinship norms.[13] In fact, the relationship between cultural affinity and political membership is "an instrumental one: the ideal was political citizenship, [and] the means to achieve this ideal was shared cultural membership" (Laborde 2008, 178). Nonetheless, republicans have enforced a notion of citizenship as abstract, of the public sphere as neutral, and of the general will—thought to represent the national community of citizens—as universal. What this means is that the supposed inability to be a Muslim and a citizen is not generated by Muslims but by republicans; the alleged contradiction between being a Muslim and being a citizen is immanent to French republicanism.

When Muslim French speak as Muslims to resist the discrimination they face—as Karima and the UFI did—they acknowledge a political fact: their interpellation and consequent exclusion as Muslims. Yet doing so precipitates what Joan Scott has called the paradox of difference. "The terms of protest against discrimination," she writes, "both refuse and accept the group identities upon which discrimination has been based" (1999, 6).[14] Even as they act as citizens and partake in a long tradition of civil qua civic associational activity, the dual nature of French citizenship as universal and particular catches Muslim French in a double bind. The particular embodied identities and attendant interests that make up the universal general will a priori exclude Muslim subjects and interests from any notion of the general, of France as a whole. As a result, Muslim French attempt to reconfigure the normative model of citizenship and upend conventional notions of who can speak for France. They proclaim themselves French citizens of Muslim faith, deliberately linking Muslim concerns—from the serving of halal meat in school cafeterias and the ability of girls to wear headscarves in public schools to job training and voter registration for mostly Muslim and Franco-Maghrebi underprivileged youth—to the national interest. They also locate the commensurability, even the equivalence, of Muslimness and Frenchness in universal principles like justice, solidarity, and fraternity. But in underscoring these concerns, and in speaking and acting on behalf of Muslims via explicitly Muslim associations like the JMF and the CMF, they reinforce the apparent nonuniversality of their identities and their demands.[15] In sum, because Muslims are excluded from the community of citizens, they are compelled to respond to this exclusion by bringing their specifically Muslim interests to the attention of the polity and by seeking political, economic, and symbolic redress. In so doing, however, they reinforce their Muslimness—and their nonabstractness and nonuniversality—reproducing their ideological and embodied difference from the community of citizens and its general will. Their demands are subsequently read as purely Muslim demands for cultural rights, and as a sign of unacceptable communalism.

Importantly, this double bind is doubled again by a series of denials. Because republicans consistently deny that legal and political tactics of exclusion target Muslims specifically, Muslims have to first point out that they are the victims of discrimination. This then gives credence to accusations of communalist thinking that in turn justify so-called neutral, anticommunalist measures. The law of March 15, 2004, for example, is coded as a neutral and general law, aimed at banning all conspicuous religious signs in public schools, even though it was clearly understood by nearly everyone in France, and especially its champions, as a response to the problem of headscarves in schools. Thus the French press, making explicit what we all knew anyway, commonly dubbed it "the law on the veil." Likewise, the 2010 law that criminalizes the wearing of clothing aimed at concealing the face in any public space is also couched in neutral language, even though all debate leading up to its passage concerned the niqab. In an attempt to forestall challenges to the law under the European Convention on Human Rights, Michèle Alliot-Marie, minister of justice at the time, insisted that the legislation did not intend to stigmatize or single out one religion. But in the lead-up to parliamentary debate about the law, the National Assembly created a commission to study the possibilities for restricting what it called the burqa, and the government asked its internal security service to count the number of women wearing niqabs in France (367, it turned out). And once again, by consistently referring to the law as "the law on the burqa," the French press made explicit what the language of the law attempted to dissimulate. At the same time, the law revealed its intended target through its various exemptions. Article 2 states that the interdiction does not apply to clothing required or authorized by other laws, nor does it apply to clothing justified for professional or health reasons or to clothing worn in the context of sports, festivals, or traditional or artistic events. The express inclusion of festivals exempts the hooded, masked robes worn by Catholic penitents for the *Procession de la Sanch*, a public street procession in southern France during the week before Easter.

This game of denial and dissimulation occurs in more ordinary spaces, too. On the day the Stasi Commission report was released in 2003, the school where I worked as a language assistant held a general assembly on laïcité and the republican school. Its timing was coincidental: the Lycée Jean Nouvel was one of 15,000 high, middle, and primary schools chosen to be part of a National Debate on the Future of the School, initiated in 2003 by the Ministry of Education. A few hundred students and teachers filled the auditorium in the late afternoon in December. As is common in the northeast *banlieues* of Paris, the students were mostly of Maghrebi, African, or Antillean descent, and they had clearly come to talk about the Stasi Commission report. However, though my fellow teachers had spent the day's lunch and coffee breaks animatedly discussing the merits and failings of the report, neither they nor the school's administration made any mention of it for the first hour of the assembly. Finally, the assistant principal, a briskly authoritative middle-aged woman who generally had a good rapport with her students, opened the floor to student questions. Samir, a baby-faced student representative, came down to the microphone. He cleared his throat nervously and announced that the students wished to discuss something that had not yet been mentioned but was on everyone's mind, and that was the veil law. A number of students clapped and cheered. Samir explained that many of the students were not necessarily opposed to a well-written law, but that "Muslims feel very targeted by this law, which is really about the veil." Most of the teachers quickly and vociferously disputed Samir's account. Many of them shot back that, first, there was no law, only a proposed law; and second, that the proposed law concerned everybody, the veil being just one of the issues. Listening incredulously to my colleagues' denials, I realized that in my bag lay a copy of that day's *Libération*, whose cover trumpeted: "The experts say yes to a law on the veil" (Coroller 2003).

When another young woman began her remarks by saying "I am Maghrebi" so as to better contextualize her sense of being a target of the proposed law, a number of teachers interrupted her to demand: "Why do you introduce yourself as Maghrebi? Why do you highlight your identity like that?" After she spoke, one of the teachers, a male professor of vocational studies, addressed her directly, asking: "Do you know which are the two days proposed by the Stasi Commission as national holidays?" The young woman answered "Aïd el Kébir and . . ." She paused, trying to recall the name of the other one, Yom Kippur. "And? And?" some of the teachers demanded in unison, as if to highlight the narrow, communalist nature of her knowledge of the law—of course she only knows the Muslim holiday!—and/or to unmask the anti-Semitism supposedly lurking within Arab-Muslim youth—of course she doesn't know the Jewish holiday! The teacher's question aimed to reveal the young woman's communalism and to position the students' desire to talk about the law and the targeting of Muslims as nothing but a sign of their communautarisme. And since combating Muslim communalism was one of the explicit justifications for the law, by exposing the presumed communalism behind Muslim students' desire to talk about it, the teachers implicitly underscored the very need for such a law.

The repeated proclamations of neutrality and universality by the teachers, Alliot-Marie, and the law itself constitute a kind of double talk. Such double talk reflects the way in which secular-republican power works through denial and dissimulation and, one could argue, self-deception, since adherents of republican neutrality are often quite sincere. These denials and dissimulations weave a vicious net around Muslim French, entrapping them in a repeating series of exclusions. Because the universal is always already the site of a privileged particular, subjects existing outside the particular-as-universal—those of marginalized racial, religious, gendered, or sexual particularities—will always speak from a subordinate position marked as irredeemably particular, from a position of difference. As a result, to claim to be both a publicly practicing Muslim and a French citizen can only be a contradiction, because the kind of subjectivity that Muslim French embody is excluded a priori from the general will and the national polity. In other words, the contradiction between universal and particular that underpins French citizenship and that systematically excludes various nonnormative subjects is displaced onto those subjects themselves, who—marked as inherently nonabstractable and therefore nonuniversal—must bear both the political and ontological burden for their exclusion from the community of citizens (to which, it should be remembered, most legally belong). Moreover, the various tactics that intentionally target Muslims and deliberately exclude them from the community of citizens are purposefully couched in neutral terms, and it is repeatedly denied that Muslims are the specific targets of these tactics in the face of all evidence to the contrary. As a result, Muslim French must first call attention to the fact that they, as Muslims, are the targets before even beginning to combat those tactics. Yet doing so elicits the charge of communautarisme, of thinking and talking too much about themselves as Muslims rather than abstract citizens. That, in turn, simply confirms the justification for their legal and political exclusion.

This is the double bind within which Karima and her fellow activists in the UFI had to formulate a response to the debate on national identity. They had to highlight the discrimination they face without overemphasizing their Muslimness and turning themselves into the *communautaristes* they are constantly suspected of being. There exists, consequently, an oscillation in the UFI's various petitions and statements between speaking as Muslims and speaking as citizens, one that republican critics like Bouzar would read as paradoxical or contradictory. That fluctuation reflects the impossibility and unintelligibility of the Muslim French subject position, an impossibility generated by republicanism's own internal tensions and its incapacity to conceive of Muslim as French, as anything but alterity and difference.

Recognition and Beyond

Given the dominant logic in France that positions Islam as always already the site of difference, one cannot but wonder about the feasibility of a politics of indifference. What are the limits not of the imagination but of the pragmatic, of the possible? After all, Muslim French politics takes place in a context in which two political logics dominate: the assimilationist republican framework of integration and the pluralist republican framework of the recognition of difference. The former seeks to render Muslim identity invisible, relegating Muslim attachments to the private sphere of belief. The latter, at least in the way it has been put into practice recently in France, seeks to publicly recognize and accommodate Muslim difference via the creation, for example, of the French Council on the Muslim Religion and the nomination of what are known as diversity candidates to various government posts and electoral lists.[16] Within existing political and administrative parameters, the political logic of recognition seemingly remains the only one that allows Muslim French to be publicly Muslim. A number of Muslim organizations, most notably the UOIF and its affiliate associations, have therefore chosen this kind of state recognition as the best means of advancing their claims to equal citizenship.

Nicolas Sarkozy's 2003 visit to the UOIF congress at Le Bourget, described in the previous chapter, was one of these moments of public recognition. Though Sarkozy proclaimed his visit to be a sign of acceptance and recognition of France's Muslim citizens, many regarded his speech as the catalyst for the 2003–4 debate about veiling in public schools. A number of Muslim French groups like the CMF and the UJM strongly criticized

Sarkozy's presence at Le Bourget, decrying the minister's heavy-handed security and antiterrorism measures that disproportionately target Arabs, Muslims, and other nonwhite immigrants. Given such criticism, I asked Farid in April 2004 whether the decision to invite Sarkozy had been a wise one, and I was flummoxed when he answered affirmatively. When I asked him why, he replied: "Because it constituted a kind of recognition by the republic, via its interior minister, of the UOIF as being within the republican framework, as being acceptable." Farid observed that although a few municipal councilors had attended the UOIF's congress in the past, Sarkozy was the first significant French political figure ever to attend. In coming, he had legitimized the UOIF, and now, Farid said, "the politicians come, officially, and recognize the UOIF." He continued: "I see [Sarkozy's] presence as a good thing. I don't share his views on everything, but I give him credit for having at least the audacity to come, to not consider us pariahs."

Farid's comments illustrate how the conventional politics of state recognition remains, thus far, the only plausible alternative to assimilationist republican policies. On the one hand, Muslim French remain wary of the reinscription of their Muslimness as pure difference, hence their desire for what Farid called the right to indifference. On the other hand, the dominant national imaginary does not include Muslims in its conception of the national interest or general will. In this context, many Muslim French feel compelled to demand various forms of symbolic, political, and legal recognition from the state in order not to remain entirely separate from the national polity.

Farid's response to my question about Sarkozy explains the otherwise inexplicable standing ovation that the minister received, despite ending his speech by warning the audience that the nation was watching them and that they should not disappoint the republic. I remember my astonishment at Sarkozy's final words, and my bewilderment at the thunderous applause that followed them. I remember, too, my confusion as I listened a year later to Farid defend Sarkozy's visit, the same Farid who had so often told me of his desire for a politics of equal citizenship beyond the recognition of difference. Yet these reactions index the extent to which Muslims are maligned in France, and the affective relief that positive recognition brings. The response to Sarkozy's speech signals the constraints of the Muslim French position, caught between a dominant politics of assimilation and an emerging politics of recognition. Farid's and the crowd's reaction attests to the limits of reconfiguring citizenship and national identity when one's legitimacy is constantly denied. Their reaction also attests to the seeming absurdity of my own advice to Karima and the UFI to speak as citizens, when they are recognized only as Muslims.

Nonetheless, Muslim French insistence on speaking as citizens and Muslims simultaneously impels us to ask what kind of alternative political possibilities can be imagined and can perhaps emerge in France. Not all Muslim French have accepted the political logic of recognition as their only viable option for redress. The CMF, for instance, criticizes assimilationist republicanism but also rejects the limited political recognition the state offers through processes like the creation of the French Council on the Muslim Religion.[17] Members of the CMF have publicly and privately denounced the council as a neocolonial enterprise intended to bring Islam under the watchful eye of the state. Younès was similarly critical of the UOIF's invitation to Sarkozy to speak at Le Bourget, arguing that it involved a kind of quid pro quo whereby the French state accorded legitimacy to the UOIF in exchange for the UOIF's silence on many of the government's draconian policies. According to Younès,

> There was a deal for the recognition of the UOIF by the government, because an interior minister who comes to speak at your place, it means that he recognizes you, and the other side of the deal was, okay, we [that is, the UOIF] are going to play the game. Let's say that tomorrow, the government tells us to do this, we will do it. It's a deal! You think that Sarkozy, he went there [to Le Bourget] in front of 15,000 people to talk about the headscarf by chance?! It's not possible, these are politicians, these guys, they have calculated strategies. He went there saying, "Voilà, I recognize you, but now let's talk about the headscarf." And since we started talking about the headscarf, we've covered up all the other problems. We've covered up discrimination at work, in housing, the failure of education, ghettos, racism, police brutality, injustice. We've covered all that up, it's like it doesn't exist!

Younès's point was not simply that the debate about the headscarf distracted attention from other pressing problems, but also that recognition and inclusion entail a form of silencing. Younès pointedly noted that the UOIF, one of the preeminent Muslim lobbying organizations in France, remained conspicuously absent in organizing against the 2004 law banning headscarves in public schools. He attributed the UOIF's aspiration for political recognition to its leaders being "what we call 'brothers of the homeland,' blédards," who, according to Younès, have "a relation of submission to authority." In contrast, he continued, "we [that is, the members of the second generation] have a more emancipated relation vis-à-vis political authority, a refusal of instrumentalization, a refusal of unhealthy deals. . . . We don't want recognition, we don't want a seat on anything. We want justice; we want equal treatment between people. Don't give us second-class treatment like you did in Algeria!"

In articulating this generational distinction, Younès made explicit the relationship I have been tracing between the unapologetic Muslim French claim to France and the critique of the recognition of their so-called difference, encapsulated by the demand for indifference. Significantly, indifference does not imply indifference toward others or toward social, political, and economic injustice; rather, it demands an accounting of Muslim French as full and equal parts of the whole, an accounting that does more than simply slot them into a political arrangement of minority satellites that leaves the center undisturbed. Younès's critique of Sarkozy and the UOIF also reflects his awareness of the costs of recognition as a political framework of redress, hinting at the ruse of reciprocity that underlies and is enacted by a politics of recognition. This ruse goes to the heart of the Hegelian dialectic of recognition on which contemporary accounts of the politics of recognition are largely based.

The Master's Problem?

Axel Honneth and Charles Taylor, the two major originators of the framework of recognition as the basis for social relations and therefore for justice, both draw on Hegel as their conceptual touchstone.[18] In Phenomenology of Spirit, Hegel traces the efforts of self-consciousness to acquire self-certainty. It first consumes other objects, then it kills another self-consciousness. Each time, however, the struggle for self-certainty proves fruitless, since it entails destroying the object necessary to confirm self-consciousness's sovereignty. Hegel's next step in this dialectic consists, famously, in positing two opposed, unequal consciousnesses: "the independent consciousness, for which the essential thing is existence-for-itself," and "the dependent consciousness, for which the essential thing is . . . existence-for-another. The former is the Master; the latter, the Slave" (1977, 115). Yet even this relationship of recognition remains unstable: searching for recognition by another self-consciousness, the master has instead found recognition through the slave, a subordinate whose recognition cannot count for the master in any meaningful way.

Taylor utilizes Hegel's master-slave dialectic as an illustration not only of our intersubjectively determined identities but also, fundamentally, of the necessity of mutual and equal recognition in processes of identity formation. He interprets Hegel's dialectic as an argument against hierarchical identities and for a politics of equal dignity. Since recognition by subordinates is not of any real worth, "the struggle for recognition can find only one satisfactory solution, and that is a regime of reciprocal recognition among equals" (Taylor 1994, 50). Though Honneth draws on Hegel's earlier writings on the struggle for recognition, he follows a parallel approach, noting that if our identities are formed intersubjectively through relationships of recognition, "an obligation to reciprocity is, to a certain extent, built into such relations" (1995, 37–38). For Taylor and Honneth, struggle occurs when the equal reciprocity of the recognition relation is not respected and certain parties—that is, marginalized minorities—are not recognized as they should be. Nonreciprocity entails misrecognition of and disrespect for marginalized minorities; the solution to negative recognition, therefore, entails positive recognition and the reestablishment of the mutual reciprocity on which intersubjective relations of recognition ostensibly depend.

But as Younès's critique underscores, the ease with which reciprocity can be established and reestablished through a process of recognition remains highly debatable. In fact, Hegel's master-slave relationship—the basis for the theory of self-certainty (or identity) through recognition—is distinctly unreciprocal and thoroughly antagonistic since, as Patchen Markell points out, the realization of self-certainty and the acquisition of sovereignty are premised on the subordination of another. Consequently, Markell argues that though we should not reduce the corpus of Hegel's thinking on recognition to the master-slave parable, we must nonetheless consider its implications for a contemporary politics of recognition, namely, that "subordination [is] a persistent possibility in relations of recognition" (2003, 119). It is precisely that problem of subordination to which Younès gestures in his criticism of the UOIF and Sarkozy. His incisive diagnosis of recognition calls our attention to the subordination that haunts the original master-slave relationship and that is reproduced through a politics of recognition.

According to Younès, the state's recognition of marginalized communities cuts an unhealthy deal, whereby political recognition is traded for silence. The reciprocity (what he terms a quid pro quo) that seems to underlie this exchange turns out to be premised on and to reproduce the structural dominance of the recognizing state. As a number of scholars have observed regarding the politics of recognition in an Anglophone context, recognition—or accommodation, as it is sometimes called—often secures the recognizer's position of power and reifies the structural organization of majority and minority. The state and/or normative majority bestows recognition on minorities and allows so-called difference to exist and perhaps even to flourish, all the while reaffirming its own place as the central source of authority and as the neutral arbiter of conflict (Hage 2000; W. Brown 2008; I. Young 2009). Liberal and republican states make democracy and justice into a matter of recognition in the first place, creating powerful incentives for others to frame their claims about inequality as recognition claims (Povinelli 2002; Markell 2003). Moreover, as Markell in particular argues, the state's tactic of bestowing recognition becomes a way to actively transform minority cultural or religious communities into forms consistent with the requirements of modern government, a process I describe in the next chapter with regard to French Islam. It is precisely these various aspects of recognition, and the relationships of inequality and subordination that even well-intentioned gestures of inclusion produce, that Younès identified as an unhealthy deal between Muslims and the French state. For him, and for the many Muslim French whose sensibilities he articulates, the state's prior co-optation of the Beur generation and the present-day co-optation of the UOIF reveal political recognition as a tactic of governmentality. As such, the inclusionary or accommodationist gesture of recognition is produced by and reproduces the nonreciprocity always already contained within the Hegelian dialectic of intersubjective recognition.

Pulling a little harder at the thread of nonreciprocity that is woven into the politics of recognition, one also begins to notice that the original intersubjectivity of Hegel's recognition relation (as interpreted by Taylor and Honneth), which was fluid and flowed between subjects, becomes fixed and flows in only one direction. The most common critique of Taylor's influential concept of the politics of recognition is that he conflates the individual subject in Hegel's theory of self-consciousness with a collective one. In so doing, his critics contend, he wrongly essentializes cultures, his primary collective subject, into pure, bounded wholes when they are, in reality, internally complex and hybrid (Appiah 1994; Benhabib 2002; Song 2007). But there are other moments of consolidation in Taylor's account as well. Taylor's narrative permanently fixes minority and majority, transforming an exchange of recognition into a demand for recognition from the minority and the bestowal of it by the majority. In Taylor's seminal essay, and in consequent debates by like-minded scholars about the politics of recognition, it is always an ontological minority that demands recognition from the majority, never the other way around. That such an arrangement seems so obvious underscores my earlier point that the politics of recognition is both premised on and reproduces an arrangement in which certain ontological constellations are fixed as either the normative majority identity ("we") or difference (everything else). Moreover, in this arrangement, the majority's identity is stable, determined, and fixed. The majority does not seem to require another subject's recognition to achieve satisfactory self-identity; that compulsion applies only to subordinate minorities.

Yet in Hegel's original story, it is the master who demands recognition, not the slave. One has to wonder, then, whether the insistence that it is minorities that demand recognition is not, in fact, a displacement of another demand for recognition, one that cannot be acknowledged, for to do so would—as with Hegel's master—undermine the arrangement of dominant and subordinate that currently holds. To acknowledge that other need for recognition, in other words, would destabilize and disrupt the sovereignty and unity of the majority, of France, a unity that is constantly, even obsessively and anxiously, being iterated and reiterated. Hence the 2009 Grand Debate on National Identity, as well as the recent surfeit of republican paeans (or is it eulogies?) to the nation, one and indivisible, with titles like *Qu'est ce que la France?* (What is France?; Finkielkraut 2008), *Comment peut-on être français?* (How can one be French?; Djavann 2007), and *Fier d'être français* (Proud to be French; Gallo 2006). One could argue that these declarations of identity are also French republican demands for recognition in a context where self-certainty and sovereignty are lacking. But the demand for recognizing France as one and indivisible, as historically, politically, and culturally continuous, as racially and religiously distinct is, in truth, a demand for the misrecognition of France, a demand for the recognition of France as something that it is not and never has been. The narrative that Arabs and Africans are new arrivals in France and must integrate stems from willful misreadings of the historical record. Consequently, republicans' demand that Muslim French accept the prior unity and integrity of France as an entity that exists without them, and within which they can be only a form of difference, requires Muslim French to fundamentally misrecognize France. And that is something Muslim French refuse to do.

Rather, by reconnecting France to the Maghreb and by imagining themselves as simultaneously Muslim and French, as I have argued, Muslim French reconfigure—indeed, unsettle and resettle—France into a robustly cosmopolitical entity, writing themselves into its past, present, and future, broadening its political horizons, and pluralizing the polity itself. It is helpful here to reflect on the political philosopher Danielle Allen's distinction between the metaphors of oneness and wholeness in conceptions of the nation. Though oneness is often used as the main metaphor to describe a people or a nation, Allen proposes instead the metaphor of wholeness. The commitment to oneness, Allen argues, has often entailed practices that make "citizens who [are] not part of 'the one people' politically invisible" (2006, 18). Wholeness offers a different vision, she contends, since the word *whole* can encompass multiplicity in a way that *one* cannot. Muslim French have a similar vision of the nation. France is conventionally envisioned through the metaphor of oneness, symbolized by Bernard Stasi's clenched fist and inscribed into the French constitution, which affirms the republic as one and indivisible. In contrast, Muslim French imagine the community of citizens through the metaphor of wholeness, as an entity Assia called *la république plurielle* in response to Stasi's exclusivist gesture. That polity is a space that cultivates not homogeneity but heterogeneity, including the possibility of radical and incommensurable heterogeneities. It allows the formerly invisible and/or hypervisible to be simply visible— that is, to be citizens. A plural republic also recognizes the legitimacy of nondominant ways of life without classifying them as essentialized difference. Finally, by conceptualizing difference not as deviation but as variation, Muslim French pluralize difference to the extent that all communities are forms of difference, an arrangement that maps onto a global heterogeneity created by God.[19] Younès, for instance, in a discussion of the CMF's participation in the European Social Forum, cited Prophetic precedents for working with non-Muslims. Recounting that the Prophet had lived among pagans, Zoroastrians, Christians, and Jews, Younès noted that the Prophet "respected them and welcomed them and spoke with them, so today, why would I be more royalist than the king? It's against my Islamic principles" to shun working with others.

A major part of the Muslim French reimagining of the polity entails a commitment to disaggregating the center. Explaining the CMF's alliances with other progressive groups, Younès spoke of finding commonalities across differences: "For example, for me, personally, on a religious level I'm not going to defend gay marriage . . . even if you say it's a universal, I don't share in this universality. On the other hand, if you say to me, 'we're going to fight for equal treatment between men and women,' I agree! 'We're going to fight for equality between rich and poor nations,' okay! . . . That is to say, I have my corpus of references and I find bridges with others. . . . We'll fight together at least according to the minimal values that we share."

As a result, Younès and the CMF work with various progressive groups on specific projects, even though they do not share the same agenda across multiple political terrains. These projects include the One School for All Collective, the Feminists for Equality Collective, and DiverCité, all of which involve activists who do defend and advocate for gay marriage. There are certainly difficulties that have to be negotiated in these spaces of radical heterogeneity, but I want to underscore the extent to which Muslim French like Younès reject any a priori notion of political unity, or oneness. Instead, they embrace a future of multiplicity, as well as the attendant potential for disagreements that this entails.

Importantly, this political ethic fundamentally unsettles existing configurations of identity and difference, majority and minority, center and periphery. In a politics of difference that reproduces a center (French identity) and periphery (Muslim difference), identity and difference are taken to be essential characteristics. But such essentialization misconstrues the fact that difference is determined only by perspective. In contrast, Muslim French conceptualize difference not in relation to a center (which no longer exists) but rather in relation to various other identities, or differences. Difference here is always relational and constantly shifting, never essential. Indeed, Muslim French seem to understand better than many political theorists the inherently relational structure of the dyad identity-difference. And by refusing their designation as essential difference, by understanding difference not as deviation but as variation, Muslim French destabilize the fixedness of identity as French and the overdetermination of Muslimness as difference. They fundamentally pluralize difference itself, diffusing the polity into various cross sections of equally different differences.[20] In the political imagination and political practice of many Muslim French, there is no fixed, normative center, only dynamic, crosscutting constellations of heterogeneous identities. Difference, as a consequence, is conceptualized in relation not to a center but to various other identities (or differences). Moreover, according to this novel politics, we all inhabit various forms of difference in relation to each other. By refusing the existence of an a priori ontological majority, the polity envisaged by many Muslim French refuses any stable, essential, or unified political formations. It also refuses a necessary link between one's religious identity and one's political commitments. The political formations and alliances that emerge out of this reconfigured political imagination and practice are always ad hoc, cannot unite everyone, and continuously shift into new constellations, new configurations of the whole. When Abdelmalek Sayad surmised, then, that "we . . . do not know how to regard or treat these new-style immigrants, and nor do we know what to expect of them" (2004, 291), he was correct on both counts. It is precisely that sense of the unexpected that Muslim French embrace; they imagine France as a future-oriented space where politics is the domain of the unpredictable.

FIELD NOTES II   Friday Prayers

The Goutte d'Or neighborhood in the eighteenth arrondissement[1] of Paris is famous for its Friday prayers. Its two small mosques—the Khalid Ibn El Walid, known as the Mosquée Rue Myrha, and the Mosquée al-Fath on Rue Polonceau—have seen their congregations grow enormously in the previous two decades, well beyond their capacity. So every Friday until recently, the roads around the mosques were barricaded, traffic was rerouted, mosque personnel laid down large rugs in the road and on the sidewalks, and hundreds of African and Arab men lined up in neat rows to pray silently. One could see this act as a moving reclamation of public space and an impressive interruption of profane time, but public bureaucrats tend to be less generous. Though the police and the municipality tolerated street prayer for years, most government officials in Paris saw it as a problem of public order and an undignified way for Muslims to pray.

With the 2001 election of the Socialist Bertrand Delanoë as the mayor of Paris, his party's project of promoting culture and the arts was linked to solving the street prayer problem, and an Institute for the Cultures of Islam (Institut des Cultures d'Islam, or ICI) was proposed. Financed in large part by the city of Paris and housed until recently in a temporary space, the ICI is a multipurpose cultural center offering art exhibitions, concerts, poetry readings, and debates. When the center's two permanent structures are completed, the ICI will also offer Muslims two large areas for Friday prayers, though this space will remain inadequate for the 3,000 or so men who pray in the Goutte d'Or on Fridays. Nonetheless, according to Daniel Vaillant, mayor of the eighteenth arrondissement, once the ICI opens, no one will be allowed to pray outside on the street.

In 2010 the street prayer issue, until then a municipal concern, took on national dimensions. First, in June a small group of extreme Right activists planned what they termed a giant aperitif of sausages and wine in front of the Rue Myrha mosque in order to protest the Friday "occupation" of the Goutte d'Or by Muslims, whom they unironically called "resolute adversaries of our wine and our pork products" ("Un 'apéro saucisson et pinard' à Paris" 2010). On December 10 of the same year, Marine Le Pen of the National Front compared street prayer to the Nazi occupation of Paris. "It's an occupation of a part of the territory," she declared. "No, there aren't tanks, there aren't soldiers, but it's an occupation nonetheless" (Lemonde.fr avec AFP et Reuters 2011). Le Pen was roundly criticized for her reference to the Nazis, but politicians of the center Right nonetheless repeated the essence of her comments: street prayer was not simply a problem of public order but also a threat to national identity. Soon after Le Pen's statement, Minister of the Interior Claude Guéant asserted: "Praying in the street is not acceptable, it is a direct attack on the principle of laïcité, and it needs to end" (Leclerc, Cornevin, and Dingreville 2011).

In August 2011 Guéant's ministry suddenly preempted the raison d'être for the ICI when the Police Prefecture declared that, come September of that year, it would no longer tolerate street prayer. The ministry proposed using a former military barracks to accommodate the mosques' overflow and brought in Dalil Boubekeur, president of the French Council on the Muslim Religion, to help persuade the leaders of the two neighborhood mosques to agree to this plan. Located on the edge of the city near the Boulevard Périphérique that encircles Paris, the barracks is 2,000 square meters and can accommodate 2,500 people; according to the ministry's plan, it would be rented for €30,000 per year and managed by a newly created association composed of personnel from the Rue Myrha and al-Fath mosques. Officially proposed as a short-term solution until the ICI is completed, the barracks mosque nonetheless threatens the administrative justification for the ICI. Vaillant has therefore both claimed credit for the barracks idea and criticized it, disparaging the heavy-handed approach of the Sarkozy government and contrasting it with the more tolerant approach that the ICI presumably represents. Many ICI staff members were dismayed by the prospect of the new mosque, pointing out the ugly symbolism of relegating Muslims to a former military barracks on the outskirts of Paris, alongside a homeless shelter and the prostitutes who work the Boulevard Périphérique.

On Friday, September 16, 2011, the ban on street prayer went into effect. The Rue Myrha and al-Fath mosques both closed that day and posted signs directing their congregations to the new barracks mosque. I visited in the morning to speak to Mohammed Salah Hamza, the rector of the Rue Myrha mosque, who was giving interviews to journalists covering the story. Inside the enormous hangar-like building split into two sections, a few men were laying out large rugs to cover the floors of both rooms. As the hour of prayer approached, thousands of men began to converge on the barracks, a twenty-minute walk from their regular mosques in the Goutte d'Or. It turned out that the barracks could not accommodate the 3,000 or so faithful who arrived to pray, and a few hundred men lined up in rows in the parking lot. Their presence outside was apparently no longer a problem of public order or dignity for the municipality, however, since they were not blocking traffic and were out of public sight. Hamza told me that the two mosques in the Goutte d'Or would close for the first few Fridays in September in order to get congregants used to going to the barracks mosque. Even though the barracks mosque is ostensibly a temporary solution, he hopes that the Muslim association running the mosque—of which he is the president—will be able to buy the space and turn the barracks into a more permanent mosque.

Three

"A Memorial to the Future"

The Goutte d'Or (drop of gold) inherited its name from the wine grown on its hillsides in the nineteenth century. In 1860 it was annexed as a suburb to the growing metropolis of Paris. It soon became a major working-class district, settled by migrant workers first from the French countryside and then from Europe and beyond. In the 1920s Spaniards, Belgians, Poles, and Italians, as well as internal migrants from Brittany, settled there. By the 1950s the neighborhood had become home to a growing number of Algerian laborers, many of whom had arrived as single men and lived in migrant-worker hostels. As they married or were reunited with their families in the 1960s and 1970s, they began to move out of the Goutte d'Or and into more permanent housing in the outer-city suburbs. By the 1980s the composition of the Goutte d'Or had changed again, with the arrival of immigrants from West and Central Africa, Yugoslavia, and Asia.

The landmarks of the Goutte d'Or testify to this layered history of working-class immigration. At the corner of Rue Saint Luc and Rue Saint Bruno sits the Saint Bernard church, site of revolutionary debates during the 1871 Paris Commune. More than a hundred years later, in 1996, the church became a politically charged space once more, when three hundred undocumented migrants, most of them from Mali and Senegal, took refuge there to demand the regularization of their immigration status. On August 23, 1996, 1,500 officers from the national security forces broke down the church doors and arrested the undocumented workers, marking a seminal moment in the political struggle for migrant-worker rights, and the Saint Bernard church remains a major political landmark in the neighborhood. A few streets down, at the Barbès-Rochechouart metro station, sits another icon of the Goutte d'Or: the Tati department store. Created in 1948 by a Moroccan businessman to cater to budget-conscious, working-class shoppers, Tati has become something of an institution, the French version of K-Mart compared to more upmarket department stores like the Galeries Lafayette and Printemps. Further north, the Chateau Rouge metro station abuts another landmark, the Marché Dejean, an open-air market offering fish, halal meat and chicken, and West African fruits and vegetables. Adjacent shops advertise African and Asian hair-care products and skin-lightening creams, and the nearby Rue Poulet is lined with African and Asian street sellers hawking vegetables and fake designer handbags. Nearby, Rue Labat is home to half a dozen Sri Lankan restaurants catering to the growing Tamil population in Paris. In the daytime, Rue Doudeauville bustles with cafés frequented by men from Cameroon, the two Congos, Senegal, and Mali. At night, African prostitutes line the streets. On weekends, young white couples stroll these same streets and sit in the neighborhood's bars, signaling the gentrification of the area that began in the early 2000s.

The Goutte d'Or, then, is changing once again. The 2001 election of Bertrand Delanoë as mayor of Paris ushered in a wide-ranging policy of "revitalizing" and "revalorizing" immigrant, working-class neighborhoods like the Goutte d'Or.[1] Police have begun to target crack dealers, crack users, and prostitutes in an effort to clean up neighborhoods known mostly for drugs and crime. Insalubrious and rundown buildings are being renovated, and new public housing is being constructed, not only for low-income immigrant families but also for middle-income populations, in the name of promoting what officials call social mixing. The Socialists have enfolded this so-called revitalization of immigrant, working-class neighborhoods into a broader policy of urban renewal in Paris, one that favors middle-class Parisians more than lower-income populations, leading to significant demographic shifts in neighborhoods like the Goutte d'Or.[2] Most notable in this project of urban renewal remains the massive investment in cultural programming (animation culturelle) that, again, caters to young, middle-class sensibilities and has made neighborhoods in northeast Paris, which were once regarded by bourgeois Parisians as dangerous and derelict, into desirable places to live and work. Delanoë's government has built a series of new cultural spaces, many of them in renovated factories and warehouses in the eighteenth, nineteenth, and twentieth arrondissements of Paris. In the

Goutte d'Or, for example, the municipality financed the construction of the Centre Musical Fleury Goutte d'Or–Barbara, a recording and concert space for young musicians. It also subsidizes a series of workshop-boutiques on the Rue des Gardes for independent young fashion designers. The most ambitious of these cultural revitalization projects remains Le Centquatre (the 104), a 39,000-square-meter space hosting artists' studios, exhibition rooms, theaters, shops, and restaurants, to which the municipal government contributed €102 million (about a quarter of its budget for public housing). Though framed as bringing culture to the masses, the urban renewal undertaken by the Socialists and Greens who control City Hall and municipal councils in northeast Paris largely privileges the parties' electoral bases: liberal, educated, middle-class urbanites in white-collar professions.

The Institute for the Cultures of Islam (Institut des Cultures d'Islam, or ICI) is part of this Socialist initiative to revitalize and bring culture to the Goutte d'Or. Established in 2006, it was housed until 2013 in a temporary space on the Rue Léon, a block away from the Rue Myrha mosque. The first of the ICI's two permanent sites opened in late November 2013 on Rue Stephenson; the second, on the site of the al-Fath mosque on Rue Polonceau, was under construction when this book went to press. The Rue Léon location has already hosted numerous art exhibitions, poetry readings, and concerts, all thematically tied to the cultures of Islam, as well as debates and conferences on political and social issues in the Muslim world. During my research there, almost all of its staff members, including its director, were white and non-Muslim,[3] and the audience for its events was largely bourgeois bohemian (bobo), although the ICI public is more racially mixed than one might find at other new sites of cultural programming like Le Centquatre. Officially, the ICI was conceived of not only as part of Mayor Delanoë's citywide plan to increase cultural programming, but also as an effort to contribute to the *vivre ensemble* (living together) in the French capital by "recognizing" and "respecting"—the two terms used most often by city officials—the city's significant Muslim presence. In addition, it fulfills the local municipality's desire for more prayer space to get Muslims off the street on Fridays and give them a place to pray in a dignified fashion. Though seemingly disconnected, these various goals—cultural programming, respect and recognition, and dignified prayer space—are linked. Revitalizing the Goutte d'Or means cleaning its streets not only of drug dealers and prostitutes but also of Muslims, those other subjects who do not use public space properly. The bestowal of respect requires that Muslims be respectable, that they learn to pray in dignified fashion and out of public sight, and that they learn the normative separation between public and private that undergirds secularity. The ICI is a site of transformation, not just of the Goutte d'Or neighborhood but of Muslims too.

In 2010 I strolled through the Goutte d'Or with Kader, who was born and raised in the neighborhood. He stopped to greet various friends and acquaintances along the way, one of them an optometrist and longtime resident. We chatted about the ICI, which many immigrant-origin inhabitants of the Goutte d'Or view with some confusion, since they are clearly not the target audience and rarely attend its events. The ICI is a space for Islam but not, it seems, for Muslims. The optometrist called the ICI "a memorial to the future," a discerning phrase that captures the strange temporality and particular spatiality of secular conversion that the ICI enacts. Intended to remake Islam into an acceptable religion in France, one that properly separates private and public space and can therefore be included within the *vivre ensemble*, the ICI celebrates an Islam of the future. But that future entails an erasure, or at the very least a transformation, in which Muslims are pushed out of public space and out of the Goutte d'Or itself. The barracks mosque is a prime example of these spatial reconfigurations: Muslim prayer has been forced out of public sight, and praying Muslims have been relegated to the periphery of the eighteenth arrondissement, alongside other marginalized subjects. And though its staff has been very critical of the barracks mosques, the ICI, too, is a memorial to the future: a site of renovation that recognizes and respects an Islam that, in being made to appear, is also being made to disappear.

Despite republican rhetoric that claims not to recognize particular, subnational communities, over the past decade the state has embarked on a very public campaign to recognize the Muslims of France as part of a broader project of inclusion. The ICI is one element of that project; the French Council on the Muslim Religion (Conseil Français du Culte Musulman, or CFCM) is another. Established in 2002 by the Ministry of the Interior, the CFCM is the organ through which Islam has been incorporated into an administrative structure that already comprises representative councils for Catholicism, Protestantism, and Judaism to help the state manage religious life. But inclusion comes with certain stipulations. After all, in order to be recognized, Islam must be recognizable—or made recognizable—as an acceptable religion. At first glance, it appears easy to distinguish between the center Right Sarkozy government's iron-fisted approach to recognition, represented by the peremptory banishing of Muslims to the barracks mosque, and the Socialists' less punitive, more open approach, represented by the ICI. Nevertheless, both initiatives seek to regulate and transform Islam in order to make it includable within the French Republic. Their tactics may differ, but both approaches are regulatory projects of the secular state.[4]

In what follows, I analyze the ICI and the CFCM together as part of the French state's attempt to transform the Islamic tradition and to refashion Muslim sensibilities in accordance with secular cultural, political, and legal norms. The state's management of Muslims has two objectives: on the one hand, to secularize Islam so as to turn it into a proper religion, one that restricts religiosity to the realm of belief, to private ritual practice, and to designated spaces like the mosque; and, on the other hand, to publicly recognize minorities as part of a politics of diversity, *le vivre ensemble*. This chapter examines the unfolding of these dual objectives and their effects, exploring how government projects seek to separate Islam from politics as well as to bifurcate Islam into the discrete domains of religion and culture. Importantly, these processes of separation are not simply discursive but also material. Secular power's intervention into religious affairs and its relegation of religion to the private sphere of belief transform and redistribute space itself, architecturally disarticulating religion from culture and politics. Despite the attempts at separation through projects like the ICI and the CFCM, however, these projects simultaneously blur and render unstable the boundaries between religion, culture, and politics that secularism seeks to erect.

Constructing Religion

According to the conventional narrative of *laïcité*, 1905 marks a watershed in the history of the secular republic. In that year the National Assembly enacted a law that officially separated church and state. Article 1 affirms that the republic guarantees freedom of conscience and freedom of worship, unless those freedoms need to be restricted in the interest of public order. Article 2 states that the republic does not recognize or subsidize any religion (*culte*).[5] With the 1905 law of separation, the state ostensibly guaranteed not only individual religious freedom but also its own neutrality, doing away with the earlier Napoleonic system of recognized religions and ensuring, at least in theory, the equal treatment of all religions before the law. Religious institutions would no longer benefit from state financial aid, although the vast religious real estate held by the state, departments, and communes after the French Revolution's nationalization of religious property, most of which belonged to the Catholic Church, would be made available to appropriate religious organizations free of charge. The law of 1905 also created a new legal entity, the religious association (*association cultuelle*). This new entity was somewhat analogous to the civil association that had been created as a legal concept in 1901, but it was also different, since—unlike civil associations—religious associations could not benefit from any government subsidies. According to the historians Jean Baubérot and Micheline Milot, the law of 1905 marks the transition from what the authors call the "emancipatory state" of antireligious republicans obsessed with liberating France from the grip of the Catholic Church to the "neutral state" championed by republican politicians invested in state neutrality and religious freedom, including the freedom to be Catholic (2011, 269). This led to a series of post-1905 laws that enabled the state to subsidize private confessional schools.[6] But we should remember that the new neutral state, and the legal and political parameters it instituted with regard to religious freedom, depended on a centuries-long transformation of religious and political life in France. Rather than two different models of secularism, then, emancipation and neutrality work together, since intervention produces the kinds of religion and religious subjects toward whom the state can be neutral.

The French Revolution dismantled the previously coextensive relationship between the state and the Catholic Church, and the Declaration of the Rights of Man and Citizen enshrined freedom of conscience and freedom of worship for citizens. The Civil Code, elaborated between 1800 and 1804, institutionalized the distinction between souls and citizens. With Christianity no longer considered something that encompassed all aspects of life, the Catholic Church had to confine itself to so-called religious activities that were now clearly distinguished from profane activities, for which the state assumed responsibility. The health and education of the population, for example, once considered the Church's domain, now came under the purview of the state. In 1806, a secondary and higher education system independent of the Church was created, and government authorization was required to open and maintain secondary private schools, including Catholic ones.

The anticlerical fervor of the revolution abated with the ascension of Napoleon I. Religion, though still considered separate and separable from politics, nonetheless became regarded as foundational to morality and was thus recognized, protected, and monitored by the state. On July 15, 1801, Napoleon signed a concordat with the Holy See, privileging Catholicism institutionally. Catholic clergy were once again paid by the state, to which they were required to take an oath of loyalty. Sundays and the principal Catholic holy days were reestablished as public holidays, though the 1810 penal code made illegal any nuptial benediction not preceded by a civil marriage ceremony. In the name of equality of religions, Napoleon also extended recognition and remuneration to Calvinism, Lutheranism, and Judaism. After 1804 Protestant ministers were salaried by the state and placed under its administrative control, as were rabbis in 1831. Under the Concordat framework, Napoleon combined freedom of conscience with the protection—and control—of religious life and the recognition of separate and discrete religions. In return for official recognition of the Catholic Church and the re-Catholicization of public space in France, he brought the Church firmly under the state's authority, rendering Catholic ritual life not so much private as simply secondary to political attachments. A similar process occurred for Judaism and Protestantism; because they were minority religions, however, their public presence was more limited.

Under the Third Republic, church-state relations were further reconfigured. In 1882 the state made education compulsory for girls and boys from age six to age thirteen, and though it allowed confessional schools to exist, secular public education became the cornerstone of republican citizenship. This and other education laws—including one that replaced the teaching of Christian morality with the teaching of civic lessons—deprived the Catholic Church of its public role in moral socialization and established the school as the privileged site for inculcating in citizens-to-be a secular morality based on the republican qua universal values of reason, freedom, and equality.[7] The 1905 law that presumably marks the beginning of what came to be called the secular republic was therefore made possible by a series of previous political interventions that had radically transformed both Catholicism and the organization of the French polity, defusing the political power of the Church and turning Catholic doctrinal and ritual life—now classified as *culte*—into a religious attachment separable from political citizenship.[8]

For Jews this process of secularization, called emancipation, was even more pronounced, and it fundamentally transformed Jewish life. Jews' incorporation as citizens into French social and political life depended on their becoming incorporable, which in turn depended on a radical reformation of Jews' relationship to community, self, and the divine. Like Muslims, Jews in France had long been considered incapable of citizenship because they were too communalist, and their communalism was both too insular and too diasporic. Emancipation and integration entailed decommunalizing

Jews. As Stanislas Marie Adélaïde, Compte de Clermont-Tonnerre famously declared in the National Assembly in 1789, "We must refuse everything to the Jews as a nation and accord everything to Jews as individuals" (quoted in Hunt 1996, 88). The rest of his declaration is less well known, though essential to the integration he advocated: "We must withdraw recognition from their judges; they should only have our judges. We must refuse legal protection to the maintenance of the so-called laws of their Judaic organization" (88).[9] Emancipation thereby remade Jewish life by dismantling Jewish law (*halacha*), which had heretofore constituted the legal, political, and ethical basis of Jewishness (Taubes 2010, 56). Disarticulating these three intertwined aspects, the secular state denied authority to the elements of Jewish law that overlapped with the public domain of civil law and turned the rest into a matter of optional, individual, private practice. Rabbis no longer had the power to adjudicate cases among Jews, except as instances of voluntary arbitration. "Like Christian religious leaders, the modern rabbi was to be a preacher and pastor rather than a judge," and he was restricted to blessing marriages, pronouncing divorces, and preaching morality in temples (Hyman 1998, 42). But the realm of marriage and divorce, too, was brought within the purview of civil law, and although Jews could still participate in marriage and divorce rites according to Talmudic prescriptions, these rites—now understood as religious rituals that were supplementary to, and always after, civil ceremonies—had no legal authority. Moreover, it became possible to remain Jewish without following any Jewish laws or submitting to any rabbinical authorities. As a result, writes the historian Esther Benbassa, "Jews were no longer tied to the community . . . nor were they required to submit to its religious obligations, themselves the foundation of the very notion of community. . . . [A]s citizens of a universalist France, they differed in no way from other Frenchmen and women, their religion being a private matter" (2001, 124). Though Benbassa notes that the "ambiguous circumstance of belonging to a religion and belonging to a people did not disappear" (125), what is significant is that Judaism nevertheless became merely a religion, and one that, disarticulated now from legal and political realms, could be voluntary and private. With emancipation, Judaism—a term that already signals the transformation and circumscription of Jewish life into a discrete entity comparable to Catholicism and Protestantism and any other ism—ceased to be a matter of legal qua ethical practice and became, though never entirely successfully, a religion.

As a religion, Judaism was recognized and regulated like other religions in order to further integrate it, and Jews, into postemancipation France.

In 1806 the state established an assembly of Jewish notables composed of rabbis and others who were nominated by departmental prefects. The assembly answered a series of questions put to it by the Conseil d'Etat, which sought to determine whether Jewish law was compatible with common law and whether Jews were sufficiently committed to the Empire. The Assembly of Notables assured the Conseil that "[our] religion orders that the law of the prince be regarded as the supreme law in civil and political matters" (quoted in Benbassa 2001, 88).[10] One year later, Napoleon replaced the assembly with the Grand Sanhedrin, based on an ancient Israelite high court active until the fifth century, though the Ministry of the Interior appointed the new institution's presidents and vice presidents. Napoleon established the Sanhedrin to create a unified religious authority for the Jews of France. Appointed by a civil power, however, the Sanhedrin's authority was of a very different order than that of its ancient predecessor, especially given that the scope of Jewish law had been severely circumscribed.

In 1808 Napoleon replaced the Sanhedrin with the Central Consistory (Consistoire Central Israélite) to serve as the official representative of Judaism and Jews in France. Though regional consistories were added, they were subordinate to the Central Consistory in Paris, which was composed of three rabbis and two lay Jews, all appointed by the government. The Consistory's responsibilities initially concerned the administration of Jewish affairs, the so-called regeneration of Jewish life, and the maintenance of social order. Over time those responsibilities were expanded to include the protection of Jewish personal and political interests, the exclusive control of all Jewish institutions, and the training of rabbis. These various transformations produced the Jew as an ambiguous category and muddled the relationship between Jews and Judaism. On one hand, Jewish law, which had heretofore constituted the basis of Jewishness, had been abolished to decommunalize Jews and turn Judaism into a religion, an optional source of tradition rather than an essential source of law and ethics. The Sanhedrin and the Consistory were therefore understood as sites of religious authority whose purview was the discrete domain of religion, a domain separate and separable from politics and public life. On the other hand, the Consistory was supposed to represent not simply Judaism but all Jews in France, even the secular ones, thereby configuring Jewishness as more than a religion. The recognition and incorporation of Jews was premised on a process of secularization that would turn Judaism into a religion, one that could be separated from political citizenship so that those who were once Jews could become French citizens. But the inherent concatenation of race and religion in the figure of the

Jew (Anidjar 2007) made that separation impossible. Jewish emancipation split the Jew across the categories of race and religion while simultaneously blurring the boundaries between those categories as well as between the domains of religion and politics.

A similar process of transformation and regulation, couched as another project of modernization and integration, occurred in French Algeria, hitherto loosely ruled by the Ottoman Empire. In Algeria, French colonial officials sought to make Islam compatible with secular colonial rule by limiting the purview of Islamic law and bureaucratizing legal and religious authority; to do so, they overhauled the entire Islamic justice system.[11] In precolonial Algeria, qadis (judges) settled disputes between two or more parties according to shariʿa and fiqh (Islamic jurisprudence). Difficult cases or serious disputes were judged through a process of consultation with the leading ʿulamaʾ, either individually or collectively, in a judicial assembly known as a majlis. Moreover, although the Muslim ruler appointed qadis, the authority of the ʿulamaʾ lay in their autonomous status as experts in religious jurisprudence. The ʿulamaʾ, rather than the ruler or his qadis, were the ultimate arbiters of Islamic law.

The colonial officials, used to dealing with a particular kind of hierarchy in which sovereignty over the law ultimately resided in the state, found this rhizomatically organized justice system, which varied from one locality to another, highly problematic. They therefore sought to rationalize it, attempting to "build an Algerian religious unity, under the control of the colonial state, on the basis of Islamic law" (Christelow 1985, 20).[12] In the latter half of the nineteenth century, the French imposed formal rules on every aspect of judicial activity, established a formal hierarchy of appeals that subordinated Muslim courts to French courts, paid the salaries of the qadis, recruited these judges on the basis of a standardized examination process, and built courthouses to serve as the physical spaces where justice would be rendered, in lieu of the marketplaces and qadis' homes that had hitherto served that function. Part of this overhaul entailed the reorganization of Islamic education. The French first confiscated the habous endowments that had sustained indigenous education and then repurposed the madrasa (Islamic school) for their own needs. After an 1877 decree, future colonial qadis were required to attend one of three official schools (now called médersas) for three years, where they would study under French and Arab teachers chosen by the colonial administration. The French used the office of the qadi, the one office in the traditional Islamic legal system where a religious official's authority is delegated by the ruler, as the model for the entire Islamic establishment in Algeria, bringing judges and scholars under the direct control of the colonial administration. The control of religious education ended the relative autonomy of the ʻulamaʼ and reconfigured the nature of their authority, which was now derived from the state. Through a process of bureaucratization and uniformization, the French transformed the judicial system and the nature of religious authority within it.

The French colonial administration also severely restricted the scope of legal and political authority in Algeria, circumscribing shariʻa to the realm of personal status—what became known as Muslim law.[13] It simultaneously established a uniform public law and multiple systems of personal status law for the different subject populations it ruled in Algeria: Muslim law for Arabs, Mosaic law for Jews, and customary law for other minorities, including Berbers. Applied to individuals on the basis of descent, these legal systems reflected the various configurations of racial and religious difference in colonial Algeria. An 1865 Sénatus-Consulte granted French nationality to Muslim colonized subjects but linked full citizenship to the abandonment of personal status law and the adoption of French civil law. Even as the French governed Muslims as a distinct legal community, maintaining the distinction between Muslim subjects and full citizens, they curtailed what fell under the jurisdiction of Muslim law. Property transactions were largely placed under French civil law, and Muslim law was "defined by, and reduced to, 'personal status,' which is to say family law matters such as marriage, divorce, and inheritance" (Surkis 2010, 553). Religious norms were thereby rendered private. Nonetheless, although Muslim law was made a discrete domain separate from secular public law, its authority was always contingent. The French maintained Muslim personal status law only on the condition that it did not violate the norms of public order and social interest. For example, though Muslim legal authorities usually handled marriages between Algerian Muslims, French courts sometimes intervened in cases of arranged or forced marriage. As the historian Judith Surkis argues, the French colonial powers simultaneously relegated Muslim law to a reified and semiprivate domain unto itself and subjected it to outside legal scrutiny (2010, 554). Furthermore, although religious law was disaggregated from secular public law and limited to so-called private matters like marriage and divorce, religion remained an essential basis for the political and legal categorization of Algerian Muslims as not French. French colonial authorities thus limited Islamic authority to the domain of private life while at the same time making Islam the basis for political and legal differentiation.[14]

Put simply, the secular state has long sought to turn Islam into a proper religion and Muslims into proper subjects, compatible with the legal, political, and ethical modalities of secular rule. The rest of this chapter recounts a similar story of reform and transformation, this time in the present. As in the past, endeavors like the ICI and the CFCM that attempt to remake Islam and Muslims draw and undo the very boundaries between religion, race, culture, and politics that are integral to secular governmentality.

"There's No Leader—That's the Problem"

When municipal officials came up with the idea for the ICI, they needed a Muslim partner since the state could not finance the construction of the prayer space within the ICI. According to a number of municipal officials, finding a reliable partner was difficult, since there was no one Muslim representative who could serve as an interlocutor with the mayor's office. "There's no hierarchy in Islam," Michel Neyreneuf, the eighteenth arrondissement's deputy mayor in charge of urbanism, housing, and sustainable development, explained to me. "There's no leader—that's the problem." The municipality approached Mohammed Salah Hamza, rector of the Rue Myrha mosque, but he did not want to take part unless he could have more leadership authority. Recounting this history, Hamou Bouakkaz, the city of Paris's deputy mayor in charge of local democracy and associational life and one of the originators of the plan for the ICI, called him a caïd, an Arabic term for chieftain used in the colonial period. The municipality refused Hamza's terms, so he refused to take part. The Rue Myrha mosque owns its location; in contrast, the al-Fath mosque uses space donated by the municipality free of charge, a fact that both Neyreneuf and Bouakkaz underlined. Neyreneuf told me that Moussa Diakité, the rector of the al-Fath mosque, had never signed a lease on the space. When I asked why not, he responded: "Have you met him?! He's a Malian peasant." Neyreneuf added that the al-Fath mosque was very badly run. "Diakité doesn't know what a checkbook is," he told me exasperatedly. "He thinks the good Lord will take care of everything. You give him money, it goes into his pocket, it comes out of his pocket." Fortunately, Neyreneuf continued, there are other leaders of the al-Fath mosque "who know what [French] society is like, what an association does, what a checkbook is, what a bank account is. . . . So it was up to them to convince Diakité" to partner with the ICI. Neyreneuf paused. Then he said: "Well, in any case, Diakité doesn't have a choice, because the [al-Fath] mosque will be destroyed" to make room for the ICI. As much, then, as the Socialists criticized the hard-line approach of the Sarkozy government with regard to the barracks mosque, their velvet glove hides an iron fist. Because the al-Fath mosque exists thanks to the municipality's largesse, it must go along with the ICI project. Municipal officials have also made it clear that once the ICI is built, they will no longer turn a blind eye to mosque overflow. As Bouakkaz put it rather pointedly when our conversation turned to Hamza, "Those not involved in the [ICI] project, well, they won't be able to count on praying in the street anymore."

As Cécile Laborde notes, "One paradox of French laïcité is that, for all its commitment to the separation of church and state and its 'privatized' and 'individualized' construal of religion, it has always, of necessity, relied on state recognition of centralized religious authorities" (2008, 47). As a result, government bureaucrats have complained for decades about the lack of a single Muslim body to serve as the state's official interlocutor in the regulation of Islamic worship and public ritual practices such as the mass slaughtering of sheep for Aïd el Kébir, the allocation of municipal permits to construct mosques, and the accreditation of imams. In a 1998 book on the difficulties of integrating Islam in France, Alain Boyer, a former official in the Ministry of the Interior's Bureau of Religions, writes of "the absence of a religious authority recognized by orthodox Islam" and the "internal theological divergences" within the Islamic tradition. All this, he complains, has led to "difficulties in finding legitimate and recognized leaders who can speak in the name of Islam" (1998, 10). Boyer is correct that Sunni Islam lacks the kind of centralized authority and hierarchy—"a real clergy," in Boyer's terms—found in Catholicism. This is even more of an issue in France, home to a multitude of Sunni, Shiite, and Sufi denominations from all over the world. Many officials and scholars believe that this diversity is a major obstacle to creating a representative body for Islam because the state is not sure to whom it should address its questions and concerns regarding the regulation of Muslim worship. Moreover, the lack of representation is thought to underlie many of the inequalities Muslims face because it makes them unable to take advantage of the benefits that the legal and political framework of laïcité affords other religions, like paying the salaries of clergy in prisons and hospitals or funding private schools. That inequality, in turn, seems at odds with laïcité's guarantee of religious freedom and state neutrality. Many Muslims make the same argument. In 1998 a group of Muslim intellectuals issued a public declaration to the president of the French Republic, calling on the government to fully integrate the Muslim community into the nation: "If the state, after decades of waiting, refuses Muslims the same means granted Catholicism, Protestantism, and Judaism, it would exclude and marginalize a whole section of the national body" (quoted in Boyer 1998, 126). In addition to public officials, then, a number of Muslims have also taken up laïcité's informal recognition of various religions as the primary means to remedy existing inequalities between Muslims and other religious communities. For the state, the creation of a representative body would enable it to recognize, institutionalize, and monitor an islam de France (a French Islam); for many Muslims, a representative body would normalize their presence in France.

The current organization of religious life remains tied to the Napoleonic system: Catholicism is represented and regulated by the Council of Bishops, Protestantism by the Protestant Federation, and Judaism by the Central Consistory. These three bodies represent their respective religions to the state and serve as the government's consultants in the management of religious life. The idea of creating a similar representative body for Islam emerged in the late 1980s from the Ministry of the Interior, then led by the Socialist Pierre Joxe.[15] In 1989 he created the Council for Reflection on Islam in France (Conseil de Réflexion sur l'Islam en France, or CORIF), which met a few dozen times in the offices of the ministry. The function of the CORIF was both clear and clearly limited. A ministerial decree brought it into being as a consultative body to respond to questions posed by the minister with regard to the exercise of Muslim worship in France. Like Napoleon's Grand Sanhedrin and a similar Council on Muslim Jurisprudence in colonial Algeria,[16] the CORIF served at the behest of the government. According to article 4 of the ministerial decree, the commission would be convened and presided over by the minister of the interior, who would also set the agenda.

As governments and interior ministers changed, this incipient representative body took various forms—the Representative Council of the Muslims of France under Charles Pasqua, the Istichara under Jean-Pierre Chevènement—until 2002, when Nicolas Sarkozy made the establishment of a permanent council one of his major goals as interior minister. In December 2002 he convened the main players of Chevènement's Istichara for two days, at the end of which he emerged triumphant, declaring that they had reached a working agreement and that elections would soon be held for the new CFCM and its twenty-five regional counterparts, the Regional Councils on the Muslim Religion. Muslim places of worship would be given numbers of delegates who could vote in the elections, with the number proportional to the size of the place of worship.[17] On the basis of a ministry census of

France's Muslim places of worship, 995 of them were accorded delegates—about 4,000 in all—to vote for the general assembly of the CFCM. Before the elections, however, Sarkozy chose a sixteen-member executive board for the council. He appointed Dalil Boubakeur, rector of the Great Mosque of Paris, as president for two years; he also selected the CFCM's two vice presidents leaders from the Union of Islamic Organizations of France (Union des Organisations Islamiques de France, or UOIF) and the National Federation of Muslims of France (Fédération Nationale des Musulmans de France, FNMF). On April 6 and April 13, 2003, the first elections for the CFCM and the regional councils were held, in which about 80 percent of the delegates voted. The slate of candidates from the FNMF emerged victorious, with the UOIF's slate a close and unexpected second. The Great Mosque's slate came in a distant third, making Sarkozy's appointment of Boubakeur to the CFCM presidency that much more conspicuous.

The stated pragmatic function of the CFCM is to regulate and ameliorate the conditions of Muslim worship in France. But it is also an effort to recognize what is often called the nation's second religion, and to do so within the existing parameters of laïcité that give the state centralized representative bodies for the major religions of France. Like Jewish emancipation and the subsequent recognition of Judaism as a religion in France, and like the reorganization of the Islamic justice system in Algeria, the CFCM is a project of transformation and domestication. As a single bureaucratic representative, it rationalizes Islam in France and locates authority in one center. It serves as well to generate—or so the state hopes—an islam de France. The CFCM does not simply represent Islam as it now exists but is one of the bodies through which a so-called moderate, modernist Islam can be made to emerge, hence the government's selection of Boubakeur as the CFCM's president, and its nomination of a number of liberal Muslims to the executive board. By creating a Muslim representative body in France, the state explicitly seeks to cut the links between Muslim immigrants and their countries of origin, bringing Islam under the authority of the French state.[18]

Living Religion Properly

Since 2006 the ICI has celebrated the final ten days of Ramadan with what it calls Les Veillées du Ramadan, a series of evening events that includes concerts, films, poetry readings, and late-night debates, and iftar, the communal meal at sundown that breaks the daily Ramadan fast. The 2010 Veillées opened on September 2 with much fanfare at the ICI's temporary Rue

Léon location. Mayor Delanoë, municipal officials, artists, intellectuals, and other visitors began to file in around 7 o'clock, and soon about three hundred people had gathered in the large courtyard, waiting for introductory remarks from the mayor and ICI officials, then a concert, and finally a debate on Islam in the media. Most of the guests were middle-class bobos; about a third were of Maghrebi origin, the rest white. A few dozen guests wandered through the exhibition rooms, looking at art installations. The theme for the 2010 Veillées was "Islam(s) of Europe," and exhibits included geometric abstractions by the Franco-Iraqi artist Mehdi Moutashar and the French minimalist pioneer François Morellet and an Arab-kitsch tearoom designed by the British-Moroccan artist Hassan Hajjaj. At the entrance to the ICI, two guards, both young Franco-African men from the Goutte d'Or, stood watch, chatting with their neighborhood buddies who were curious to know what was going. Since they were not on the guest list and had no interest in either the concert or the debate, they lingered outside, peering in occasionally.

Earlier in the evening, I and a group of journalists attended a small press conference with the ICI's director, Véronique Rieffel, where she explained that public authorities had created the ICI "in the spirit of laïcité, in order, above all, to enable citizens to live their culture, their religion, and their faith." Rieffel called the ICI an open door and declared that it had been inspired by "a laïcité that does not exclude the Other." The ICI would serve the needs of Muslims in the neighborhood who "are searching for a dignified space to pray." Rieffel noted that when one thinks of Islam, communautarisme often comes to mind. Invoking Edward Said's classic Orientalism (1979) and Thomas Deltombe's more recent L'islam imaginaire (Imaginary Islam; 2005), she reminded journalists that the stereotypical image of Islam remains a creation of the West. Asserting that Paris is an anticommunal city, she declared that the 2010 Veillées theme would be an exploration of the linkages between the West and Islam in order to dismantle stereotypes about Islam. Finally, she implicitly addressed critics of the ICI who argue that the Paris city government has no business building prayer space, since the 1905 law prohibits secular public authorities from funding religion. "Of course there will be separate [that is, nonstate] financing for the religious aspects of the ICI," she insisted. She then affirmed that "the cultures of Islam do not concern only the people of Islam, they concern everyone."

Though the 1905 law of separation forbids the state from financing the construction or maintenance of religious sites built after 1905, it also guarantees the freedom of religion. Operating in the administrative crevice produced by that tension, ICI officials defend the institute as being within the purview of laïcité, framing the problem of street prayer and the lack of adequate prayer space as an infringement on the religious freedom of Muslims in Paris.[19] Bouakkaz told me that although the state cannot recognize or remunerate any religion, the law also guarantees that "no one is prevented from practicing his religion." In a long conversation with me about the ICI, Rieffel also invoked the framework of laïcité, asserting that "this law solves the problems of praying in the street and enables people to live their religion properly [vivre leur religion correctement]." Like the English term properly, the French term correctement is polysemic: it can mean both decently and correctly. Rieffel used correctement to mean "in a dignified fashion," repeating the trope of dignity that underpins the criticism of street prayer and justifies the need for the ICI. But her turn of phrase also hints at the disciplinary purpose of the ICI, and of laïcité more generally, to remake Islam into a proper religion and Muslims into proper religious subjects who live their religion correctly.

According to its mission statement, the ICI will offer its public "the necessary tools" to understand Muslim cultures and deepen their knowledge of Islam (quoted in Davidson 2012, 213); the target audience of the ICI is therefore both non-Muslim and Muslim. One aim is to dispel stereotypes about Islam and present the relationship between Islam and the West as a dialogue between civilizations rather than a clash. As Neyreneuf explained, the ICI lets "non-Muslims discover that Islam isn't just about the veil and polygamy." The ICI also aims to teach Muslims more about Islam. Neyreneuf put it in the following terms: the ICI will enable Muslims to develop "a view of Islam that is much vaster, much more serious, more rigorous than the slogans one hears, the idiocies one hears, from the UOIF and others." Bouakkaz was even more explicit about the disciplinary nature of the ICI. His goal, he told me, was "to create the mosque within the ICI in order to destroy it [the mosque]." A few minutes later, he declared: "Most people think five years ahead; I think fifty years ahead. I am thinking about the future of France."

For many politicians on both the Left and Right, France's successful future hinges on the emergence of an islam de France.[20] Although some Muslim French already practice what they would call French Islam, what distinguishes that Islam from the islam de France imagined by secular-republican politicians is the latter's imbrication in a bipartisan politics of recognition and, concomitantly, a binding relationship with the state. Sarkozy couched his 2002 visit to the UOIF congress as an inclusionary gesture of recognition of the nation's Muslims. As he would later make explicit, such inclusion depends on the emergence of an *islam de France*. "Let us make sure," he declared, "that *islam de France* is what it must be, that is to say a religion of tolerance and of openness" (quoted in Bonnefoy 2003, 28). Sarkozy's statement has three implications: first, a desire for a French Islam, one that would distinguish itself from traditional Islam through its tolerance and openness; second, the sense that Islam has yet to take the form necessary for its inclusion in the French Republic; and third, the work required—including that of the state ("us")—to bring about that necessary form. Like the emancipation of French Jews, then, the project of recognizing and including Islam in the republic is a disciplinary project of secular governmentality, one that seeks to refashion Islam and Muslims in ways that make them recognizable to the secular state. As Patchen Markell (2003) has astutely observed in regard to Jewish emancipation in Prussia and to contemporary multicultural politics, the state has often used recognition as a tool to remake subjects in conformity with the requirements of modern political rule.

In contemporary France that means teaching Muslims about the nature and limits of religion, a domain separate and distinct from culture. The division between religion and culture, or between *culte* and *culture*, underpins the legal and political framework of *laïcité*. The category of the religious association instituted by the 1905 law of separation, which benefits from tax breaks but is ineligible for any state subsidy, remains legally distinct from the cultural association (*association culturelle*), a legal entity created by a 1901 law, which can receive various forms of financial aid from the state. This split between religion and culture underpins the organization and structure of the ICI, and its staff and public officials are careful to point out that the municipal government is subsidizing culture, not religion. Though initially set up as a foundation, which made it easier for that government to fund it directly, the ICI soon became a cultural association under the 1901 law. Since the Paris municipality cannot directly finance the construction of any spaces designated for religious worship—even though one major purpose of the ICI is the creation of prayer space—it helped to formalize a local Muslim religious association established under the 1905 law that would use private donations to finance the construction of the parts of the ICI dedicated to religion. The city plans to contribute approximately twenty million euros toward the ICI's construction, though technically that money must be used only for the ICI's cultural aspects; another six to seven million euros would come from its partnering Muslim association to pay for the construction of prayer space. When I told Bouakkaz that I could not imagine how a group of poor Muslim immigrants would procure that kind of money, he dismissed my concerns: the municipal government "is going to build everything. Even the religious part will be built in advance [and bought later by the Muslim association]. We're not going to delay the project because the Muslims have no money." Bouakkaz contended that the municipality had to act as if its Muslim partner had the adequate finances, or else the project would never see the light of day. "We understand that the Muslim community is poor, divided, and incapable of doing this on their own," he explained. "So we're going to try to make this project happen." Unsurprisingly, the local Muslim association was unable to come up with the necessary funds before the first permanent site on Rue Stephenson opened, and the Great Mosque of Paris stepped in instead. In 2013, the Société des Habous des Lieux Saints de l'Islam, which runs the Great Mosque—and is, incidentally, an association established under the law of 1901—purchased the prayer space for €2.2 million.

The architecture of the ICI mimics the financial and administrative separation it makes between religion and culture. Though the Rue Léon location does not have a space for prayer or other religious activities, the future ICI will consist of two sites, one at Rue Polonceau and one at Rue Stephenson, and each site will have separate spaces designated for culture and religion. The Polonceau site will also house a research center and a café, and the Stephenson site will offer a hammam. According to its mission statement, the ICI will encompass three poles of activity: cultural, religious, and intellectual—each "clearly identifiable on a spatial level . . . to distinguish between the sacred spaces reserved exclusively for Muslims and 'profane' spaces open to all" (quoted in Davidson 2012, 215). Indeed, in the newly opened Stephenson site, the "sacred space" for praying is clearly separated from the rest of the ICI. To get there, one must walk across the lobby and exhibition space, through a doorway and up a set of stairs; a sign by the door helpfully notes "prayer room" (salle de prière), with a small arrow pointing up the stairs. Religious space, understood as the place where Muslims will pray on Fridays, ostensibly mirrors the space of the mosque. In fact, the site on Rue Polonceau long occupied by the al-Fath mosque will become one of the ICI locations. But in the Islamic tradition, the mosque is dedicated not only to praying but also to the cultivation and propagation of other aspects of social life. In most of the Muslim world, and for many centuries, mosques have been sites of education, business transactions, and even troop levying (Messick 1996; Metcalf 1996). The al-Fath mosque—destroyed in December 2013 to begin building the second ICI site—was a space in which men came to pray, socialize, and network, sitting and chatting in small groups. As historians of mosque architecture demonstrate, multiplicity of purpose and flexibility of space have been central to the Islamic tradition (Qureshi 1996). Within a secular imaginary, however, a mosque is like a church: the designated site of religion only. The ICI architecturally performs and actualizes that designation.

The government's investment in constructing a mosque inside the ICI reflects the state's particular notion of religion within the framework of laïcité. As John Bowen asserts, the state "support[s] religion by facilitating worship in properly built houses of worship but strictly control[s] any 'leakage' of religion" into other, un-authorized domains (2009, 31). The state recognizes that religion entails communal, ritual practice outside the private sphere of the home, but it also makes sure that these enactments of religion remain confined to designated spaces: the Christian church, the Jewish synagogue, and the Muslim mosque for what is understood as everyday religion, with a few exceptional forays into public space for festivals and processions. Additionally, parallel to the secular state's recognition of the mosque as the site purely of Muslim worship (rather than of economy and politics, too) is the understanding that it is the only legitimate space of religion outside the home. This produces a very specific politics of visibility. Though building mosques remains a fraught process, government officials have nonetheless sought, as Sarkozy put it repeatedly, to bring Islam "into the light." Mosques signal the presence of Islam in France, and for many politicians on both the Right and Left, inclusion hinges on enabling Muslims to pray in mosques that are, in common political parlance, "worthy of the name" (digne de ce nom). At the same time, this investment in Muslim visibility is also a practice of surveillance and circumscription.[21] The desire to bring Islam into the light emerges from a widespread anxiety about so-called underground Islam (islam des caves). Politicians and pundits routinely speak out against this unregulated Islam, practiced in basements and utility rooms in the banlieues and propagated by self-appointed imams, as the seedbed of extremism and fundamentalism. The semiprivate existence of this Islam makes secular republicans nervous precisely because it remains out of public view. Muslims must not pray conspicuously in public, but they must not pray too inconspicuously either; they must be neither too visible nor too invisible. Furthermore, with the mosque, and especially Friday prayers, designated as the sole legitimate domain of nonprivate religion, other forms of public religiosity—wearing headscarves, requesting halal meals outside the home, or praying at work or school—become excessive, a leakage of Muslim religion into domains beyond its circumscribed confines of mosque and home.

Though the transformation of Muslim space is an end in itself for projects like the ICI, these spatial reconfigurations aim to transform Muslim habitus as well. One of the goals of the ICI is to give Muslims a better, fuller, and truer sense of Islam as not only religion but also, though separately, as culture. Members of the ICI's staff recognize that the working-class public served by prayer space and the bobo public served by contemporary art installations do not often overlap. Nonetheless, a number of ICI personnel pointed out to me that putting prayer space inside the larger areas of the two future cultural sites would mean that Muslims coming only to pray would inevitably walk by exhibits; the staff members hoped the Muslims would thus have their minds opened to the aesthetic pleasures of the cultures of Islam. The ICI's mission, then, is to bring culture to working-class immigrants and to inculcate them in the aesthetics of modernity.

Paralleling the impetus to teach Muslims that Islam constitutes more than just religion is, paradoxically, an impetus to teach them that it is only a religion, with a proper location and a proper way of practicing. When I remarked to Neyreneuf that the future ICI prayer space would not, in fact, accommodate all the people who now pray in the street, he responded that the ICI mosque might have multiple services. "There could be three services," he said, "one at 11:00, one at noon, and one at 1:00. I mean, I don't know the exact hours. Noon, 1:00, 2:00." I must have looked surprised—the timing of the five daily prayers usually follows the trajectory of the sun—for Neyreneuf quickly added: "Well, it's more dignified than praying in the street." He told me that the Muslim religious association that the ICI had originally partnered with was already working on this solution. Neyreneuf admitted: "I don't know if it will work very well, because for a traditional Muslim, he absolutely has to pray at prayer time. But these are nonetheless things that can evolve." He noted that in any case, there would be no overflow permitted in the street: "The people who can't get in, they won't get in, and that's it. And they will find other habits. Anyway, praying at the mosque is not obligatory, so they can pray at home." Neyreneuf thereby explicitly stated one of the goals of the ICI, which is to change Muslims' habits and the way they conceptualize and practice religion. Praying at the mosque, Neyreneuf asserted authoritatively, is not obligatory, contrary to what many "traditional" Muslims believe. Neyreneuf and the ICI hope to make Muslims understand that prayer must take place either in the mosque or in the private sphere of the home.

The precise ways in which the municipality both protects and regulates praying reveal the contours of laïcité and its spatial organization of religion and religious freedom. On the one hand, many government officials consider praying an important Muslim practice that falls under the purview of laïcité's guarantee of religious freedom. On the other hand, praying publicly in the street is not simply a traffic problem and an undignified way to pray but also, as Minister of the Interior Guéant put it, "a direct attack on the principle of laïcité" (Leclerc, Cornevin, and Dingreville 2011). Outside the designated space of the mosque, praying contravenes laïcité. Within the so-called sacred space of the mosque, however, where it is separate from all other aspects of Muslim social life, Friday prayer becomes the central element of Islam and deserving of legal and political support. The structure of the ICI, with its particular organization of space and time, helps define the nature and limits of proper religion. It also seeks to cultivate Muslim habits of religious practice that accord with this definition and those limits. In addition to producing the contours of religion, the ICI's architecture mimics the relationship imagined—if never fully secured—between religion and culture: religion is not only a discrete entity unto itself but also a domain surrounded by the larger sphere of culture. Thus the secular project of remaking Islam disarticulates Muslim religion from Muslim culture and teaches Muslims the difference between religion and culture. It also disaggregates religion from politics. At the very same time, laïcité makes this disaggregation impossible. Secular political rule is subtended by two imperatives: to separate religion from culture and politics, and to regulate religion (and culture) through political intervention. Enacted together, these dual imperatives actually render untenable any boundary between religion and culture, or between religion and politics.

Exigencies of Inclusion

On the evening of September 2, 2010, a large, stylishly dressed crowd gathered in the courtyard of the ICI on Rue Léon for the inauguration of the 2010 Veillées du Ramadan. Drinks and hors d'oeuvres in hand, the guests around me spoke admiringly of the art installations and the arabesque aesthetic of the courtyard. Soon, the ICI's president, Hakim El-Karoui, took the stage to open the festival. A tall, thin man in his forties, El-Karoui is a Franco-Tunisian investment banker and was a speechwriter for former prime minister Jean-Pierre Raffarin. (Named president of the ICI for his fund-raising potential, El-Karoui was forced to step down a year later when it became public that he had been advising the Tunisian dictator Zine el Abidine Ben Ali during the spring 2011 revolution.) El-Karoui welcomed the audience, then addressed the ever-present issue of communalism. He observed that although Muslims sometimes close in on themselves as a community, the ICI constituted *une ouverture* (an opening), one that "comes with a certain exigency," though he did not specify what he meant. Next came Mayor Delanoë, who invoked the importance of *laïcité*, which he defined as tolerance, and who declared the ICI a space of *vivre ensemble*. Delanoë closed by saying: "Let us respect one another. Let us love even that which is Other."

To create the *iftar* meals for the 2010 Veillées, the ICI had invited two cultural programmers who call their craft *la boulettologie moderne*, a play on words that could be translated as modern mixology. The *boulettologues*, or mixologists, defined their craft to me as "the bringing together of various different ingredients to create an amalgam." During the press conference just before the inaugural ceremonies, the mixologists explained their approach for the Veillées: they had sought to go beyond the *chorba* (soup) and *brik* (savory pastry) that comprise a traditional Maghrebi *iftar*, which they and Rieffel found too clichéd. They looked instead to Al Andalus, when Muslims, Jews, and Christians lived together in medieval Moorish Iberia. The mixologists had, they said, "undertaken an immense voyage in space and time," and they sought to recreate an authentic experience from that voyage. To the room full of journalists, they served lime juice made from a twelfth-century recipe that was supposed to liberate one's faith, and the intricate meals they offered each night to the ICI's visitors adhered closely to Moorish standards, including a distinct lack of salt. Meals were communal, served in large dishes, and guests were purposely not given silverware. The mixologists explained that they wanted to create a kinesthetic encounter and that they wanted eaters to use their hands so that those who were unfamiliar with such a practice would be compelled to ask their more knowledgeable neighbors for assistance. Food, they said, "is supposed to help us ask questions," and they hoped each guest would ask herself, "What is happening in this voyage that I am taking?" The mixologists asserted that their goal was to get patrons to think about how to share a meal.

Since the ICI had only five full-time staff members, it recruited a dozen volunteers to help mount the 2010 Veillées. Volunteers set up and cleaned up, staffed the entrance and the exhibition rooms, and circulated with water jugs so that guests could wash their hands before and after *iftar*. Ranging in age from the early twenties to the early forties, most of the volunteers were either white French with careers in cultural programming who were seeking professional experience and were also interested in the cultures of Islam, or nonwhite French of Maghrebi descent, some of whom were also in cultural programming, lived in Paris without their families, and were intrigued by the concept of the ICI and wished to celebrate Ramadan communally. All the Franco-Maqhrebi volunteers were fasting during Ramadan, though not all considered themselves Muslims; for many, Ramadan was an important but bounded moment of ritual life. Almost all were middle-class professionals with working-class parents, a group sometimes called the *beurgeoisie*. Miriam was a director of social services for the national railroad company, Fahim worked for the Ministry of Sports, Hanaan was an accountant, and Abdelazziz was finishing a PhD at Sciences Po. I also volunteered that year, and in conversations with me, many of the Muslim volunteers seemed puzzled by the mission of the ICI, especially its continuous attempt to separate but encompass religion and culture. Hanaan, for example, enjoyed the musical performances during the Veillées—Titi Robin and Jeanne Cherhal, Natasha Atlas, the Transglobal Underground, and a flamenco recital—but she did not see their connection to Islam. "I was expecting something more, well, Islamic," she told me. Muslim volunteers were particularly put off by the *iftar* meals. Having spent their lives breaking the Ramadan fast, they felt insulted that cultural programmers with no prior knowledge of *iftar* or Ramadan had determined their regular culinary ritual practices to be clichéd.

Fahim, a volunteer in his late twenties, offered a particularly thoughtful assessment of the ICI: "In a context in which Islam is so maligned, the ICI, even with its bobo side, deserves to exist to at least deconstruct stereotypes." He enjoyed the late-night debates and the focus on how Islam is lived differently in different parts of the world. But he found the *iftar* "too intellectualized [and] too folkloric." *Iftar* is a fundamental part of Ramadan, he continued, and Ramadan is a fundamental part of Islam. *Iftar* therefore has a precise ethical foundation. It constitutes a moment of reflection, of thinking about the day that one has spent fasting, "so breaking the fast with electro-dub music [instead of a call to prayer], that denatures things." Fahim also did not enjoy the lack of silverware. "It's not a bad idea in itself," he observed, but he thought it replayed colonial stereotypes. "We don't eat with our hands in the Maghreb," he said, but stereotypes hold that "Islam, it's about Arabs, that is to say, savages [who don't know how to use utensils]." Fahim acknowledged that this was not the mixologists' intent and that the *iftar* was supposed to create a positive experience of sharing, but he found that problematic as well: "It's like, 'it's great, we're going to eat like them!' It's folklore." He recalled an argument with Kamel, the sole Muslim member of the ICI staff at the time, who insisted that the ICI was a cultural, not a religious, center. "But come on," Fahim complained, "it's called the Institute for the Cultures of Islam, not the Institute for Fashionable *Iftar!* We've submitted to the exigencies of [non-Muslim] whites."

One key element of *le vivre ensemble* is openness. Delanoë, Rieffel, and other public officials often speak of the ICI as an open door and a space of openness. The religious association that the ICI intially partnered with was called the Association of Muslims of Openness (Association des Musulmans de l'Ouverture, or AMO). The recurring theme of openness opposes another common term, *le repli* (the closing in on oneself), which Muslims are often accused of in France. In her remarks to journalists at the inauguration, Rieffel noted pointedly that Paris was an anticommunal city. In so doing, she explicitly referenced the widespread accusation of Muslim communalism; her subsequent description of the ICI as an open door sought to undercut the link between communalism and Islam. Rieffel speaks often of the need to deconstruct Orientalist stereotypes of Islam; to demonstrate the diversity within Islam; to show the Islamic genealogies of European arts, architecture, and philosophy; and to prove that Islam has a place in Paris and, more broadly, in France. Rieffel and all the ICI staff members are sincere in their desire for a France that is more tolerant, respectful, and open to Muslims. But as El-Karoui noted cryptically in his inaugural remarks, openness comes with a certain exigency. The recognition of and openness toward Islam on the part of public authorities require that Islam be recognizable and open. Only by declaring themselves Muslims of openness can the ICI's Muslim partners prove themselves worthy recipients of the municipality's recognition and financial largesse.

In fact, *l'ouverture* means both openness and opening. The government's call for *l'ouverture* demands that Muslims open up to the gaze of outsiders, in part to determine whether they deserve to be partners in the *vivre ensemble* being created. One of the Ramadan activities the ICI offered during the 2010 Veillées was a guided visit of the Goutte d'Or and its mosques, couscous restaurants, and pastry shops. On a Sunday afternoon, about twenty people, all but two of them white and non-Muslim, gathered at the ICI. Staff members informed visitors that women were encouraged to cover their heads when they entered a mosque, but it was not an obligation if it made anyone uncomfortable. Though the tour stopped by the Rue Myrha mosque, we were not allowed inside; Hamza, the rector, pointedly came out and spoke to us on the street. We then made our way to the al-Fath mosque, where Moussa Niambelé, one of the mosque leaders, was waiting. He said that although women were encouraged to cover their heads, they were not obligated to do so. Two out of the ten women entered the mosque bareheaded, much to the consternation and discomfort of mosque regulars. However, to have insisted that women cover their heads, a common practice in mosques, would have marked the al-Fath mosque as too communalist, too fundamentalist, too exigent. The position of exigency, of making demands, is clearly reserved for the non-Muslim partner in this *vivre ensemble*.[22]

The other key element that constitutes le *vivre ensemble* is sharing. Inaugurating the 2010 Veillées, Mayor Delanoë declared Ramadan "a moment of generosity, of solidarity, and of sharing in the Other [*partage de l'Autre*]." But what, exactly, is shared? For starters, food. About eighty patrons came every evening to partake in the *iftar* that the two mixologists created. Most of them had not been fasting during the day, so their experience of Ramadan was restricted to this meal and the festive ambiance. The commencement of each *iftar* was announced by electro-dub music rather than the traditional call to prayer heard elsewhere in the Muslim world, though it wasn't immediately clear to either the fasting or the nonfasting guests what the music signified. The previous year, readings from the *Quran* followed by a French translation had broken the fast, but critics had complained that a secular institute had no business propagating religion. Conscious that public funds financed the *iftar*, the ICI had already ruled out the prayer that also normally breaks the Ramadan fast. Fasting Muslims therefore found themselves in an odd predicament: having come to break their fasts with an *iftar*, they could not carry out the other ritual practices to which *iftar* is linked and that together constitute Ramadan. The Rue Léon site has no separate space for praying, and doing so in the public parts of the ICI would have been awkward. Those who wanted to pray before eating had to find a private room, provided by Kamel, the only person on the ICI staff who had any sense of the various ritual requirements surrounding *iftar*. Except for Kamel, the ICI staff members also seemed unaware that the Muslim volunteers might want to eat before they could help with the ICI *iftar* since they had been fasting all day. Many ducked away to pray, eat a quick snack, and drink some water before returning to help; Kamel, a paid employee, felt compelled to keep working, and he often took his meal much later at night, when all the volunteers ate together.

My point is not to criticize the ICI, as some have done, for propagating a folkloric Islam to French bobos. Rather, it is to think critically about the nature and limits of *le vivre ensemble*, and how the kind of recognition the ICI bestows on Muslims fits in the parameters of secularism. ICI officials and employees genuinely seek to respect and share with the Other, but the mixologists' question remains pertinent: how does one share a meal, a ritual practice, a religious experience? How does one share in the Other, as Delanoë put it? Respect requires that the Other be respectable, just as sharing requires that the Other's practices be sharable. Within the paradigm of *le vivre ensemble*, acceptance depends on sharing and openness; practices that cannot be shared by all become more difficult to include. Predictably, attendees shared films, concerts, poetry readings, and art installations—all of them catering to liberal and progressive sensibilities—and, of course, food. And that food was a thing of the past: guests did not partake in *chorba* and *brik*; rather, they shared platters of food that were eaten by Andalusian Muslims more than six hundred years ago. The mixologists and Rieffel sought to conjure up a time of peaceful coexistence between Muslims, Christians, and Jews, of which Al Andalus has become the ideal representation for liberal Europeans. But the actual culinary practices of many Maghrebi Muslims currently living in Paris were ignored. Rieffel explained to me that she and the mixologists sought to avoid the cheap exoticism of *chorba* and couscous. Yet those dishes are not exotic to the vast majority of Maghrebi-origin Muslims, thus Rieffel's gesture of sharing is simultaneously, if unintentionally, one of exclusion. As Fahim noted, the ICI's *iftar* was aimed not at fasting Muslims but at nonfasting non-Muslims. The *iftar* was indeed a voyage, in the mixologists' terms, but one that comforted rather than disrupted the voyager's world by taking her to a faraway place and time. There, the voyager could mingle with fantasy Muslims of Al Andalus and feel like a good, tolerant liberal without having to deal in any substantive way with Muslims of the present. The language of otherness that both Delanoë and Rieffel used is telling: respecting and sharing with and in the Other requires that Muslims remain Other, but comfortably so.

Explaining her vision for the 2010 Veillées, Rieffel told me that she had wanted to find another way to conceptualize *iftar*, to do something interesting with the ritual. For Rieffel, *iftar* is a ritual unto itself, linked certainly to Ramadan, but not inextricably so, which meant that it could be played with, made more interesting. For most Muslims, however, *iftar* is one practice in a chain of daily rituals that constitute them as Muslims during Ramadan. *Iftar* becomes a very different kind of practice depending on whether one has fasted or not. But *iftar* can be shared only if it has, as Fahim put it, become an intellectual exercise, abstracted from its affective and ethical moorings.

To conceptualize and to live Islam as a set of authoritative norms with con-comitant ethical practices and to imagine an interconnected relationship between practice, norm, and the divine—as many Muslims do—renders these practices unsharable to those without some prior relationship to the Islamic tradition. Thus a sharable Islam must be imagined very differently, first by confining unsharable ethical practices like praying to the mosque, and then by locating everything else under the sign of culture. The tempo-rary site of the ICI, because it is purely cultural, has no room for prayer. And in the permanent ICI, such ritual practices will take place in the part reserved for religion.[23] Unlike prayer, however, iftar could be reconceptu-alized as culture and included in a municipality-funded Ramadan festival. So far I have translated Delanoë's phrase partage de l'Autre as sharing or par-taking in the Other, but partager also means to divide, to take apart.[24] One could therefore translate the phrase not as sharing in, but as dividing up the Other—namely, into religion and culture. Although culture can be publicly celebrated, religion must remain bounded, not necessarily private but cer-tainly not public—banished, like the barracks mosques, to the outer edges of the city, or, like the ICI's prayer space, to clearly demarcated spaces out of public sight.

Disaggregating religion from culture and confining religion to its designated space reconfigure Islam into a recognizable religion, a religion recognizable as religion. The notion of religion found in contemporary Euro-American politics, law, social life, and academia emerged in the post-Reformation West. As Talal Asad writes, in early modern Europe religion became a transhistorical phenomenon, an essential and distinct form of human experience shared across various cultures and geographies. Reli-gion was conceived of as "a distinctive space of human practice and belief," one that had a particular and "autonomous essence [that was] not to be confused with the essence of science, or of politics, or of common sense" (1993, 27–28). Soon European scholars developed the attendant notion of world religions—Christianity, Judaism, Islam, Hinduism, Buddhism, and so on—that are all specific and discrete instances of the meta category of religion (Masuzawa 2005). But, as Asad and Masuzawa argue, the purport-edly universal definition of religion in fact relied on a distinctively Christian epistemology and ontology. Though Christianity became just one of many world religions in this new secular paradigm, it provided the model for the category of religion itself. The emphasis on belief as the definitive aspect of religiosity, the centrality of text in the semiotic configuration of knowl-edge and subjectivity, and the possibility of separating political power and religious authority are all defining elements of the modern category of religion, pointing to its Christian genealogy. Moreover, the political and legal regulation of religion that is definitive of secularism depends on a prior definition of religion, which in turn both necessitates and produces the transformation of ethical, social, political, and legal lifeworlds into the mold of religion. This secular remaking of what is called, a posteriori, the religious life of non-Christian communities has refashioned other "religions" into forms analogous with Christianity.

The ICI and CFCM are part of this long secular project of transformation, and, unsurprisingly, Christianity constitutes religion prime, against which Islam is compared and into which Islam is being transformed. The entire structure of the CFCM relies on an organization of religious authority premised on Catholicism, one that assumes a clear hierarchy and a unified voice on doctrinal matters. From the government's perspective, the rhizomatic organization of authority in the Islamic tradition prevents Muslims from accessing the benefits accorded to Catholicism, Protestantism, and Judaism. The CFCM was created to unite and consolidate the doctrinal diversity and decentralized authority of Islam into a single representative body that can speak in the name of Islam. To be included in the French Republic, Islam must take the proper form of religion, as Judaism had to do in a previous era. Because Islam is unlike Christianity, it must be made analogous; it must be translated and transformed into a bona fide religion so that it can be recognized and included. It is therefore unsurprising that municipal officials have proposed multiple services modeled after Catholic mass to solve the overattendance of Friday noon prayers in the Goutte d'Or; this solution Christianizes and transforms the temporal logic of Muslim prayer. Nor is it surprising that government officials have fixated on training imams—most analogous to priests—as the key to producing an *islam de France*. In addition, officials see the mosque (and the temple and the synagogue) as analogous to the church, not only as the one space for religion outside the domain of private belief but also as a space cleared of politics, culture, law, economy, and so on. At the same time, as Boukkaz declared, the government's goal is to build a mosque within the ICI in order to tear that mosque down eventually. Like the churches that fewer and fewer Christians attend in Europe, the mosque will, he hopes, become obsolete. What remains unclear is whether, like the Christians who simply became French, the target population of this rehabituation process will ever stop being Muslim.

In an essay on translation, Dipesh Chakrabarty (2000) observes that modern social science works through a framework of abstract, generalizing categories. Used to translate and compare particulars across geographical space and historical time, a general category transforms singular phenomena into specific instantiations of a more general abstraction. In his example, historians translate, analogize, and compare the otherwise incommensurable activities of Bolivian miners and Indian weavers through the mediating category of labor. But Chakrabarty cautions that labor is a key category in the imagination of capitalism, and it is therefore neither abstract nor general. The Indian weavers' activities that historians describe, which incorporate the agency of gods and spirits, remain ultimately incommensurable with the secular modern category of labor. Because the translation of the weavers' god-inhabited practices into labor requires a reworking, it produces something of the uncanny, an excess that seeps out of this new framing as labor. Translation, contends Charkrabarty, always already fails to turn the weavers' god-inhabited practices into proper labor.

Religion, of course, is another ostensibly universal category used by social scientists that turns out to have a singular, Christian genealogy, and the attempt to translate Islam into the two separate domains of religion and culture is similarly fraught. Though the administrative and spatial organization of the ICI attempts to render religion and culture separate, those two domains intertwine in the very institutionalization of the ICI. Because the state cannot finance the construction of religious buildings, the ICI helped formalize a Muslim religious association (the AMO) to raise funds for the spaces of the ICI that would be dedicated to religion. Ironically, however, when the AMO was created, it comprised three cultural associations, one of which manages the al-Fath mosque. In fact, most French mosques—supposed to be spaces of religion only—are managed, usually with the blessing of public officials, by cultural associations under the law of 1901 rather than religious associations under the law of 1905, since the former are easier to register. The barracks mosque is managed by a cultural association created for that purpose and headed by the rector of the Rue Myrha mosque (which is also managed by a cultural association). Even the Great Mosque of Paris is, legally, an association under the law of 1901, established in 1926 as the Muslim Institute of the Paris Mosque precisely so that the French state could finance its construction without running afoul of the 1905 law of separation. (That cultural association bought and now manages the prayer space within the ICI at Rue Stephenson.) This legal and political subterfuge persists. As part of their continuing mission to create an *islam de France*, public officials have actively sought to circumvent restrictions on financing the construction of religious buildings. A 1991 Interior Ministry report on immigration concluded that publicly funding mosques and prayer rooms was preferable to having them financed by immigrant Muslims' countries of origin. It therefore proposed subsidizing projects that combined religion and culture to get around the law of 1905. As much as the division between religion and culture is a constitutive separation under *laïcité*, it is never quite secure.

The blurring of boundaries in a secular project intended to erect them occurs in the CFCM as well. In describing the creation of the council, Boyer explained that the lack of a centralized authority makes it difficult "to find legitimate and recognized leaders who can speak in the name of Islam" (1998, 10). Boyer has a point, but his formulation of the problem is interesting in and of itself: its underlying basis assumes that religious authorities should be able to speak in the name of Islam. Boyer does not simply mean that religious authorities should serve as the middlemen between the divine and the faithful, but that religious authorities should speak on behalf of the faithful (or the religion) to the state. He and other public officials see the rhizomatic structure of Islamic authority as a problem because it prevents the existence of a unified entity with whom the state can communicate. According to this secular logic, religious authorities not only interpret text and establish ethical and legal guidelines; they also represent a demographic constituency. Although the separation of religion and politics so central to secularism requires that Muslim religious authorities restrict themselves to theological or doctrinal domains, their status as representatives to the state actively brings them into public and political domains. The transformation of religious authority from an interpretive to a representative function is evident in the CFCM and in the state's delegation of authority to Muslim bureaucrats rather than to formally trained religious scholars. The first vice presidencies of the CFCM went to leaders of the UOIF and the FNMF. These men may be devout Muslims, but their qualifications to head the CFCM come from their organizational skills in running two of the largest Muslim federations in France. The first president of the CFCM, Boubakeur, was formally trained as a medical doctor; the second, Mohammed Moussaoui, is a professor of mathematics.

The transformation of religious authority into a democratically representative function raises the question of which constituency that authority represents: individual Muslims, the Muslim community, or Islam in France?

In October 2002, in one of his first addresses to the Istichara formed under Chevènement, Sarkozy stated that the CFCM, then not yet in existence, "concerns the Muslim religion and not Muslim culture . . . and even less the representation of the French Muslim community" (Sarkozy 2002). At the same time, Sarkozy, other government officials, the press, and many Muslims themselves often speak of the CFCM as the Muslim community's representative body. In one 2003 radio interview about the CFCM, Sarkozy and the journalist Jean-Pierre Elkabbach alternated between numerous appellations (Sarkozy 2003). Elkabbach noted: "The practicing Muslims of France have at last elected . . . their religious council." Sarkozy agreed: "Finally there is an organ that represents the Muslims in all their diversity." "Religious Muslims," Elkabbach corrected. "The Muslim religion," Sarkozy replied. Sarkozy also repeatedly stated that "the five million Muslims in France have finally become full citizens," thanks to the establishment of the CFCM (quoted in Sellami and Vézard 2003). His number is significant: it grounds the notion of a Muslim in something beyond religiosity, since various polls have shown that only 10–30 percent of the five million people counted as Muslims consider themselves practicing.[25] At the same time, the government's decision to organize elections for the CFCM around mosques implicitly linked mosque attendance—that is, ritual practice—to representation, and therefore to an idea of who counts as a Muslim (Bowen 2004, 53n4). Given that it is primarily men who attend mosques, women were seemingly excluded from representation.

The election itself resulted in much confusion about whether the CFCM represents the Muslim religion or Muslims themselves. Muslims and non-Muslims alike criticized the CFCM and the election process as undemocratic and unrepresentative, since the delegates who voted were chosen by mosques. Such a notion of democratic representation invokes a distinct kind of secular-national legitimacy and authority that differs from the bases for religious legitimacy and authority, even as the latter are understood within a secular notion of religion. The CFCM's defenders, including members of the government, parried the accusation of nonrepresentation by contending that the CFCM is not supposed to represent all Muslims. In an interview with the newspaper Le Parisien, Sarkozy reminded readers that "the CFCM is a religious authority, not an organ representing the whole community of Muslim faith" (quoted in Sellami and Vézard 2003). Yet the CFCM's composition is based on bureaucratic rather than religious authority. Furthermore, even though it is supposed to be analogous to the state's other religious interlocutors, the structure of the CFCM differs considerably from the Central Consistory and the Council of Bishops. The latter, which represents and manages Catholic worship, consists of bishops who accede to the council via channels of authority and hierarchy specific to the Catholic Church. The Central Consistory and its chief rabbi represent and organize the Jewish religion, while the Representative Council of Jewish Institutions of France, a sociocultural association, represents the Jewish community in a more capacious sense. In contrast, the CFCM is composed for the most part not of religious scholars but rather leaders of large federations that were established under the general 1901 law governing associations, not the 1905 law regulating religious associations and institutions. In addition, the scope of the CFCM encompasses doctrinal, bureaucratic, and community-relations functions. The government has demanded an opinion from the CFCM on whether or not wearing the hijab is a religious obligation for Muslim women; it has asked the CFCM to organize the slaughter of thousands of sheep for Aïd el Kébir in keeping with the demands of public hygiene; and it has called on the CFCM to consider issues like Islamic militancy, inner-city violence, and the conflict between Israel and Palestine—all of which, according to a Bureau of Religions official, are "questions related to Islam, even though Muslim worship is not directly concerned" (Terrel 2004, 91).

The CFCM's existence therefore raises the thorny question of who counts as a Muslim. Does the category of Muslim fall into the realm of religion and theology, culture and demographics, or politics and economics? And what would it mean to encompass all three? These questions become even more complicated with the emergence of secular Muslims who, critical of the participation of so-called fundamentalists (that is, the UOIF) in the CFCM, have formed a series of explicitly secular representative bodies—the French Council of Secular Muslims, for example—that they claimed represented the silent majority of Muslims in France. This silent majority obviously extends beyond the practicing or even believing Muslim to everyone of Arab-Muslim or African-Muslim origin. In a similar vein, government officials, academics, and the media increasingly refer to the five to six million Muslims in France, clearly invoking an ethno-racial community rather than a strictly religious one, or at least making it difficult to delineate between religious and ethno-racial classifications.

The ICI repeats these conflations between race and religion. ICI staff members identified many of the artists responsible for the films, concerts, art installations, and dance recitals during the 2010 Veillées as Muslims, connecting them to Islam by their ethno-racial and national origins as Arab, Moroccan, Algerian, and so forth. To the staff, these artists were culturally

Muslim if not religiously so. I do not deny the inspiration many of these creators draw from Islamic artistic traditions, or the long intertwining of Arab and Islamic cultural life. Indeed, some of them, like artist Hassan Hajjaj and dancer Héla Fatoumi, critically reflect on their identity as Muslims in the post-9/11 world. I simply want to underscore how the term *Muslim*, encompassing ethno-racial, religious, and cultural indices, has become the first choice of marker to identify this particular minority population. Though cultural difference and cultural attachment are valorized rather than denigrated in the ICI's rhetoric, its notion of culture nonetheless draws on a Europe-wide discourse that constructs culture as a reified ontology. Culture is not explicitly biological, but it remains tied to descent and phenotype. The culture concept at work in Europe depends on a racialized notion of difference that combines race, religion, and culture to produce the figure of the Muslim. It also, of course, produces the European as a figure—though always unmarked—of racial, religious, and cultural particularity.

These confusions and conflations between race, culture, and religion result from conflicting objectives on the part of the French state. On the one hand, attempts to secularize Islam are intended to transform it into a proper religion. Within the secular imaginary, religion is largely a matter of private belief; its manifestation through ritual practice must be in the private sphere or the sacred space of the mosque. On the other hand, the establishment of the CFCM and the ICI draws on a multicultural politics of recognition based on ethnicized notions of community and difference, with the state publicly recognizing minority ethnic, racial, cultural, and religious identities to promote integration, social peace, and a general *vivre ensemble*.

The irony is that the classifications of race, ethnicity, culture, and religion, as well as the very possibility of separating them into discrete categories, are products of secular modernity.[26] Yet secularization has also confused and conflated ethno-racial and religious designations, transforming the term *Muslim* from a theological notion into an ethno-racial category rooted in modern conceptions of the nation—hence the increasingly essentialized alterity of Muslims. The very attempt to secularize Islam by disaggregating it into religion, distinct from culture or race, destabilizes any boundary between religion and culture or race. The contemporary secularization of the Islamic tradition in France relegates acceptable religiosity to the realm of individual belief or the sacred space of the mosque, a relegation that many Muslims embrace. It also cultivates cultural forms of Islam in which culture becomes folkloric practice and embodied identity, as evidenced in the use of the recently coined phrase *of Muslim culture (de culture* musulmane), in state projects like the ICI, and in the fact that the term Muslim now refers to people coded twenty years ago as Beurs, thirty years ago as Arabs, and forty years ago as immigrants. Furthermore, the distinction between religion and culture that contemporary secularism seeks to enact intersects with the equally foundational distinction between religion and politics. Within the secular configuration of space, public expressions of Islam outside the designated space of the mosque must take place under the sign of sharable culture; those that do not—like the headscarf, an unsharable ethical practice—become forms of religious fundamentalism, defined as an excess of religion that is neither religious nor cultural, but rather political. However, the relegation of Islam to the designated space of the mosque or to the private sphere of belief never quite eliminates Muslim alterity, which is increasingly recoded as cultural and racial.

The current slippage between Muslim as a religious, cultural, and racial category draws on and reproduces a historical conflation. In colonial Algeria, even as the French state sought to secularize Islam and limit Muslim religious and legal authority, native (indigène), Arab (arabe), and Muslim (musulman) were overlapping categories in legal, political, and social domains. Muslim was a political and legal category, not just a religious one.[27] In fact, though the French sought to limit Muslim law to the private sphere, they were convinced that Islam had such a hold on the faithful that public and private could never be entirely separated (Davidson 2012). French officials saw Muslimness as an innate, embodied, and physical quality; as a result Muslims could never become secular—their religiosity was as innate as race. The contemporary construction of the figure of the Muslim is therefore saturated by France's history of attempting to render religion into a discrete domain of existence and of interpellating its colonial subjects in ways that knotted race, religion, and culture together.

In the Western-Christian imagination, the conceptualization of Islam has long oscillated between religion and race, and between theology and politics. Christian theologians like Thomas Aquinas posited Muslims as the political and external enemy of Christianity (as opposed to Jews, its theological and internal enemy) (Anidjar 2003). For these Christians, Islam had no theological basis, and Aquinas compared the Prophet to a political criminal. Yet, as Aquinas's classification suggests, Islam was not properly political either. As Gil Anidjar argues, Islam was both a political enemy and the enemy of the political in Christian thought. Always in excess, it was neither politics nor religion, a framing that has been repeated ad nauseam since 9/11. Within this logic, Islam is a form of political power that mistakes itself for a religion, yet it is not properly political either, since its political power—the power of its God and its rulers—is despotic. What Islam cultivates, or so the story goes, is political subservience. In contrast to Islam, Europe knows how to separate and properly embody the domains of politics and religion, being both pure politics (the secular state) and pure religion (Christianity).

Islam's oscillation in the North Atlantic imagination between religion and politics—its neither-nor quality—parallels its oscillation between race and religion in nineteenth-century Orientalism. For scholars like the philologist Ernest Renan, Judaism and Islam were race-religions, also called national religions. Whereas Judaism was seen to admit its racial particularity, Islam was classified as a race-religion masquerading as a universal religion, transgressing its proper racial and national (read: Arab) boundaries (Masuzawa 2005, 199). In contrast to true world religions, Islam had only universalist pretensions, actualized through political violence. Islam could not be a proper religion because it was both too racial and too political. Its religious dimension was excessive; it entailed violent fanaticism rather than religion. Once again, Islam was a political enemy of the West and an enemy of the properly political. And again, in contrast to Islam stood Christianity, a truly universal religion of global salvation. In the classificatory schema that defined *religion*, Christianity was the model religion. But this is unsurprising, given that Christianity was the model for religion.[28]

Predictably, then, contemporary and historical attempts to secularize Islam and turn it into a proper religion engender a series of slippages between culture, race, religion, and politics. These slippages reproduce Islam as a failure, incapable of separating religion and politics or of distinguishing between religion and culture or race. That failure, however, does not stem from the internal structure of Islam, as critics often contend. Rather, it is premised on the North Atlantic imagination of Islam as neither properly religious nor properly political. That premise, in turn, hinges on the intertwining of what we now call race, religion, culture, and politics in Christendom, and on the fraught separation of these domains as Christendom became secular Europe. Secularism demands the disaggregation of these domains and their reconfiguration as distinct and separate. Thus Christianity became a religion; politics took the form of the secular state; whiteness became a matter of race, though always unmarked; and culture emerged as the public presence of Christian ritual life, the surplus of Christianity that stayed public after belief went private. But these ostensibly distinct domains nonetheless remained intertwined, the discreteness of one premised on its relation to the others and to the whole configuration of race, religion, politics, and culture. Hence the long and unmarked racial basis of Christianity, secularity, and European culture in colonial and postcolonial contexts; the Christian underpinnings of secular modern law and politics; and the ease with which whiteness, Christianity, and secularity come together in the contemporary construction of European culture.[29] Put another way, the constant excesses produced by the secularization of Islam emerge not because Islam cannot separate religion, race, culture, and politics, but because Christianity, secularity, and Europe cannot.

Playing Politics

Though the barracks mosque was officially presented as a short-term solution to the problem of Muslim prayer until the ICI is completed, Hamza wants to turn it into a more permanent prayer space. Sidelined by city officials for his refusal to take part in the ICI, he has used the recent street prayer controversy to reassert himself as a major player in matters pertaining to Islam in the eighteenth arrondissement. He currently heads the association that runs the barracks mosque and, as a result, now controls one of the largest mosques in Paris. Hamza's wily political maneuvering disappointed and frustrated many of the ICI staff members and municipal officials, who criticized him for playing politics. One staff member told me she did not understand how he could favor the barracks mosque, given its marginal location and the heavy-handed tactics that the interior minister used to create it. Bouakkaz called Hamza a caïd, a chieftain. And Neyreneuf claimed that although Hamza and Diakité, the "Malian peasant" rector of the al-Fath mosque, were quite different, they had one thing in common: their desire to remain in power.

But Hamza is not the only one playing politics. Interior Minister Guéant's unexpected resolution of the street prayer problem cannot be divorced from the context of a national election campaign in which preserving French national identity by upholding laïcité became a major theme in Sarkozy's re-election bid. Similarly, Marine Le Pen's initial comments about the Muslim occupation of Paris are located in the wider context of national elections and the particular political moment in which she made them, when she was running for the presidency of the National Front. As for the Socialists, they have made it clear to Hamza that his refusal to participate in the ICI project comes at a cost: as Neyreneuf put it, "street prayer on Rue Myrha, that's over." Little surprise, then, that Hamza took so keenly to the barracks mosque proposal. In addition, his expansionist vision is aligned with a paradigm of Muslim authority put in place by the French state itself. Because mosques have now become the basic electoral unit for the CFCM, and square footage determines the number of delegates a mosque is awarded, the control of mosques has taken on some political importance (Bowen 2009, 25). By maneuvering to control one of the largest mosque spaces in Paris, Hamza is simply playing the game of religion-as-politics that has been institutionalized by the secular state.

The notion that Hamza politicizes religious matters perpetuates a widespread secular-republican discourse that distinguishes between real religion and politicized religion, between Islam and Islamism, and, ultimately, between religion and politics. Prior to the passage of the 2004 law banning headscarves, politicians and pundits routinely classified the headscarf as the politicization of otherwise private religiosity. "The wearing of the veil is not the manifestation of piety or modesty," proclaimed Alain Juppé, then head of the Union for a Popular Movement party and a former prime minister, "it is a militant act sustained by a veritable fundamentalist propaganda" (quoted in Guiral and Schneider 2003). Françoise Hostalier, a former official in the Ministry of Education, was equally certain: "To wear the Islamic veil is not a religious gesture but a political gesture" (2003). And, as Alain Billon, an advisor on Islam for the Ministry of the Interior, put it, "public opinion knows how to make the distinction between Islam and Islamism" (quoted in Bonnefoy 2003, 10).

These statements gesture to the way the distinction between religion and politics maps onto the distinction between real Islam and false Islam. The good Muslim–bad Muslim division that Mahmood Mamdani (2005) so aptly analyzed has theological import, and it is increasingly common to hear republican politicians claim that Islamic fundamentalists distort the true teachings of the Quran.[30] Yet this distinction between true and false Islam has a suspended temporality that is evident in Sarkozy's discussion of the CFCM as a bulwark against terrorism: "If anyone thinks that I am being naïve about the reality of Islam, I remind [them] that in the space of a few months, I had twenty-six people detained for undertaking antirepublican activities under the cover of Islam. We must not confuse the Muslim faithful and these people" (quoted in Bonnefoy 2003, 28). Although Sarkozy suggests that those extremists and terrorists undertaking antirepublican activities are not part of the Muslim faithful, he simultaneously refers to the "reality of Islam," which clearly encompasses terrorism and antirepublican activities. In Sarkozy's framing, terrorists do not simply work under the cover of Islam; they are part of "the reality of Islam." His ambiguous statement makes more sense when paired with another comment he made about the CFCM: "Let us make sure that islam de France is what it must be, that is to say a religion of tolerance and of openness" (quoted in Bonnefoy 2003, 28). The current reality of Islam, Sarkozy implies, is that it does not yet separate religion and politics, and is not yet tolerant or open. Consequently, the state must work to ensure that Islam becomes a real religion. However, given the history of Islam's always already excessive status in the Christian and secular imaginary, the process of making Islam into a religion will always fail; the suspended temporality of Islam as religion is a permanent condition, and the project of reform never ends.

These determinations by secular political authorities of what constitutes real religion are not a contradiction of secularism but rather its operationalization. Secular states seek to separate the religious and the political and to relegate religion to its designated and discrete realm. But in order to undertake this act of disaggregating religion, secular political and legal authorities must remake lifeworlds so that religion, politics, and culture can be separated. This second imperative of regulation constantly undoes the first imperative of separation, producing the very intersection of the religious and the political that defines secular rule. The criticism that Hamza plays politics is ironic, given the massive political, financial, and affective investment by public authorities in the construction of the ICI, and in the remaking of Islam more generally. The very criticism of Hamza for not knowing that politics has no place in religious matters constitutes one small moment in the ongoing reformation of Islam by political authorities, as they attempt to turn it into a proper religion.

Indeed, the criticism of Hamza might be read as a deferral, a symptom of the unease that these competing imperatives of secular rule produce. In my conversations with Neyreneuf, I was struck by the constant alternation between his desire to transform Islam into a manageable religion and his sense that doing so overstepped the boundary between religion and politics that laïcité seeks to erect. Describing the rectors of the two neighborhood mosques, Neyreneuf told me: "These are people with whom it's hard to work. If we had the choice . . . but we don't have the choice because we are in the framework of the law of 1905, we are not supposed to meddle in their affairs." If we had the choice, Neyreneuf seems to say, we would simply build the mosque ourselves, but since we have to keep religion separate from politics, we have to work with the Muslim peasants and chieftains we find. Neyreneuf's narrative reproduces the competing imperatives of secular political rule, but it also evinces a flicker of tension that interrupts his narrative, an interruption I have re-created with an ellipsis.

The ICI is precisely a project of "meddl[ing] in their affairs," underscored just minutes earlier in the conversation, when Neyreneuf declared that the ICI mosque could have many services, that praying in a mosque is not obligatory, and that traditional Muslims would eventually evolve and change their habits. Neyreneuf had begun our conversation by insisting that the ICI did not have a religious vocation, but except for these momentary declarations of disavowal, our conversation consisted of him telling me what needed to change in the Muslim community and how these changes would occur or had occurred. Neyreneuf clearly recognized that the ICI constitutes a project of transformation and rehabituation, and that it is necessary because the institutional, political, and ritual forms Islam currently takes present difficulties for the secular state. He acknowledged, in other words, that laïcité intervenes in and regulates Muslims' affairs even as he punctually disavowed that intervention. His criticism of Hamza for confusing religion and politics speaks to the imperative of separation that laïcité seeks to enact. But that criticism also displaces an unease produced by the other imperative of secular rule—namely, the definition and regulation of Islam, a form of meddling that seemingly contradicts the distance that political authorities are supposed to keep from the domain of religious life. The dual imperatives of secularism mean that the boundaries between religion, culture, and politics that the state attempts to secure through projects like the ICI and the CFCM are simultaneously rendered unstable. Yet even as the imperative to regulate is enacted, it is also explicitly disavowed, and the tension between the two competing imperatives of secularism is displaced and thereby deferred. The problem of blurring boundaries is shifted onto Muslims, who become the peasants, chieftains, and fundamentalists incapable of disaggregating religion, culture, and politics, and who consequently must have the regulatory force of secular rule brought to bear on them in order to reform them. For an Islam of the future to emerge as a proper, secular religion, Muslims of the present must be remade, and made to disappear.

Four

Reconfiguring Freedom

In early 2004 a group of activists formed the One School for All Collective (Collectif Une Ecole pour Tous et Toutes) to contest the proposed law banning conspicuous religious signs in public schools, and to provide legal counsel and educational support for students expelled as a result of the law. The collective brought together various overlapping constituencies: Muslim French associations, anticolonial and antiracist groups, progressive feminists, and members of the Green Party and the Revolutionary Communist League. It also included activists from Paris's small community of Sikhs, whose turbans became an unintended target of the new law. I was a member of the collective, opting to serve on the Legal Subcommittee alongside Céline and Nadia, two Muslim French women; Malika, a self-declared Algerian feminist; Najette, a Franco-Tunisian lawyer; and Jaswant, an energetic middle-aged Sikh man. We met weekly in a café in the eleventh arrondissement of Paris in early 2004, with copies of legal codes and conventions piled in front of us as we searched for ways to legally challenge the law. The collective was divided over how to proceed. Most secular activists felt that the law contravened the right to education. Many Muslim French and Sikh activists, however, considered it an attack on the right to religious freedom.

Jaswant was particularly outraged by the law, which would require Sikh boys to remove their turbans in public school. He declared that the five Ks of Sikhism, including *kesh*, or uncut hair, "are not optional—they *are* the faith [ils sont la foi]."[1] Since Sikhs cannot cut their hair, they must wear a turban. Moreover, Jaswant contended, "when a Sikh cuts his hair, his beard, soon, he begins to eat meat, to drink alcohol . . . he loses his soul." Jaswant did not mean that the same loss of faith that would lead a Sikh to cut his hair would also lead him to drink alcohol and eat meat, but rather that the practice of not cutting one's hair produces and sustains one's faith in the first place, and to cut one's hair would destabilize one's ethical self and one's relationship with the divine. For Jaswant, the turban holding a Sikh's uncut hair is not an optional sign of Sikh religiosity but a necessary part of being Sikh. Nadia, a member of the Collective of French Muslims, was also disturbed by the law. Though she did not wear a headscarf, she was a practicing Muslim and did not understand how she was supposed to repress this fundamental aspect of herself in public. "If I believe," she said, "how can I stop believing in different places? . . . That's not possible." Many of us felt that the most relevant way to challenge the law would be to advocate for the fundamental right to religious liberty, presumably protected by the French Declaration of the Rights of Man and Citizen, the European Convention on Human Rights and Fundamental Freedoms, and other international conventions.

It turned out that we were wrong. As we began to delve deeper into French and European law, we discovered that the French constitution and the European Convention on Human Rights distinguish between the right to conscience, which is inalienable, and the right to expressions or manifestations of conscience, which can be subject to restriction. Neither Céline, Nadia, nor Jaswant understood practices like veiling and wearing the turban as optional expressions of belief; rather, they considered them religious duties, as did most of my other practicing Muslim French interlocutors. Nonetheless, the headscarf and the turban—considered to be expressions of conscience—fell outside the purview of the inalienable right to conscience. After a series of meetings, we came to the conclusion that we simply had no way to challenge the law via a defense of religious liberty, and we turned our attention and resources elsewhere.

This chapter unpacks the conundrum we faced, tracing how secular assumptions about freedom, authority, choice, and obligation make Muslim French religiosity unintelligible in law and public discourse. I begin by examining how the debate about the French Islamic revival, and the veil specifically,[2] depends on and reproduces a series of oppositions between choice and constraint, personal autonomy and religious authority, and self-realization and external norms. As I go on to show, Muslim French challenge these binaries by conceptualizing practices like veiling, praying, and fasting as both modes of personal freedom and authoritatively prescribed acts necessary to becoming a proper Muslim subject. Yet the same oppositions that pervade public debate about the headscarf also underpin secular law and political discourse regarding religious freedom. This makes it difficult, if not impossible, for Muslim French to articulate what it means to wear the veil in a way that is intelligible within dominant legal, political, and ethical frameworks.

Submission or Emancipation

Various justifications have emerged for banning the headscarf in public schools: the veil violates the avowedly secular, neutral space of the public school; it represents an unacceptable form of communalism and is just the tip of the iceberg of a larger Islamist threat; and it symbolizes the submission of women to patriarchal religious authority.[3] The third justification has carried the most affective and legal weight and takes two forms.[4] Some critics (more in 1989, fewer in 2003 and 2004) argued that young girls' fathers, brothers, or Muslim community leaders were forcing them to wear the veil, and that the secular republic and its laws needed to emancipate them (Augé 2004; Long and Weil 2004). Other critics, mindful of studies showing that many young women choose the headscarf, advanced a more nuanced argument, one that reappeared in later French debates about outlawing the niqab. These critics argued that the veil, even if worn as a matter of choice, perpetuates normative religious authority, polices female sexuality and prescribed gender roles, and reinforces patriarchal communal norms not only on the veiled woman in question but on all Muslim women around her. In a May 2003 editorial, one of the first explicit calls for a law banning headscarves, Catherine Kintzler, Pierre-André Taguieff, Bernard Tepe, and Michèle Tribalat wrote that the veil reduces a woman "to a particularity that she has not chosen" (Kintzler et al. 2004, 37). Moreover, they argued, "religious conviction, because it pertains to freedom, cannot be manifested as an absolute (or as a nonnegotiable norm) at public school—the key site where the freedom of the citizen is formed—thus it certainly cannot entail the seizure of a part of the population in the name of authoritatively regulated sexual roles" (38; see also Weil 2004).

These intellectuals quite forcefully pitted freedom, represented by the school, against normative authority, represented by the veil, and they were not the only ones to do so. In another editorial, Suzy Rojtman, Maya Surduts, and Josette Trat, three longtime feminist activists, dismissed arguments that defended the headscarf as a choice: "Whatever the individual sense given to the wearing of the veil by a minority of young Muslim girls . . . wearing the veil has the same sense in all monotheistic religions the moment it is presented as a binding religious prescription. It is in no way a symbol of emancipation" (2004). All these critics' arguments depend on a clear opposition between emancipation and religious authority and on an understanding of the headscarf as fundamentally oppressive because it is worn, even if by choice, as a religious prescription.

In contrast to those who see the headscarf as a form of submission to religious authority, numerous French sociologists have argued that the veil is a form of empowerment and emancipation (Gaspard and Khosrokhavar 1995; Tietze 2002; Venel 2004). Many assert that by becoming a practicing Muslim and participating in Islamic civil associations, young women can cloak their desires—for work, education, and freedom—in a veil of Islamic legitimacy, enabling them to escape traditional customs like forced marriage and domestic servitude without breaking completely with their families and community. According to Nancy Venel, "under the cover of religion and altruism, [young veiled women] enjoy a relative autonomy. . . . Through the veil, young women get around all parental suspicion with regard to their chastity and the rectitude of their conduct. The veil allows them to occupy a space of liberty outside the family cell . . . and to invert the traditional relations of authority within the family" (2004, 188). These scholars also emphasize that the kind of rigorous Islam practiced by second-generation youth often is the result of a willed, individual choice, not the habitual reiteration of parental norms. In fact, a number of analysts hold that the defining feature of the French Islamic revival is the individualization of religiosity (Khosrokhavar 1997b; Roy 1999 and 2007; Venel 2004). Olivier Roy, for instance, maintains that the absence of Islamic religious authorities who could "state what is the norm," and the lack of social, communal, and juridical coercion have all made religiosity a fundamentally individual experience, so that "at the end of the day, it is the believer who decides, not the law, and not the society" (1999, 70 and 91). Roy describes the kind of modern religiosity central to liberalism and republicanism, in which one chooses one's religion by following one's inner voice rather than conforming to the exterior rules of religious authority.[5]

In contemporary France, where the majority of the French public views the headscarf as the ultimate symbol of women's submission to patriarchal authority, the aforementioned sociologists of French Islam have tried to normalize the veil, portraying Muslim women as modern, even quasi-feminist subjects. Nonetheless, these scholars reproduce the same analytical schema as secularist critics of the veil: choice opposes constraint, and autonomy emerges in resistance to or in the absence of normative authority. It is true that many young Muslim French women value personal freedom and conceptualize human agency as the capacity to author one's own life. But they also seek to submit to God's will by undertaking certain normative, obligatory practices like veiling, praying, and fasting. Although I recognize the political efficacy of arguing that the veil is a personal choice, not an imposition, such a reading misses crucial aspects of a specific kind of Muslim French subjectivity. Propagating a secular interpretation of veiling as emancipation—in which personal autonomy is the opposite of social and religious authority, and internally generated choice is the opposite of external constraints—ironically does a political disservice to practicing Muslim French women. Framing the headscarf as a freely chosen expression of the wearers' religious belonging may mark these Muslim women as conventionally modern religious subjects, but it simultaneously restricts their ability to articulate what it means to wear the veil as a religious duty.

"To Be Modern Is to Say 'I'"

Héla grew up in a Franco-Tunisian family that did not practice Islam, the kind of family that always served wine at dinner. When she was sixteen, she began to read more about Islam in books she purchased at small Islamic bookstores around Paris. She also began to read the Quran in translation, since her formal Arabic was weak. She soon decided that she wanted to become more practicing. She started slowly: first she stopped eating pork and drinking alcohol, then she began praying five times a day, and after four years she put on the hijab. "You have to be ready to wear the headscarf," she observed. "You have to understand the philosophy behind it, just as you have to understand the philosophy behind all the other interdictions. And at a certain point, I needed to wear it. My love for God was such that I needed to wear it."

My interview with Héla was the first one I conducted during my fieldwork, and she became one of my closest friends in Paris. In December 2002 we joined a group of other women for dinner at an Iranian friend's house. Héla, who was studying social movements in Iran for her PhD in sociology, had recently got a job in Qom teaching French. The job was through a

Catholic relief agency, which everyone—including Héla—found very funny. Fariba, who had fled Iran for Paris in the 1990s, proceeded to warn Héla that Qom was a cultural backwater full of ultraconservative religious types who would not take kindly to Héla's patterned headscarves. Héla declared that she would refuse to wear a chador, and that she had verified with the agency that she would not have to. Pauline seemed surprised, but Héla insisted that a verse in the Quran states quite specifically that religion cannot be compelled, and that putting on the headscarf, in whatever form, must be a personal choice based on personal conviction.

Héla's understanding of veiling as a practice of personal conviction is common to Muslim French. Most of my Muslim interlocutors considered veiling necessary for cultivating a relationship with God. They were equally adamant that practices like praying, veiling, and fasting cannot be compelled by others but must instead be chosen according to one's inner convictions. Khadija, another practicing Muslim whose parents came to France from Tunisia in the 1970s, has lived in metropolitan Paris all her life and was a part-time journalist studying for her master's degree in communications. "I would never tell a woman to veil obligatorily—no way," she said. "Because it's really something between you and God." As I was told repeatedly by a number of Muslim French women and men, quoting the Quran, "there is no coercion in religion."[6]

Muslim French argue that practices like veiling must be the result of an active, reasoned, conscious choice and not the repetition of habitual actions.[7] One must understand the reasons behind a practice—its doctrinal basis and pragmatic or theological function—for it to be meaningful and effective. Consequently, although my interlocutors are happy to have parents who pray and fast at Ramadan, they are critical of what they perceive as their parents' lack of understanding as to why praying and fasting are necessary. Given their conceptualization of the relation between intention and meaningful practice, moreover, Muslim French find that forcing anyone to pray, veil, or fast is not only ethically problematic but also pragmatically useless. As Héla contended, a practitioner should undertake ethical practices only when she is spiritually ready, which requires careful and critical deliberation. In addition, each practice commands a different level of readiness. The emphasis on thorough knowledge of the theological foundations for particular actions explains why bookstores are so central to the French Islamic revival and accounts for the growth of institutes that teach Islamic studies.

Khadija's and Héla's comments were echoed by members of al-Houda, a local association in Rennes that does civic outreach and meets biweekly to study the Quran and Quranic exegesis. When I worked with them, most of the women were between eighteen and thirty-five years old, and they came from varying ethno-racial and class backgrounds. One evening, we gathered at the home of Monique, a convert and stay-at-home mother of two small children, to discuss the headscarf and the role of individuals in interpreting God's will. Amira, a feisty high-school student with a cherubic face, took the lead in our conversation. Only eighteen years old, she exuded independence. Her Iraqi parents had fled Saddam Hussein's regime in the 1980s, and Amira had grown up in the Rennes banlieues with her sisters. She began by noting that there are different levels of obligatory practice in Islam, and veiling, though required, does not carry the same obligation as the five pillars of Islam. She referred to her friend Thérèse, who does not consider the headscarf an obligation. "She sees it like that," Amira said, "and I consider her as much a Muslim and as practicing as me." Amira paused, then went on:

> But now, we as individuals, what do we do with a verse in the Quran that we read? For example, the question of the headscarf. In the context in which we live, is [the verse] still applicable? We have to ask questions. For me, personally, my approach with the headscarf was to study the positions of the schools, Sunni and Shiite, to research religious scholars' opinions. And you know what? There's a certain unanimity on this question. Now, these scholars are men, they are interpreting in a political context that we must not ignore, but they nonetheless have proof, they are relying on the sources. [Pause.] There was a time when I really questioned the veil, but then I asked myself, "Is it really me asking these questions? Is it me who is interrogating my faith? Is it me who is asking myself whether I want to wear the veil and whether I am sincere, or isn't it really society?" . . . And it was this that led me to keep [the veil], because I said to myself that it isn't really my faith doing the questioning, it's Western society in general and French society in particular that are always singling me out. . . . But at the time, I really had a moment where I wanted to take it off because I thought, this is something imposed by men. I am obeying because I fear God, and men are using my fear of God to make me submit to a command. . . . But then I realized that when I pray and when I put on my veil, everything makes sense. The headscarf, for me, makes sense. . . . And that's when I said to myself that while it was legitimate to ask myself all these questions, I was putting into question something that does me good. . . . Now, I think as women,

it's important that we make sure we aren't used by men, that we remain vigilant on this question because there are women who submit to pressure, there are women who wear [the veil] because there are men who impose it on them, so that they do not live it as an intimate relationship [with God]. . . . And in my opinion, we must be very vigilant about this. The question to ask is: Do we grow in our faith? What does [the veil] bring to our spirituality? And if it brings nothing, then there's a problem.

Amira's comments indicate the extent to which she tries to distinguish her own desires from those of others. She maintains that women must be especially vigilant to make sure men in positions of authority do not abuse their power. In fact, she reached a point in her life when she almost removed her headscarf, fearing it had been imposed on her by a patriarchal interpretation of the sources. But she realized that her questioning of the hijab emerged from French society's norms rather than from her own convictions, and she decided to keep veiling because it fulfills her own spiritual needs and desires.

Hélène, another member of the group, nodded while Amira spoke. A convert of Guadeloupian descent in her mid-twenties, Hélène was a social worker and lived alone in Rennes. She explained that her decision to veil was not driven by external factors like her family. Rather, "it is truly the desire [la volonté] to apply what I consider as emanating from the Transcendent, a desire to please Him and be closer to Him, that makes me wear the veil." She noted that veiling had been difficult because the headscarf poses such a problem for French society, "but I really disregard how others look at me because it is my relationship with God that is in question in my choice to wear the veil. I believe it's important, in order to become the subject of one's life [devenir sujet de sa vie], to not conform to the opinion of others, because to do otherwise would be self-alienation. Thus the importance in holding fast to my convictions."

Hélène's sense that becoming a full subject entails the authorship of her own life was reiterated by Saida Kada, then a member of the Collective of French Muslims, which coformed the One School for All Collective. To many Muslim French, Kada is a model citizen: a practicing Muslim who works, cares for her children and husband, and actively participates in political and civic life. In a treatise she wrote with the anthropologist Dounia Bouzar on Muslim women in France, Kada contends: "To be modern is to say 'I'—to not let the clan decide for you, to use reason to put into question ancestral traditions" (Bouzar and Kada 2003, 199). "Freedom," she writes, "comes with the access to knowledge, and liberation with the ability to speak. . . . We [Muslim women] must not let others speak in our place" (15). For Kada, freedom means the ability to speak for oneself, to be the subject of one's own life story, not the object of someone else's version. What Kada, Khadija, Amira, and Hélène all invoke is a sense that human agency is grounded in the capacity to lead one's life according to one's own desires and choices, a conception of agency familiar to secular-republican and liberal sensibilities.

These women's attitudes toward veiling seemingly validate the sociological analyses that portray the headscarf as very much a choice, as well as part of a more general form of individualized religiosity that privileges one's inner voice over the external rules of religious authority. Yet a closer look at the beliefs and practices of women like Khadija, Amira, and Hélène demonstrates that, ultimately, they upend such a distinctly oppositional relationship between the self and authority, and between personal freedom and norms. By linking self-realization to the realization of the Transcendent will—which requires submission to certain religious obligations—these Muslim French women fundamentally reimagine the relationship between norms and the self. For them, the true self is realized not against social and religious authority but rather through it.

Reconfiguring Freedom

In the middle of Burgundy sits the sleepy village of Saint-Léger-de-Fourgeret, site of the European Institute for Human Sciences (Institut Européen des Sciences Humaines, or IESH), an unaccredited center for the study of Arabic, Islamic theology, and Quranic recitation. Most of the 160 or so students live in sex-segregated dormitories; student couples, along with teachers and staff members, live in the large château that also houses the institute's administrative offices. When I visited in 2004, forty students were studying theology, another twenty-five were studying Quranic recitation, and the rest were studying Arabic. Though most were Muslim French, there were also students from other countries in Europe and a few men from the Maghreb. At €2,600 per year, attending the IESH is a major investment, and many students stay for only one or two years. Linked institutionally to the Union of Islamic Organizations of France (Union des Organisations Islamiques de France, or UOIF), the IESH was designed to serve two constituencies. It provides courses and an Islamic environment for young men and women who want to learn Arabic and deepen their knowledge of Islam. It also runs a more rigorous four-year program in Islamic theology and jurisprudence, entirely in Arabic, for postbaccalaureate students interested in becoming experts in Islamic law.

The place feels thoroughly rural. The IESH compound overlooks rolling hills spotted with bales of hay, and reception for cell phones is next to nonexistent. It also feels thoroughly Islamic. Women are required to wear the headscarf, so even those few who do not usually wear it put it on while at the IESH. In the dining hall, a makeshift barrier divides the room, and men and women eat separately; they also avoid contact with each other outside the classroom. The small mosque has separate entrances for men, who pray on the ground floor, and women, who pray on the second floor, and the call for morning and evening prayers is broadcast over loudspeakers in the dorms.

One morning, four female students and I sat on the floor in Zeynep's room, talking about the IESH and my research. Zeynep, who was born in Turkey and had come to France at the age of five, was finishing her second year of Islamic theology. She had already dressed for the day, in a black *abaya* and black headscarf; the other girls were still in T-shirts and sweatpants, their hair uncovered. I asked them why they had come to the IESH, and Zeynep responded that she wanted to deepen her knowledge of Islam. She also wanted to read the *Quran* in Arabic, and "it annoyed me that I couldn't before because it's the word of God, and I wanted to understand." Samia, who lived in Belgium, answered that even though her parents practiced Islam, she wanted to know more about her religion. For example, she said, "though I fasted during Ramadan, I didn't know the real sense of it." She also wanted to be able to respond to questions about and criticism of Islam from non-Muslim Belgians. Fouzia, who was born and raised in Paris, agreed, although she observed that it was not just non-Muslims talking: "People say lots of things, anything and everything, and here, in this context, in Europe, we are a bit lost." She meant that she and other young European Muslims, mistrustful of the so-called customary practices of their parents, are not sure whom they should listen to and which beliefs and practices are authoritative. Sites like the IESH are islands of authoritative knowledge in an ocean of competing discourses about Islam emanating from Muslims and non-Muslims alike.

Our conversation returned to Ramadan, and I asked Samia what she meant by its "real sense." She responded that fasting enabled the practitioner to feel what the poor felt, and that it was also a reminder of God, a way of loving God. Zeynep agreed, adding that fasting developed patience.

"You don't wait for recompense," she said. "You're patient for God. Before I started practicing, I was nervous, but since, I have become patient. When my friends do something annoying, I don't say anything, I'm patient with them."

Zeynep's reference to her love for God (amour de Dieu) was a theme I heard repeatedly at the IESH, especially when students spoke about donning the headscarf. In a different conversation, Zeynep told me that her love of God grows through prayer. "It's the one time when you're with God, one on one," she said. "It's when you kneel down to pray that you're closest to God. When you're on your knees with your head to the ground, you feel like God is most high. I feel closest to Him when I do my supplications [invocations]." She added that before she became a practicing Muslim, she was always very lonely, even though she had no familial or material problems: "Inside, there was always something—I didn't feel at ease, there was always a lack." And she understood now why she had felt this lack, this unease: "When we are out and about, we forget about [God], but we know that we are forgetting something." She paused, then said: "God created us so that we could adore Him."

Most analyses of the Islamic revival in France, and of the headscarf especially, involve psychosocial and functionalist explanations, accounting for why Muslim French turn to religious revivalism.[8] In contrast, I am interested in the nature of Muslim French subjectivity, and particularly in the self's relation to normative authority. Recall Amira's description of how she came to wear the headscarf. On the one hand, her comments indicate the extent to which she watches over herself in order to distinguish her own desires from those of others. In fact, she reached a point in her life at which she almost took off the headscarf because she felt that it might have been imposed on her by a patriarchal male elite. On the other hand, however, she ultimately recognizes veiling as an obligation, accepting the authority of religious scholars to interpret the sources correctly. Although her acceptance of this obligation relies on her internal feelings of self-fulfillment—"when I put on my veil, everything makes sense," as she said—Amira is equally persuaded by the arguments and authority of established Islamic scholars. Her sense of self-fulfillment becomes coextensive with the obligation to veil.

Consider, too, the following explanation by Khadija of how and why she decided to wear the veil:

I understood from the books [I read] that I had to cover [my hair], and during the first year of university, I said to myself, "Khadija, you can't stay like this [unveiled]." I talked to the sisters, I read books, and the books were clear, they said that God had written in the *Quran* that the headscarf was obligatory. . . . And the fact that God required it, and that there was a logical explanation—well, I said to myself, "Khadija, you're going to veil." And I put on a simple headscarf, where you could see my neck. You know, I had a real problem at the beginning. And then, little by little, at the end of a year, I started to wear the headscarf like this [a piece of thick fabric covering her head, neck, and ears].

Amira's and Khadija's accounts elucidate how many pious Muslim French understand the relationship between self-directed choice and normative authority. Significant, for example, is their reliance on the authority of accepted texts. One of the most salient features of the Islamic revival is the production, circulation, and consumption of religious manuals and recorded sermons by preachers, many of whom have no classical training at religious institutions; these audiovisual and written manuals often detail the proper Islamic behavior for men, women, and children. Many scholars contend that the increased availability of texts and modes of Islamic reasoning, as well as the absence of state and judicial enforcement of religious law, has shattered traditional authority in Europe (Khosrokhavar 1997a; Roy 1999; Bouzar 2001). In so doing, they echo arguments about the Islamic revival in the Middle East that circulation of religious knowledge in the mass media has democratized authority (Eickelman and Piscatori 1996; Eickelman and Anderson 1997; Starrett 1998). Though the mass circulation of religious knowledge has certainly shifted religious authority from the restricted domain of the 'ulama' to a public domain, religious authority has not necessarily been shattered. Rather, in Europe, it has been resituated in nontraditional figures like Tariq Ramadan and his fellow preachers and intellectuals.[9] Furthermore, the availability of religious manuals in the French vernacular actually helps propagate authoritative norms of piety, as Amira's and Khadija's religious transformations attest. And, as the existence of the IESH and other similar Islamic institutes suggests, Muslim French actively seek out sites of authoritative knowledge and interpretation.

One of the texts that most influenced Khadija to veil was Fatima Naseef's *Droits et devoirs de la femme en islam* (Rights and duties of the woman in Islam; 1999). Another popular book is *Être musulmane aujourd'hui* (Being a Muslim woman today; 1999) by Malika Dif, an influential speaker on the Islamic conference circuit in France. These and other manuals detail the role of women according to the Islamic tradition, outlining what is expected of a woman and what she should expect from others. The manuals have two particularly striking features. The first is their constant reference to "the Muslim woman" (la femme musulmane), indicating that there is a correct model of female piety derived from the Quran, the Sunna, and the behavior of the Prophet's wives, which ordinary Muslim women should emulate. The second, related feature of these texts is the frequent occurrence of the verb devoir, which means "must," "have to," or "have a duty to," as in: "The woman must, above all, surround her family with attention and care. . . . She must watch over the physical and psychological health [of her family]" (Dif 1999, 41). The prevalence of the word devoir highlights the fact that certain types of behavior, including practices like veiling, are necessary to becoming the kind of Muslim woman who is delineated in these texts. Books like Dif's and Naseef's underscore the lacunae in analyses of Muslim French revivalism that herald the individualization of religion, the end of normative authority, and the emphasis on unconstrained, individual choice. Although it is undoubtedly "the believer who decides" (Roy 1999, 91), the believer is nonetheless guided by religiously authoritative texts and arguments that explicitly state the norms. According to these norms, the headscarf, like other practices, is both a choice and, importantly, an obligation, a divine prescription incumbent on all Muslim women.[10] The choice here lies in whether or not to accept the obligation of veiling.

The following example of a conversation with Nawel nicely elucidates the particular relationship between individual choice and obligation at work in Muslim French religiosity. At the time, Nawel was a twenty-year-old student getting an associate's degree in communications and working as an intern for the UOIF. She and I were having coffee when I asked her why she wore a simple headscarf tied in a large knot that covered only her hair, rather than a fuller headscarf that covered her neck as well, or even the niqab. She responded: "The niqab, it's not my thing, although I respect the girls who wear it, just as I respect those girls who don't wear anything [to cover their hair]." Nawel thereby reaffirmed the importance of respecting individual believers' personal choices, including the decision to veil or remain unveiled. I then said, referring to the practice of veiling: "So you have to cover the hair, and if you want, the neck and ears . . ." Nawel interrupted me sharply. "It's not 'If you want,'" she said. "It is the ears and the neck [that have to be covered]." Nawel's point was that one does not simply veil according to one's personal predilections. Proper veiling, an obligation in itself, has a specific, authorized form; the act of choosing lies in whether one opts to follow the divine injunction or not. In fact, the general goal for pious Muslim French like Nawel is to undertake willingly what is necessary. For example, Naseef writes that it is a woman's duty to maintain her house in proper order, and that this duty must be assumed voluntarily: "In the authentic hadiths about women's work in her household, it is said that the wife must accomplish these household tasks willingly and without any coercion" (1999, 185). One must transform religious obligations into desire, so that the desire to perform duties flows naturally from within the self.

Khadija used texts like Naseef's and Dif's to work on herself, and the transformation she underwent is similar to the process of ethical self-cultivation previously theorized by Saba Mahmood (2005) in her ethnography of the Egyptian women's piety movement.[11] Recall that Khadija began by wearing a simple headscarf that covered her hair because although she realized that veiling was obligatory, she was not ready to wear a fuller veil. As she said, "You know, I had a real problem at the beginning. And then, little by little, at the end of a year, I started to wear the headscarf like this [covering her head, neck, and ears]." Khadija's desire to veil came about by purposefully working on herself through other ethical practices like praying, reading, and discussing the headscarf with other Muslim French. Over the course of a year, Khadija disciplined her desire so that she could sincerely and freely undertake the requirements of a pious Muslim woman. Moreover, what connects desire and obligation—what turns obligation into desire—is love of God. Through practices like praying, fasting, and veiling, Muslim French augment their love of God, which in turn makes them want to please Him and to continue to become better and more practicing Muslims.

Turning obligation into desire through self-discipline reflects a broader conception of the self and of its internal malleability through external practices. In a half-day conference sponsored by the French League of the Muslim Woman (Ligue Française de la Femme Musulmane, LFFM), Dif applied this relationship between internal desire and external practice to the question of marriage. About forty or so Muslim French women had gathered in the women's section of the UOIF mosque in La Courneuve on a Saturday afternoon in May 2004 to hear Dif. "Marriage," she told us, "is a process and a difficult engagement" for which one must prepare properly. She quoted the Prophet's dictum that "marriage is a form of servitude," an axiom she would repeat three more times in her lecture. "My sisters," she said, addressing the audience, "you need to understand what undertaking a marriage means.

Marriage is not the culmination but the beginning of a difficult life" that unites two different personalities. "The goal is to live in harmony under the satisfaction of God," she declared. "To attain that objective, one has to go through a series of hardships." Dif noted that men and women must work to bring their behavior into line with what is required of a good Muslim husband and wife: "Marriage necessitates the smoothing of one's comportment in order to conform with the teaching of Islam."

The relationship between disciplinary practice and desire emerged particularly clearly in Dif's discussion of love. She warned that many women dream of a grand love affair, but that the basis for a good marriage is affection and respect. Love, she declared, evolves over time, and unless a couple takes a very long time to get to know each other before marriage, they often marry before love between them exists. "Love is born with time," Dif continued, "and each person in the couple brings a small rock to construct this edifice. He who loves the most is he who gives the most. One has to make an effort." Dif here invoked a model of companionate marriage in which men and women nonetheless may marry without love, possibly without even dating, and certainly without premarital sex. Love, according to Dif, occurs after marriage and is cultivated through acts of ordinary devotion that range from a smile to doing the housework to passing the remote control with patience. These gestures do not result from preexisting love but are necessary steps to cultivating marital love, itself necessary for a lasting marriage. Through these outward practices, the Muslim wife brings herself to love her husband, and vice versa.

Dif's lecture itself is part of the cultivation of Muslim piety, and the self-directed religious education undertaken by the women who came to listen to her is common to the French Islamic revival. In addition to formal institutes like the IESH, conferences, lectures, and workshops sponsored by national organizations like the UOIF, LFFM, and Muslim Presence or smaller local associations and mosques are a mainstay of the Islamic revival. These gatherings feature figures like Ramadan, Dif, Hassan Equioussen, and Tareq Oubrou (a scholar and imam based in Bordeaux), who speak on topics ranging from the religious duties of Muslims in Europe to the political governance advocated in the Quran to the Prophet's treatment of women. Although these events certainly mark the intellectualization of European Islam (Roy 1999) and what Dale Eickelman and James Piscatori (1996) and Gregory Starrett (1998) have called the objectification of the Islamic tradition more generally, acquiring knowledge is equally a process of ethical self-cultivation. Conference going is a disciplinary practice like praying, crucial to cultivating a properly pious Muslim French self. Through workshops and lectures, as well as through practices of reading, deliberation, and discussion, Muslim French educate themselves about their religion; deepen their knowledge of the divine and of divine injunctions; and learn, both from texts and from each other, how to be a properly practicing Muslim. The intellectual, affective, and ethical registers of subjectivity are conjoined here and sustain a feedback loop: to learn more about Islam is to cultivate one's love for God, which propels better practice and more learning, and so on.

Khadija had told me that cultivating piety is a long path, and over the course of my fieldwork, I came to recognize the basic steps. Most of my interlocutors began what they called their spiritual journey (cheminement spirituel) by reading, attending conferences, and talking to friends and acquaintances with greater knowledge of the Islamic tradition. Then they began praying intermittently, increasing over time the regularity of their prayers to five times a day. Initially, many found it difficult to rise for the dawn prayer (fajr), but they slowly brought themselves to do it every day. They also began to dress more modestly and change other behaviors—eating halal, for example, and carrying spare change to give to homeless people—and they often took their cues from those who were more advanced on their spiritual journeys. Most of the practicing Muslim women I knew prayed regularly for months and sometimes years before putting on the headscarf. This temporal gap highlights the intellectual and physical disciplinary process through which, step by step, these women turn themselves into proper Muslims.

Certain forms of prescribed behavior—fasting, praying, and veiling, in particular—are essential to realizing the authoritatively prescribed model of virtuous female piety. As Zeynep declared, fasting during Ramadan cultivates the virtue of patience. The constant feeling of hunger also produces humility in the face of divine omnipotence as well as a commitment to justice for the poor and the hungry. Djamel, a member of the Muslim Students of France, expanded on the necessity of certain practices: "When I pray, I am reminded of God, who is all-powerful, and who is my creator, and I realize that I am a tiny part of this huge presence, and I feel humble. When I fast during Ramadan, it's not just because that's what you do if you're Muslim. You need to know why. And you fast during Ramadan in order to remember how fragile you are as a human, and to remember that there are people who do not have enough, who are suffering, and it teaches you the importance of justice. It makes you more and more just in your own life toward others, even toward people whom you don't know."

Similarly, veiling is part of a larger ethical project of self-making. Many of my Muslim French interlocutors not only consider modesty a fundamental aspect of being a pious Muslim woman, but they also see veiling as necessary to cultivate modesty. Irène, a member of al-Houda in Rennes, explained the relationship between modesty and veiling: "Unfortunately, I don't yet have a good grasp of modesty, so I hope that it will come about through wearing the veil. . . . I don't have that base, that notion of modesty. It makes me sad, but it's like that. . . . But I know that by wearing the veil, it helps me to have a certain modesty, even in my way of speaking or comporting myself. So I put it on hoping, and it worked out. Each time you take a step toward God, He takes ten steps toward you." By veiling, Irène has completely changed her physical comportment, down to the way she speaks. In this particular configuration of the relationship between interiority and exteriority, mind and body, and piety and practice, actions like veiling, praying, and fasting do not simply signify Muslim piety but are integral to achieving that piety. As Mahmood has argued in her seminal work on the Egyptian mosque movement, "the importance of these practices does not reside in the meanings they signify to their practitioners [and to others] but in the *work they do* in constituting the individual" (2005, 29 [emphasis in original]). Mahmood contends that for the women she worked with, it is impossible to acquire piety without performing certain practices in a prescribed way. "Outward bodily gestures and acts," she writes, "are indispensable aspects of the pious self in two senses: first in the sense that the self can acquire its particular form only through the performance of the precise bodily enactments; and second in the sense that the prescribed bodily forms are necessary attributes of the self" (133). Wearing the headscarf is not just a sign of one's modesty but also, fundamentally, an ethical practice necessary to making the mind and body modest. And once put on, the veil becomes essential to its wearer's sense of self.

What Muslim French women enact, then, is a complex relationship between norms and desire in which social and religious authority are not opposed to the true self but lead to its cultivation and realization. When Kada asserts that "freedom comes with access to knowledge" (Bouzar and Kada 2003, 15), she means that freedom—understood as the realization of one's true desires—depends on knowledge of God's will, since what the self desires is sutured to what God wants for the self. As Ramadan writes, "if it is clear that there is no choice without liberty . . . it must be added that there is also no choice without knowledge and understanding. Choice and ignorance are antithetical terms" (1999, 316). One cannot make choices for oneself without understanding who one really is and what one really desires, and that depends on understanding the divine will, which in turn depends on trained religious scholars who can properly interpret the textual sources. This attitude explains the modernist revivalist return not only to the sources but also to the authority of trained exegetes, both classical and contemporary, to interpret them.

In addition, although self-realization and self-liberation remain fundamental goals for women like Khadija, Amira, and Hélène, the two principles are anchored in the Islamic concept of fitra, the natural capacity within each individual to know God. Self-realization is understood as the rediscovery of one's original knowledge of God, and self-liberation as the enactment of God's will. When Hélène asserts that becoming the subject of one's life means not conforming to others' opinions, she articulates the idea that liberation from others is integral to self-realization, and that it is achieved by submitting to God's will, knowable to humans through the Quran and the Sunna. Ramadan puts it in similar terms. Muslim spirituality, he writes, is the return to one's true, God-connected self, which is a form of liberation, but one that requires awareness, discipline, and constant effort (2004, 119). "Islamic teaching," he continues, "has given us concrete tools to help us succeed in this work on ourselves. . . . The daily requirements of Muslim practice give us the direction and the first steps along the way to freedom" (120). Self-realization is possible only by actively submitting to religious discipline and remaking oneself according to Islamic norms, extracted from the sources through centuries of authoritative interpretation. Furthermore, practices like praying, veiling, and fasting are not only signs that intentionally index a Muslim identity; they also, as Ramadan reiterates, are necessary to cultivate the Muslim self.[12] Ramadan and the Muslim French women he appeals to conceptualize self-realization as the enactment of the Transcendent will, and as dependent on, rather than constituted in opposition to, social and religious authority. In so doing, they reiterate freedom and self-directed choice as essential ethical values and as constitutive of the modern self. Yet they also reconfigure secular notions of personal autonomy and modern religiosity so that normative religious authority and inner, individual desire are not opposed, but rather inextricably linked.

The kind of religiosity Muslim French inhabit, with its distinct configuration of personal autonomy, authority, and the self, was unintelligible on the discursive and legal terrain on which debates about the ban on headscarves were waged. Within the legal and moral framework of religious freedom, Muslim French women were compelled to defend the headscarf as either a choice or an obligation—it could not be both.

Secular Law and Religious Liberty

As a result of the 1989 Conseil d'Etat ruling that headscarves did not in themselves present a problem in the secular public school, administrators were not legally allowed to institute general bans on religious head coverings as part of a school's rules of conduct (*règlements intérieures*). At the Lycée Jean Nouvel in La Courneuve, teachers and administrators routinely complained about the 1989 decision because they could not include the veil in the rules that otherwise forbade head coverings (*couvre-chefs*) like caps and hats. "They get away with it because it's religious," grumbled Anne, an English teacher. When I asked her if she saw a difference between the headscarf worn by her student Naveeda and the do-rags she made her male students remove, she replied, "I suppose they are different. I mean, the headscarf is religious, isn't it? It means more to her." Nonetheless, Anne wanted all head coverings banned.

During my first week at the school in 2002, some teachers had invited a representative from the local board of education to speak to them about how to deal with the problem of the headscarf. The representative acknowledged that girls were legally allowed to wear the headscarf as a form of religious freedom. He did, however, offer some tips about how teachers could get around this legal technicality by linking the headscarf to safety issues. For instance, a girl in chemistry class could be told that if she wears her hijab, she cannot take part in any experiments, adversely affecting her grade. As Anne told me, the school "has to play these students at their own game." Though some teachers remained unfazed by the headscarf, others felt the students' recourse to the letter of the law contravened the spirit of *laïcité*. They therefore sought to find ways to counter the headscarf while remaining within legal limits.

The 2004 law made their maneuverings obsolete, closing what many saw as a loophole in schools' rules of conduct. At a June end-of-year meeting of Jean Nouvel's administrative council, made up of teachers, administrators, and parental representatives, the principal, Monsieur Thomas, discussed changes to the rules of conduct. Henceforth, a section on *laïcité* would include a ban on conspicuous religious signs, in addition to the ban on head coverings (located in a different section of the rules). One of the teachers inquired about the Sikh turban, and the principal replied that Sikh students would have to wear a net over their hair knot rather than a turban. Besides, he observed, the turban is not religious but cultural. Regardless, it would be banned, either as a head covering or as a conspicuous religious sign, since religiosity no longer made a difference in adjudicating the rules of conduct.

A parental representative then asked how expulsions of veiled schoolgirls would proceed, and the principal responded that according to the law, there would be a short period of dialogue before any expulsion. The representative observed bitterly: "This dialogue is not really a dialogue. The law was made to expel." Monsieur Thomas shot back that "the dialogue is not a negotiation. The law is nonnegotiable." The dialogue, he continued, "would point out the stakes—that is to say, the possibility of the girl's removal from school. And after that, it's her own free will. It's up to her to make the choice. I'm not the one who's going to make the decision."

If we on the Legal Subcommittee of the One School for All Collective felt sure that the ban on headscarves in public schools constituted a violation of religious freedom, proponents of the law were equally insistent that it did not and, moreover, that it constituted an important defense of religious liberty. They drew on two key themes that permeate French political discourse and French and European law: a semiotic understanding of practice as the expression of belief, and a related notion that freedom of conscience means freedom of choice.

French politicians and intellectuals in favor of the ban argued repeatedly that restricting the wearing of the headscarf and other religious signs did not constitute a violation of religious liberty because the believer could continue to believe—on the inside. As Zaki Laïdi, a political theorist, put it, "there are a thousand ways for a Muslim woman who aspires to wear the veil to wear it on the inside without wearing it on the outside" (2004, 159). Gisèle Halimi, an influential feminist lawyer, similarly argued that under the terms of laïcité, "faith, thought, conscience . . . can be expressed," but "behaviors, religious 'prescriptions,' basically signs and insignia, in other words, practice . . . must be banned" (2003, 66). Here, Halimi draws a stark distinction between conscience (or faith) and practice, the latter clearly delineated as a sign of the former. Halimi and Laïdi, like other proponents of the ban, thus invoked the conventional secular relationship between conscience and practice that consists of two related ideas: first, religious practices comprise the outward manifestations—"signs and insignia"—of an

already constituted conscience; and second, as inessential, exterior representations of conscience, practices have no effect on interior conscience
itself. According to this logic, banning a practice like veiling does not constitute a violation of religious liberty because if the practice-as-sign presumably has no effect on the believer's conscience, neither would its disappearance. The ban was therefore envisioned not as a restriction on veiled
women's conscience, but rather as a limitation on their right to manifest
that conscience. Although Muslim girls and other religious students would
no longer be able to express their beliefs in certain ways as a result of the
law, proponents of the ban argued that they would nonetheless remain free
to believe whatever they wanted to believe, exercising their right to conscience. As Laïdi noted, Muslim girls could continue to wear the headscarf
"on the inside." Significantly, then, proponents of the law did not contend
that religious liberties must sometimes be curtailed in the name of public
order; rather, they did not see the ban on headscarves and other religious
signs as an attack on religious liberty at all.

This logic is not only dominant in French public discourse about the
headscarf, but also undergirds French and European legal conventions pertaining to religious liberty. According to article 10 of the Declaration of the
Rights of Man and Citizen, "none shall fear for his opinions, even religious,
as long as their manifestation does not trouble the public order as established by the law." The European Convention on Human Rights and Fundamental Freedoms, to which France is a signatory, echoes the Declaration.
Article 9(1) of the European Convention guarantees to all "the right to freedom of thought, conscience and religion" as well as the right "to manifest
[one's] religion or belief, in worship, teaching, practice and observance."[13]
However, like the second clause above from the Declaration, article 9(2)
immediately places certain limitations on the latter freedom: "Freedom
to manifest one's religion or beliefs shall be subjected to such limitations
as are prescribed by law and are necessary in a democratic society in the interest of public safety, for the protection of public order, health or morals,
and for the protection of the rights and freedoms of others." Like Halimi
and Laïdi, the European Convention differentiates between conscience and
its manifestation or expression, protecting in absolute terms what is often
called the *forum internum* of personal beliefs and religious creeds (Evans
2001, 72). According to the legal scholar Peter Danchin, the *forum internum*
"is a narrower concept than the commonly understood meaning of the term
'private sphere.'" The *forum internum* "encompasses the *internal* space of personal thought, conscience, or belief, and not those *external* spheres, even if

nonstate and therefore technically 'private,' such as places of worship, the school, or the family, where religious belief may be communicated or acted upon" (2008, 261 [emphasis in original]). Instituting what Danchin calls a mind-action distinction, the European Convention and other major rights conventions distinguish between thought and conscience, on the one hand, and action related to belief, on the other hand. Although the realm of the *forum internum* is inviolable and the right to conscience inalienable by any state law, the right to manifest one's conscience is alienable, since a restriction on the manifestation of conscience is not considered a restriction on conscience itself.[14]

A specific, secular understanding of the relationship between belief and practice underpins this distinction between conscience and its manifestation, an understanding that has a Christian, and especially Protestant, genealogy.[15] One of the effects of the Protestant Reformation and subsequent secularization of Europe was the emergence of belief as the authentic site of religion. Disciplinary practices of the body, once considered even by Christian authorities as integral to cultivating proper piety, came to be thought of as second-order expressions of belief (T. Asad 1993). The resulting configuration of the relationship between belief and practice holds that religious practices are neither as integral to religiosity as are beliefs, nor do practices produce belief. Thus a restriction on practices (like wearing the headscarf) does not necessarily constitute a violation of religious liberty, defined as one's right to have religion or belief. Practicing Muslim French do not share this notion of practice as a contingent expression of belief. They see the practice of veiling, like the practices of praying and fasting, as a religious duty integral to the cultivation of Muslim piety. Their conception of veiling, however, as well as the particular subjectivity in which it is embedded, remains largely unintelligible within human rights law. Because the headscarf is posited as an expression of conscience or belief—a sign—the right of French girls to wear headscarves in public schools is not necessarily protected under the aegis of religious liberty.

Importantly, there is one exception in European law that considers the manifestation of conscience, rather than simply the *forum internum*, an inalienable form of religious liberty: when a religion requires certain practices.[16] The apparent capacity of European law to protect required practices and acts of worship would seem to apply to practicing Muslims who claim that wearing the veil is a religious duty. However, the European Commission and European Court of Human Rights have understood the notion of required practice in a very particular way. The Commission and Court have generally been unwilling to accept the so-called subjective assessment of individual applicants about religious requirements, preferring instead to rely either on the opinion of recognized religious authorities or on the Commission's or Court's own definition of what counts as a required practice. This approach privileges members of hierarchically structured and heavily centralized religious traditions like Catholicism, at the expense of less institutionally centralized traditions like Islam or Buddhism (Edge 2000; Evans 2001). It also disadvantages members of minority religions, whose tenets are probably unfamiliar to European judges. Finally, it diminishes the claims of an individual who either does not accept all the teachings of an established religion or who believes that her religion places demands on her additional to those deemed necessary by the Court or by Court-recognized religious authorities.

The Commission's and Court's approach to what is religiously required, and its privileging of religious authorities to define norms, initially seems to contradict the secular affirmation of modern religiosity as a fundamentally individual enterprise that allows an individual to interpret religious requirements for herself. However, the Court's approach and the secular affirmation of individualized religiosity both assume an oppositional relationship between autonomous and authority-imposed actions. According to the terms of this relationship, individually inspired choices emerge in the absence of authority, religious or otherwise, and religious obligations or requirements are defined and compelled by established normative authority. We have returned, then, to the same interpretive paradigm so common to analyses of Muslim French religiosity, which depict the veil as either actively compelled by religious authorities, and therefore not a legitimate individual choice, or as "chosen" according to a "personal reading of religion" (Venel 2004, 86), and therefore a form of individualized self-expression.

Within such a paradigm, central to European analytical and legal understandings of modern religiosity, it becomes difficult, if not impossible, to articulate a practice like veiling in a way that makes sense to most secular republicans. For Muslim French, the veil is both a self-directed choice and a religious duty. An external authority cannot impose veiling, which must be undertaken willingly, according to the dictates of individual conscience. Veiling is also necessary for cultivating the kind of pious Muslim self that religious authorities delineate. However, secular law and public discourse consistently compel Muslim French to categorize the veil as either a choice or an obligation. Consider the following exchange, which took place during a January 2004 televised debate on the proposed law banning headscarves

("Dieu et la république" 2004). Leila Babès, a sociologist and vocal critic of veiling, insisted that wearing the headscarf was not a religious prescription. Quoting verses of the Quran, she maintained that the hijab was meant only for the Prophet's wives and was not a major pillar of the faith, and that the Quran advocated only modesty for Muslim women, not the headscarf. Saida Kada replied: "What Leila Babès says about the veil not being a religious prescription is her point of view; other women have a different point of view." Kada added that she had no desire to impose the veil on anyone, and that she had come to realize that the headscarf was an obligation through her own spiritual journey. Kada's intervention was completely ignored. The debate's moderator changed the subject to the unequal status of women in Muslim countries, Babès claimed that the Quran advocates cutting off thieves' hands, and Bernard Stasi lamented "the return to religion, [to] fundamentalism," seemingly embodied by Kada.

This exchange highlights two essential elements of the problem Muslim French women face in claiming that wearing the headscarf is a religious duty. First, the debate surrounding the doctrinal status of the hijab, and the open question of whether wearing the headscarf constitutes a religious prescription, is precisely what disqualifies it from being a religious requirement protected by the European Convention. Ironically, Muslim French women's commitment to the validity of internally generated desire and their refusal to dictate wearing the headscarf for all Muslim women—that is, an ethical attitude that coincides with secular liberal and republican norms—are precisely what disqualify their religious practices from secular law's protection. Second, the exchange exemplifies a secular tone deafness to the multiple meanings of the term *obligation*. When Muslim French women say that they wear the headscarf because it is a religious obligation, secular critics assume either that their fathers, brothers, and other male religious leaders demand it or that these women believe that the veil should be imposed on all women. In public and private debates about veiling, secular critics could not conceive of it as a truly autonomous choice if it was also an obligation. For these critics, any reference to obligation entailed either the negation of one's personal autonomy or the negation of all women's freedom. There was simply no room in the secular French imagination, or in European and French law, to conceptualize obligation as a personal ethical commitment. Consequently, to speak publicly of wearing the headscarf as a religious duty or obligation was, essentially, to declare oneself a fundamentalist and to disqualify oneself as a legitimate participant in public debates about the law. Not surprisingly, then, most Muslim French women speaking about the headscarf to a secular audience did so through a language of personal choice and individual freedom. Such language was not disingenuous; it simply foregrounded one dimension of the practice of veiling. However, it unexpectedly undermined their case for the right to religious liberty.

To illustrate how this happened, I turn to the second assumption central to secular republicans' insistence that the ban on headscarves upheld religious liberty: that freedom of conscience means freedom of choice, an assumption best exemplified by Patrick Weil's defense of the 2004 law. Weil, a historian and member of the Stasi Commission, admits that the veil "remains for some an individual sign of [religious] belonging [that is] freely chosen" (Long and Weil 2004). Elsewhere, he notes that the European Convention on Human Rights "recognize[s] the right to publicly express one's religious beliefs" (Weil 2004, 143). So how and why should the headscarf be restricted? Because "in the schools where some girls are wearing the headscarf, Muslim girls who do not wear it are subject to strong pressure to do so [by religious groups]. . . . In the view of these groups,[17] composed mainly of males, these girls are 'bad Muslims' or 'whores,' who should follow the example of their sisters and respect the prescription of the Koran" (143). Weil continues: "Muslim girls who do not want to wear the scarf also have a right of freedom of conscience, and they constitute the large majority" (144). It remains unclear how the headscarf constitutes such an enormous source of pressure if the large majority of students do not (and do not even want to) wear it. Nevertheless, Weil's point is that the headscarf impinges on the freedom of conscience of nonveiled girls. He concludes that although numerous international conventions recognize the right to publicly express one's religious beliefs, they also authorize "the limitation of the expression of religious faith, especially in the case of problems of public order or attacks on the rights and on the freedom of conscience of others" (144).

Weil's argument was not unique; the notion that the headscarf impinges on the consciences of nonveiled girls and constitutes a violation of their religious liberty was one of the most rhetorically and legally effective justifications for the headscarf ban. Loubna Méliane, at the time vice-president of sos Racisme and a founding member of the feminist group Neither Whores nor Doormats, put it in the following terms: "We live in a secular republic that guarantees the respect for every person and for his or her convictions. . . . Unfortunately, the young girls who demand to wear the veil in school are proselytizing and making the other young girls feel guilty" (2003b). Similar testimonials in newspapers and magazines attested to the apparent pressure nonveiled women felt to conform to patriarchal Muslim codes of sexuality that the veil supposedly represented, and that rendered nonveiled women disreputable whores. For its critics, the headscarf policed the sexuality not only of veiled girls but also of nonveiled girls, circumscribing their choices and, therefore, their freedom of conscience.[18]

Weil, Méliane, and other like-minded proponents of the ban understand freedom of conscience as the freedom to choose, but as the political philosopher Michael Sandel (1998) has argued, these two concepts are not identical. Sandel contends that freedom of conscience has traditionally meant the freedom to exercise religious liberty without suffering civil penalties, protecting those who are constrained by duties they cannot renounce, even in the face of conflicting civil obligations. When religious liberty comes to mean simply the right to choose one's beliefs freely, the result is a devaluation of claims by those for whom religion is not a matter of choice but of duty.[19] When religious convictions are understood as choices or personal preferences, and religious liberty as the capacity to choose freely with regard to religion, performing a religious duty is reduced to making a religious choice.

This reduction underpins Weil's arguments in favor of the headscarf ban, for he clearly understands freedom of conscience as the right to choose without any external pressure or social coercion. According to this logic, any external pressure (for example, the presence of veiled girls) diminishes individuals' right to choose freely, violating their freedom of conscience. Given the present-day hegemony of this logic in France, it became discursively and politically impossible for Muslim French women to defend wearing the headscarf as anything but a choice. And many did defend the headscarf as an internally driven choice, unmediated by external authority. A number of my interlocutors who had previously spoken of veiling as necessary to their practice of piety foregrounded religious freedom as the right to choose. Dalila, a friend of Héla's, told me that Muslims needed to stop talking about the compulsory dimension of the veil. "Yes, it's an obligation," she said, "but we need to focus on the problem of religious liberty, on our rights that are being violated. Talking about the religious aspect, well, there are people who say it's not an obligation, and you get into an argument with them. We should focus on the fact that it's a violation of a person's right to practice their religion freely." Dalila's framing underscores the limited ground of argumentation that Muslim French women have to make their claims. She repeats the dominant secular-republican framing that religious liberty does not entail the fulfillment of an obligation but the free exercise of a practice or belief, disembedded from its ethical context. The significance of that practice, and the justification for the right to practice it, no longer hinges on its ethical import but on its status as a self-driven choice.

Kada similarly maintained that veiled women in France "would simply like to be able to live out their choices, without having someone impose some kind of truth on them, whatever it may be" (Bouzar and Kada 2003, 26). In an editorial on the website *oumma.com*, a writer named Felwine Sarr likewise voiced outrage at the denial of the fundamental right to choose one's beliefs for oneself: "The question here is not about knowing whether the veil is a Quranic prescription or obligation. We only need to say that these Muslim women who want it (wearing the veil must not be imposed on anyone) have the freedom to wear it, whatever their own reading of the Text, and as long as their freedom does not infringe on that of another" (2003). Sarr's point is that the question of whether the veil is a Quranic prescription should be irrelevant before the law; that question remains, of course, absolutely relevant to practitioners of veiling, since it forms the basis for the practice. Yet Sarr's total excising of obligation in this defense of veiling is an instructive indication of the contemporary political landscape in which Muslim French women must make their claims.

Les filles voilées parlent (The veiled girls speak) is a collection of interviews with young women who have been forced to remove their headscarves at school or at work. Like Kada and Sarr, a number of the interviewees use the language of choice to express their frustration. Naima complains that at her high school "there are girls dressed in gothic style, in the latest fashion, in miniskirts or low-slung jeans with their thong showing, Nike, Adidas, and Reebok everywhere, but we, we aren't allowed the right to our veil. It's called 'a religious sign' even though it's just a piece of clothing. Where is the justice in this law?" (quoted in Chouder, Latrèche, and Tevanian 2008, 19). Naima clearly means to problematize the fact that school officials do not take issue with signs of rampant consumerism and overt female sexuality yet find the headscarf unacceptable. But to do so, she has to minimize the import of the hijab, calling it just a piece of clothing. A young university student, Jihene, expresses her frustration in similar terms: "It's just a piece of cloth. . . . If I go to school, it's to learn, not to show my headscarf. I put on a headscarf, another girl puts on a pink sweater: it's exactly the same. I want to be hired for my professional competence, without everyone being fixated on my headscarf" (47). Naima and Jihene are clearly responding to a dominant discourse that constitutes the headscarf as aberrant, fundamentalist, out of the ordinary, and ostentatious. They attempt to make the headscarf ordinary and unremarkable. They do so by portraying the decision to wear it as a choice like any other, asking secular France to respect their choices as self-directing, autonomous subjects.

Herein lies the rub. In efforts to normalize the headscarf, young Muslim French women have to deemphasize its Islamic character. Disembedded from its location in a wider set of ethical norms, the headscarf is a choice like any other. But that disembedding makes it difficult to argue either legally or ethically for the headscarf's special status as a religious practice. As even Anne, the teacher, said, recognizing its particularity, "the headscarf is religious, isn't it? It means more to her." Once the headscarf becomes just a piece of cloth, akin to a do-rag, the choice of whether to wear it is no longer a question of religious freedom.

But even Muslim French women who underscored the specifically religious aspect of their choices were caught in a bind. Framing the veil as a religious choice, Muslim French demanded that the government protect their right to religious freedom. Yet having to articulate the veil exclusively as a religious choice (rather than as a religious duty as well) paradoxically undermined their case for religious liberty because it enabled politicians and public intellectuals (like Weil) to emphasize veiling as simply a choice, akin to a personal preference. When religious convictions become a matter of choice, "it is difficult to distinguish between claims of conscience, on the one hand, and personal preferences, on the other. Once this distinction is lost, the right to demand of the state a special justification for laws that burden religious beliefs [and practices] is bound to appear as nothing more than 'a private right to ignore generally applicable laws'" (Sandel 1998, 91). Moreover, the transformation of religious conviction into religious choice made veiling and not veiling coextensive choices. And for Weil and the Stasi Commission, the right of one group of girls to exercise their religious choices seemingly impinged on the capacity of another group to make their own religious choices in an unconstrained manner (T. Asad 2006). Since one person's freedom ends where another's begins, the decision was made to protect unveiled girls' freedom of religion, understood as the right to choose freely in the absence of pressure produced by other girls' headscarves.

I want to emphasize how much this dominant understanding of conscience as choice relies on an oppositional relationship between personal autonomy and social and religious authority. There exists no discursive space in which to conceptualize or articulate practices like veiling, which most veiled Muslim French women consider a religious duty, although one that cannot be coerced, and which entails a very different relationship between desire and social and religious authority. When the practice of veiling is turned into a free choice, as it must be in order to make it discursively and legally intelligible to the secular majority—to claim that wearing the headscarf is an obligation is to out oneself as a bona fide fundamentalist— Muslim French women lose the capacity to express the ethical stakes of what it means to wear the headscarf as a religious obligation. That, in turn, enables lawmakers to argue that restricting headscarves in schools does not constitute a violation of religious liberty. In having to defend the veil as a choice, it becomes impossible for Muslim French to articulate, in a way that is intelligible to a secular public, the fact that it is indispensable to their religiosity and their sense of self, and to convey the point that a restriction on veiling is not simply a limitation on personal preference, but rather a profound disarticulation of their very selves.[20]

At the same time, framing the headscarf as both a personal decision and a religious obligation constitutes a kind of double talk (un double discours), thought to represent either an incoherent subjectivity or an insidious plot to mask a fundamentalist agenda with liberal or republican language. As John Bowen writes, "The multivocality of 'obligation' has become a frequent sign of the 'double-talk' of Muslims who say, to other Muslims [and non-Muslims], that wearing hijâb is a divine injunction and obligation, and, to non-Muslims [and Muslims], that there is no compulsion in Islam, and that it is up to women to decide what to do" (2006, 176).[21] Of course, Muslim French women's understanding of the hijab as both an internally driven choice and a religious duty makes sense when one conceptualizes self-realization and religious normativity as linked. Within the secular-republican imaginary, however, where self-realization emerges against normative authority and autonomous choices are made in the absence of constraint, Muslim French women occupy a no-man's-land of discursive and legal unintelligibility.

The Mosque and the School

Every year in mid-June, the permanent commission of the administrative council at Lycée Jean Nouvel meets to discuss the previous year and the upcoming one. The hallways of the school, usually teeming with boisterous students and harried teachers, are oddly quiet. When I entered the meeting room on the second floor, the principal, Monsieur Thomas, was already there, along with the assistant principal, the guidance counselor, the accountant, two parental delegates, and three teachers. The 2003–4 year had been a difficult one at Jean Nouvel, and the headscarf controversy had led to much consternation. Jean Nouvel had also hosted a series of debates about secularism and student motivation, part of the national Grand Debate on the Future of the School initiated by the Ministry of Education. Not surprisingly, much of the business for the permanent commission concerned those two themes. After some discussion about the general lack of motivation affecting all students, we moved on to the issue of laïcité and the headscarf.

"It's very clear," the principal declared. He directed us to the second page of the new rules of conduct, which now incorporated text from a Ministry of Education directive (circulaire) about the interdiction of conspicuous religious signs like headscarves, yarmulkes, and small crosses. Monsieur Thomas announced that even if the school's administrative council, scheduled to meet a week later, did not adopt the new rules of conduct, the law would still apply. After having decisively pronounced the law's clarity, Monsieur Thomas proceeded to speak at length, and quite emotionally, about how difficult the beginning of the new school year would be. A number of veiled students and their parents had agreed to abide by the law, but one girl, Naveeda, and her father were adamant that Naveeda would not come back to school unveiled. Monsieur Thomas seemed deeply affected by Naveeda's case, declaring regretfully that the law "will not address the human dimension." He told us more about Naveeda, a sixteen-year-old of Pakistani descent who had worn the hijab since the sixth grade. Excluded from her science class for more than a month at the beginning of the school year because she would not remove her headscarf, she had already experienced a very difficult junior year. She had excelled as a sophomore, Monsieur Thomas reminded us, but her grades had fallen so dramatically in the past year that her teachers suggested she repeat her junior year, though in a different track, switching from the prestigious scientific track to the much weaker technical one. "Let's be clear," the principal said. "It's going to be very difficult." We all fell silent, pondering the fate of this once-brilliant student who would likely not return to school at all the next year.

Later, I continued to talk about the situation at Jean Nouvel with a social science teacher named Gilles. An erudite and thoughtful man in his early fifties who had taught at Jean Nouvel for ten years, Gilles described the changes he had witnessed over the years. "The kids' behavior has got much worse," he lamented. "They behave as if they are at home, as if the school is not a different place, a special place." He blamed Americanization and the culture of television, and in particular the growing popularity of reality shows like Star Academy and Loft Story that promote instant fame and fortune. He complained that the students no longer had any concept of hard work, patience, and long-term goals; instead, they simply wanted instant gratification. These complaints were voiced repeatedly by many of his colleagues, who saw the republican school foundering, its preeminent mission of forming good French citizens increasingly threatened by funding cuts; overcrowding; efforts to bring the French education system into line with European Union standards; and students who thought of themselves as consumers, with attendant consumers' rights. As we talked, Gilles focused his lament on what he regarded as the bad influence of the UOIF mosque just around the corner from the school. He declared: "Before, girls who wanted to wear the veil would take it off at the school entrance. Now, they claim it as their 'right'!" He maintained that Muslim girls get "all this talk about rights" from the mosque. He added that he increasingly felt as though students, who now look to the mosque for guidance, were questioning the school's authority. "Our students," Gilles proclaimed, "are caught between the authority of the republic and its ideas and the religious authority of the mosque."

What most disturbs secular-republican critics of the Islamic revival is Muslim French submission to explicit norms and correct behavior, which ostensibly contravenes the basis of modern, secular, democratic citizenship. "Can one draw inspiration from sacred texts in order to become [a] democratic [subject]?" Dounia Bouzar asks in "Monsieur Islam" n'existe pas ("Mr. Islam" does not exist; 2004, 155). She, like many others, thinks not. Attacking what she calls the normativity of the Islamic revival, Bouzar finds deeply problematic young Muslims' acceptance of the principle that norms stem from texts, both revealed and exegetical. These Muslims "do not put the norm into question," Bouzar writes, but rather transform it into a life ethic, an attitude she finds antithetical to what she claims is the "critical spirit" and "individual thinking" of secular modernity (94). According to Bouzar, who simply repeats a common criticism of practicing Muslims, by submitting to the beliefs and practices of Islamic normativity, Muslim French lose the ability to think for themselves, abdicating the moral autonomy that defines the modern, sovereign subject who forms the basis of secular democracy. In her discussion of the Islamic revival, Bouzar puts into play once again a series of oppositions between emancipation and discipline, freedom and authority, and individuality and the norm—oppositions central to the self-narrative of secular modernity, and especially to French laïcité.

Yet republicanism has long struggled with how, as Jean-Jacques Rousseau put it, to make men what they ought to be without depriving them of the free will that defines them as human (1972, 1988). Rousseau was not the only Enlightenment thinker to grapple with this problem. John Locke's defense of individual freedom, both political and moral, was coupled with a deep anxiety about the passionate excesses to which humans are naturally prone (Mehta 1992; see also Locke 1968, 1975, and 2003). Rousseau and Locke rehearse a certain anxiety in French republicanism and Anglo-American liberalism about the relationship between freedom and social morality and, concomitantly, between freedom and norms. And it is no coincidence that the two political thinkers perhaps most associated with republicanism and liberalism, respectively, meditated not only on the question of freedom but also on education, a disciplinary process they both believed necessary for the cultivation of freedom.

There has always been a tension in modern liberal and republican political philosophy between the authoritative political institutions necessary to social stability and the constraints those institutions seemingly place on the natural freedom of the individual. But as Uday Mehta demonstrates in *The Anxiety of Freedom*, his masterful treatise on Locke's political thought, the tension between authority and freedom is not only external, underlying the relationship between institutions and the individual. It is also immanent to individual freedom, since authority is actually essential to cultivating proper freedom. In other words, disciplinary authority does not simply constrain freedom from the outside; it is integral to producing freedom. For Locke, true freedom emerges through actions willed by reason; the realization of freedom turns on the actualization of reason, which in turn hinges on acting according to the laws of nature (Mehta 1992, 138). And it is the capacity to reason, and therefore to be free, that is natural, not its actual exercise. "To the extent that being naturally free turns on knowing natural law and thus its limits," Mehta writes, "which in turn involve actualizing the capacity we have to reason, we are forced to acknowledge, as Locke acknowledges, the importance of education as the process through which the capacity to reason [and therefore to be free] is actualized" (122). Moreover, the self-disciplinary process of actualizing one's capacity for reason requires submitting to the reason of others: "The experience of submission to others is thus a necessary precondition for being able to submit to one's own reason, and hence a precondition for self-discipline" (138). If liberty is the ability to follow one's free will, that will is one that has been carefully disciplined by law and by education (158).[22] Indeed, the molding of the will required for the formation of the subject of freedom requires the specific experience of submitting to authority. For Locke, this experience—what he calls education—occurs through the submission to parental discipline. What interests me here, however, is not the particular site of authority to which the free subject-to-be must submit, but rather Locke's notion that the experience of submission to authority lays the groundwork for freedom through the cultivation of rationality and self-discipline in the child.

If parents are the site of education and disciplinary formation for Locke, the school is that site for Emile Durkheim, writing in France a few centuries later, at the height of the Third Republic. Durkheim, too, was concerned with how the social collectivity would proceed, especially without the moral anchor of Catholicism, and how to establish norms to ensure the functioning of familial, vocational, and civic life. In *Moral Education*, he takes up the question of how to create a free, moral citizen with an inclination for collective life.[23] For Durkheim, discipline forms the basis of morality: "Through it and by means of it alone are we able to teach the child to rein in his desires, to set limits to his appetites of all kinds" (2002, 43). Without discipline, passions and inclinations will end up ruling the individual, rather than the other way around. "Moral discipline," Durkheim continues, "performs an important function in forming character and personality in general. In fact, the most essential element of character is this capacity for restraint . . . which allows us to contain our passion, our desires, our habits, and subject them to law" (46). Discipline requires a moral authority from which to emerge and entails repetitive behavior that regularizes conduct. Moreover, discipline produces self-discipline, for the goal of discipline is to produce citizen subjects who bring their will and desire in line with the law. "Morality," writes Durkheim, "appears to us under a double aspect: on the one hand, as imperative law, which demands complete obedience of us; on the other hand, as a splendid ideal, to which we spontaneously aspire" (96). The objective of moral discipline is to turn duty into desire, to make citizen subjects want to aspire spontaneously to that which they should do. Education turns discipline into self-discipline by teaching what Durkheim calls knowledge and science, which cultivate not passive resignation but enlightened allegiance: "Conforming to the order of things because one is sure that it is everything it ought to be is not submitting to a constraint. It is freely desiring this order, assenting through an understanding of the cause" (115). Like Locke, Durkheim appeals to reason in turning submission to authority into the means of self-actualization. Conforming to moral rules that one rationally knows are good—through knowledge and science—does not constitute submitting to a constraint, because one has come to *want* to do what one *should* do.

In fact, Durkheim argues explicitly that this process of disciplining the citizen does not constitute a violation of her freedom. "Self-mastery is the first condition of all true power," he contends, "of all liberty worthy of the name" (2002, 45). And this self-mastery is necessary for achieving man's nature, which "cannot be itself except as it is disciplined" (51). The capacity for containing our inclinations, acquired in the school of moral discipline, "is the indispensable condition for the emergence of reflective, individual will. The rule, because it teaches us to restrain and master ourselves, is a means of emancipation and freedom" (49). A few pages later, Durkheim writes that "'rules' and 'liberty' are far from being exclusive or antithetical terms. The latter is only possible by virtue of the former" (54). True freedom necessitates a will that is not ruled by desire and inclination, which in turn requires a process of authoritative discipline that produces the self-mastery on which emancipation depends. Furthermore, according to Durkheim, nondemocratic societies may rely on external regulation alone, but democratic societies have to turn discipline into self-discipline, to make external regulation internalized. Thus the anxiety about social peace, and about the concomitant relationship between freedom and authority, emerges in a context of democratic freedom, where subjects cannot simply be compelled to do what is right but must rather be disciplined to turn the moral imperative into willed self-direction.

What this discussion of Locke and Durkheim underscores is the intertwining of authority, discipline, and freedom in the liberal and republican traditions, an intertwining that echoes statements about discipline, knowledge, and freedom that Ramadan, Kada, and my Muslim French interlocutors make. These parallels make the common secular-republican critique of Muslim French piety—the critique of submission to normative authority—somewhat confounding. I am obviously not the first to point out the tenuousness of the secular opposition between emancipation and discipline, freedom and authority, and individuality and the norm. Numerous poststructuralist critics have argued that inner desire, even for freedom, is produced through disciplinary or regulatory powers.[24] Nonetheless, the near-hegemonic espousal of an opposition between freedom and authority by contemporary republicans remains particularly curious in France, where the state's explicit role in forming free citizens has consistently blurred any a priori boundary between disciplinary authority and individual freedom.

Laïcité is and has been a modality of government with concomitant practices, authorizing discourses, and political and legal institutions that aim to create particular kinds of ethical and political sensibilities and forms of sociality. Since the Third Republic made schooling compulsory for boys and girls in 1882, the secular school in particular has been a privileged institution for producing normative, albeit "free," subjects inculcated in a secular morality based on the positivist and humanist values of reason, freedom, and equality (Baubérot 1997; T. Asad 2006; Surkis 2006). The school is a place where, through a series of disciplinary techniques, individuals are stripped of their passions and regional and religious customs and imbued with the particular moral, social, and political values and commitments—to patriotism, civic equality, liberty, and social solidarity—that make men and women French citizens (Weber 1976; Baubérot 2000; Silverstein 2004). In fact, Fadela Amara, one of the cofounders of Neither Whores nor Doormats, describes in laudatory terms how she was taught the importance of democracy by a teacher who wielded a rod and, with it, the threat of physical punishment for disobedient students.[25] Amara invokes the regulatory nature of the secular public school and the way in which the democratic and free citizen is produced through discipline, even violence. What is ironic is that, like Bouzar, Amara is a vocal critic of the headscarf as a symbol of the submission to normative authority.

In *The Politics of the Veil*, Joan Scott (2007) proposes that the recent headscarf crisis indexes a deep-seated anxiety about the problem that sexual difference poses for republican political universalism. This chapter brings me to a parallel conclusion about a different set of anxieties and the deferral of a different problem. I wonder if criticism of the religious authority and normativity of Islam defers a set of tensions inherent to a secular-republican project that emancipates individuals from various forms of authority (the Catholic Church, custom, and so on) by bringing the normative disciplinary authority of the school to bear on its subjects. The headscarf indexes the relationship between authority and freedom that is central not only to the Islamic tradition but to republicanism as well. At the same time, it signals the waning of that authority and the school's inefficacy in disciplining citizen subjects.

The shift in thinking between 1989 and 2004 by many republicans is indicative of that waning, or at least of a sense of waning, and of a concomitant anxiety about the authority of the republican school. During the first headscarves affair in 1989, many republicans were sure that keeping veiled Muslim girls in school would lead them to remove their headscarves themselves. The authority of the school, these republicans reasoned, could discipline Muslim girls into citizens who would aspire willingly to the normative imperatives of secular-republican morality and sociality. By 2004 many of these republicans had changed their tune and were advocating an outright ban on headscarves. Their faith in the republican school to create proper citizens seemed shaken, given that Muslim French were now willingly submitting to a different disciplinary authority. Gilles's lament that students "are caught between the authority of the republic and its ideas and the religious authority of the mosque" signals this wider anxiety about the obsolescence of the school as the preeminent site for creating republican citizens, beset as it is by underfunding, overcrowding, and decentralization, as well as by decreasing respect for the social status of teachers.

If the headscarf is read as a symptom of the failing authority of the school, however, it is simultaneously a reminder of the relationship between autonomy and authority that has been so central to French secularism and republicanism. By disturbing the viability of a strict distinction between normative authority and personal autonomy, practicing Muslim French women reveal the intensely intertwined relationship between discipline and freedom that has been crucial to the secular-republican project. On the one hand, secular republicans hitch their criticism of the headscarf and the efflorescence of Islamic normativity to a nostalgia for the authority of the republican school, cultivator of emancipated citizens. On the other hand, and simultaneously, the consternation about Muslims' ostensible lack of freedom helps sustain a secular fantasy of personal autonomy, deferring an underlying anxiety about the very interconnectedness of autonomy and authority that continues to haunt the republic. What is particularly ironic in this context, then, is that Muslim French appear to be the true heirs to the Third Republic. If most contemporary republicans disavow the norms and social discipline required for the practice of moral and political autonomy, Muslim French recognize the necessary relationship between discipline and self-mastery set forth by the likes of Durkheim and, before him, Rousseau. One might even argue that Muslim French are some of the only real republicans left in France.[26]

FIELD NOTES III   A Tale of Two Manifestos

On February 16, 2004, the left-wing daily *Libération* published a petition called the *Manifeste des libertés* (Manifesto of liberties), signed by 619 men and women "of Muslim culture [and] believers, agnostics, and atheists" ("Manifeste des libertés" 2004). Most signatories were journalists, academics, and political party officials. The petition denounced "the declarations and acts of misogyny, homophobia, and anti-Semitism . . . that are done in the name of Islam." It called for equality between the sexes and opposition to the Islamic veil, invoking the signers' personal experiences: "In various countries, we have seen the violence, even death, inflicted on friends and those close to us because they refused to wear [the veil] . . . and there is, behind this supposed 'choice' claimed by a certain number of veiled girls, a desire to promote an Islamist society, based on a militant ideology that is active on the ground and that declares values we want nothing to do with." The petition called for a "halt to homophobia" that the signatories ascribed to the chronic chauvinism of "fundamentalists" who want "women behind the veil and homosexuals behind bars," and who see "any man in favor of equality between the sexes as potentially a subman, a faggot." In contrast, the signers declared, they recognized "the liberty of homosexuals to lead their lives as they wish," adding that "as long as an individual does not contravene any laws protecting minors, the sexual choices of each person concern only that person and not the state." Next on the list of Islamic evils was anti-Semitism, which the petition also strongly condemned. The manifesto ended by observing that although "young people of immigrant origin have been considerably held back in social promotion and face discrimination," they nonetheless must choose between two paths: "either rediscover the force of a living laïcité . . . or find themselves in a fictional umma" that will "create an inegalitarian, repressive, and intolerant society." "This second choice," concluded the signatories, "is not ours."

It was not clear to whom the petition was addressed. Although it called on Muslims in France to renounce Islamic fundamentalism and embrace republican laïcité, it was also clearly aimed at a broader audience, since Libération is hardly the daily of choice for working-class, nonwhite populations. In fact, the petition seemed to stage a French version of the good Muslim–bad Muslim narrative described by Mahmood Mamdani (2005).[1] Written and signed by secular Muslims adhering to the values of laïcité, the petition publicly admonished so-called fundamentalists and their potential allies among Franco-Maghrebi youth for their misogyny, homophobia, and anti-Semitism, an admonition performed for the wider French public of Libération and beyond. This indictment presented the current problem with Islam—namely, bad fundamentalist Muslims—as well as the possibility of Islam's redemption by good secular Muslims.

Later that year, a very different manifesto entitled Inch'Allah l'égalité (Equality, God willing) was circulated (see Collectif Féministes 2005). Written by the newly created Feminists for Equality Collective (Collectif Féministes pour l'Egalité, or CFPE), which brought together longtime white feminists and younger Franco-Maghrebi and Muslim French feminists, the manifesto's title was sincere and purposefully provocative. It signaled the collective's commitment to bridge feminist goals and Muslim religiosity[2] and it boldly rebutted a secular-republican feminism that remains hostile to public religiosity and especially to Islam. In fact, the CFPE and its manifesto emerged out of that hostility, and the story of the collective's formation illustrates the kind of division that has cleaved the French feminist movement but has also assembled a somewhat unlikely coalition of feminist activists.[3]

In 2004, while the law banning conspicuous religious signs was being debated, the National Collective for Women's Rights (Collectif National pour les Droits des Femmes, or CNDF) began to plan for the yearly International Women's Day march. The CNDF, headed by the prominent feminists Maya Surduts and Suzy Rotjman, brought together a number of large organizations, including the Coordination of Associations for the Right to Abortion and Contraception, Family Planning, and the Lesbian Coordination. Smaller activist groups would also participate in the demonstration.

In early 2004 the CNDF held a meeting, run by Surduts and Rojtman, to finalize the text of the *appel* (call to march) and to nail down logistical details. A number of veiled feminist activists from the One School for All Collective (Collectif Une Ecole pour Tous et Toutes, or UEPT) attended that meeting, much to the chagrin of some others in the room. Mainstream feminists were already divided about how to address the proposed law on headscarves. A number condemned the veil and supported the law, while others criticized both the veil as an instrument of women's sexual oppression and the law as a divisive electoral tactic. The eventual text for the *appel* emerged as a compromise: it neither supported nor censured a ban on headscarves in public schools, but it denounced the veil, linking it to the violence suffered by women worldwide. Needless to say, the UEPT feminists were unhappy with the final version, though their efforts to plead their case were shouted down during the organizational meeting. Some mainstream feminists held that veiled women should not even join the International Women's Day march. That position prompted members of the Pink Panthers, a radical LGBTQ association, to declare that no woman should be blocked from participation in a demonstration for women's rights, and if UEPT activists were kicked out of the march, the Pink Panthers would also withdraw. The UEPT members ended up not signing the group's name to the collective text, though its members did march with their own text echoing all the points of the *appel* except for the section on the headscarf. In its place, the UEPT inserted a passage condemning a sexist law that would deprive young girls of an education. On March 8, International Women's Day, the UEPT had difficulty accessing the procession, and a number of UEPT activists recall not only being blocked from joining the march but also being insulted by other marchers, who shouted that they should be ashamed to be at a feminist gathering and should go live in Iran, Saudi Arabia, or Afghanistan. Finally, activists from the Pink Panthers, the Green Party, and the Revolutionary Communist Youth League let the UEPT contingent into the procession.

In part as a result of these kinds of disputes with other feminist groups, and of ongoing discussions within the UEPT about questions pertaining to gender and religion, UEPT activists founded the CFPE in June 2004. Though restricted to women, the new collective cut across ethno-racial, religious, class, and generational lines, bringing established feminists like Christine Delphy and Monique Crinon together with younger activists, many of them Muslim French. The primary purpose of the CFPE was to combat discrimination against women and to fight for women's equality without positing a singular or universal model of women's emancipation. Many members of the collective later recounted that they wanted to bring Muslim and non-Muslim women together to demonstrate that there was no contradiction between being a Muslim and being a feminist. Crinon told me that "the common reference of feminists is in the process of being constructed, and it will take place through the crossing of different currents." All the members recognized that they would not be in agreement on everything, but, as Crinon put it, "what unites us is the conviction and a profound agreement on the fact that there is a patriarchal system in which men are in a position of dominance. Not men as individuals, but a general system." Drawing on poststructuralist and postcolonial theories of gender equality, a field in which Delphy has long been an important voice, the collective sought to critically examine and expand the very definition of emancipation; to engage in robust but respectful discussions about gender, religion, and equality; and to address the matter of gender discrimination in relation to other forms of discrimination. In short, they sought to pluralize feminism. Hence the careful choice of their name: Collectif Féministes (collective of feminists) rather than Collectif Féministe (feminist collective). In April 2004 the group adopted a charter stipulating their goals and called it *Inch'Allah l'égalité*.

Five Of Mimicry and Woman

The *Mariannes d'aujourd'hui* (Today's Mariannes) exhibit opened on Bastille Day—July 14—in 2003, the culmination of a five-week march across France by the newly created association Neither Whores nor Doormats (Ni Putes ni Soumises, or NPNS). Galvanized by the October 2002 murder of Sohane Benziane, a young woman from a housing project in Vitry-sur-Seine (near Paris) who was burned alive by a male acquaintance, NPNS organized the march to protest the living conditions of immigrant-origin women in the *banlieues*, especially their lack of sexual freedom and equality. The *Mariannes* exhibit was unprecedented. Mounted on the façade of the Palais Bourbon, seat of the National Assembly, it consisted of fourteen color photographs of young women from the march, many of them Arab or black. Each large portrait featured a young woman wearing the red cap of liberty (*bonnet phrygien*) and/or the tricolored rosette (*cocarde*) of Marianne, the emblem of the French Revolution and the original *citoyenne*. Numerous politicians attended the exhibit's inauguration, which, like the Benziane murder and the NPNS march, was heavily covered by the media.

The protest march and *Mariannes* exhibit coincided with the national debate about headscarves in public schools, and the two leaders of NPNS, Loubna Méliane and Fadela Amara, became vociferous proponents of the ban. They were prominently featured in newspaper articles and on radio and television programs between 2002 and 2004, joined by Chahdortt Djavann, an Iranian dissident and writer. Echoing Ayaan Hirsi Ali in Holland,

Necla Kelek in Germany, and Irshad Manji in North America—other "secular Muslim" and "ex-Muslim"[1] critics of conservative Muslim-immigrant communities—Amara, Méliane, and Djavann claimed to be ideally suited to speak on behalf of their sisters silenced by patriarchal Islamic fundamentalists. All three women published popular autobiographies describing their difficult personal experiences with Islam—*Ni putes ni soumises* (Neither whores nor doormats; 2003), *Vivre libre* (To live free; 2003a), and *Bas les voiles!* (Down with veils; 2003), respectively.

A year after the *Mariannes* exhibit, the National Assembly again celebrated the work of NPNS when it awarded Amara its 2004 Political Book Prize for her autobiography. In 2005 the prime minister's office agreed to finance the production and distribution of an NPNS guide on respect for women aimed at male youth in the *banlieues*. And on International Women's Day in 2006, in partnership with a number of corporate donors—including the Philip Morris Foundation, Dassault Aviation, and Pinault-Printemps-Redoute—and in the presence of the president of France, the mayor of Paris, and public figures on the Left and Right, NPNS inaugurated a Maison de Mixité (house of mixing), located in the twentieth arrondissement of Paris and imagined as a space for men and women to come together for various social activities. The leaders of NPNS have translated their embrace by the media and public into political positions in the two main parties: Amara was junior minister for urban policy in Nicolas Sarkozy's conservative government, and Méliane became an official in the Socialist Party. Sihem Habchi, who replaced Amara as president of NPNS, was appointed in that capacity to the now-defunct High Authority for the Fight against Discrimination and for Equality, the government's antidiscrimination commission; in 2011 she became the spokesperson for the short-lived presidential campaign of the Socialist politician Arnaud Montebourg. The NPNS movement's current and former leaders were also early and vocal supporters of the 2010 law banning niqabs in all public spaces.

Much ink has been spilled over the headscarf. Yet alongside the paradigmatic menace of the veiled woman (la musulmane voilée) and the incommensurable difference she embodies has appeared another kind of Muslim woman in the French public sphere: the secular Muslim woman (la musulmane laïque). This chapter examines French politicians' and the French state's unexpected valorization of, as Amara puts it in her autobiography, "a handful of young women from the housing projects" (Amara 2003, 35). What are we to make, I ask, of the National Assembly's interest in sexual freedom and equality for women of color? What are the state's investments in the *musulmane laïque?* My goal is not to dispute or justify the sexism and gender violence that propelled the formation of NPNS, but rather to attend to the asymmetrical political and media focus on sexism and violence in the *banlieues.* Rather than offer a history or ethnography of the movement itself (see Benabdessadok 2004; Winter 2008), or of secular Muslim subjectivity (see Fadil 2011), I examine the production, reception, and circulation of these exceptional—meaning both singular and exemplary—citizens in French public and political life in order to trace key discursive and institutional logics within French secularism and French republicanism. In other words, I read NPNS's unprecedented fêting by the public and politicians as symptomatic of, and an ideal site to better analyze, broader trends in secular-republican rule. This chapter explores how the state's embrace of sexually liberated Muslim women reveals the twinned imperatives of inclusion and exclusion that underpin secular-republican power and produce both commensurable and incommensurable forms of Muslim difference. It also attends to the particular historicity of NPNS's emergence, locating the state's investment in NPNS within larger patterns of neoliberal sovereignty and the new nexus of sexuality and secularity.

Exceptional Citizenship

The extraordinary public celebration of NPNS is impossible to understand without attending to the politics of sex and secularity, what Joan Scott (2011a) calls sexularism. Secularism is increasingly posited as the best guarantee of women's sexual freedom and equality, and as what distinguishes the West from the woman-abusing rest. Significantly, as a number of scholars note, ex-Muslim or secular Muslim women in Europe and North America have emerged as important actors in constructing this distinction (Mahmood 2009; E. Fassin 2010). What remains unexamined is why ex-Muslim or secular Muslim women like Hirsi Ali, Manji, and Amara have become so crucial to reaffirming the values of secular Western civilization in contrast to those of its Muslim enemy. Why have these women emerged as such powerful totems in the narrative of secularism? Why are the affirmation of sexularism and the defense of sexual freedom and equality so consistently mediated through ex- or secular Muslim women? How is it that a few non-white women have come to best embody the norms of sexual equality and freedom said to define French and Euro-American culture?

This section takes up those questions by integrating secularity's relationship to sexuality and to Muslim difference into a broader logic of secular-republican power in France. The public emergence of Amara, Méliane, and NPNS, and their political fêting as exemplars of successful republican integration, is ineluctably tied to the claims to universality made by secularism and republicanism, and therefore to the universal-particular dilemma that haunts both ideological and political formations. Even as secularism and republicanism claim that their social and moral sensibilities and political and legal arrangements are universal, they remain ontologically particular. This means having to deal with the problem of difference in its various instantiations: Jews, Muslims, women, Arabs, Africans, queers—and the list goes on. In addition, even if the universal-particular dilemma has played out differently within them, republicanism and secularism have come to mean increasingly the same thing for their proponents, precisely through the question of sexuality. I return to the problem of universal versus particular within secularity at the end of the chapter; for now, I want to examine that dilemma within republicanism, and republicanism's consequent investment in exceptional citizens like Amara and Méliane.

The competing imperatives to universalize and particularize simultaneously are foundational to the structure of republican citizenship (Wilder 2005; see also Blanchard, Bancel, and Lemaire 2005). That tension is perhaps best exemplified in "What Is a Nation?" (1990), a lecture delivered by the philologist Ernest Renan at the Sorbonne in 1882, ten years after France's defeat in the Franco-Prussian War. Renan described the modern nation as constituted by "the possession in common of a rich legacy of memories" that "presupposes a past" and by "present-day consent, the desire to live together" (19). He also called the nation a daily plebiscite, distinguishing between the still primordial and inherently particular nation form of the German enemy and the contractual, universal French nation (Brubaker 1992). Renan's formulation of the modern nation, understood as a political relation between citizen and state, undergirded republican ideology in the mid- and late nineteenth century—including the ideology of much of the colonial civilizing mission—and still provides the basis for contemporary mainstream republican theorizing about citizenship and immigration (see, for example, Finkielkraut 1987; Schnapper 1994; Taguieff 2005).

Renan, however, was not only a scholar of the nation. His philological work on Semitic languages also exemplifies mid-nineteenth-century thinking about the linkages between language groups, races, and religions (Masuzawa 2005; Olender 2008). For example, Renan and other philologists believed that the supposed structural rigidity of the Arabic language mapped onto the inherent fanaticism of Islam and the inflexibility of the Arab mind, compromising the civilizing mission's potential to turn Arab natives into French citizens. With the discovery of incommensurably different Arabs, the republican colonial project was confronted by the limits of its universalist promise. But all was not lost, for Orientalist thinking like Renan's was also integral to the formulation of the nineteenth-century Kabyle myth in Algeria, which portrayed Kabyles (also known as Berbers) as the original, proto-Christian inhabitants of the territory who were racially, linguistically, religiously, and culturally distinct from Arabs. Distinguishing between incommensurably different Arabs and commensurably different Berbers, the colonial republican project considered Berbers prime candidates for civilizing (Lorcin 1999; Silverstein 2004).

The tension between Renan's inclusive notion of the nation and his exclusive racialism—between the universalizing and particularizing imperatives of republicanism—is actually contained in his conception of the nation form itself.[2] For Renan, the nation is both a voluntary political community bound by contract and a historical community bound by memory; Janus-faced, the nation looks simultaneously to the past and future. On the one hand, French values like liberty, equality, and fraternity are universal and therefore open to voluntary adoption by those who are not necessarily a part of France's past. On the other hand, a sense of French national identity emerges out of the French people's already constituted particular history, one that assumes an a priori positing of a discrete people. More than simply a rational political unit, the nation is also a cultural, ethno-racial, historical, and affective entity.

A number of republican public intellectuals, most notably the well-respected political sociologist Dominique Schnapper, have restaged this ambivalent relationship between contractual and cultural citizenship. Laying out the contemporary republican model of citizenship in La communauté des citoyens (The community of citizens), Schnapper contends that "the nation is defined by its ambition to *transcend particular affiliations*—biological, historical, economic, social, religious, or cultural—*through citizenship*, to define the citizen as an abstract individual, without identification and without particular qualifications" (1994, 49 [emphasis in original]). Yet Schnapper believes the nation-state cannot coalesce through rational political citizenship alone; also needed is a sense of preexisting identity linked to the historical and cultural particularity of each national entity. The philosopher Julia Kristeva echoes Schnapper's overarching point in a treatise entitled *Nations without Nationalism*, originally published as "An Open Letter to Harlem Désir" (Désir was president of SOS Racisme, which at the time was pressing for immigrants' right to difference). There, Kristeva explicitly identifies the French nation as both "contractual" and "cultural" (1993, 40). This duality underpins French nationality law as well, which since the French Revolution has combined *jus sanguinis* (blood citizenship), in which citizenship is accorded to the children of citizens no matter where they may be born, and *jus solis* (territorial citizenship), in which citizenship is accorded to individuals born in France.

Since the late 1980s political parties on both the Left and the Right have sought to restrict the principle of *jus solis*, largely in response to the rise of the National Front, which claimed that Muslim immigrants from North and West Africa were undermining French values and threatening national identity (Favell 2001). In 1993 the conservative government revised the nationality code so that those born in France to foreign parents would henceforth have to file a formal request between the ages of sixteen and eighteen to become a French national. The revision also made it possible to deny such requests on the basis of a criminal record (Feldblum 1999). Similar restrictions on nationality and naturalization have continued into the twenty-first century. For example, under center Right and Socialist governments, the period of time a foreign spouse must wait before applying for French nationality has steadily increased, from six months to one year in 1998, and then to four years in 2006. Under recent additions to the civil code, the Ministry of the Interior can deny French nationality to an applicant—even one who has otherwise met all other relevant criteria—on the basis of insufficient assimilation (*défaut d'assimilation*), defined as a lack of respect for the host society's values of tolerance, *laïcité*, liberty, and equality. These various revisions and restrictions are part of a larger set of political discourses and practices aimed at protecting French identity against the supposedly incommensurable values held by Muslim immigrants from North and West Africa.

Dominant republican politics concerning immigration and citizenship has clearly moved toward the racially and culturally essentialist positions of the National Front.[3] This is a sometimes explicit strategy to court National Front voters, a process that journalists and progressive critics and academics have noted (Chombeau 2005; E. Fassin 2006; Tevanian 2007; L. Levy 2010). Nonetheless, despite the increasingly essentialist tenor of republicanism, there remains a fundamental distinction between the racial and cultural chauvinism of the National Front and that of mainstream republicans, one that goes back to the dual character of republican citizenship as both cultural and contractual. It is important to underscore this distinction not only because it is crucial to understanding republican ideology and its forms of governmentality, but also because it helps make sense of the emergence and political success of a few exceptional secular Muslim women.

In assessing this distinction between mainstream republicanism and integralist chauvinism, it is instructive to revisit Kristeva's *Nations without Nationalism*, particularly the discursive structure of her argument about French identity. Kristeva contends that the French or European[4] attitude of pluralism and openness to foreigners is due to a specific history: namely, the Greek polis, Christianity, Judaism, and the Enlightenment. Thus European values like democracy, liberty, equality, and pluralism are particular, formed in the crucible of European history that remains distinct from the history of "the Arab 'nation'" across the Mediterranean (1993, 45). Yet, even as she restricts these values to Europeans, Kristeva simultaneously unlocks them for non-European immigrants. "The right of foreigners to be integrated," she claims, "is a right to participate in this contractual, transitional, and cultural [French] nation" (47). Elsewhere she writes: "Let us not be ashamed of European and particularly French culture, for it is by developing it critically that we have a chance to have foreigners recognize us as being foreigners all, with the same right of mutual respect" (38). By coming to Europe, foreigners can give up their essentialist, particularist rootedness and embrace Kristeva's enlightened position. That embrace of French national values is a chance not only for foreigners, however, but also for France. After all, Kristeva writes, "*we* [French] have a chance to have foreigners recognize us as being foreigners all"—that is, to recognize the universality of the pluralist principle of mutual respect.[5] Why would such recognition on the part of foreigners be a chance for France? Because it would fulfill republicanism's universalist ambitions and establish the universality of its principles. Importantly, the universalizing imperative of republicanism depends on assimilated foreigners, whose acceptance of republican values proves the latter's universalist promise.

Recent historical and anthropological scholarship has proposed that universalism and particularism, and assimilation and difference, are not opposites but rather two sides of the same coin, and that together they constitute the continual avowal and disavowal of difference that forms the basis of French national identity (Balibar 1991b; Silverman 1992; Silverstein 2004). Extending these arguments, I want to highlight the discursive necessity of commensurable difference to republicanism. Kristeva's short treatise illuminates not only the dual nature of republican citizenship—its cultural and contractual forms—but also how the French Republic's historical particularism and principled universalism both exclude incommensurable forms of difference and, simultaneously, depend on commensurable ones.

Contemporary republicanism's investment in commensurable difference illustrates how, even as it moves toward the extreme Right's chauvinism, it remains distinct from the latter. Although many republicans propose a fundamental incommensurability between the values of Islam and those of the post-Enlightenment West, they also insist, in contrast to most extreme Right neoracists, that individual Muslim immigrants can, and must, surmount the barriers between the two opposed civilizations.[6] This distinction may seem minor, but it is significant, for it goes to the heart of republican citizenship's ambivalence toward difference. On the one hand, republicanism denies national belonging to those who do not embody secular French values, and it excludes forms of incommensurable difference that it deems threatening to the racial and cultural nation. On the other hand, the very universality claimed for French values like liberty, equality, tolerance, and secularity means that all forms of immigrant-Muslim difference cannot be excluded wholesale. These dual imperatives of exclusion and inclusion generate a bifurcated Muslim difference. Discursively and ideologically, then, republicanism produces and depends on commensurable forms of difference, and on foreigners and immigrants, in a way that the integralism of the extreme Right does not. Exceptional citizens like Amara prove the universality of French values by underscoring their desirability and transferability to the not yet French. They also forestall claims about the inherent exclusiveness of French national citizenship extolled by the extreme Right and criticized by the radical Left.

The republican project's fashioning of and dependence on a few paradigmatic assimilated subjects is not new. For much of its existence, the French colonial state refused citizenship to most of its colonized subjects in North and West Africa, usually on the basis that these natives were not yet civilized enough to properly exercise the rights of citizens (Conklin 1997; Lorcin 1999; Blanchard, Bancel, and Lemaire 2005; Le Cour Grandmaison 2005; Wilder 2005). But natives were not completely denied citizenship. The colonial state practiced a form of selective assimilation, opening citizenship to a few exceptional individuals who demonstrated French cultural competence (Wilder 2005). Gary Wilder understands these exceptional citizens as effects of republicanism's universalizing and particularizing imperatives, which made it impossible for the imperial republic to ever extend full citizenship to Africans as Africans because they were always already culturally particular. Instead, the republic could offer citizenship only to exceptional individuals. But these exceptions, beyond simply being effects of the republic's duality, also helped sustain the republican project despite the contradiction at its core. Even though it was thought to be impossible and undesirable to make all Africans and Arabs citizens, selective assimilation underscored the republican principle that a West African or Algerian subject could become a French citizen (Conklin 1997; Shepard 2006). Thus the tension between particular and universal that underpins secular republicanism was displaced onto the ostensible barbarity and incommensurability of African and Arab-Muslim difference. The exceptional few who became citizens were testaments to the universal promise of republican citizenship and to the seeming failure of other Africans and Arabs to embrace universal qua French values, forestalling the contradiction at the heart of the secular-republican project. These exceptional citizens of the nineteenth and early twentieth centuries prefigure the ideological production and effectiveness of secular Muslims like Amara, Méliane, and Djavann. And the consistent production of these exceptional subjects underscores how they are not ancillary to republican rule but integral to its operation.

Interestingly, the autobiography plays an important role in the contemporary logic of exceptionality and has become essential to the public fêting of secular Muslim women. Those who circulate in the Euro-American public sphere have written popular, often best-selling autobiographies: besides the books by Amara, Méliane, and Djavann, there are Ayaan Hirsi Ali's *Infidel* (2007), Irshad Manji's *The Trouble with Islam Today* (2003), and Azar Nafisi's *Reading Lolita in Tehran* (2004). These autobiographies all read like conversion narratives, telling the story of a Muslim woman's embrace of secular-republican values (especially sexual values) and subsequent emancipation from the clutches of Islam. These "native testimonials" (Mahmood 2009, 194), which portray Muslim culture at home and abroad as inherently undemocratic and misogynist, are cited by politicians and media pundits as indisputable evidence of Europe's Muslim problem, and they have become key to the propagation and legitimation of a sexual "clash of civilizations." The 2002 Stasi Commission hearings—at which Amara and Djavann were invited to testify—and subsequent debate on Muslim girls in headscarves demonstrate how personal experience now trumps sociological or anthropological analysis. Only one sociologist of the many scholars working on Muslim French women was called before the commission, which seemed to have taken to heart Djavann's contention on the back cover of her autobiography: "I wore the veil for ten years. It was the veil or death. I know what I'm talking about" (2003). The privileging of personal experience over expertise—in fact, the transformation of personal experience into expertise—explains the political influence and professional success of secular Muslim women like Amara, Djavann, and Hirsi Ali.

Even if they would not qualify as works of sociology, however, autobiographies like Amara's do play a sociological role, one that goes to the heart of secular Muslim women's exceptionality. Amara's autobiography mixes the personal, political, and sociological, recounting Amara's personal history, the rise of the NPNS movement, and the rapidly degrading social conditions in the *banlieues*. Its hybrid nature underscores its pseudo-ethnographic aspirations and the politics of representation crucial to the genre. That politics relies on an ambiguous, even contradictory, notion of exemplarity underpinning the exceptionality of secular Muslim women. Amara's autobiography is supposed to double as ethnography—a description of the life and worldviews of young, immigrant-origin women in the *banlieues*. This is precisely why personal experience can stand in for sociological expertise. Amara presents herself and is read as one example of a numerically significant sociological category: the secular Muslim woman. At the same time, Amara also represents an aspirational model, an example of what not yet emancipated, not yet secular, and not yet French women of immigrant origin might become. As the back cover of Loubna Méliane's autobiography (2003b) proclaims, "with all her energy, Loubna emerged from the ghetto, like a ray of hope for all the housing projects." Yet the particular racial and religious underpinnings of Frenchness make the not yet a permanent ontological position for these women, hence the very exceptionality of figures like Amara and Méliane. This second aspect of their exemplarity—the example as aspirational model—undercuts any notion of representativeness that Amara or Méliane claim, revealing the secular Muslim woman to be a purely political construction rather than a sociological class. It is this fiction of representativeness, and my argument about the secular Muslim woman as a political category, that I index with the term "like" when I repeatedly use the phrase "secular Muslim women like Amara."[7]

Save the Muslim Woman

Amara's *Ni putes ni soumises* was written in collaboration with Sylvia Zappi, a journalist for *Le Monde*, and published in 2003; an English translation appeared in 2006.[8] Part autobiography, part social analysis, and part indictment of Islamic patriarchy, it remains an odd read, unexpectedly juxtaposing depictions of racism and social marginalization alongside glowing statements about the French Republic's commitments to liberty, equality, and fraternity. The first chapter recalls how Amara's parents, like so many other North African immigrants recruited to rebuild France after World War II, were relegated to a transit city before finally being settled in Herbet, a cité (housing project) where 90 percent of the population was Algerian. At school, she and other children from the cité were constantly singled out as Arabs, and one of her teachers forced Amara to identify herself as a foreign student even though she was by law a French citizen. Amara poignantly recounts the death of her youngest brother, Malik, who was run over by a drunk driver when she was fourteen years old. "I saw how the cops were able to mistreat people simply because they were Arabs," she writes, describing how the police roughed up her mother, bullied her father, and called her family boug-noules, a racial slur used for Arabs (Amara 2006, 53–54). Nonetheless, Amara maintains an idealized view of the republic. She contends that even though she and her family lived with "discrimination, exclusion, [and] racism . . . deep down I knew with certainty that this was not France. My own France . . . is the France of the Enlightenment, the France of the republic, the France of Marianne. . . . In short, the France of liberty, equality, and fraternity" (48–49).

The next few chapters move from chronicling Amara's own story to a quasi-sociological description of the deteriorating gender and generational relations in the banlieues. Amara finds that constraints on young women of immigrant origin are no longer imposed by fathers but rather by older brothers, who have extended their authority beyond their own sisters to all young women in the projects. These older brothers now monitor girls' comings and goings, police their sexuality and romantic dalliances, and verbally insult and sometimes physically assault girls. Women "who [dare] break the rules" by showing off their "femininity . . . [are] treated as whores" (2006, 65). Amara maintains that poverty, racism, and exclusion from French society have "generated an incredible rage" (68) within young men, and that they assuage their feelings of powerlessness by dominating the only thing they can—namely, women in the housing projects. These first parts of the autobiography criticize the state for having "abandoned" and "neglected" the immigrant suburbs (84, 64), pointing out that "the deterioration [of gender relations] took place during a period of mass unemployment that hit the housing projects hard" (62). But Amara abruptly shifts focus midway through the book from a structural critique of government policy to the presence of Islamist groups that enforce reactionary codes of morality on women. Without much elaboration about these groups, she turns to a discussion of the headscarf—"the most visible and telling evidence of this lapse into obscurantism" (98)—denouncing it as a "symbol of women's oppression" (98) worn by the new "soldiers of green fascism" (74). And she calls on the state—the same one she has just criticized—to take the initiative against this menace: "The state, guarantor of secularism, must protect its fundamental values and responsibilities at school and elsewhere" (99).

Intentionally or not, Amara's autobiography repeats a well-worn colonial narrative of "white men saving brown women from brown men" (Spivak 1988, 297). Maghrebi-French women are increasingly figured in popular and political discourse as the victims of Arab-Muslim men (Guénif-Souilamas and Macé 2004; Raissiguier 2008; Ticktin 2008).[9] Politicians and the mainstream media, fueled by Samira Bellil's autobiography *Dans l'enfer des tournantes* (In the hell of gang rapes; 2003), have portrayed gang rapes as a common occurrence in the *banlieues*. In addition, a semantically catchy *voile-viol* (veil-rape) parallel underpins debates about veiling, propagated by Djavann, who compares veiling to rape in her autobiography, and by Habchi, co-author of *Ni voilée, ni violée* (Neither veiled nor raped; 2011). Behind the sexually oppressed *musulmane voilée* and the sexually emancipated *musulmane laïque* stands another figure: the sexually pathological Arab man, what Nacira Guénif-Souilamas and Eric Macé call *le garçon arabe* (2004).

Indeed, as I noted above, the massive media attention to NPNS coincided with the death of Sohane Benziane, the young woman burned alive by a male acquaintance, reportedly in retaliation for something Benziane's boyfriend did to him. In the mainstream press and in public statements by NPNS, Benziane's murder came to represent a general problem of sexual violence in the *banlieues*, violence attributed implicitly and explicitly to Maghrebi-French and African-French men. In *La racaille de la république* (The republic's trash), coauthored by her NPNS colleague Mohammed Abdi, Amara pairs Benziane's murder with the attempted murder of eighteen-year-old Shérazade Belayni, who in November 2004 was set alight by a young man whom she had rebuffed romantically. Amara writes: "It is imperative that this kind of murder not become ordinary, that we do everything so that this kind of crime does not begin again in our country. . . . History is repeating itself, I said to myself: Sohane, Shérazade . . . When is it going to end?" (Amara and Abdi 2006, 60–61 [ellipsis in original]). Remarkably, Amara implies that nonwhite immigrants have somehow brought sexual violence back to France, even though sexual and domestic violence never went away and cuts across distinctions of race, class, and religion (Mucchielli 2005). Between 2005 and 2006, for example, 410,000 women were the victims of violence by a partner or former partner, and in 2006, 137 women were killed by their spouse or partner. Incidentally, the immigrant hub of Seine-Saint-Denis may have one of the highest rates of nonlethal domestic violence in France, but rural areas—including bastions of Frenchness like Champagne-Ardenne, Limousin, and Franche-Comté—are disproportionately represented when it comes to men murdering their former female partners.[10] And Sohane Benziane's murder was soon followed by that of Marie Trintignant, a well-known actress, killed in August 2003 by her white French boyfriend Bertrand Cantat, the lead singer of the popular rock group Noir Désir. An autopsy showed that Trintignant had been punched in the face nineteen times, and she died of multiple head injuries after spending several days in a coma.[11]

Nonetheless, Amara's references to "this kind of murder" and "this kind of crime" repeat a dominant narrative that attributes sexual and domestic violence to the aberrant sexuality and delinquency of Arab-Muslim and black men in the *banlieues*. Amara does not categorize or analyze gendered violence in a national context; rather, she underscores its religious, cultural, and racial specificity.[12] If domestic and sexual violence perpetrated by white French men is largely understood as a sign of individual and even momentary psychosis—as Cantat's was—the same kind of violence in the *banlieues* signals a collective cultural pathology, one that marks the incommensurable difference of black and brown male bodies from white ones. The logic of incommensurable and commensurable difference operates through a sexual matrix to produce both *la musulmane laïque* and her opposite, *le garçon arabe*. It is through, or more precisely against, the incommensurable sexual pathology of the Arab-Muslim male that the secular Muslim woman emerges as an exceptional, commensurably different citizen.

NPNS reproduces a victimizer-victim structure, perpetuated ad nauseam by the media and politicians, in which Arab-Muslim men are sexually violent offenders or, at the very least, oppressors who deny women their femininity. Consequently, freedom, defined by Amara and NPNS as sexual liberation and female self-expression, means liberation from Arab-Muslim men—or, in Amara's terms, from "reactionary patriarchal traditions" (2006, 69) and "fundamentalist Islam" (95). In this structure, Arab-Muslim men become hyperagentive oppressors and Arab-Muslim girls their passive victims. And this is when the white male saviors, in Gayatri Spivak's classic phrase, return. Although the women of NPNS believe themselves to be agents in the salvation process, they nevertheless accept their auxiliary role in the state's campaign to save brown women from brown men. Consider these comments by Jean-Louis Debré, then president of the National Assembly, when he inaugurated NPNS's *Mariannes* exhibit by asking rhetorically: "Who other than [the National Assembly], after all, better embodies the values of the liberatory and protective republic to which women from the housing estates wish to pay homage and of which the deputies are the guarantors?" ("l'Assemblée Nationale" 2003). Debré reinscribes a masculinist symbolic order in which the state and its mostly male legislators protect women, especially brown women, who then must pay homage to their protectors. He thereby adroitly recuperates the liberatory initiative demonstrated by the women of NPNS—who, after all, have managed to save themselves—turning the *Mariannes* exhibit into a celebration of the emancipatory republic.[13]

Carceral Emancipation

Ironically, the sexual emancipation of women in the *banlieues* has largely taken a carceral form: saving Muslim women means punishing Muslim men and, to a certain extent, their veiled accomplices. The headscarf law of 2004 and the niqab law of 2010 were justified as necessary to promote sexual equality. They were also part of a broader law-and-order paradigm, one that first emerged in the mid-1970s under Valéry Giscard d'Estaing's center Right government, continued under various Socialist cabinets, and accelerated with Sarkozy's election as president in 2007. Combating insecurity (*insécurité*)—an amorphous concept that encompasses violent crime, delinquency, and so-called incivilities—has become a priority for both the Left and Right, with successive governments outdoing each other to enact new laws and expand police and judicial powers (Jobard 2005; Terrio 2009; Wacquant 2009). In 1993 lawmakers initiated the first complete revision of the French penal code since 1810, ushering in a new penal model in which the aim of imprisonment and probation is to control rather than rehabilitate at-risk populations (Terrio 2009). The new model gives police and prosecutors additional powers, expands the bases for provisional detention without charge, and permits identity checks without probable cause. Following the now-discredited "broken windows" theory propagated in New York City, it also entails the systematic repression of petty crime and public order violations in target neighborhoods (Terrio 2009, 74; see also D. Fassin 2011).

These carceral tactics are largely enacted in the *banlieues*, referred to as lawless zones (*zones de non-droit*) by many politicians and journalists, and they disproportionately target men of color. Though the carceral state began to emerge before the alleged Islamic threat, the contemporary rhetoric of security and attendant carceral tactics are entangled in a broader antiterrorist logic, one that started in the mid-1990s with the civil war in Algeria and that has increased in the wake of the American-led War on Terror. In the space of the *banlieues*, and in the bodies of brown and black men, the dual threats of delinquency and fundamentalism—always inflected by the threat of sexual violence—come together. Delinquent young men, it is held, are the prime recruits for Islamic fundamentalism and eventually terrorism; to combat delinquency is thus to combat fundamentalist terrorism.

Carcerality, as many scholars have observed, has become a defining feature of neoliberal governance. Replacing welfare assistance, criminalization and incarceration are now the primary means used to manage the contradictions and insecurities generated by social and economic policies (LeBaron and Roberts 2010, 26). Indeed, Loïc Waquant (2009) contends that economic deregulation and carcerality are mutually constitutive and interconnected elements of neoliberalism: the rolling back of the welfare state necessitates the penal state as a control mechanism for managing the devastating effects of deregulation. Through carceral practices, neoliberal states reassert their authority over law and order just as they withdraw from organizing the economy. It is unsurprising that at exactly the same time as the French state began to deregulate and denationalize its economy, it also began to expand its domestic carceral powers.

Furthermore, those targeted by the carceral state as criminals are constructed via a logic of individual responsibility that is crucial to neoliberal ideology. Eliding the social and structural causes of deviance, neoliberal carcerality criminalizes nonnormative social behavior and sees various forms of deviance as free choices made by bad individuals who must be held entirely accountable for their actions and punished by the law-and-order state. Although acknowledging the effects of poverty and unemployment on youth, for example, Prime Minister Lionel Jospin nonetheless asserted in 1999: "As long as we accept sociological explanations and don't question individual responsibility, we will not solve these problems" (quoted in Terrio 2009, 115). And in 2002, during a debate on delinquency, the Socialist legislator Julien Dray, a longtime supporter of NPNS, commended the policies of the center Right government then in power, arguing that "a delinquent is a delinquent. . . . If you do not choose where you were born, you do choose your life and, at a given moment, you choose to become a delinquent. Whence society has no other solution than to repress these acts" (quoted in

Wacquant 2009, 10). The new bipartisan logic of individual accountability shifts the burden of responsibility from the state onto individuals and, in so doing, disavows the state's role in creating the conditions that have left these individuals with few choices in employment, education, and housing. In addition, this logic of individual responsibility is, crucially, sexed: black and brown men are irredeemably agentive criminal and sexual offenders, while black and brown women are their victims.[14]

At the same time, the new emphasis on individual responsibility exists alongside what Susan Terrio calls an analytic of cultural pathology (2009), in which violence (especially sexual violence) has a collective, cultural origin. The cultural pathology model—recently deployed by sociologist Hugues Lagrange (2010)—holds that the social structure and values of many non-European immigrants produce young people incapable of accepting and integrating mainstream French values. Though the tropes of individual choice and collective, cultural pathology seem contradictory, French politicians and pundits use them together to denounce delinquency and sexual violence. In fact, the choices that Arab-Muslim men make to become delinquents and *violeurs-voileurs* reinforce the seeming pathology of their religious and cultural communities of origin and their incommensurabilty as French citizens.

As their media and political success demonstrates, the women of NPNS have played an important role in justifying and perpetuating this twinned discourse on delinquency and sexual violence, offering their personal experiences as indisputable evidence of a culture of sexual pathology that requires strong state action to punish men and protect women in the *banlieues*. The cultural pathology model of delinquency relies on the construction of immigrant families as sexually aberrant, positing sexual violence and sexual repression—purportedly engendered by polygamy, forced or arranged marriage, and an overinvestment in women's honor—as the immigrant norm that remains fundamentally at odds with the secular French values of sexual freedom and equality. In identifying what caused the deterioration of gender relations in the *banlieues*, Amara points to "the fact that in immigrant families patriarchy is embedded in the way the family operates." "My parents always made their daughters assume responsibilities from which their sons were exempt," she continues, though "I do not hold it against them; they were conditioned to act this way by their culture" (2006, 67–68). She does, however, blame immigrant patriarchy for turning young men into "spoiled," "overprotected" "kings" (68) and young women into virtual prisoners. She also blames immigrant-origin boys for their lack of respect for women. Although this was "normal in a patriarchal society" like that of her parents, the same attitude among youths (*chez les jeunes*) is "a thousand times worse, because they don't have the excuse of being conditioned by a patriarchal society. They have grown up here, in a 'free and equal' society, and that makes all the difference" (Amara and Abdi 2006, 22–23). In France, accordingly, despite the collective, cultural origins of their sexual pathology, these youth choose to become sexual delinquents. And just as their immigrant parents need to stop coddling them, so does the French state. Echoing the dominant law-and-order paradigm of both major political parties, Amara argues that "we have to end the sentiment of impunity that exists among certain minor delinquents" (117), adding that "those who screw up must pay. At a certain moment, when prevention [that is, community policing] doesn't work anymore, these youth must be brought to justice and punished in proportion to the crime committed" (125).

In short, NPNS exemplifies a form of carceral feminism. The term, coined by critics of U.S.-based campaigns against sex slavery, describes "the commitment of abolitionist feminist activists to a law and order agenda and . . . a drift from the welfare state to the carceral state as the enforcement apparatus for feminist goals" (Bernstein 2007, 128). Carceral feminists focus not on the socioeconomic structures that often drive sexual violence and sexual exploitation, but rather on groups of deviant men who oppress women. They thereby rely on law making and incarceration as the primary mechanisms for ensuring sexual freedom and gender justice. Like carceral feminist organizations elsewhere, NPNS is a strong ally of the neoliberal state, authenticating a mainstream discourse about "the lost territories of the republic"[15] that justifies the state's carceral, law-and-order response. The proposals that have been put forth by NPNS to combat sexual inequality and sexual violence in the *banlieues*—guidebooks preaching respect for women, the creation of the Maison de Mixité where men and women can socialize together, calls for more community policing, and appeals for strong political and legal action against supposed Islamist infiltration of the *banlieues*—underscore two approaches to delinquency that reinscribe a neoliberal logic. First, the leaders of NPNS not only seek to make delinquent young men pay for their actions but also locate prevention in changing individual sexist attitudes, not social and economic conditions. Even as Amara explicitly attributes sexual violence and juvenile delinquency to the ravages of economic dislocation, she and NPNS reproduce a logic of individual responsibility in offering solutions. And second, Amara and NPNS appeal to the carceral state—both the soft power of community policing and the hard power of the penal system—to ensure sexual equality and freedom. More-over, in shifting the focus to the threat of Islamic fundamentalism, NPNS helps to obfuscate the root causes of social degradation in the *banlieues* and attributes the deterioration of gender relations to a lack of secularism. As a result, NPNS exemplifies and validates the reigning political discourse that the reassertion of secular values will best solve the problems of the *banlieues*, especially the problems of sexual violence and inequality.

Save the Republic

The success of Amara's autobiography, and of the movement itself, was pre-dictable. Propagating a tripartite narrative of female Muslim victim, male Muslim oppressor, and emancipatory state, Amara and NPNS confirmed—and did so as authentic spokeswomen from the *cités*—what the mainstream media and politicians already averred about the need to reassert the republic's authority in its lost territories. What remains particularly inter-esting about Amara's autobiography, nevertheless, is that it also serves as an autobiography of the republic. In fact, behind the immigrant-Muslim woman stands another victim: the republic itself. Like many of the auto-biographies by prominent secular Muslim women, Ni *putes ni soumises* nar-rates the victimization of Muslim women by Muslim men as, ultimately, the victimization of the republic by Islam. Indeed, Amara's narration simply makes explicit a broader underlying political logic. And by saving the Mus-lim woman, the republic also saves itself.

Consider the arc of Amara's autobiography (mirrored by that of the move-ment as a whole), and the shift from a critique of the government's failure to prevent or deal with problems like poverty, unemployment, and racism to a single-minded focus on the menace of Islamic fundamentalism and its op-pression of women. After chronicling the deterioration of social conditions in the *banlieues* in a chapter titled "From Neighborhood to Ghetto," Amara turns in the next chapter to conservative Islam, which, she contends, has "offered young men a theoretical framework and tools with which to op-press young women" (2006, 97). Significantly, this chapter is called "Ob-scurantism, the Key to Regression," suggesting that Islamic obscurantism, and not the government's "policies of social segregation" (84) indicted in the previous chapter, constitutes the "key" to the *banlieues*' problems. More-over, Amara ends this chapter on Islamic obscurantism by depicting not the *banlieues* but the republic as being under threat, "tested on all fronts to resist religious inroads" (98). By moving so quickly from a description of social disintegration caused by the state's own policies to an excoriation of patriarchal Islam and the headscarf, Amara obscures the structural causes of social malaise and displaces the state's responsibility for them onto fundamentalist Islam. She thereby turns what began as a biting critique of socioeconomic degradation into a treatise on Islam and *laïcité*, advocating "the reaffirmation of secularism" (99) as the solution to the problems in the *banlieues*. Amara initially held that a law banning headscarves in public schools was unnecessary and unwise, but she reversed her position after her autobiography's first edition. In the postscript to later editions, Amara links the headscarf to polygamy, female genital cutting, sexual inequality, cultural relativism, and anti-Semitism—the multifarious evils of "green fascism"—and presents NPNS as "carry[ing] on our unrelenting combat to preserve secularism, equality, and a plurality of social identities" (162). The fight to protect women's rights has been transformed into a battle to protect the secular republic.

In following her discussion of social breakdown in the *banlieues* with calls for action against Islamism in general and the headscarf in particular, Amara adheres closely to, and also justifies, the dominant law-and-order logic of the neoliberal French state. Amara and NPNS buttress a government discourse that treats the Islamic menace as the central challenge facing not simply the *banlieues* but the republic itself. They also enable the government and media to reframe social disintegration and sexual violence in the suburbs as a symptom of the decline of secularism, rather than the result of decades of regressive social and economic policies. When Amara won the National Assembly's Political Book Prize in 2004, the day of speeches and panels devoted to her book barely touched on any kind of socioeconomic dispossession or on the structural transformations that have led, as Amara herself contends, to the erosion of gender and sexual relations. The event concentrated instead on how to defend *laïcité*, and four of the five panels had titles like "Daily Threats to *Laïcité*" and "The Future of *Laïcité* in France." The trope of defending an embattled *laïcité* and the very integrity of the republic became the perceived crux of Amara's book and of the NPNS movement. Books like hers—written by unimpeachable native experts— have thereby helped forge a political consensus about the need to secure France against Islamic *communautarisme*, as well as about the need to reestablish the authority of the republic by banning the headscarf.

The emergence of this narrative of the republic as victim takes place in a particular historical context. The sense of national anxiety that so consistently undergirds French debates about Islam, and the insistence on defending laïcité and reestablishing the authority of the republic, occur in a time when the republic's sovereignty seems increasingly challenged by globalization, European integration, regional decentralization, and consumerism, all of which are driven by neoliberal capitalism. Étienne Balibar has called this predicament "the impotence of the omnipotent" (2004, 135), while Wendy Brown (2010) refers to the "waning sovereignty" of nation-states that are now subordinate to the vagaries of a neoliberal capitalism that makes national borders irrelevant. The recent epidemic of wall building and border enforcement by nation-states in Europe and elsewhere, Brown contends, does not signal the reestablishment of national sovereignty so much as reveal its waning. Escalating policies of containment—walls, fences, and exclusionary legislation—that attempt to regulate the boundary between us and them are forms of sovereignty as political theater and have, Brown writes, "a Wizard of Oz quality" (2010, 25). They are purely symbolic practices that underscore the state's lack of sovereignty, its impotence rather than its potence as a sovereign.

The restoration of the French Republic's authority through various legislative practices that regulate Islam certainly has a symbolic quality as well as a synecdochal one. Consider Djavann's op-ed in *Le Figaro* in defense of the law banning headscarves in public schools: "We needed a quick blow, a strong symbolic act, [and] the new law was necessary. It will buttress secular Muslims in France and extremists will have no choice but to submit to it" (2004). Djavann's reference to the symbolic nature of the law invokes the double meaning of the term. As detractors pointed out, targeting a few thousand teenage girls in hijab would hardly solve the problem of Islamic extremism in France. The law was merely symbolic. But Djavann also draws on another meaning, where a symbolic ritual act in one domain (the school) will have real effects in another (society at large). For Djavann and other proponents of the 2004 law, its goal seemed to be not the eradication of Islamic extremism but the restoration of the republic's sovereignty, understood as its ability to make extremist Muslims submit to its authority. Hence, too, the synecdochal quality of the law: acting quickly and decisively as a sovereign in one domain (the *banlieues*), the French state seemed (and was seen) to reestablish its sovereignty in all domains. Importantly, too, the symbolic reassertion of sovereignty through the containment of certain spaces and bodies does not simply mask its real disappearance elsewhere (as some contend); that reassertion has real effects, and not only on the lives of black and brown subjects. Like many rituals, the symbolic enactment of law and order in the space of the *banlieues* proves efficacious, reaffirming state sovereignty within national and cultural borders and, concomitantly, allaying the anxieties precipitated by the waning of national sovereignty across political and economic ones. When the embattled Muslim woman stands in for the embattled republic, its emancipation of her serves to reassert the republic's own sovereignty and restore its waning authority. By saving Muslim women, the republic ostensibly saves itself.

The Ruse of Neoliberal Sovereignty

I use the word *ostensibly* for a reason. Balibar and Brown are correct that the political rationalities and economic policies of neoliberal governance have undone key aspects of nation-state sovereignty. But political sovereignty is not entirely waning; rather, it is being reconfigured, resituated, and narrated anew (Harvey 2005 and 2007; Wacquant 2009). The project of neoliberalism combines market-friendly policies like labor deregulation, capital mobility, deflation, and trade liberalization with the retraction of the welfare state, the devolution of government, the privileging of a managerial political and cultural ethic, the individualization of responsibility, and the emergence of an expansive carceral apparatus. This project, as well as the opening of borders to transnational capital, is a political decision made and instituted by the governing elites of European nation-states who circulate between national government positions and supranational ones.[16] In fact, the narrative of impotence that Brown and Balibar emphasize is also a self-narrative that neoliberal states perpetuate: they proclaim the purported separation of the political and the economic and disavow their sovereignty over, and responsibility for, the market economy and its effects on social life. In short, the political discourse of waning sovereignty is a ruse of neoliberal power.

After all, neoliberalism ushers in not so much the end of political sovereignty as its purposeful reorganization into a new political, economic, and legal form. As part of the project of integration into the European Union, European states reconfigured themselves to "redefine and lock in the relationship between the political and the economic and, more specifically, to reconstruct the terms through which political action and regulation action are deemed possible in a capitalist society" (Gill 2003, 66). In France neoliberal transformations began in the mid-1970s under the center Right government of Giscard d'Estaing. The Socialists came to power in 1981, and by 1983 they, too, had begun to adopt a policy of economic deregulation, competitive disinflation, and balanced budgets, shifting away from the previous *dirigiste* sensibility of the Left and parts of the center Right (Clift 2003). The elimination of capital controls in the late 1980s facilitated the expansion of production abroad, and the liberalization of France's financial markets led to the growing presence of foreign investors, which led, in turn, to the dependence on and vulnerability of French financial markets to foreign investment (Clift 2003). Moreover, though some sectors were protected, consecutive center Right and Socialist governments opened up domestic industrial markets to foreign competition. As in the rest of Western Europe, these political and economic transformations led to high, and rising, structural unemployment, which had skyrocketed from 8.3 percent in 1983 to 12.6 percent in 1997. But a major aspect of neoliberal political and economic transformations in France was the tacit acceptance that the government could, and would, do very little about high levels of structural unemployment. The terms of the 1992 Maastricht Treaty prioritize deficit reduction over welfare protection, and France's integration into the European Union has meant following this new political and economic logic. After 1983 unemployment went from being one of the main priorities of national economic policy to the principal anti-inflationary tool and adjustment mechanism of the French economy. As the political economist Ben Clift notes, "the strategy followed [by both the mainstream Right and Left] has been, quite simply, to achieve disinflation and increased competitiveness through higher unemployment" (2003, 183). As a result, between 1990 and 1999, the unemployment rate for people ages 15–24 who were looking for a job rose from 19.9 percent to 25.6 percent. During the same period, in what are known as sensitive urban areas (*zones urbaines sensibles*, or ZUS), populated largely by immigrants and their children, it rose from 28.5 percent to nearly 40 percent. Precarious work—temporary jobs, short-term contracts, and training programs—has also risen sharply: in 1990, one in ten workers held precarious positions, while in 1999 one in seven did, and in the *banlieues* in 1999 about 20 percent of work was precarious. Forty-two percent of young people in the ZUS in 1990 were either without work or doing precarious work; the figure had risen to 60 percent by 1999.[17]

The paradox of neoliberal sovereignty is that the transfer of control over the economy from the *dirigiste* state to transnational capital and the technocratic expertise of the European Union was itself a sovereign political decision made by the governing elites of various nation-states. In other words, it is through the purposeful reconfiguration of modern sovereignty that the French Republic's authority (in certain legal, political, and economic domains) has been reconstituted outside institutions of the nation-state, resulting in increased capital mobility, European integration, regional decentralization, and consumerism—all processes that fundamentally disrupt the national values of equality, unity, and social solidarity on which the French welfare state has long been based (Holmes 2000). The anxiety continually articulated by French governing elites about globalization, Europeanization, and the loss of French identity—which propels anti-immigration and Islamophobic legislation as well as numerous national debates about the future of French identity—is an anxious disavowal of responsibility by elites for their role in that loss. Brown's analytic metaphor of containment as political theater is therefore apt, though not in the *Wizard of Oz* sense in which she and others use it to describe a semblance of sovereignty that is not actually present. Successive French governments disavow their active role in bringing about the transformations they now decry, and in dismantling an earlier organization of political economy to produce the social conditions these elites now proclaim themselves unable to control and that necessitate, they also claim, the law-and-order state. The political theater lies in this denial of responsibility and its relocation elsewhere—namely, in the uncontrollable and incommensurable bodies, culture, and religion of the *banlieues*. Put another way, the political decisions that have made social and economic life uncertain for many, in the *banlieues* and beyond, are both obfuscated and symbolically resolved through the punishment of sexually aberrant immigrants and delinquents. Republican sovereignty is therefore reasserted, but only in very particular domains. And declarations of the need to restore the republic's authority through law and order have had an effect: the French public has become heavily invested in the battle against crime and insecurity, despite a corresponding downward trend in actual criminal behavior (Jobard 2005). In 1997, 9 percent of the public found combating violence and criminality to be a political priority; in 1998 that number had risen to 14 percent, in 1999 to 30 percent, and in 2001 to 46 percent, overtaking unemployment for the first time as the problem most people identified as requiring urgent government action (Robert and Pottier 2004). Thus the neoliberal state not only denies its role in creating the conditions that underlie crime and delinquency, but it also relocates responsibility within individual criminals and reasserts its authority by punishing those criminals, symbolically restoring order to the social world.

The discourse of sexual victimhood exemplified by NPNS has played a key role in the political theater of neoliberalism. Indeed, NPNS has become both an ally of and an alibi for the French state in this shell game of sovereignty. First, by reiterating a neoliberal carceral logic that locates criminality in the individual choices of Arab-Muslim men and in the collective pathology of their religious and cultural communities of origin, NPNS authenticates and legitimizes the state's disavowal of its own responsibility for creating the socioeconomic conditions that underlie delinquency, most notably unemployment or precarious employment and overcrowded, failing schools. Second, if we take seriously Loïc Wacquant's contention that neoliberalism produces an increasingly capacious carceral apparatus precisely to handle the devastating effects of economic deregulation and the retraction of social welfare, the alibi-like nature of NPNS becomes clearer. The carceral feminism of NPNS helps rationalize an expanding penal state as the most effective means of managing the *banlieues* and emancipating immigrant Muslim women; surveillance and incarceration seemingly ensure security, sexual freedom, and sexual equality, allowing (a few exceptional) Muslim women to flourish by punishing and cordoning off Muslim men. By locating responsibility for the problems of the *banlieues* in the delinquent bodies and patriarchal culture of its residents, the native experts of NPNS justify the state's expansion of a carceral regulatory system necessary to neoliberal political rationality without a concomitant acknowledgment of the other, deleterious effects of that political rationality.

In other words, the carceral feminism of NPNS enables the state to proclaim its impotence over the market economy and, concurrently, to reassert its sovereignty within national borders and restore the secular values that purportedly constitute French national identity. Recall Debré's comments at the *Mariannes* exhibit declaring the National Assembly the best embodiment of the "liberatory and protective republic," to whom it was only natural that women from the housing projects would want to pay homage. Even as Debré publicly recognizes a movement seeking to bring attention to the effects of the state's political and economic abandonment of the immigrant *banlieues*, he positions the state and its representatives as the guarantors of liberty and security in those spaces. He congratulates himself, his colleagues, and the republic for a job well done in the face of all evidence to the contrary—namely, the very existence of the NPNS movement. The discourse of insecurity and sexual deviance, perpetuated by successive governments and authenticated by the *banlieues* spokeswomen of NPNS, allows the state to reaffirm sovereignty in certain spaces (the *banlieues*) while denying it in others (the economy). By saving Muslim women, the republic not only saves itself by reasserting its waning sovereignty, but it also simultaneously saves face by disowning its responsibility for that waning. The state's investment in liberating Muslim women, then, is crucial to the disavowals and reinstatements—disavowals under the guise of reinstatements—on which neoliberal power hinges.

Debré's comments illustrate, too, the secular-republican management of French sexism and misogyny. Aided by the culturalist rhetoric of NPNS, Debré and his colleagues displace these enduring problems onto Arab-Muslim culture and reaffirm the republic's commitment to sexual equality. As the radical feminist philosopher Christine Delphy observes, Debré "kills two birds with one stone: the alterity of other sexists is confirmed, while absence of sexism [among non-Muslim French] is proven by the alterity of sexists" (quoted in Kemp 2009, 30). As Delphy suggests, sexuality has become a discourse of border control in France (Ticktin 2008), so that deviations from the norm—veiling, polygamy, gang rape, arranged or forced marriage, and domestic or sexual violence—are taken as signs of deviant Muslim cultural alterity. Moreover, these enactments of aberrant sexuality are not simply understood as un-French but as unsecular. As *liberté* and *égalité* have largely been redefined as sexual liberty and sexual equality (E. Fassin 2010), and as republican *laïcité* has been repurposed as the political arrangement that best guarantees sexual liberty and sexual equality, sexuality has become a key site of concern and regulation in secularism's self-narrative of progress and cultural exemplarity. The dual production of incommensurable and commensurable difference so integral to secular-republican rule now maps onto a distinction between aberrant and normal sex. Secular Muslim women like Amara play a crucial role in this nexus of sex and secularity, not only by attesting to the liberatory nature of the secular state but also by managing the tension between universal and particular that is at the heart of secularism as a global project.

If, as I have argued, the emancipated secular Muslim woman emerges in relation to the incommensurable alterity of the patriarchal, sexually deviant Arab-Muslim man, she is also consistently juxtaposed against the veiled Muslim woman. In televised debates about the 2004 and 2010 veil laws, for instance, secular Muslim women like Amara, Méliane, and Habchi were often seated next to or opposite women in headscarves or (more rarely) full veils.[18] A prime example is an October 20, 2003, episode of the debate show *Ripostes* titled "Is *laïcité* under attack?" It featured four white men (two of them journalists, the other two politicians) and two nonwhite women: Méliane of NPNS and Siham Andalouci of the Collective of French Muslims.

From the beginning, the veiled Andalouci was relentlessly attacked by Méliane, who had clearly been invited as Andalouci's counterpart. And part of the contrast was sartorial. While Andalouci wore a long-sleeved turtleneck and matching headscarf, Méliane was dressed in a fashionable blouse that left her shoulders bare and her bra straps visible.

The staged juxtaposition of these two prototypes effects a double symbolic move. First, given that public Muslim piety is understood in conventional academic and political discourse as a sign of the failure of republican integration, the conspicuous visibility of secular Muslim women like Méliane affirms the efficacy of the republican model of integration. The presence of veiled subjects like Andalouci, whom Méliane repeatedly called a fundamentalist and accused of not being a proper French citizen, is symbolically and politically countered by integrated figures like Méliane. Note the irony of this disavowal: even as the NPNS movement brings attention to the dire conditions in the cités, conditions that signal the republic's failure to integrate its nonwhite subjects into French society, Méliane and her colleagues offer themselves up and are eagerly read as signs of the republic's success at integration. Second, secular Muslim women like Méliane, whose bodily comportment and embrace of heteronormative sexuality demonstrate their integration, underscore a dominant narrative of successful integration through successful sexuality that reinforces the heterosexual norms foundational to secular republican citizenship (J. Scott 1996 and 2005; Surkis 2006). Moreover, the fact that the juxtaposition of veiled and unveiled female bodies was staged during an episode of Ripostes titled "Is laïcité under attack?"—and it was clear by whom—indicates how sexual and secular norms have come to be coextensive.

Particularly striking is how so many musulmanes laïques embrace normative secular notions of femininity and agency, echoing a dominant discourse that regards veiling as sexually abnormal and fundamentally repressive. In a discussion of the headscarf, Méliane once remarked: "It's better to wear a skirt and take up [assumer] one's femininity than to hide it behind a veil in order to avoid the gaze of others" (2003b). Decrying the headscarf as a "means of oppression, of alienation, [and] of discrimination" rather than an act of religion, Amara similarly contends that during her adolescence "it was considered natural for us to wear short skirts, tight-fitting jeans, low-cut blouses, and short T-shirts," all modes of dress she defines as "showing off our femininity" (2006, 100, 65). Amara bemoans the "reactionary" pressure exerted on young women and lauds those who rebel: "They try to resist by being themselves, by continuing to wear revealing clothing, by dressing in fashion, by using makeup, sometimes outrageously. They want to live in modern society, to exist as individuals, and to command personal respect on equal footing with young men" (75). Méliane and Amara identify certain aesthetic practices like wearing makeup and short skirts as essential to femininity, consequently defining femininity as sexual desirability to men.[19] Méliane and Amara also naturalize this mode of femininity, so that wearing revealing clothes corresponds to taking up one's natural qualities and desires as a woman and as an individual. Furthermore, they posit wearing makeup and revealing clothes as acts of sexual liberation and sexual equality, as fundamental to turning immigrant-origin women into agentive individuals on an equal footing with men. Equating a particular mode of heterofemininity with individual autonomy and sexual equality—values that define the modern, secular woman—Méliane and Amara propose that to be secular is to be sexually normal, and vice versa.

The heterofemininity Méliane and Amara embrace and reproduce was on full display in the *Mariannes* exhibit, which consisted of fourteen close-up photographs of individual women from the NPNS march, aged between twenty-two and thirty-four. Every photograph was accompanied by a few sentences about what the original Marianne symbolizes for the new one. For Awa, "Marianne is an ambitious woman who wants to flourish where she lives." To Riva, Marianne represents "the opposite of selfish individualism" and is "someone who believes in progress." Gladys thinks that "Marianne is above all a woman: she doesn't deal with human relations through violence." Linda believes that Marianne is "a woman of the heart, whose initial attitude toward others is positive and warm." Alice thinks of Marianne as "a protective mother, turned toward the future." And Safia worries that "Marianne, today, might be in danger," that "*laïcité*, justice, equal rights, we have to make an effort to defend them." These words invoke key themes of republican citizenship, such as collective coexistence, progress, and leadership. They also conjure a very specific idea of modern womanhood: "Marianne is tough but gentle, firm but just, combative but caring" (Winter 2009, 237). Remarkable in this republican mise-en-scène is how much that notion of modern womanhood reproduces a traditional, heteronormative sexual order that insists on the integrality of sexual difference.

Many of the young women begin by affirming Marianne as first and foremost a woman (*une femme*): Marianne is an ambitious woman; Marianne is a woman of the heart; Marianne is a woman of her times. As Gladys notes, "Marianne is above all a woman." The ability to model oneself on Marianne hinges on one's female sex—men, it seems, cannot be like Marianne—and the ostensibly abstract citizen of republicanism is already cleaved in two. As a result, the values ascribed to Marianne remain firmly rooted in traditional femininity. For all her rebellion, Marianne remains "a protective mother," "soft and reassuring," "positive and warm," and because she is "above all a woman," "she doesn't deal with human relations through violence." In one image, Linda cradles a rooster meant to symbolize the *coq gaulois*, the Gallic cock that is Marianne's masculine symbolic counterpart in representations of France, underscoring not only Marianne's role as nurturing mother of the (male) republic but also the dual, sexed organization of symbolic representations of citizenship and the French nation. And, in addition to being nurturing, the modern Marianne must also be beautiful. The introductory text for the exhibit explains that Marianne symbolizes strength, intelligence, freedom, and generosity, and that "she is also a young, beautiful woman" ("l'Assemblée Nationale"). The text affirms that the photographs seek to portray the new Marianne as "serious and preoccupied" with the problems in the *banlieues*—the reason for the NPNS march—"but also sure of herself, smiling and feminine, in the image of the young women in this country." Moreover, the text continues, the photographers who shot the new Mariannes were instructed to "respect and valorize the very contemporary beauty and femininity of 'Today's Mariannes,'" and to allow them to become 'reference images' for the new generation" of *banlieue* women.

So what norms of contemporary beauty and femininity should young black and Arab women from the *cités* aspire to? Four of the new Mariannes are dressed in outfits that leave their shoulders bare, all except one wear lipstick, and seven of them are quite heavily made up with blush, eye shadow, eyeliner, and bright lipstick. Since the portraits are head-and-shoulders shots, it is unclear if they also wear short skirts, that other essential marker of femininity, according to Amara. Most of the women are stylishly dressed, and one, Awa, wears a fashionable tulle ruff in red, white, and blue that might be found in a couture magazine. In fact, the photographs are strikingly commercial, resembling billboard advertisements for high-end Parisian department stores like the Galeries Lafayette and Printemps.[20]

The commercial quality of the exhibit and its affirmation of what the introductory text terms "the right to femininity" signal NPNS's imbrication within and affirmation of a broader current of mainstream republican feminism in France, what Guénif-Souilamas and Macé (2004) call neofeminism (see also Kemp 2010). Avowedly postpolitical, neofeminists understand the question of sexual equality as resolved except in the *banlieues*; defend beauty, seduction, fashion, and maternity as fundamental pleasures of femininity;

and see female autonomy as a woman's right to express her natural femininity. Even as neofeminists defend gender equality in the name of universal citizenship, they simultaneously reestablish the link between sex and gender that was undone by earlier feminists like Simone de Beauvoir and Monique Wittig, positing an integral relationship between the female-sexed body and the feminine gender, the latter now positively rather than negatively valued (Guénif-Souilamas and Macé 2004, 33). Neofeminists reject structural analyses of sexism and regard women's autonomy as a question of personal freedom and the right to choose one's lifestyle. As a result, neofeminists cannot criticize or combat structural inequalities, and they propagate the consumer culture within which neofeminism remains institutionalized. A prime example of this intersection of naturalized femininity and freedom as consumption remains the December 2003 petition against the Islamic veil, launched by the French version of the magazine Elle. Nestled among advertisements for the perfume, makeup, lingerie, clothing, and diet regimens that the magazine offers women to make them prettier, sexier, and thinner, was a call for a ban on headscarves in public schools in the name of sexual equality. Elle can simultaneously champion hypernormative femininity and sexual equality thanks to the idea of a natural or biological sexual difference that underlies the femininity of women and the masculinity of men. To express one's self, and therefore enact one's autonomy, is to express one's feminine sexuality, and vice versa. When Méliane speaks of "taking up one's femininity" (2003a) she invokes the notion that femininity is already within the female self biologically and ontologically, waiting to be brought forth and properly expressed. It is precisely this logic that allows Amara to call the headscarf "an instrument of power over women used by men" by noting that "men do not wear the headscarf" (2006, 100), while at the same time describing cité women's wearing of short skirts and makeup as a way of "affirming their femininity" and "being themselves" (75).

NPNS reproduces this naturalized heterosexual symbolic and moral order through a series of juxtapositions. Take its name, for instance: Neither Whores nor Doormats. Amara writes that the phrase emerged in response to the expression "all whores except my mother," which illustrates the way men regard women in the banlieues (Amara 2006, 112). Nonetheless, it is telling that the organization's name reaffirms a normative sexual order that understands proper female sexuality in a very specific way. The juxtaposition of Méliane and Andalouci on the stage of a television program, and of the whore and the doormat in NPNS's name, underscores how the heterofemininity embraced by the members of NPNS and other neofeminists is produced through an explicit contrast with two sexually abnormal figures: the veiled doormat (la soumise) and the whore (la pute). Within this dominant framework of heterofemininity, la soumise represents repressed sexuality and a lack of femininity, while la pute represents an excessive sexuality that breaches the bounds of proper femininity: "Prostitutes who claim to have sex for money out of choice are disturbing because they have separated sexuality from desire . . . [while] Muslim women who choose to veil create confusion because they have opted out of a mainstream vision of female sexuality as overtly and publicly alluring" (Kemp 2009, 26–27). Both the doormat and the whore refuse to play the game of seduction that remains foundational to republican feminism à la française (J. Scott 2007; Sciolino 2011).[21] The doormat refuses by making her body unavailable to men's gaze—by hiding from it, in Méliane's terms—and the whore does so by turning seduction into an economic transaction. Similarly, the sexual abnormality of the unfashionable soumise emerges from her refusal to participate in consumerist heterofemininity, while the pute takes consumerism too far, commodifying her own body. To be sexually normal—and therefore fully secular—is to be ni pute, ni soumise. The semantic juxtaposition enacted by NPNS reiterates a broader regulatory regime, evidenced by recent laws criminalizing both prostitution and veiling (Ticktin 2008). Thus the symbolic politics of NPNS's name merely makes explicit a wider secular republican logic about sex and secularity.[22]

Sexual Difference and/as Secular Universalism

Sexual difference has long posed a problem for republican universalism. Joan Scott's seminal work highlights the various and largely futile attempts that feminists, republican thinkers, and legislators have made to reconcile sexual difference (the embodied particularity of sex) with the abstract equality of citizens that republican ideology extols. Scott problematizes the emancipatory narrative in France that laïcité has liberated women and ushered in gender equality. She points to enduring gender inequalities as well as the fact that "the equality that secularism promises was always—still is—troubled by sexual difference, by the difficult, if not impossible task of assigning ultimate meaning to bodily difference between women and men" (2011a, 95). She goes on to posit, as she has elsewhere (2007), that "one effort at resolution—the one we are now witnessing in dramatic form in relation to Islam—is the displacement of the problem onto unacceptable societies with other kinds of social organization" (116). NPNS and the Today's Mariannes exhibit represent a striking illustration of this displacement.

Covering the façade of the Palais Bourbon, the fourteen photographs of the new Mariannes symbolically affirmed the republic's commitment to sexual liberty and equality, although inside the National Assembly—behind the façade—those commitments have never quite materialized. The National Assembly remains mostly male and almost completely white. While the 2000 parity (parité) law has increased women's participation in politics, its effects have mostly been at the local level; a gender gap persists in the National Assembly and Senate. Moreover, sexism in the halls of political power, ranging from the glass ceiling to sexual harassment and sexual violence, remains a major problem for female politicians and staff members, epitomized by the catcalls directed at cabinet minister Cécile Duflot by male legislators as she spoke in the National Assembly in 2012.

But the presence of these new Mariannes not only displaces the tension between sexual difference and universal equality, it also diffuses that tension. The contradiction between difference and equality in relation to the problem of sex is both displaced onto the alterity of Islam and temporarily worked out through the production of secular Muslim women. Ostensibly emancipated by laïcité, these secular Muslim women become its alibi. They smooth out the troubled relationship between sexual difference and gender equality through their neofeminism—which posits sexual difference *as* gender equality—and underscore the universality of republican secularism through the particular heterofemininity they inhabit. What is especially significant about NPNS, and the republican ideology that the organization reflects and reproduces, is how sexual difference, and the particularity that women are thought to embody by the very materiality of their sexed bodies, has become the grounds for claims to universality. This development marks a new moment in republicanism's engagement with the problem of sexual difference. The parité movement, which claimed the universal subject as sexed, as male and female, already comprises one reconfiguration (J. Scott 2005). Neofeminism extends the logic of parité in a different direction, positing a set of moral, social, and aesthetic norms as universally integral to the second sex. If the logic of parité maintains the possibility of abstraction, neofeminism does not: the materiality of sexual difference corresponds to the differences between femininity and masculinity. Where paritaristes split gender and sex, neofeminists collapse gender into sex once again.

Republicanism (and liberalism more generally) has long identified masculinity with the universal and femininity with the particular, hence the problem of conceiving of women—once known simply as "the sex"—as abstract political citizens. Hence, too, the series of gendered distinctions—between public and private, reason and passion, and politics and religion—that have come to anchor liberal democracy. "When reason becomes the defining attribute of the citizen and when abstraction enables the interchangeability of one individual citizen for another, passion gets assigned . . . to the sexualized body of the woman," writes Scott (2011a, 95). Men take their places as equal citizens in the public sphere of politics while women are confined to the domestic sphere, their appearance in the public sphere signaling sexual and political disorder. At the same time, men's own "existence as sexual beings is at once secured in relation to women and displaced onto them" (97; see also Surkis 2006). Thus, as Scott points out, the public-private distinction so crucial to laïcité and to its normative organization of religious life rests on a prior arrangement of masculine and feminine, one that consistently figures women as the site of difference in relation to the abstract universality of men qua citizens.

It is ironic, then, that women's essential sexual difference has become the sign of secularism's universality and that sexual difference, embraced now as the emancipatory taking up of one's natural femininity, has come to manage the tension between universal and particular that is integral to secularism. Like republicanism, secularism claims itself as universally normative, as the best political arrangement for guaranteeing democracy, equality, freedom, and so forth. At the same time, secularism also claims to be culturally particular; emerging out of a specific Christian history and imbued with specific commitments to sexual equality and liberty, it defines the West against various civilizational Others. Secular Muslim women enact the working out and deferral of this tension within both republicanism and secularism. If femininity has historically been the site of the particular in the republican tradition, now, as republicanism intertwines itself with sexularism, femininity does a different kind of work. Recall that colonial-era évolués were largely men of color; though brown women's bodies were the ground on which claims to civilization and barbarism were adjudicated, brown women were never considered possible citizens themselves. Rather, individual Arab and African men proved their exceptionality, their potential to be abstracted from their race or religion, through their attitudes toward native women, the latter always configured as an indistinguishable group.

The new évoluées are, significantly, individual women, and their exceptionality and assimilability reside precisely in their embodied sexual difference.[23] Even as sex and gender norms have come to signal the particularity of European secularism, secular Muslim women's embrace of those norms nonetheless reaffirms secularity—and its normative sexuality—as the site of the universal. That embrace also serves to diffuse republican racism (republicanism's cultural form) by underscoring the possibility that subjects of difference—namely, Arab Muslims—can transcend their particularity to become bona fide abstract citizens, thereby confirming the universality, or at least the universalizability, of republican citizenship. Women like Amara, Méliane, and Djavann, exemplars of republican integration and paradigmatic secular subjects, manage the tension between universal and particular that underlies republicanism's and secularism's self-narratives of universality. It is for this reason that secular Muslim women in particular, rather than non-Muslim women or secular Muslim men, have emerged as the new avatars of secular-republican values.

The Necessary Traces of Difference

The question remains, of course, whether the deferral of the universal-particular dilemma, and attendant attempts to include secular Muslim women in the nation, entails the successful erasure of these women's particular racial, cultural, or religious difference. Can a few paradigmatic foreigners, to use Kristeva's terms, actually be transformed into abstract French citizens? Can exemplary figures like Amara ever transcend their difference to become truly universal republican citizens?

Consider again the *Mariannes* exhibit, which drew those fourteen young women from the march into the republic's fold, presenting them as modern exemplars of Marianne. The mainstream press and politicians nevertheless insisted on identifying these young women not simply as Mariannes, but as *Mariannes black-blanc-beur* (black-white-Beur Mariannes), and on emphasizing that they were housing project girls (*filles de cité*) from the immigrant suburbs (*issues des banlieues*). The consistent racialization of these women at the moment of their celebration as citizens underscores the extent to which they are, like their exceptional nineteenth-century predecessors, effects of the dual universalizing and particularizing imperatives of republicanism that place subjects of difference in what Catherine Raissiguier (2008) and Wilder (2007) call an impossible predicament: they must, yet they cannot, assimilate.

I would go further: this impossible predicament is not only generated by republicanism's dual imperatives, but it also sustains and performs the universalism of republicanism, as well as of secularism. Today's Mariannes are, like Amara, paradigmatic subjects symbolizing the universality of secular-republican citizenship, exemplary figures who have apparently transcended their communal origins and their Muslim immigrant difference. But, paradoxically, the universal citizenship that they represent depends on the concurrent production, erasure, and reproduction of commensurable forms of difference, since it is precisely the existence of such a difference that makes its erasure meaningful. It is only by marking the new Mariannes' difference—their race, religion, and immigrant origins—from the purportedly universal norm that their adherence to this norm makes any sense as a narrative of transcendence to universality. As representations of secular-republican citizenship's universal promise, women like Amara and her fellow marchers must be simultaneously similar and different, for it is the moment of transition from difference to nondifference that performs universality. The process of erasure must leave a trace so we can know that erasure has occurred. These women's difference must be overcome in order to fulfill citizenship's universal promise, but in fact it cannot ever be overcome: the universality of secular-republican citizenship depends on that moment of transition, which depends in turn on the coexistence of difference and nondifference.

Like colonial mimic men, then, these exceptional citizens are full not only of promise but also of menace, for they reveal the contingency of secularism's and republicanism's claims to universality. The colonial strategy of mimicry, writes Homi Bhabha, aimed to create "a reformed, recognizable Other, as *a subject of a difference that is almost the same, but not quite*" (1994, 126 [emphasis in original]). However, the project of mimicry, of creating English Indians or Arab évolués, contained within itself an immanent threat to the transformative force of colonial power, for "to be Anglicized [was] *emphatically* not to be English" (128 [emphasis in original]). The fact that colonial subjects could only ever be "not quite" fundamentally ruptured the progress narrative of the civilizing mission from within: mimicry "quite simply mocks its power [the power of French republicanism or English liberalism] to be a model, that power which supposedly makes it imitable" (128). The power to which Bhabha refers is the universalism of the colonial project, articulated variously as republicanism, liberalism, and Christianity. The raison d'être of the transformative logic that underpinned the colonial project, and that continues to underpin contemporary republicanism and the French model of integration, lies precisely in its claims to universality. Yet the difference that cannot be abstracted from exceptional figures like Amara, a difference necessary to underscore the transformative potential of republicanism and secularism and required for the assertion of universality, is at the same time the difference that destabilizes and renders contingent those very claims to universality. The unabstractability of Amara's

Muslim difference makes a mockery of secular-republican citizenship. It reveals the fact that the impossibility of exceptional citizens' impossible predicament is actually an effect of the impossible universalism—and thus the contingency—of secular republicanism and republican secularism.

That impossibility of abstraction is reflected in the interpellation of Amara as a secular Muslim. As much as she is celebrated as a model of integration and as a paradigmatic secular-republican citizen who has cast aside her particular identity to embody (I use that term purposefully) the abstract universalism of secular-republican citizenship, she is consistently demarcated by terms that signal her bodily and civilizational difference. The same politicians, journalists, and public intellectuals who laud her as a model citizen usually refer to her with supplementary terms like *beurrette* (politically acceptable slang for second-generation Arab woman), *fille d'immigrés algériens* (daughter of Algerian immigrants), *d'origine immigrée* (of immigrant origin), and *d'origine maghrébine* (of Maghrebi origin). Even the term secular Muslim, or *musulmane laïque*—though suggesting a distinction between commensurably secular and incommensurably nonsecular Muslims—actually underscores Amara's difference. She is not secular like other secular French, who do not require supplementary qualifiers, precisely because she remains intractably Muslim. Hence the position in which secular Muslims like Fadela Amara find themselves: ostensibly abstracted into universal secularity—secular—yet consistently racialized as particular—Muslim.

To fully grasp France's Muslim question in all its complexity, therefore, requires attending in tandem to the intertwined processes of secularization and racialization, and to these processes' imbrication in and reproduction of sex and gender norms. This allows us to productively analyze how Muslims in France are variously excluded from and included in the secular-national community of citizens. The politicized presence of veiled Muslim and secular Muslim women in the public sphere is not an oppositional occurrence; the two figures are inextricably interlinked effects of the tensions of a secular-republican citizenship that produces and depends on both the incommensurable difference of the veiled woman and the commensurable difference of the unveiled secular Muslim woman. And just like their pious Muslim counterparts, secular Muslim women are caught in the contradictions and tensions of secular republicanism despite themselves. *La musulmane voilée* and *la musulmane laïque* may be positioned as opposites, but only together do they make sense and do their symbolic and ideological work for the secular-republican project.

Six Asymmetries of Tolerance

The excitement at the first meeting of the Feminists for Equality Collective (Collectif Féministes pour l'Egalité, or CFPE) in April 2004 was almost palpable. The women at the table were a motley collection: longtime white and Maghrebi veterans of feminist movements in France, Algeria, Morocco, and Tunisia; younger Franco-Maghrebi members of Palestinian and anti-racist movements; white anarchists and communists; and young Muslim French activists, many veiled and most of them members of Muslim civic associations.

Tensions within the collective soon emerged, however. During a meeting in October 2004, members began to discuss the impending anniversary of abortion's legalization in France. Established feminist organizations like the Coordination of Associations for the Right to Abortion and Contraception and Family Planning were preparing a large demonstration on January 17, 2005, to celebrate the thirtieth anniversary of the 1975 law decriminalizing abortion and to issue a call (*appel*) for better access to abortion and contraception. Many CFPE members who had fought to legalize abortion in the 1970s, and for whom the right to abortion remains a key feminist principle, wanted the collective as a whole to sign the *appel*. Most of the practicing Muslim members were hesitant and wanted to discuss the ethical dilemma of advocating for abortion rights. Reaction to their hesitation was fierce. Many non-Muslims and nonpracticing Muslims in the CFPE accused them of hypocrisy, claiming that since secular feminists in the collective had respected and supported Muslim women's right to wear the headscarf as a fundamental right to choose what to do with one's body, the latter should, in turn, respect and support the right to abortion for the same reason. The issue was not about defending abortion, they contended, but about defending women's right to choose.

Nabila, who had joined the CFPE at its inception and eventually became its president, was one of the hesitators. Born in Argenteuil, a working-class suburb of Paris, she had studied at the Sorbonne and been heavily engaged in associational activism, doing volunteer work with at-risk adolescents. She recounted to me her dilemma, and the drama that had unfolded within the CFPE in late 2004: "The feminists who weren't Muslim said, 'yes, we support you on the question of the headscarf, but are we going to see you demonstrating on the question of abortion?' It was almost a summons: 'we give you this, we're there [for you], what are you going to do [for us] in exchange?'" But Nabila felt torn between her religious community and her feminist colleagues. "After all, with my headscarf," she said, "I represent the Muslim community to a certain extent. I have my own principles, my own position on the question of abortion, but in a demonstration for the right to abortion, my presence might lead others to draw a particular conclusion." Nabila feared that non-Muslims and Muslims alike would read her presence at an abortion rally as representing a general "Muslim position."

Beyond the problem of representation, Nabila and other practicing Muslim women did not feel completely comfortable supporting the unrestricted right to abortion. "The problem," she told me, "is that there are specific conditions for a woman to abort [according to Islamic norms].[1] Abortion in all cases is not possible" to support. Yet Nabila found the debate in the collective framed as a seemingly simple question: "'Are you for or against [the right to abortion]?' But we couldn't answer that question without thinking it over!" Nabila described the pressure she felt to decide, and quickly, even as she felt incapable of doing so without more reading, discussing, and reflecting with others. She also noted that she and many of her Muslim colleagues had never really talked about abortion. All the practicing Muslim women in the group recognized the logic of the secular feminists' argument that since the latter had supported the right to veil without defending the veil itself (which a number of them still find troubling), Muslim women should support the right to abortion even if they are ethically opposed to the practice. Nonetheless, many of the practicing Muslim members of the CFPE felt trapped (piégé), a predicament that others in the collective dismissed as hypocrisy.

A similar argument about reciprocity and hypocrisy occurred in relation to the issue of same-sex marriage. When the question of supporting queer sexualities arose in CFPE meetings, a number of Muslim French felt unsettled by demands to explicitly endorse the right to same-sex marriage. Nabila noted that the insistence on reciprocity came not from the Pink Panthers or the Furieuses Fallopes, two radical queer collectives, but from what she called classical feminists inside and outside the collective. As we talked, it became evident that homosexuality was a difficult issue for Nabila. "You don't touch the fundamental rights of gays and lesbians, the right to legal residence, the right to work—we are at their side on that," she said. The right to marriage was trickier: "I have a really good friend who's queer, we see each other all the time, we argue, we love each other. I would never want her to be hurt . . ." Nabila trailed off, and when she continued, her speech was full of hesitations: "But the right to marry, it's a subject that is [pause] rather more complex. [Pause.] I mean, you shouldn't stop people from [pause] building a life, living together." She paused again, then said, "I don't know. I simply don't know."

Our conversation clearly discomfited Nabila, not necessarily because we were talking about homosexuality but, I think, because she associated me with her secular feminist colleagues and felt she had to justify herself to me. Though I demanded nothing explicitly, Nabila correctly recognized the representational burden she carries as a Muslim. I had talked previously about this burden with Amira, another member of the CFPE, and I later learned that though she was initially very active in the collective, she and a few other Muslim French women eventually left it because of other members' inability to understand the dilemmas and impasses that practicing Muslims faced. When we discussed the matters of reciprocity and hypocrisy with regard to same-sex marriage, Amira observed: "It will be yet another test: they single you out for the headscarf, you are summoned to respond. Now, they single you out for this, and you are ordered to respond."

This chapter explores the nature of the summons both Nabila and Amira invoke, analyzing the ethical and political predicament Muslim French women like them face within a dominant French and European discourse about homosexuality, homophobia, and Islam. Over the past decade, the treatment of gays and lesbians has become a defining feature of the "clash of civilizations" discourse, a way of distinguishing the progressive West from the backward rest, and especially from Muslim societies. In Europe, Muslim immigrants' intolerance—their presumed homophobia, anti-Semitism,[2] and misogyny—has increasingly justified the political, cultural, and physical exclusion of Muslims as proper citizen subjects. The subtitle of the 2004 Manifesto of Liberties discussed in Field Notes III—"Being of Muslim Culture and against Misogyny, Homophobia, Anti-Semitism, and Political Islam" ("Manifeste des libertés" 2004)—reveals how Muslims are compelled, or summoned, to prove their secularity, modernity, and commensurability by denouncing the triumvirate of intolerance attributed to Islam. The ostensible bigotry of Muslim immigrants and their children has led politicians and pundits across the European political spectrum to claim that liberal Europe has tolerated Muslim intolerance for too long. The 2004 murder of the Dutch filmmaker Theo van Gogh by a Dutchman of Moroccan descent reinforced many European (and American) commentators' sense that multicultural tolerance was destroying purported European values like freedom, individuality, equality, and tolerance—and the very fabric of Europe—by allowing Muslim intolerance to exist.

After the van Gogh murder, the Franco-German television show *Le forum des Européens* (Forum of Europeans) ran a January 2005 episode titled "Radical Islam: What to Do?" ("Islam radical" 2005). A segment on the murder and the rise of radical Islam in Holland asked: "Tolerance—has it become too permissive?" Bruce Bawer, a conservative gay American living in Norway and an active critic of multicultural policies in Europe, published a *New York Times* op-ed titled "Tolerant Dutch Wrestle with Tolerating Intolerance," asking: "By tolerating Muslim intolerance of Western society, [is] the Netherlands setting itself on a path toward cataclysmic social confrontation?" (2004). In another op-ed, called "Why Tolerate the Hate?," the self-styled "Muslim refusnik" Irshad Manji wrote: "Neither the watery word 'tolerance' nor the slippery phrase 'mutual respect' will cut it as a guiding value. Why tolerate violent bigotry?" Manji added: "The ultimate paradox may be that in order to defend our diversity, we'll need to be less tolerant" (2005).

These liberal critics ask why Europeans should tolerate Muslims when the latter are intolerant of the liberal-democratic values that presumably define Europe. In France, where tolerance is glossed as *respect de l'autre* (respect for others), center Right politician Nadine Morano elaborated the flip side of this discourse: Muslims will be tolerated only when they prove themselves tolerant. Morano explained: "We must respect the other as soon as he respects the law, as soon as he respects the terms of his entry into France . . . [and] he accepts our traditions."[3] Morano and Manji thereby invoke one of the great paradoxes of the liberal ethic of tolerance—namely, the intolerance of intolerance in the name of tolerance. Within the liberal-democratic tradition, tolerance reaches its limit at intolerance, at which point the ethical commitment to tolerate can, and even must, be abrogated to preserve the value of tolerance itself.

In what follows I take up how this paradoxical logic of tolerance interpellates Muslim minorities in Europe, and in France specifically, focusing on claims of Muslim homophobia.[4] I do not intend to dispute or justify the existence of illiberal Muslim beliefs and practices, including homophobia; I wish instead to examine the political and cultural work done by the logic of tolerance, and to inquire into its immanent tensions and paradoxes. Late liberalism's complicated relationship with its queer and Muslim subjects has been the site of recent theorizing (Massad 2002; Arondekar 2005; Puar 2007; Butler 2008). Most scholars rightly regard the liberal state's embrace of certain queer subjects and the emergence of homonormative (Duggan 2004) and homonationalist (Puar 2007) ideologies, on the one hand, and the production of Muslims as irrevocably homophobic, on the other hand, as twinned processes. These processes, scholars argue, sustain and reproduce heteronormative kinship, racial, sexual, and gender norms across national and transnational borders. This chapter both overlaps with and expands such theorizing, focusing on how the secular-liberal imperatives of tolerance and *respect de l'autre*, despite their immanent contradictions, secure Europe and France as unified entities. I analyze how Muslims in France are summoned to be tolerant, respectful subjects, and how their apparent inability to comply renders them illegitimate as French or European citizens. I also explore how the impasse that women like Nabila and Amira reach actually replays a tension underlying the secular imperative of tolerance between the simultaneous commitments to procedural reason and to deeply held ethical and affective norms—a tension that is ultimately displaced, I argue, onto Muslims. Although previous chapters have focused on Muslim minorities in France, this chapter takes up the question of Islam in Europe, and therefore the question of Europe itself. And though I conducted ethnographic research for this chapter before the recent legalization of same-sex marriage in France, the questions that the research raised remain pertinent.

Unmanageable Tensions

Amira, already active in the Rennes-based association al-Houda, joined the CFPE after hearing about it at a Paris meeting of the One School for All Collective. She found intriguing the idea of gathering different kinds of women in solidarity and debate, and she was excited to discuss with other feminists issues like the reproduction of norms and the definition of freedom. She also looked forward to thinking more about her own relationship to Islam, which she had been doing already in al-Houda. Preternaturally intelligent and articulate for her age (eighteen at the time), she was elected vice president of the CFPE, and she returned to Rennes to enroll her colleagues from al-Houda in the group too. Al-Houda comprised practicing Muslim women of different backgrounds and ages. Its members met on a regular basis to study Islam; they also joined with other associations to defend the rights of illegal immigrants and battered women, and they worked with mosques on charity efforts like providing meals to the poor and homeless. Once when I visited her in Rennes, Amira took me to a daylong occupation of an asylum shelter to prevent police from deporting a Bosnian couple. Two other members of al-Houda—Amal and Suzanne, Amira's sister and best friend—joined us, along with five white French activists.

A few days later, al-Houda met as a group to discuss whether to join the CFPE. Monique, a white convert in her late thirties, hosted us in her home. During the meeting, her Algerian husband tended the garden and occasionally checked on the stew that was cooking in the kitchen. The couple's two children played as we sat in the living room. Amira began the conversation by noting that the new association's name was *Collectif Féministes pour l'Egalité* rather than *Collectif Féministe*—the Collective of Feminists for Equality rather than the Feminist Collective for Equality—signaling its commitment to a plural rather than unitary feminism. Amira next read out the collective's founding charter, which included, among other objectives, "to fight against the discriminations suffered by women and for the equality of rights; to refuse the idea of a single model of liberation and emancipation for women . . . [and] to fight for the emancipation of women by respecting their political, social, religious, and sexual choices." She then opened the floor to debate. Amal wanted to know why the label *feminists* and not simply *women* was used. Irène, a soft-spoken white convert in her late twenties, asked: "Do we really have that much in common with feminists, especially given the history of feminists in France?" She was alluding to the tradition of mainstream secular feminism that, suspicious of religious normativity, has been very critical of Islamic revivalism. Amira responded that although mainstream feminists' reaction to the headscarf was certainly a problem, "I don't think we should spit on the entire feminist movement in France." Hélène, a social worker of Guadeloupian descent in her mid-twenties, added that it was important to realize that, "like all movements, there is no one way of thinking for all feminists." After more animated discussion about the history of feminism in France and whether it was inherently anti-religious, Amira asked Amal for her definition of feminism. Amal was hesitant: "I don't know, maybe I need to read more, but for me, it's the fight for homosexuality, the fight for abortion." Hélène responded that feminism was not a fight *for* homosexuality, but she allowed that "it's true, it's an important question, because if you read some e-mails from the [CFPE], there's the question of homosexuality that certain members claim." A woman named Zainab then said: "You see, refusing the idea of a single model of liberation and emancipation of women, okay, I agree. But what does that phrase *mean*? It means accepting all models!" "Of course!," retorted Monique. "Of course! We cannot want others to accept our model without accepting the model of others." "But hang on," replied Zainab, "you can't accept *everything*." The meeting ended with an agreement to table temporarily any decision to join the CFPE, but members were free to join individually.

After the meeting, we spoke more informally about homosexuality, which, according to all of the women, the *Quran* forbids. However, as Amira pointed out, there is no unanimous position on how to treat gays and lesbians: "Homosexuality is considered a sin, and as a Muslim, you impose on yourself the discipline not to be gay.[5] But that doesn't mean that the person in front of you who's gay, that you lack respect for him or try to take away his freedom." As we spoke about the rights of gays and lesbians, we returned repeatedly to the question of the limits of respect and tolerance. Irène best articulated the dilemma for these women: "When you are very open toward non-Muslims, sometimes you no longer find yourself in your own values. We are obliged to be open to the world, because it's unhealthy to live otherwise, enclosed. But we are at the same time obliged to return to the sources. . . . There are limits one cannot cross. For example, we spoke about homosexuality. You cannot tell me I am *for* homosexuality, that isn't possible. [Pause.] Obviously there is much thinking to do. But it's clear that for me, defending homosexuality is inconceivable."

A few months later, Amira, who had enthusiastically defended the CFPE and its charter during the al-Houda meeting in Rennes, found herself facing Irène's dilemma when the celebration of legalized abortion arose. Amira attended the January 2005 demonstration, though she noted later: "Had I not been a part of Feminists for Equality, I would never have been there. It's not that I didn't consider it [abortion] a right, but in my situation and my communal context, it's something that isn't even debated." As Amira observed, most Islamic scholars hold that abortion is permitted under certain conditions, such as when a woman's life is in danger, or when a serious deformity makes the fetus unviable. She continued: "There isn't a dogmatic position, it's not a matter of sacrilege in Islam. . . . But the rule is the right to life. The exception is the right to abortion." Amira therefore had to think very seriously about supporting the unrestricted right to abortion. Yet for many feminists in the collective, "the right to abortion, it's a historic right, it's part of the paradigm of French feminism, it's unavoidable." Amira understood and respected this ethical position, but she nonetheless lamented the way the abortion question had unfolded in the CFPE, and particularly how the ethical dilemmas of practicing Muslims were never entirely addressed: "I think the Muslim women just wanted to leave aside this debate. They kind of said to themselves, 'it's better that we don't have this debate because [the secular feminists] are going to realize that we don't have the same positions.' And I think the non-Muslims took [the issue of abortion] for granted. So there was no basic dialogue on this question. Look, it's not a problem in itself if we're not in agreement. But we have to discuss it. We have to know where each of us stands in this conversation." Amira felt that, instead of having a frank discussion about the bases for their position, and the ethical and political stakes involved for the collective's various components, Muslim women were silenced, even if unintentionally.

Partly as a result of the abortion controversy, Amira left the collective a year after she joined, and after asking herself a series of questions: "'Why I am participating? What is my priority? Is it my community? Am I participating freely or I am ceding to pressure? Am I being a feminist the way I want to be, or I am being a feminist the way others want me to be?' Because, on the one hand, I had found allies in a very difficult context [the 2002–4 headscarf debate], and I didn't want to lose them. But at the same time, I didn't want to spend my life justifying myself on a whole series of subjects." After leaving the collective, she and the other members of al-Houda spent two years in what Amira called "a spiritual and communal retreat [un repli communautaire, spirituel]." They stopped working with non-Muslim associations, focused entirely on local activities, and got back in touch with fellow Muslims from the Rennes community. It was, Amira said, "a period of recentering within the community," a process she found reenergizing, enabling her eventually not only to work with non-Muslim partners but also to pursue a PhD at the prestigious School for Advanced Studies in the Social Sciences (École des Hautes Études en Sciences Sociale) in Paris. By referring to this period as a repli communautaire, Amira resignified and valorized what is otherwise a highly negative term in French public discourse, portraying her communal withdrawal as precisely what allowed her to reemerge into the public sphere and work with non-Muslims. Looking back, she observed:

> Of course I want us to fight together, to be in diverse engagements together. But in terms of practice, to manage all this, to be in a situation where I can say what I really think, I need to have my communal anchoring. . . . It's important that I and my community develop interpretations of Islam that are not sexist or rigid. And that isn't easy. It's a lot of work. And if I'm constantly confronted with the fact that I'm in a collective with non-Muslims, participating in debates that seemingly have nothing to do with Islam, then I'm always going to be on the defensive, and it's unmanageable. There are tensions that are unmanageable.

Echoing Irène's earlier rumination on the risks of unexpected partnerships, Amira remarked, "When you have one foot within your own community, and one foot outside, it's really very difficult."

The dilemmas of working with others and of the limits of respect extended beyond the women of al-Houda. Though Muslim French are routinely accused of being intolerant communautaristes, I was struck by how often the term respect came up in conversations with my Muslim French interlocutors. For instance, the discourse of respect de l'autre undergirded much of the criticism of the 2004 headscarf law. Younès[6] and I were sitting in a small café in Saint Denis one day. Dressed in his usual slacks and slightly rumpled sweater, he was sipping orange juice and gesticulating as he spoke. He argued that certain principles are universal—namely, "justice, respect de l'autre, alterity." "You know," he said, "I'm not trying to say that the National Assembly should become the National Assembly of Muslims, I'm not trying to say we should remove the president and install a caliph. . . . I'm just saying, very simply, that one must respect my identity. My identity, whatever it is. I'm not going to make war on the atheist. The Buddhist, the Catholic, the Jew, the Protestant—each has the freedom to believe." He went on, pounding on the table for emphasis: "In what name am I going to deny you your difference? I don't have the right to deny another's existence. I don't have the right to lack respect for someone—in what name?!" With this, Younès implicitly invoked the reasoning behind Muslim French criticism of the 2004 law—that if a girl chooses freely to wear a headscarf, what right does the state, or anyone else, have to deny her that choice? As Younès demanded incredulously, "in what name are you going to impose something that goes against the freedom of a person to choose?"

Respect de l'autre is therefore an important political concept in the defense of Muslim beliefs and practices that differ from dominant French norms. Although many republican politicians and intellectuals tend to represent Muslim demands as part of a separatist effort to create differential rights and obligations for Muslims, most Muslims use the language of tolerance, respect for diversity, and respect for autonomous individuals' choices. Moreover, Muslim French understand respect for diversity as a universal value, exemplified by the fact that the principle of respecting human differences exists in many traditions, including Islam. In discussing their commitment to diversity and *respect de l'autre*, many Muslim French would ask me, rhetorically, why God would create different kinds of people if not to bring them together to know each other.[7] Differences between humans, they argued, are divinely ordained, and their respect for human diversity constitutes part of their respect for God's creation. As noted in chapter 2, Younès drew on the example of the Prophet to underscore Islam's ostensible commitment to diversity: "In the time of the Prophet there were pagans, Zoroastrians, there were Christians, there were Jews . . . and [the Prophet] respected them and welcomed them and spoke with them." He added that it was against his Muslim principles to deny human diversity. For Muslim French, the Islamic recognition and valorization of heterogeneity proved that Islamic and republican ethical imperatives are not merely compatible but ultimately the same.

The imperative to respect differences and individual life choices is not simply a way to make a case for Muslims' rights, however; the obligation of *respect de l'autre* holds for Muslim French as well in their treatment of others. Many Muslim French are adamant not only that veiling must be willingly undertaken, but also that unveiled women deserve the same respect as veiled women. Moreover, different forms of veiling are equally worthy of respect if the wearer is fulfilling her own desire. Recall Nawel's response (in chapter 4) when I asked her why she didn't wear the niqab: "The niqab, it's not my thing, although I respect the girls who wear it, just as I respect those girls who don't wear anything [to cover their hair]." As for Amira, she found the niqab impractical in social interactions, and she argued that neither the Quran nor the Sunna prohibits a woman from showing her hands, face, and bodily extremities. She also noted that in France, wearing the niqab is contradictory to its original purpose of modesty, since it actually attracts attention. She then added: "But I think it's really a spiritual undertaking for [niqab wearers]. And I respect it, truly. I respect those girls who wear it, because it's truly their choice and their vision of things." Although Amira found niqab wearers' interpretation of the sources incorrect, she nonetheless respected their beliefs and practices if they were arrived at autonomously.

Given the imbrication of Muslim French in dominant ideologies that celebrate the primacy of individual autonomy, it is unsurprising that *respect de l'autre* has become a deep ethical and political commitment for them. And the obligation to respect and the obligation to work for justice—Younès's two universal principles—lead a number of Muslim French to participate in various progressive social justice movements, often alongside non-Muslims who may share their social justice goals but nonetheless lead very different social and sexual lives. In the course of this civic engagement, the obligation to respect other people's life choices sometimes runs into other, competing obligations that test the limits of the ethical and political principle of respect. Thus the difficulty some members of al-Houda experienced with the CFPE's charter. Irène, Zainab, and Amal were clearly uncomfortable with the implications of the collective's broad commitment to respect women's choices, which entailed respecting sexual choices they could not agree with. They supported the idea of refusing a single model of women's emancipation, but they immediately saw that grounding this refusal of singularity in the principle of *respect de l'autre* meant accepting all kinds of choices and sexual modes of being, including same-sex intimacy. And as Irène put it, "there are limits one cannot cross. . . . You cannot tell me I am *for* homosexuality." Yet the ellipses and pauses in Irène's monologue, and her own acknowledgment that "obviously there is much thinking to do," suggest that as much as "defending homosexuality" made her uncomfortable, so did the refusal to respect gays and lesbians. Irène's arrival at this impasse between the imperative to respect others' sexual choices and a set of moral norms that disapprove of certain sexual practices clearly distressed her, for she recognized her own hypocrisy. And Irène's predicament—the arrival at this impasse and the concomitant recognition of one's hypocrisy—is not exceptional. Amira once recounted her experiences in the CFPE and the quid pro quo expected: "I remember having this conversation at the beginning with an activist who said to me, 'I protested with you all on the question of the veil, and I am waiting for you [Muslim women] to protest with me on the question of homosexuality.'" And, Amira added, "in their logic, it makes perfect sense! Within this way of seeing things, it's a completely logical demand!"

That demand took on national dimensions when Noël Mamère, then mayor of Bègles and a prominent member of the Green Party, married Bertrand Charpentier and Stephane Chapin in the first same-sex civil marriage in

France, which was illegal at the time. The Green Party had made same-sex marriage a prominent part of their election campaign. It had also consistently supported the right to wear headscarves in public school and was the only party to vote almost unanimously against the 2004 law. The Greens therefore asked their progressive Muslim colleagues to support the cause of same-sex marriage in the name of respecting individual rights and freedoms. Many Greens argued that since they had supported Muslim women's right to wear the headscarf even though they may have disapproved of veiling, Muslims should support the right of gays and lesbians to marry even if they disapproved of homosexuality. The Green Party's arguments were not unreasonable; as Monique of al-Houda pointed out, Muslims cannot expect others to accept and respect their ways of life without accepting and respecting others' identities and choices.

Many critics seized on the inability of Muslims to resolve this problem as a sign of hypocrisy or, more ominously, of a conscious Muslim double talk that uses liberalism's tools to further an illiberal agenda. In a 2005 interview with Tariq Ramadan, the journalist Aziz Zemouri raised the issue of homosexuality. Ramadan noted that for Islam, like all other religious traditions, "homosexuality does not correspond to the divine command with regard to sexual relations. Thus I do not promote it. That is the general and explicit principle concerning homosexuality. As for my position regarding gays and lesbians, it is clear: I respect them and I respect their choice. I cannot agree with what they do, but I respect who they are" (quoted in Zemouri 2005). Zemouri then invoked the Bègles marriage. Mamère and the Greens voted against the law banning headscarves, Zemouri reminded Ramadan: "However, when [Mamère] tried to promote individual liberty by organizing a gay marriage, he didn't find the same support" among his Muslim colleagues. "Mamère and his supporters felt they were advancing individual liberty," Zemouri continued, adding: "Does your partnership only extend in one direction?" Ramadan replied that the two issues were quite different; one concerned negative liberty and the other positive liberty.[8] "In the case of the law on religious signs," he observed, "it was about restricting in a discriminatory fashion the exercise of individual liberty," while gay marriage promotes new liberties through the enactment of a new law.

Ramadan, like his Muslim audience, attempts to navigate the reciprocity demanded by *respect de l'autre*. Having grounded their claims to a minority Muslim identity in the imperative of *respect de l'autre*, Muslim French are called on to follow that imperative to its logical conclusion. Many critics read their subsequent impasse as pure hypocrisy, since they demand respect for their own nonnormative beliefs and practices in the name of individual liberty yet are intolerant of gay and lesbian ways of life. Hence the question: have secular-liberal foolishly Europeans tolerated intolerant and illiberal Muslims and, in so doing, jeopardized the liberal values of tolerance and respect, and thus the very core of Europe itself? Hence, too, the solution: secular-liberal Europeans must not tolerate (always already intolerant) Muslims unless and until they have proven themselves tolerant—that is, secular and liberal.

But that question and its solution elide the fact that Irène's impasse is actually internal to liberalism. Indeed, the very structure of her reasoning, and of Ramadan's as well, is eminently liberal. Recall Irène's feeling of being caught between two competing obligations: to be open to the world, as she said, and to follow Islamic traditions that condemn the practice of homosexuality. It is easy to dismiss her problem as one of simple Muslim intolerance or too fundamentalist an approach to textual sources. But Irène's difficulty in respecting and accepting homosexuality replays one of the nagging questions of liberalism: what are the limits of tolerance and *respect de l'autre*? Irène's worry—that when you are open to the world, you sometimes lose yourself and your own values—echoes the philosopher Charles Taylor's statement that "there are substantial numbers of people who are citizens and also belong to [a] culture that calls into question our philosophical boundaries. The challenge is to deal with their sense of marginalization without compromising our basic principles" (1994, 63). Or, as Zainab put it in Rennes, "You can't accept *everything*."

In other words, Irène's dilemma emerges precisely because Muslim French like her adopt and redeploy the liberal logic of tolerance and *respect de l'autre* to make a case for the acceptance of their minority beliefs and practices. In so doing, they reproduce an impasse central to that logic between the obligation to respect individuals' autonomy (their agency and their choices) and the obligation to moral norms, what Taylor calls "our basic principles." Elizabeth Povinelli glosses the late-liberal iteration of this problem as the impasse between the obligation to public reason—the sense that one arrives at a shared understanding through rational argument—and the obligation to moral sense.[9] In a multicultural context, this translates into an impasse between the simultaneous obligations "to value diversity and to repudiate immorality" (2002, 4). As Povinelli observes, "when people have moral obligations, they seem to have them independent of the way they arrive at critical rational conclusions. People seem to be had by them rather than to have them. In the procedural ideal of critical rational discourse, reasoned public debate occurs prior to a judgment. . . . But moral sensibility works as an a priori type of 'knowledge'" (9). Although these two obligations are ultimately supposed to coincide for liberals, moral sense is precisely not subject to public reason and debate (236). This may explain why Amal and Irène fell silent when Monique told them their moral position was illogical.

Within liberalism, the limits of tolerance are breached at two procedural junctures: when actions are not the result of autonomous agency, or when actions harm another person (Nicholson 1985; Weale 1985). Thus the limits of tolerance should be—and, liberal theorists argue, can be—determined on procedural rather than substantive moral grounds, on the basis of right rather than good (Rawls 1971). When reading liberal political philosophers writing in defense of cultural tolerance or *respect de l'autre*, however, one is struck by the ever-present, self-explanatory category of the intolerable. Tolerance based on respect for individual autonomy goes only so far. There are always limits, and they are obvious to legitimate members of the national, moral community. Take the example of female genital cutting (FGC).[10] If one were to follow the procedural logic of liberalism, in which respect for cultural difference is based on respect for individual autonomy, then as long as adults consent consciously to cutting, there should be no cause for interdiction of the practice. The same applies to polygamy, face veiling, the immolation of widows, and a host of other practices that transgress North Atlantic sensibilities. Yet for many liberals, these practices are wrong, even abhorrent. As such, they are not open to rational debate about procedural issues like consent and choice. These practices offend moral sensibilities on a visceral level that is well beyond the reach of reason. And if consent for these practices is really not the result of social pressure—liberalism's escape hatch from the intractability of the impasse between procedural reason and moral sense—then there is surely something deeply wrong with the practitioners.

Consider the liberal philosopher Michael Walzer's treatment of female genital cutting and attempts by France to criminalize it. Responding to an anticriminalization petition, Walzer writes:

> As with the suttee [widow immolation], it is important to get the description right: clitoridectomy and infibulations "are comparable . . . not to the removal of the foreskin but to the removal of the penis," and it is hard to imagine circumcision in that form being treated as a matter of private choice. In any case, the infant girls are not volunteers. . . . Toleration surely should not extend to ritual mutilation, any more than it does to ritual suicide. . . . In other sorts of cases, where the moral

values of the larger community—the national majority or the coalition of minorities—are not so directly challenged, the excuse of religious or cultural difference (and "private choice") may be accepted, diversity respected, and nonstandard gender practices tolerated. (1997, 63)

Walzer's comments could be mined in many different ways, but let me focus on the interplay between his commitment to the procedural principle of autonomous individual choice and his clear moral revulsion at the practice of genital cutting. The petition in defense of FGC makes an argument about private choice that Walzer is compelled to engage. Yet he simultaneously engages the argument and dismisses it in the same breath. "It is important to get the description right," he tells us, noting that FGC is tantamount to the removal not of the foreskin of the penis but of the penis itself, and "it is hard to imagine circumcision in that form" being treated as a matter of choice, let alone a choice that anybody in his or her right mind would make. Interestingly, Walzer is adamant that we must "get the description [of FGC] right," but he offers no reasons why one might cut one's daughter or undertake the practice oneself. Walzer's argument here pertains to affect, not reason. After stirring up our moral revulsion at such a practice, Walzer reverts to procedural arguments, noting: "In any case, the infant girls are not volunteers." "In any case" defers the tricky moral questions raised by voluntary genital cutting. We do not have to deal with these questions, Walzer says, because this practice is not voluntary and therefore is intolerable. But the placement of "in any case" is telling: it comes between Walzer's exposition on the horror of FGC and his statement that "toleration surely should not extend" to this kind of "ritual mutilation." "In any case" is an afterthought, a nod to the procedural in the midst of an affective appeal to majority notions of the moral good. The word surely summons an existing moral community to recoil in horror and then bring down its righteous condemnation on "ritual mutilation." As Walzer himself notes later, the case of female genital cutting directly challenges the moral values of the liberal majority community, values that must be protected from the procedural framework of rational critical debate. Walzer here experiences an impasse between his commitment to tolerance based on procedural claims of individual autonomy and his visceral attachment to certain moral norms; ultimately, he rejects the former for the latter.

In another consideration of cultural difference, Alain Touraine restages Walzer's suspension of procedural reason. Un nouveau paradigme: Pour comprendre le monde aujourd'hui (A new paradigm: Understanding the world today) attempts to delineate the limits of cultural pluralism in what Touraine terms a postsocial modernity based on *respect de l'autre*. A political sociologist and public intellectual who served on the Stasi Commission, Touraine has long represented a faction of republicanism that sees itself as open to difference, and he calls for the respect and recognition of cultural rights, within limits: "Concretely, we can only recognize cultural rights on the condition that [others] accept our fundamental principles, that is to say, belief in rational thought and the affirmation of personal rights on which no society and no state has the right to infringe" (2005, 295–96). Touraine never explains what he means by "belief in rational thought," nor does he define the personal rights (*droits personnels*) that all must accept. But he does make explicit what "we" cannot tolerate or respect: "Must we 'understand' the stoning of unfaithful women, arranged marriages, or female genital cutting? No, of course not [Non, *bien sûr*], despite the declarations of radical cultural relativists" (296–97).

Touraine repeats, using almost the exact phrase, Walzer's rhetorical sleight of hand. Touraine's "of course not" functions in much the same way as Walzer's "surely" by conjuring into being a particular moral community of affect, one that does not need to be told why certain practices are problematic. Touraine thereby invokes the procedural imperative of rational public debate without having to actually partake in it. As a result, he does not have to open himself up to the possibility that practices like FGC, stoning, and arranged marriages might be explainable via rational thought and personal rights. Or that such debate might put into question the rationality of routinely accepted practices in the post-Enlightenment West (for example, permanent punitive incarceration, breast implants, and the genital mutilation of male infants). Instead, when confronted with practices that offend his moral sensibilities, Touraine shuts down reasoned public debate in the very name of rationality and individual rights, masking his affective commitments in the guise of a public reason so obvious that it need not be explained. Like Walzer, Touraine will not submit his affective, moral attachments to critical rational discourse and, when confronted with the impasse between procedural claims and visceral attachments to certain moral sensibilities, he suspends the former with a simple "of course." Touraine's and Walzer's recourse to affect—to disgust—via the invocation of the obvious ("surely," "of course") have their roots in the thought of John Stuart Mill, one of the earliest liberal theorists of individual respect. Near the end of *On Liberty*, Mill reserves the state's right to restrict freely chosen acts that do not directly harm others: "There are many acts which, being directly injurious to the agents themselves, ought not to be legally interdicted, but which, if done publicly, are a violation of good manners and, coming thus within the category of offenses against others, may rightly be prohibited. Of this kind are offenses against decency; *on which it is unnecessary to dwell*" (1978, 97). Mill's commitment to abstract, procedural reason dissolves, just like Walzer's and Touraine's, in the face of threats to the majority's sense of decency.

It turns out, then, that the impasse of al-Houda's members mimics the impasse that plagues liberal theorists like Walzer and Touraine. The structure of the conundrum that Muslim French like Irène and Amira face with regard to homosexuality reproduces a tension immanent to *respect de l'autre* (and tolerance) between the commitment to respect individual choices and the attachment to moral norms. In fully inhabiting certain ethical and political imperatives of republicanism—here, the obligation to respect individual autonomy—Muslim French reproduce its aporias. They ground their claims to identity in the principle of *respect de l'autre*, not because it is politically efficacious but because it makes sense to them ethically. Yet in so doing, they inevitably reach a point at which the commitment to value individual choices must be suspended for another kind of attachment, since respect always has limits. As Zainab, Walzer, and Touraine would agree, you can't accept everything.

Most liberals and republicans, however, understand the Muslim French discovery of that impasse between procedural reason and moral sense as a sign of Muslims' incapacity to be legitimate French (and, more broadly, European) citizens. When Muslims reach this impasse, they are treated as irrational and intolerant, which in turn justifies their exclusion from the moral and political community of Europe. By inhabiting not only the imperative of *respect de l'autre* but also its limits, Muslim French confirm their belonging as French and European and, simultaneously, disqualify themselves from the ethical and political community of France and Europe. In fact, a liberal impasse is explicitly Islamized; rather than signaling Frenchness, it becomes that which makes Muslims not French. And by marking that impasse as a Muslim problem, as a consequence and sign of specifically Muslim intolerance, secular liberals not only displace their own dilemma onto Muslims but also justify the exclusion of Muslims from France and Europe. After all, besides affective judgments that are not subject to public reason, the one practice that can explicitly, legitimately, and reasonably suspend the imperative of tolerance is intolerance itself.

In sum, the Islamization of the impasse integral to *respect de l'autre* effects a triple move. First, in turning a liberal conundrum into a Muslim problem of intolerance, the discourse of Muslim homophobia defers a dilemma constitutive to liberalism by displacing it onto Muslims. Second, by treating that impasse as purely Muslim intolerance, the discourse of Muslim homophobia enables tolerant liberals to suspend any obligation to tolerate or respect Muslims, now marked as intolerant subjects. And third, by refusing to tolerate intolerant Muslims, liberals reaffirm their commitment to the foundational principle of tolerance.

Asymmetrical Demands

Although there exists a symmetry between the conundrum al-Houda's members face and the impasse Walzer and Touraine experience, the imperative of respect and its attendant aporias interpellate Muslim French in highly asymmetrical ways. Walzer and Touraine may experience an impasse between their commitment to procedural reason and their attachment to moral norms, but they are not summoned to resolve it, as Muslim French are. Walzer and Touraine do not struggle with their discomfort at being stuck; as part of the moral majority, they can appeal to the obvious to gloss over any tensions in the ethic of respect without having to justify their intolerance of practices that offend their moral sensibilities. Such comfort in discomfort does not extend to Muslim French like Irène and Amira. The previous section examined the imperative of *respect de l'autre* through the symmetry between Muslim French and liberal conundrums; this section traces the asymmetries that a discourse of *respect de l'autre* produces.

There is, after all, something odd about the demand that Arab Muslims, a racial and religious minority, be tolerant of others, a gesture normally reserved for a powerful class or majority.[11] As Susan Mendus (1989) observes, the act of toleration necessitates that the actor (the tolerator) have the power to influence the behavior of the object of her action (the tolerated). Mendus writes that we may be said to tolerate only in those circumstances where, although we disapprove of an act and have the power to persecute someone for committing it, we refrain from doing so. This definition of tolerance, or toleration, underpins John Locke's seminal 1689 *Letter Concerning Toleration* (2003), the cornerstone of the liberal doctrine of tolerance. For Locke, toleration entailed the state's neutrality toward minority religious communities and subjects. The act of toleration was generated by, and reinscribed, the state's power over its subjects. According to a Lockean notion of toleration, it makes little sense to classify individuals as tolerant or intolerant, as we do now, or to demand tolerance from marginalized minority communities.

The contemporary liberal demand that individuals and minorities be tolerant, especially of other minorities, reveals both a transformation in Locke's logic of tolerance and a dissimulation of power in the late-modern configuration of secular tolerance.

The fact that tolerance has become a matter of *respect de l'autre* signals this transformation and dissimulation. *Respect de l'autre* is the French gloss on a global discourse. As Walzer explains, the two main contemporary definitions of *tolerance* identify it first, as the principled recognition that others have the right to live as they choose, even in unattractive ways; and, second, as the expression of openness to others, "perhaps even respect, a willingness to listen and learn" (1997, 10–11). The shift away from Lockean toleration as an action of the state entails the intensification and individualization of tolerance, now understood as respect for others rather than mere forbearance, and as an endeavor incumbent on the individuals who comprise society. Though concerned with protecting individual autonomy, Locke emphasized the autonomy of the individual in relation to the state; toleration therefore meant state neutrality toward religious beliefs. Contemporary tolerance, and especially of social and cultural differences, continues to emphasize respect for the autonomous individual, but it has become concerned as much, if not more, with relations between individuals as with relations between state and individual. This new configuration traces its roots back not to Locke, then, but to Mill and his defense of individual freedom in *On Liberty*. There, Mill writes against the power not only of the state ("the magistrate") but also of public opinion and society: "Protection . . . against the tyranny of the magistrate is not enough; there needs [to be] protection also against the tyranny of prevailing opinion and feeling, against the tendency of society to impose, by other means than civil penalties, its own ideas and practices as rules of conduct on those who dissent from them" (1978, 4). Since liberalism largely views society as comprising unencumbered individuals, protection of the individual against the pressures of prevailing opinion means protection against other individuals, what Mendus calls "social pressure" (1989, 9).[12] Hence the contemporary imperative that all individuals—presumably equal—be tolerant of each other. Hence, too, the emergence of a new pair of opposites: *respect de l'autre* and intolerance.

The new paradigm of *respect de l'autre* explains the heretofore puzzling demand that individual Muslims, members of a marginalized religious minority, be tolerant of others. Nonetheless, we should continue to attend to the peculiarity of that demand, for the individualization entailed by *respect de l'autre* has significant political effects, dissimulating the nature of secular state power captured by Locke in his earlier treatise on toleration. For Locke, a marginalized Muslim minority would not have had the power to tolerate or not. Only a very individualized understanding of tolerance, uprooted from a Lockean embeddedness in unequal relations of power between state and minorities, accounts for demands on Muslims in Europe to be tolerant. Yet the abdication of the state in matters of tolerance remains, as Wendy Brown (2008) reminds us, a practice of the state, signaling a particular neoliberal moment in which the discourse of tolerance has been depoliticized in two related ways. First, as Brown argues, contemporary tolerance and respect de l'autre reduce structural and historical inequalities to a problem of different beliefs and practices that need to be tolerated or respected, substituting affect for political solutions (see also Jakobsen and Pellegrini 2004). By turning structural inequalities into a matter of personal attitudes, the discourse of tolerance both dissimulates the state's role in producing and maintaining these inequalities and recasts the state as neutral arbiter among warring minorities: Muslims versus queers, Muslims versus women, Arabs versus Jews, and so on. Second, the demand that Muslims be tolerant and respectful (of gays and Jews especially) makes sense only within a neoliberal or late-liberal conception of society that transfers responsibility for social relations away from political institutions and onto private individuals, understood as self-governing subjects interacting one-on-one on a level playing field.

Put simply, respect de l'autre, a position incumbent on all citizens, effaces the structural discrimination Muslims suffer. The French state's policing practices disproportionately target and incarcerate young Muslim men; Muslim children attend crowded, underfunded public schools; Muslim families are disproportionately represented in public housing projects; and Muslims are themselves the targets of Islamophobic intolerance, as is clear in the growing instances of physical assault, verbal abuse, job discrimination, and legal sanction. Ironically, as the state has legitimized same-sex partnerships in France, marriages involving Muslim citizens and immigrants have been subjected to increasing scrutiny and legal restriction (E. Fassin 2010; Surkis 2010). In such a context, demanding that Muslims respect their fellow citizens obscures the state's abandonment of certain populations. It also creates a chimera of equal citizenship where Muslims, like all citizens, must be respectful. Even when all evidence points to the fact that Muslims are not like all citizens, an individualized discourse of respect de l'autre sustains a fantasy of equal citizenship. Moreover, when homophobic Muslims fail to act like good citizens and take up their equal responsibility for tolerance, it is ostensibly that failure, rather than their prior exclusion, that disqualifies them from being full French or European citizens.

There are other asymmetries in the discourse of Muslim intolerance as well, demonstrated by the quid pro quo nature of demands made on progressive, practicing Muslim French and by the cascading series of terms—respect, accept, defend, embrace, promote—that interpellate them. Consider Ramadan's statement quoted above: "I respect [gays and lesbians] and I respect their choice. I cannot agree with what they do, but I respect who they are." At first glance, Ramadan's position resembles the Christian discourse of love the sinner, hate the sin. However, he invokes not love and hate, but respect and disagreement. He claims to respect gays and lesbians as individuals but cannot agree with the moral rightness of their intimate practices. His framing echoes the somewhat counterintuitive distinction made by al-Houda's members between respecting and accepting difference. There, the notion of respect means having respect for the individual who is making a choice or undertaking a particular practice, but not necessarily for the choice or practice itself. The notion of acceptance, on the other hand, indicates agreement with the legitimacy of the choice or practice. For the women of al-Houda, respect entails the capacity to tolerate—to accept the existence of—practices they find morally wrong because they have a basic respect for the human agent and her right to do as she wishes. However, these women are called on to agree with the rightness of practices they find morally wrong. When Irène declares somberly that "defending homosexuality is inconceivable," she clearly feels compelled to do more than simply accept its existence and remain indifferent to the practice in her own actions.

Irène might be misreading what is expected of Muslims, but given how little power Muslims in Europe have to affect LGBTQ rights, her reaction testifies to how they are indeed expected to do more than simply tolerate the practice and respect the individual. A conversation with Amira helps illuminate the demand made on Muslim French. Speaking about the January 2005 demonstration for abortion rights, Amira distinguished between recognizing the right to abortion and actively advocating for it: "From the moment that [the right to abortion] is recognized, it's not going to be a primary cause [for me]. And recognizing the right to abortion, that's not a problem, but I'm not going to fight for abortion." She felt the same way about queer rights—that as long as "people are not being persecuted for being gay, as long as they are free," the fight against homophobia is not her priority. Yet the need for Muslim French to attend abortion and LGBTQ-rights rallies was presented as a quid pro quo arrangement: as Amira's colleague said, "I fought along-side you all on the question of the veil, and I am waiting for you [Muslim women] to fight alongside me on the question of homosexuality." Amira's practice of respect de l'autre as a form of live and let live is not enough; she is expected to fight (militer) for something that is not a priority for her. This demand exceeds both tolerance, understood as silent disapproval, and respect de l'autre, or respect for individual differences. Whether one finds Amira's decision not to fight for LGBTQ rights disappointing with regard to social justice and coalition building is beside the point; she is clearly being asked to do more than respect. Her difficulty in doing more than simply respect, however, is read as a refusal to practice even simple respect. Though she actually fulfills the basic requirement of respect de l'autre, she and Muslim French like her continue to be seen as intolerant Muslims.

Particularly asymmetrical in this demand is the fact that progressive Muslim French are already in excess, ethically and politically, of the tolerance exhibited by liberals like Walzer and Touraine. Earlier I showed how Irène reproduces the impasse integral to respect de l'autre, but now I want to point out how her reaction is also quite different. Firstly, Irène is clearly dismayed by her arrival at this impasse; she wants very much to overcome it, but she cannot. She recognizes the logic in accusations of hypocrisy—we can't expect people to respect and accept our way of being in the world if we don't respect and accept theirs—and she wants to be open to the world, but she doesn't know quite how to deal with the resulting ethical quandaries. Even as she states that it is "inconceivable" to defend homosexuality, she also observes that "obviously there is much thinking to do." These reflections parallel Nabila's: even as she hesitated to fully support the right of gays and lesbians to marry, she nonetheless acknowledged an epistemological uncertainty. Calling the subject a complex one, she confessed, "I don't know. I simply don't know." Similarly, many of the practicing Muslim women in the CFPE called for a respectful debate on abortion rights, not so that they could reiterate their position but so that they might be persuaded to take a different view. Contrast Irène's and Nabila's uncertainty with the sureness ("surely," "of course") with which Walzer and Touraine dismiss what makes them uncomfortable and reassert the validity of their positions. Irène is sure that there is a lot of thinking to do; Walzer and Touraine are equally certain that there is no need for more thinking, or even talking. Rather than recognize or engage with the impasse they find themselves at, they simply dismiss it by displacing their visceral discomfort, which they refuse to submit to debate or even reflection, onto the absolute intolerability of the practices that generate discomfort. Whereas Irène recognizes and grapples with her logical and ethical inconsistencies, Walzer and Touraine act as if there is no impasse between visceral attachments and public reason.

Moreover, unlike Walzer and Touraine, Irène and other members of al-Houda do not seek to ban those practices that generate discomfort. Indeed, the latter's live-and-let-live version of respect de l'autre seems to enable ad hoc, heterogeneous coalition politics—politics actually practiced by al-Houda and other Muslim French associations—that neither the liberal tolerance of Walzer and Touraine nor the love the sinner, hate the sin paradigm of evangelical Christianity would easily permit. Amira is happy to work with queers, abortion rights activists, and women who have had abortions; she just doesn't want to engage actively on behalf of their causes. She appreciates that her fellow queer and feminist activists fought against the ban on headscarves in public schools, but she cannot return the favor, so to speak, when it comes to fighting for gay marriage and abortion rights. The fact that she will not militate for these issues does not mean, however, that she wants to restrict them. Unlike Walzer and Touraine, she does not summon the state's legal arm to resolve her moral conundrum by making illegal that which she must, but cannot, accept.[13]

In contrast, Walzer and Touraine clearly favor banning those practices they cannot accept, practices they brand intolerable. They thereby reveal the underlying, asymmetrical power structure of respect de l'autre and tolerance that belies the relationship between individuals that both discourses invoke. Walzer writes explicitly in favor of criminalizing female genital cutting, summoning the state to act on behalf of his personal discomfort, his inability to respect. One would guess that Touraine, too, would argue for banning practices he deems unacceptable, regardless of whether practitioners consent to them, because his disapproval is fundamentally not premised on consent. In fact, when he was on the Stasi Commission, Touraine voted for a ban on headscarves—even those freely worn—in public schools. For most liberals, personal moral disapprobation for truly intolerable acts must be turned into—and, given the nature of democratic electoral politics, have been turned into—legal interdiction. For Walzer and Touraine, the question is not whether to respect, accept, or even militate, as it is for Muslim French progressives, but whether to respect or ban. Though respect de l'autre seemed at first glance to have drifted away from the statist roots of Lockean toleration, it turns out to be just as imbricated in political power. Liberal intolerance of certain nonliberal practices carries significant political and legal effects that refute the symmetry invoked by respect de l'autre.

Furthermore, the demand for respect de l'autre and the practice of intolerance unfold in asymmetrical ways. Thus Walzer and Touraine are understood to exercise the proper kind of tolerance and respect de l'autre, and to properly exercise their intolerance for "obviously" intolerable practices like female genital cutting and arranged marriage. In contrast, the Muslim French conundrum—one that both mimics and exceeds what liberals like Walzer and Touraine face—becomes representative, in the dominant French and European imaginary, of a general Muslim intolerance that continuously undermines the viability of Muslim French as citizens.

Asymmetrical Inclusion

Reading recent commentary on the Muslim immigrant presence in Europe reminds one that Samuel Huntington's clash of civilizations theory (1993) has had a long shelf life. In the wake of van Gogh's murder in 2004, Bawer wrote that Holland, and Western Europe generally, was "a house divided against itself" (2004).[14] "The division was stark," he continued. "The Dutch had the world's most tolerant, open-minded society, with full sexual equality and same-sex marriage, as well as liberal policies on soft drugs and prostitution; but a large segment of the fast-growing Muslim population kept that society at arm's length, despising its freedoms." The Dutch, Bawer claimed, needed to "act decisively to protect their democracy from the undemocratic enemy within." In an article on Turkish "honor killings" in Germany, the author and playwright Peter Schneider echoed Bawer's concerns, writing of "a new Berlin wall" and a "parallel society growing" within Germany (2005). After the London subway bombings in June 2005, David Rieff, a Fellow at the World Policy Institute and a contributing editor to the New Republic magazine, contended that Europe faces the immense challenge of preventing its "multicultural reality from becoming a war of all against all," adding that this challenge "makes all of Europe's other problems, from the economy to the euro to the sclerosis of social democracy, seem trivial by comparison" (2005). Later in the decade, Angela Merkel and Nicolas Sarkozy—the latter once a proponent of affirmative action—declared multiculturalism a failure.

These dire warnings echo the rhetoric of many French republican writers from the mid-1980s onward (see, for example, Finkielkraut 1987; Jelen 1997; Kintzler 1998). At the same time, most Left-leaning republicans in France are usually careful to pay lip service to a distinction between Islam and Islamism (the latter is also termed "political Islam" or "radical Islam"). Despite these claims of distinguishing between Islam and Islamism, the constant slippage in political discourse and television and print media between terms like *islam*, *islamisme*, and *intégrisme* (fundamentalism) marks Islam itself as an inherently foreign and potentially violent entity (Deltombe 2005) and Muslims as a perversely sexualized and racialized population (Hamel 2003; Puar 2007). Take, for instance, Caroline Fourest, an influential queer feminist journalist who claims to speak not against Islam but against Muslim fundamentalism and all fundamentalisms. Tellingly, though, she saves her harshest critique for Islamism, "the most reactionary and regressive movement of the last few decades" (2005, 10).[15] She has also criticized the French government for working with the Union of Islamic Organizations of France and condemning the 2005 Danish caricatures of the Prophet. Writing with Corinne Lepage and Pierre Cassen, she wonders: "If these two pillars, the law of 1905 and the freedom of expression, fall or at least begin to crumble, with what weapons shall we defend ourselves against an obscurantism that is none other than a new totalitarianism?" (Fourest, Lepage, and Cassen 2006). Fourest is hardly alone in worrying about the future of Enlightenment Europe. Writing immediately after van Gogh's assassination, Daniel Schneiderman, a Left-leaning French media critic and journalist, insisted on the indispensable value of freedom of expression. He warned that the French should pay attention to Holland's problems, suggesting that "this luxury" that the French take for granted "may be taken away from us"—presumably by Muslims. "Yes, we must cherish our Voltaire . . . while everywhere the skies darken," he asserted, adding that "Europe, at least, must remain an enchanted parentheses where all images and words are allowed" (2004).[16] The Franco-German television channel ARTE was more succinct. Anne-Sophie Mercier opened one program on radical Islam with the broad question: "Is Islam soluble in modernity?" ("Islam radical" 2005). In another she asked, "Muslims and non-Muslims—can they still live together?" ("Musulmans" 2006).

For many liberal and republican critics, Muslim obscurantism and Muslim intolerance, more so than the intolerant obscurantism of any other group, endanger the very fabric and future of Europe. Concomitantly, Muslim disapproval of homosexuality and Muslim opposition to same-sex marriage are interpreted as signs of a moral qua civilizational clash between Islamism (often simply Islam) and Enlightenment Europe. Contrast this bombastic civilizational rhetoric with the way republican politicians and the French media take up non-Muslim opposition to same-sex marriage, and to homosexuality more generally. After all, Muslims do not have a lock on homophobia. The 1999 debate on the legalization of civil unions (PaCS),[17] reactions to the 2004 Chapin-Charpentier marriage in Bègles conducted by Mayor Mamère,[18] and more recent debates in 2012 and 2013 on the legalization of same-sex marriage and gay adoption (l'homoparentalité) have made this clear.

Though it occurred earlier than the 2012–13 debate, a January 2006 episode of *Ripostes* ("Homos" 2006) on the matter of same-sex adoption is instructive: it illustrates both the nature of conservative opposition to same-sex marriage and adoption, and the way mainstream liberal republicans nonetheless understand this opposition as a political question about equal rights and discrimination rather than a form of intolerant homophobia or a civilizational difference. The *Ripostes* debate featured a number of politicians, including Mamère of the Green Party and Jean-Marc Nesme and Christine Boutin of the center Right Union for a Popular Movement (Union pour un Mouvement Populaire, or UMP). Boutin's politics have long intersected with her Catholic faith; at one point during the parliamentary debate on the PaCS, she clutched a Bible as she spoke. Numerous times on *Ripostes*, she and Nesme outlined an orthodox Catholic argument—quite similar to many practicing Muslims' position—against same-sex marriage and gay adoption, based on a fundamental biological difference between men and women that Nesme called "the foundation of society." Boutin affirmed: "Between a man and a woman, there is a difference. And this difference, which we can see, was translated into law. . . . Today, the cultural [i.e., the law] and the biological are in the process of moving further and further away from each other. . . . We are in the process of rupturing the basic heterosexual biological reality" via the law.

Serge Moati, the program's host, explicitly refused to paint Boutin's and Nesme's position as homophobic. When introducing Nesme, Moati was at pains to note that the UMP's positions against same-sex marriage and gay adoption "have nothing to do whatsoever with any homophobia—you are fighting for the interests of the child." One may beg to differ, given that another UMP deputy, Christian Vanneste (who was not on the show), had recently asserted that "homosexuality is a threat to the survival of humanity" (quoted in Deram 2012). Boutin had similarly declared in the 1999 PaCS debate that "all civilizations that recognized and justified homosexuality as a normal lifestyle have only ended in decadence" (quoted in Portelli and Richard 2012, 146). But Nadine Morano, a third UMP deputy on *Ripostes* who actually supported same-sex marriage at the time, defended Vanneste, averring that "personally, [his words] shock me, but I don't think he did it because of homophobia. His point was perhaps misunderstood." Mamère, on the other hand, called Vanneste's statements homophobic, but his criticism of the UMP's opposition to same-sex marriage and gay adoption remained surprisingly muted. The Right's position, Mamère argued, treats gays and lesbians as a "subcategory of citizen who cannot benefit from the same rights as everyone else because of his sexual orientation. That's a form of discrimination." Nothing was said during the debate about upholding French, European, or universal values, and the UMP's position was not criticized—not even by Eric Verdier, an LGBTQ activist and president of the adoption rights association Coparentalité—as backward or antimodern, only as discriminatory and politically wrongheaded.

That pattern was largely repeated when the Socialist Party introduced a bill in November 2012 to legalize same-sex marriage and gay adoption. Opposition was fierce: the UMP strongly contested the law, massive demonstrations were held in cities across France, and Catholic clergy (joined by their Jewish and Muslim counterparts) spoke out against it. Again, this opposition to the law was couched in terms of sexual difference and filiation. "The problem is not homosexuality, but human filiation," declared Frigide Barjot, one of the principal organizers of the demonstrations against the law (termed *Manif pour tous*, or demonstations for all).[19] Echoing former pope Benedict XVI's discourse of "human ecology," Barjot went on to say that "to make a child, you need a man and a woman," making gay parenting "totally contrary to reality" (quoted in Erlanger 2013). Opponents of same-sex marriage and gay adoption repeatedly invoked their concern for the well-being of the family, the "basic unit of society" (Boutin 2013), and for the integrity of natural procreation. "If there is such passion on the part of the French in the debate on marriage for all," declared the Christian bioethicist Jean-René Binet, "it's precisely because they feel that what is hidden behind the problem goes far beyond the simple question of marriage, love, and sexuality. The real issue is the structure of filiation and of transmission within our society" (quoted in "Mariage homosexuel" 2013). Binet contended that the debate was not about homosexuality or homophobia, "which are questions that have been resolved since homosexuality [was] legalized and homophobia criminalized," but about attempts to create "a totally artificial [structure of] filiation based on individual will."

Those who view heterosexual marriage and procreation as the basis of human society refuse to see themselves as homophobic. For them, "to maintain the distinction between homosexuality and heterosexuality does not imply any discrimination: it is simply to preserve the difference between the sexes and the principle of the family" (E. Fassin 2008, 40–41). Even many mainstream proponents of the law understood opposition to it as political (not civilizational) and as entirely normal and justifiable. In an online forum, Socialist Minister for the Family Dominique Bertinotti maintained that she was not surprised by the mobilization against the law, "since all social reform provokes lots of passion and debate. These reforms affect intimacy, so everyone feels concerned" (quoted in Béguin 2013). Asked if there was a homophobic climate in France, Bertinotti responded that only after "the debate had reached its limits" and ended in the National Assembly and Senate did "we [see] a rise in homophobic remarks." The preceding five months of massive opposition to the law based on heterosexist and Catholic notions of natural law and filiation apparently did not, for Bertinotti, constitute a climate of homophobia, only one of passionate debate. For Bertinotti and others, the division between those who oppose same-sex marriage and those who support it remained an inherently political rather than civilizational gap between Right and Left. Some commentators even contended that the UMP's opposition to the law wasn't really about homophobia at all; it was simply a way to distinguish Left and Right, given their indistinguishable positions on immigration and the economy (see, for example, E. Fassin 2013). Despite their willingness to discriminate against gays and lesbians, then, politicians on the Right remain fundamentally within the moral and political fold of France and Europe; their Frenchness or Europeanness is rarely questioned by the mainstream Left or the media.

In fact, mainstream media and politicians often termed parliamentary discourse and public demonstrations against same-sex marriage and gay adoption as constitutive of rather than counter to French democracy. In an article titled "Le 'peuple veto'" (The people veto), *Le Monde* integrated the demonstrations against same-sex marriage into a long line of post-1968 new social movements, including protests against education, welfare, and employment reforms (Courtois 2013). When Barjot declared that if President "Hollande wants blood, there will be blood" and Boutin predicted impending "civil war" (quoted in Sicard 2013), many people felt that both women had gone too far, but their belonging to France was never questioned, and neither of them faced police scrutiny or sanction (as one might imagine would be the case for similarly violent remarks by Muslims). They were simply referred to as "hotheads" (quoted in Berthe 2013) who needed to "calm down" (Sicard 2013). Similarly, when Fourest was violently harassed by white, right-wing opponents of same-sex marriage—ironically, Fourest was on her way to a colloquium titled "Toward a Modern Islam?"—she merely termed their actions "over the top and out of proportion" (quoted in "La journaliste Caroline Fourest 'traquée' par des anti-mariage gay" 2013). Unlike Muslims, apparently still inching their way toward modernity, these protestors did not prompt Fourest to question the modernity of Catholicism, and certainly not that of France. And most mainstream commentators were confident that Barjot and her ilk would calm down. "I am confident that our co-citizens will return to reason and good sense," Bertinotti declared. "I think the climate of violence will quickly subside" (quoted in Béguin 2013). Nicolas Gougain, spokesman for the federation Inter-LGBT, echoed the minister's confidence; in two years, he said, "it's going to seem surreal that we had this whole debate" (quoted in Erlanger 2013).

Contrast this generous attitude with earlier reactions to Muslim opposition to same-sex marriage, an opposition couched in the biological and theological logic of Catholics. Many of the same critics who see the Catholic position as political rather than purely homophobic, and as evolving rather than intractable, configure a similar Muslim position in moral and civilizational terms, and as incapable of progressing. Liberal critics of Muslim homophobia wonder whether Islam is "soluble in modernity" ("Islam radical" 2005) and whether, as a journalist for Le nouvel observateur did, Islam can "ever be modernized" (Esber 2006). The distinction between homophobic Catholics and homophobic Muslims operates through spatial and temporal matrices that feed back into each other. Because European modernity is held, even by staunch secularists, to have emerged out of Christianity,[20] the latter is figured as both always already within Europe and capable of transforming itself; concomitantly, because Christianity contains within itself the possibility to modernize, to become that which it is already (namely, European), it naturally belongs in Europe. In contrast, because Islam is always already not Europe, it has long been thought incapable of transformation, and this Orientalist trope persists in contemporary political thought. Conversely (and tautologically), because it is incapable of transformation and modernization, Islam cannot belong in Europe. With regard to homophobia more specifically, Muslims, it is held, have always been and therefore always will be homophobic. Any attempt to prove otherwise must be made immediately. Hence the circumscribed temporality within which Muslim French like Amira and Nabila must decide whether or not to fight for gay rights. They do not have time or space to think or to debate, the kind of time and space—on television and in the National Assembly—offered to Catholics. As Puar rightly observes, "cultural difference is embodied by Muslim homophobia and sexual repression as a distinct ontological reality" (2007, 139), with Muslims figured as inherently civilizationally and racially Other. Muslim homophobia, and the inability of certain Muslim French to defend homosexuality, serves to confirm their a priori status as non-European rather than to establish it after the fact.

The disproportionate and civilizational stakes of Muslim homophobia enact a particular representational burden on Muslim French, who are, as Amira noted, consistently summoned to respond to the accusation of intolerance and constantly monitored for any signs that confirm their non-belonging. Again recounting her experience in the CFPE, Amira observed that there was no strategy on the part of non-Muslim feminists to instrumentalize their Muslim colleagues. But Muslim French women nonetheless felt the pressure of having, as Amira had put it earlier, one foot in their own community and one foot outside it. She pointed out that secular feminists in the CFPE were equally "torn within their feminist movement, because they were told, 'Yeah, but your Muslim women, they'll never march with you for queers, they'll never march with you for this or that issue.' So in some ways, and without even really wanting to, they had to ask us to demonstrate our good faith." As a result, secular feminists expected that Muslim French members should and would march with them for abortion and gay rights and were disappointed and frustrated when Muslim French did not always meet that expectation, or met it with hesitation. Amira added that Muslim members, too, were torn: "We, on our side, we had found allies, and we didn't want to lose them, because this project that we have in common is enriching. But I think that we weren't in the same rhythm, in the same logic. . . . Everyone saw the huge stakes of the collective, Muslim women with non-Muslim women. It was a huge thing, and [yet] in a way, no one really understood the stakes, myself included."

Amira gestures here to the tremendous pressure on everyone involved, Muslims and non-Muslims alike, to make the CFPE a successful venture in a political climate anticipating its failure. The mainstream feminist reaction to the One School for All Collective and the CFPE—for example, excluding veiled women from the Women's Day and January 31, 2005, demonstrations—reflected the assumption that practicing Muslims subscribe to an inherently intolerant and sexist worldview and cannot be feminists or queer allies. For most non-Muslim French, Muslim French are intolerant until proven otherwise, an a priori positioning that explains why Muslim French members of the CFPE felt compelled to justify themselves, demonstrate their good faith, and prove their respect for others. This positioning also explains other members' subtle desire to see their practicing Muslim colleagues do precisely all that. Given these high stakes, few Muslim French felt comfortable having the discussions they had initially hoped for in a heterogeneous collective with conflicting ethical and political positions, discussions afforded other communities with less representational baggage. When practicing Muslim French requested such a dialogue, they were quickly silenced. Nor could they appeal for time. As Amira put it, "there was no way to take any time for reflection" on the question of abortion. She had wanted to explain her hesitation in marching for abortion rights, and why a classic feminist slogan like "my body belongs to me" did not sit well with her. ("Spiritually, my body does not belong to me," she said.) But, "consciously or unconsciously, the political stakes were such that we didn't want to disrupt [the strategy of a united front] to enter into foundational debates." Amira thought it would have been productive to talk about the ethical norms driving various members of the collective. She continued: "On questions of norms, of our relationship to our bodies . . . there really is a need for a group discussion, a free one, where our speech is entirely free." And as demonstrated by our very frank discussion of the CFPE charter, members of al-Houda are not afraid of such potentially fraught, uncomfortable debates among friends. But the space and time—the freedom—for that kind of discussion do not exist. As a result of what Amira called the unmanageable tensions of being caught between two communities, she and a number of Muslim French decided to leave the CFPE.

That sense of unmanageable tensions was common to many Muslim French members of the collective. Like Amira, Nabila also used the term torn (tiraillée) to describe her sense of being caught between her religious community and her feminist colleagues. She understood her secular colleagues' investment in her presence at an abortion rally, which would show dubious mainstream feminists that Muslims could, in fact, be feminists and queer allies. Consequently, she feared a double mediation of her attendance: first, that because the headscarf stands for Islam in so many public debates, non-Muslims would read Nabila's veiled presence as taking a position on behalf of Islam as a whole; and second, that anticipating this reaction, and blaming her for contributing to it, other Muslims would also read her presence as a statement about Islam, rather than about her own ethical position, and "certain people would say, 'that's not true, Islam is against abortion!'" Ismahane Chouder, another veiled member of the CFPE, put these women's dilemma in similar terms: "For me, [abortion] is an established right, which is recognized and codified with precision in Islamic jurisprudential texts. But I was obliged to take others' perceptions into consideration. What was problematic for me was the public visibility of Muslim women in a demonstration, where they would be unable to explain the nuanced reasons for their presence, unable to underline the difference between being 'for abortion' and 'for the right to abortion'" (quoted in Chouder, Latrèche, and Tevanian 2008, 313–14).

Chouder and Nabila gesture to the Fanonian representational burden (Fanon 2008) that I examined in more depth in chapter 1, a burden that assigns communal responsibility onto and radically disindividuates Muslim French. Always already fixed to a particular community, Chouder and Nabila are responsible for their bodies, their religion, and their ancestors. They cannot speak only for themselves. Correspondingly, any decision by women like Amira and Nabila not to fight for gay marriage, or not to attend an abortion rally, confirms the intolerance and misogyny of which Muslims are always suspected. The converse, however, does not hold. Despite Nabila's fear that other Muslims would see her as claiming to speak for Islam, and despite secular feminists' hope that her presence would dislodge preconceptions about practicing Muslims' intolerance, unanticipated progressive acts by individual Muslim French—such as attending a queer rights demonstration—are usually read as just that: individual acts. They do little to undermine the dominant sense that Islam is not only essentially intolerant (and misogynistic and anti-Semitic) but also fundamentally incapable of evolving.

Deferring Europe

What remains particularly striking in the discourse about the need to protect European values from Muslims is the indeterminacy of these values. Terms like *tolerance, freedom, equality, democracy, respect for individual rights,* and *secularism* circulate as keywords tied to the overarching term *European values,* but their meanings are hazy, abstract, and implicit (Blommaert and Verschueren 1998, 85–86). In a communication on European identity, the European Commission once declared that Europe's "cultural dimension" was "characterized by a pluralist humanism based on democracy, justice and liberty" (quoted in Shore 2000, 26). But the Commission left those terms undefined. Did it intend to give immigrant nonnationals the vote as part of its commitment to democracy? Was it committing to a model of redistributive justice? What kind of liberty did it have in mind? Moreover, what makes tolerance, freedom, democracy, and equality as European values? Does Europe have a monopoly on these values? And why are European values those of tolerance, freedom, democracy, and equality and not, say, totalitarianism, genocide, and colonial rule, all of which constitute important moments of European history? To paraphrase the journalist Gary Younge (2004), are Dutch values those exhibited by Anne Frank's protectors or by the neighbors who turned her in to the Nazis? Are French values those of the Resistance or of Vichy?

Jan Blommaert and Jef Verschueren argue persuasively that the vagueness of European values allows for demands on immigrants that cannot be imposed on autochthonous Europeans, enabling the majority to keep declaring minority members "unintegrated" (1998, 86). Going a step further, I would argue that the vagueness of European (and Belgian, French, Dutch, and so on) principles and values also defers an anxiety about the lack of consensus on what constitutes European values, a lack of consensus that problematizes the very notion of Europe as more than a geographic designation. The discourse of European values not only constructs Europe but also keeps at bay the differences that consistently threaten to render its seams visible, even tear it apart. That discourse maintains the illusion of Europe as a naturally existing cultural entity rather than one whose production and reproduction require constant and careful work. By keeping terms like *democracy, tolerance, freedom,* and *equality* in the realm of abstract principle, cosmopolitan European liberals do not have to confront either the varied and contradictory meanings of these terms for various kinds of Europeans or the fundamental nonexistence of a unified European identity.

Take, for example, the paradox of claiming tolerance and *respect de l'autre* as essential European values. One does not have to look very far to realize that Europe's history and its present social and political realities belie such a notion. The electoral success of extreme Right parties—the National Front in France, Vlaams Blok in Belgium, and Freedom Party in Holland—indicates that a substantial part of the European voting public is racist and xenophobic rather than respectful of others. With regard to the intolerance of gays and lesbians in particular, it is absurd to think that homophobia is restricted to Muslims, or that only socially conservative Muslims oppose same-sex marriage. Witness the recent mass, sometimes violent, protests against marriage equality in France. In addition, the Vatican has made preventing same-sex marriage a priority, and in 2005 it issued a document to be used by seminaries that states that although the church "profoundly respects homosexuals," it "cannot admit to the priesthood those who practice homosexuality, present deeply rooted homosexual tendencies or support the so-called 'gay culture'" (quoted in Fisher 2005). I recognize, of course, that many of the secular-liberal critics of Muslim intolerance find the Catholic Church and the UMP as intolerant as Muslims. But neither Catholic bishops nor conservative French politicians and activists have had their belonging to Europe questioned. Rarely does one hear calls for the expulsion of intolerant Catholics from tolerant Europe. In fact, the campaign against same-sex marriage sees itself as upholding true French values. Nor do Catholic priests, even foreign ones, fear deportation from France for their views on homosexuality or even for their active participation in a sexist institution like the priesthood, which expressly forbids women the same right of participation. Immigrant imams, on the other hand, can be and have been deported for their views on women and gays.

Homophobic practices and utterances on the part of Jean-François Copé, leading member of the UMP, and Pope Benedict XVI seemingly do not constitute true European values even as both men remain fully European. Because white Christians are always already European, their homophobia is considered a political problem, not a civilizational one. Moreover, Copé and Pope Benedict carry no representational burden: their homophobia, and the homophobia of other bona fide Europeans, does not constitute a stain on Europe, on all Christians, or even on all Catholics because that homophobia remains individualized even when it is socially dominant, and even when it emerges in collective gatherings like public demonstrations. Vanneste may be an actual representative in the National Assembly, but his rampant Catholic homophobia—excused by his colleague Morano as a misunderstanding—apparently does not represent France.

These dissimulations signal not just hypocrisy but also a broader pattern of deferral and displacement that I want to trace through a reading of Uni Wikan's *Generous Betrayal*, explicitly framed as a critical inquiry into the limits of tolerance with regard to Muslim immigrants in Europe. Though she highlights not homophobia but the subjugation of women, another pillar of unacceptable Muslim difference, Wikan, a Scandinavian anthropologist, elucidates the kind of logic at work in similar critiques of Muslim homophobia. Wikan calls for an end to Swedish society's tolerance of Muslim immigrants' oppression of women, represented by honor killings and forced marriages. "Sweden has been extremely generous . . . in opening its arms to immigrants and refugees," Wikan writes, but the presence of foreigners who do not respect the freedom of others has forced Sweden to ask itself: "What should be the limits to tolerance?" (2002, 93–94). How should Sweden deal with immigrants who cling to "an old-fashioned culture imbued with 'honor' and 'shame'" to such an extent that "a deep depreciation of women . . . is culturally endorsed" (95–96)? Wikan then backtracks, wondering whether it makes sense to attribute violence against women to immigrants' culture and religion when there are, she admits, thousands of immigrants who live in Sweden as law-abiding citizens and who condemn crimes like honor killings. Furthermore, Wikan notes, "Sweden has its share of indigenous wife abusers. Violence against women is nothing exotic, it is a common problem . . . [and] when Swedish men are found guilty of violence, it is explained in individual or structural terms. So why call on 'culture' just because the perpetrators are immigrants?" (96).[21]

Wikan's answer to her own questions reveals the logic of the liberal championing of European values like sexual freedom and equality, and the deferrals and displacements that such a championing entails. In the paragraph following her questions, Wikan quotes Jan Hjärp, "a highly respected authority on Islam" who "put[s] it bluntly: 'True, Swedish men also kill their wives—but they are not applauded for it'" (2002, 96). Wikan does not discuss whether or not Hjärp's contention is true, or how his contention answers Wikan's original question as to whether Muslim immigrants' "culture" should play any explanatory role, when most Muslim immigrants abide by Swedish law and condemn rather than applaud violence against women. She simply tables the issue of Swedish domestic violence and concentrates on clan loyalty and the honor-shame complex that is supposedly endemic to Middle Eastern societies. In a later chapter in which Wikan discusses the " 'disproportionate share of the costs of multiculturalism' " borne by immigrant women and girls, she claims that "gender equality—an entrenched value of modern democracies—is at stake" (156). Notice what Wikan does in these two instances: she defers the problem of the existence of Swedish wife abusers who contradict the "entrenched" Swedish value of gender equality by reaffirming the principle of gender equality, and then she displaces the burden of violence onto Muslims by turning to anecdotal examples of immigrant violations of that principle. In the face of empirical evidence that Swedes also beat their wives—gender equality may be an entrenched value, but it is clearly not an entrenched practice—Wikan simply repeats that gender equality is a fundamental Swedish value and turns her attention to immigrants, rhetorically shifting the problem of violence onto immigrant Muslim culture. In Wikan's and similar arguments about tolerance and gender equality as Europe's constitutive values, the gap between European ideal and European reality—Europeans' actual practices—is continually suspended by reiterating tolerance and gender equality as regulating ideals or values. Yes, some Swedish men also beat their wives, Wikan admits, but gender equality remains our value. Yes, intolerance of gays and lesbians exists among some Europeans, but *respect de l'autre* remains our value.

Wikan and others are able to manage this gap between the ideal and the empirical through two mutually contradictory operations of individualization and communalization. On the one hand, violence and intolerance inflicted by bona fide Europeans are held to be individual acts that do not reflect on European or Christian culture more generally. Domestic or antigay violence at the hands of white Europeans is presented as either individual pathology or excessive passion (Mahmood 2009, 204). White Europeans carry no representational burden; when it comes to utterances and practices that violate the values of tolerance and gender equality, not even Pope Benedict represents Europe. On the other hand, similar acts and utterances by Muslims are communalized. A Muslim cannot represent only himself or herself; Muslims are "understood to be compelled by 'their culture,' irrationally and blindly acting out its misogynist [and homophobic] customs and traditions" (204). These simultaneous operations—the individualization of European behavior and the communalization of Muslim comportment—produce radically different reactions to the same acts and utterances. Homophobic and misogynist Europeans are targeted for individual opprobrium, while Islamic culture as a whole is targeted for reform, exclusion, or eradication.

Wikan's treatise reveals another process that helps manage the contradiction between European ideal and European reality—namely, the active displacement of that contradiction onto Muslims. Recall Wikan's maneuver referred to earlier: although she claims to address the problem that Swedith men also beat their wives, in fact she simply deflects the issue by turning her attention to Muslim immigrants. That rhetorical sleight of hand is indicative of a broader ideological and political displacement in which a focus on Muslim intolerance reaffirms Europe's commitment to tolerance in the face of so-called autochthonous Europeans whose actions muddy the barbarism-civilization distinction mapped onto, respectively, Muslims and Europeans. Europe's inability to reconcile its supposedly constitutive value with the actions of Europeans is deferred through a critical focus on Muslim intolerance; it is Muslims who become almost solely responsible for the problem of intolerance in Europe.

At the same time, we should be careful not to put too much stock in the ideal of European tolerance either. As I demonstrated above, individualization and communalization produce an asymmetry in representations of Muslim versus European intolerance. But the individualization of European homophobia, and the ascription of homophobia to a few individual Europeans who will eventually evolve, has other effects as well. Eric Fassin has taken up the common-sense distinction between an explicit, psychological homophobia that is condemned by most republicans and an implicit, ideological homophobia (or heterosexism) that goes largely unnoticed. He writes: "Everyone loves homosexuals in general, and many have homosexual friends in particular. No one [in mainstream politics], however, will go so far as to demand strict equality between sexualities in terms of the law. . . . In short, in France today among enlightened folk, no one is a homophobe (in the first sense), and everyone is (in the second sense)" (2008, 79). The focus on homophobia as a personal attitude individualizes and psychologizes a structural phenomenon of discrimination and inequality, dissimulating existing heterosexist laws and political and moral discourses that have little to do with either individual or communal Muslim homophobia. Janet Jakobsen and Ann Pellegrini (2004) make a similar assessment of American hate-crimes legislation, where the focus on individual, pathological hate serves to mask a heterosexist social order, turning homophobia into an exceptional problem outside or in excess of the normal course of things. Furthermore, the attribution of homophobia to Muslims and, more grudgingly, to a few not yet evolved Christians obscures the power of the French state, and of the powerful majority of secular republicans, in propagating a social order premised on the heterosexual norm, evidenced in the normalization of homosexual intimacies via heteronormative institutions like monogamous marriage, a process Lisa Duggan aptly calls homonormativity (2004; see also Warner 1999). The focus on Muslim intolerance, like the paradigm of respect de l'autre itself, disguises the actual structure of secular modern rule, dissimulating an asymmetry not only between the secular-republican majority and Muslims, but also between the heterosexual majority and those who practice queer forms of intimacy.

In sum, consistently focusing on Muslim homophobia, and emphasizing respect de l'autre as that which promises a free and equal society, has a number of effects. First, it particularizes homophobia as a Muslim problem, not a European one, and in the process reaffirms the distinction between Muslims (who are not European) and Europeans (who are not Muslim). Second, it shifts the burden of the contradiction between the ideal of respect de l'autre and its nonpractice by Europeans—always figured as an exceptional minority of homophobes and racists—onto Muslims, who are held accountable for the problem of intolerance in Europe. Third, the focus on Muslim homophobia, and on the speech and actions of a nondominant minority, occludes the structural homophobia and heterosexism of France and other

European nations. Existing legal and political inequalities between hetero-
sexuals and queers are underpinned by a twinned secular-republican and
Catholic logic—one that is shared, incidentally, by many Muslims—that
holds the heterosexual couple to be the foundation of the social and natural
order.[22] The displacement of homophobia onto French Muslims obscures
the heterosexual norm that continues to underlie the legal, political, and
moral configuration of modern France.

Lastly, the various displacements and dissimulations sketched above
maintain a certainty about France and Europe as unified, naturally existing
entities, a certainty that in fact is being cast ever more in doubt. In an essay
on European liberals' definition of Europe as a secular space of freedom
and modernity, distinct from the temporalities and values of nonwhite immigrants, Judith Butler writes of the cultural homogeneity required by such
a definition. That homogeneity in turn requires "a set of cultural norms that
are understood as internally self-sufficient and self-standing. These norms are
not in conflict, open to dispute, in contact with other norms. . . . The pre-
sumption is that culture is a uniform and binding groundwork of norms,
and not an open field of contestation" (2008, 5). But European culture is an
open field of contestation, oscillating between the acceptance of homosexuality and the reiteration of the heterosexual norm, between the ideological
commitment to *respect de l'autre* and the practice of intolerance, between the
promise of equality to all and the suspicion of difference. Europeans may
speak of cultural homogeneity and demand that immigrants assimilate into
European norms and values, but what those values are, what Europe stands
for, and who counts as European are not as self-evident as the discourse of
European values and European civilization makes out. The anxious reiteration of European values and of cultural homogeneity signals not an existing
fact but its discursive, legal, and political production. There remains a per-
formative quality to the discourse of European values, and to Europe itself,
that reveals the fundamental instability—indeed, the nonexistence—of a
unified European identity.

Like Butler, Puar writes that gay marriage "has become a steep but necessary insurance premium in Europe, whereby an otherwise ambivalent if
not hostile populace can guarantee that extra bit of security that is bought
by yet another marker in the distance between barbarism and civilization,
one that justifies further targeting of a perversely sexualized and racialized
Muslim population. . . . Gay marriage reform thus indexes the racial and
civilizational disjunctures between Europeans and Muslims" (2007, 20).
Puar continues: "While the conflict is increasingly articulated as one be-

tween queers and Muslims, what is actually at stake is the policing of rigid boundaries of gender difference and kinship forms most amenable to their maintenance" (20). Given the impasses, disavowals, and deferrals I have traced in this chapter, and in this book as a whole, I would go further than Puar: the boundaries between civilization and barbarism that are supposed to map onto Europeans and Muslims are policed so rigidly precisely because they are so tenuous. Using Puar's notion of "that extra bit of security" in a somewhat different way, I would argue that the focus on Muslim homophobia functions as the fail-safe keeping at bay thorny questions about the fragility of the distinction between barbarism and civilization, questions that fundamentally destabilize the ideas of Europe and of Europeans. Indeed, what has interested me throughout this book is how European secularism coalesces despite—or, more precisely, through—its immanent contradictions and tensions. The impasse between the commitment to respect de l'autre and the visceral attachment to moral norms, and the displacement of that impasse onto Muslims, reveals once again both the tenuousness of Europe and how its tensions are deferred and disavowed to consolidate a unified, if contradictory, secular formation.

Epilogue

It is commonplace to hear that secularism offers the best hope for a tolerant world in which we can all live together. As previous chapters have demonstrated, however, secular tolerance is less open to alterity than it imagines itself to be, and in fact it reproduces a series of asymmetries. But what are the alternatives? What are other possible ways of living together justly, respectfully, and noninjuriously? Could these ways of living emerge out of a set of ethics and politics that bypass the epistemological and political terrain of secularity?

The political philosopher William Connolly proposes critical responsiveness (1999) and agonistic respect (2005) in place of liberal tolerance. Where liberal tolerance reinforces the structure of a dominant majority and subordinate minorities, agonistic respect and critical responsiveness decenter it. In addition, and unlike liberal tolerance and the politics of recognition, critical responsiveness "*involves acceptance of some risk to the stability of your own identity*" (2005, 31 [emphasis in original]). Critical responsiveness toward others implies a disruption of the ethical and political truths that one holds to be self-evident. It does not work on an abstract level but rather on a visceral register of subjectivity. Like agonistic respect, critical responsiveness occurs as a process of negotiation, a back-and-forth between competing and contradictory ideas, beliefs, feelings, sensibilities, convictions, and bodily sensations. Such a process is often spurred into action, Connolly contends, by specific political and social movements "that purport to show

how implicit assumptions of naturalness or universality in elements of your own identity often impose otherwise unnecessary injuries upon others" (146). He discusses the example of euthanasia, writing:

> Suppose you habitually assume that death must come when God or nature brings it. A new political movement by those who claim the right to doctor-assisted death when people are in severe pain or terminally ill shocks you to the core. You concur with those critics who accuse the doctors of death of cruelty to the dying and lack of respect for the fundamental design of being. But later, when the shock of the new demand wears away a little, your concern for the suffering of the dying in a world of high-tech medical care opens a window of exploration of other possibilities. . . . You continue to affirm, say, a teleological conception of nature in which the meaning of death is set, but now you acknowledge how this judgment may be more contestable than you had previously appreciated. . . . [Through a process of critical responsiveness w]hat was heretofore nonnegotiable may now gradually become rethinkable. (1999, 146–47)

Moreover, writing against a secular formation in which faith must remain private, outside politics and the public sphere, Connolly argues that an ethos of agonistic respect can, in fact, emerge "between multiple constituencies honoring different final faiths" (2005, 123). He writes:

> In a relation of agonistic respect, partisans may test, challenge, and contest pertinent elements in the fundamentals of others. But each also appreciates the comparative contestability of its own fundaments to others. . . . An ethos of agonistic respect grows out of mutual appreciation for the ubiquity of faith to life and the inability of the contending parties, to date, to demonstrate the truth of one faith over other live candidates. It grows out of the reciprocal appreciation for the element of contestability in these domains. (123)

I find Connolly's framework of critical responsiveness productive for thinking about the possibilities of coalition politics and justice in France, and the potential for rich and robust ways of living together and being in common. At the same time, though Connolly's is by no means a secular-liberal position, he seems to assume that agonistic respect flows from doubts about the basic fundaments of one's faith, perhaps even doubts about the possible existence of one overarching or transcendental truth. I certainly appreciate his evocation of the contestability of all truth claims as the basis for his paradigm of agonistic respect—namely, the element of doubt that he claims exists in faith—but this proposition would be a difficult one to maintain for the many people, including my Muslim French interlocutors, who do not doubt that God's truth exists in the fundaments of Islam. Is it possible, then, for people like those with whom I worked to engage in an ethos of critical responsiveness? Could agonistic respect emerge out of a position of deep conviction as well as one of ultimate doubt?

I want to suggest that it could. Take the example of Nawel, my student at Lycée Jean Nouvel. I once asked her what it meant to be a good Muslim. She replied: "First of all, it's not up to me to say who's a good Muslim and who isn't, because, really, it's not up to me to judge." She listed a few practices such as praying and fasting during Ramadan, and then she said: "If you understand and you practice, that's already a lot. So I don't think you can say who's a good Muslim and who isn't. I can't even say for myself if I'm a good Muslim, but in any case, I try to be." I began to ask another question, but she stopped me, saying: "I'd like to return to something for a second. To say who is a good Muslim and who isn't, and to say whether I am [a good Muslim], that means making a judgment. I think, really, the only person who can judge, in any case, for me, is God." During all our conversations about Islam, ethics, and politics, Nawel usually prefaced her statements about the exigencies of her faith with "For me . . ." This should not be taken to mean that for her there exist no authoritative prescriptions and proscriptions emanating from the will of the Transcendent. It was Nawel, after all, who insisted that the Quran, understood as the word of God, obliged a practicing woman to cover not only her hair but her head and neck as well. Rather, what Nawel invokes is the possibility for agonistic respect to emerge not from doubts about the Transcendent or from the contestability of truth(s), but instead from a position of conviction in a divine truth and a concomitant notion of nonsovereignty on the part of the human subject. It is not that Nawel has doubts about her own faith, or about the existence of a transcendental and universal truth. Rather, it is precisely as a result of her conviction in an omnipotent and all-knowing Transcendent that the nonsovereignty of her own status as a human being is confirmed. Because she is convinced that God exists, and that only God judges, she refuses to judge others.

For Muslim French like Nawel, the possibility of agonistic respect emerges not out of doubt so much as out of epistemological and ontological modesty, out of the nonsovereignty of the Muslim subject. Taking the position of human nonsovereignty one step further, one could also see how the possibility of agonistic respect can arise from the sense that although God may be infallible, and although God's truth exists in the Quran, the human capacity to interpret God's truth, the truth of the world, is and always will be imperfect. Indeed, the notion of human nonsovereignty has always been a fundamental part of the Islamic tradition, and epistemological modesty has defined the basis of the relationship between divine truth and divine justice and its instantiation in human law, politics, and ethics. In the practices of ijtihad and fiqh, the human interpreter's relationship to the truth of the Quran and the Sunna has long been asymptotic (Messick 1996; Hallaq 2009b).

In fact, the preceding chapters describe how Muslim French practice a form of critical responsiveness in their everyday lives. They consistently participate in social justice and prodemocracy projects with others, Muslim and non-Muslim alike, working together on the concerns they share and bracketing those they do not. And, as a consequence of having to negotiate between the competing and contradictory sensibilities and ethical positions that ensue, they constantly put the stability of their own identities at risk. Let me return in closing, then, to the conversation between the women of al-Houda (discussed in chapter 6) about whether or not to join the Feminists for Equality Collective. As we saw, a major sticking point for many of the women was the question of homosexuality and the collective's mission to fight for the emancipation of women by respecting their sexual choices.

After about half an hour of dialogue regarding the new collective, Amal was still hesitant. The following is a transcript of the resulting conversation between Amal, Amira, Suzanne, and Monique.

AMAL: But I'm against homosexuality . . .

SUZANNE: I'm not for homosexuality. But it's not about judging the homosexuality of people. We don't judge. Frankly, the question of homosexuality doesn't concern me.

AMAL: It's not a question of judging. But what are you going to support? Total sexual liberation?

SUZANNE: No, it's not that. It's about the right they have to exist, to be respected like any other human being.

AMAL: But that's normal!

AMIRA: You really think it's as obvious as that?

SUZANNE: It's not obvious at all! There was someone in the north of France who was burned alive [because he was gay]. You understand? Burned alive!

AMAL: But we as women have nothing to do with that. Besides, you don't find that in the banlieues. And it's not our concern.

MONIQUE: But it *is*—we live in a non-Muslim country, and we're maybe confronted more than in a Muslim country with questions like these, on homosexuality. We could choose not to talk about it, but then, when it happens, with you, people close to you. . . . It can happen, perhaps, to our children, because they're growing up in a society where it's normal, so what do you do? You're going to reject your child because he sleeps with another man?

Amal was somewhat subdued after this. The conversation about whether to join the collective continued until it was tabled for another week, and the meeting moved on to other administrative matters.

My views on sexuality and same-sex marriage differed markedly from those of most of my Muslim French interlocutors, and I was rendered uncomfortable and vaguely embarrassed by these kinds of conversations. As an anthropologist, one comes to have an investment in and respect for one's interlocutors, but on questions of sexuality, my values were quite distinct from those of many Muslim friends and acquaintances. I transcribe this segment of our conversation not to underscore the tolerance or intolerance of the women, nor to justify their position. Rather, I do so because I was struck by Suzanne's mention of Sébastien Nouchet, who was doused with gasoline and set on fire in his backyard because, police suspected, of his sexual orientation. Suzanne's comment, which summoned Amal's attention to the very real costs of being queer, reminded me of Connolly's example of the euthanasia debate, which I had read a few years earlier. By invoking the physical and emotional injuries involved, it seemed to me that Suzanne, and to a certain extent Monique, was appealing to Amal on what we might call a visceral register of subjectivity, quite different from the register on which Amal's arguments against joining the collective were taking place. Suzanne and Monique seemed to be conjuring up an affective response in Amal, one that appealed to Amal's compassion and her ethical commitment to caring for others.

In distinguishing between democracy as the political system of a state and democratic sensibility as an ethos, Talal Asad writes that the latter "involves the desire for mutual care, distress at the infliction of pain and indignity, concern for truth more than for immutable subjective rights, the ability to listen and not merely to tell, and the willingness to evaluate behavior without being judgmental toward others" (2012, 56). He contends that although democracy as a political system is fundamentally exclusive, a democratic ethos is fundamentally inclusive. Asad rightly links the exclusivity of the democratic state to the jealous guarding of its sovereignty, though he does not explicitly attribute the inclusivity of a democratic ethos to a very different attitude toward sovereignty. I want to suggest that there might be a link between the two. A notion of human nonsovereignty produces a certain epistemological and existential modesty, which in turn generates an attunement to and care for others without judgment, an attunement vital to a democratic ethos. What is particularly interesting about Nawel and the political and ethical position she invokes is that she is not an activist, unlike Amira. Yet she, too, occupies a subjective orientation to the divine that opens up a set of political and ethical possibilities with regard to working with others, often thought to be foreclosed to deeply and publicly religious people. Although it remains problematic that justice-oriented responses often have to emerge from a place of injury—that it is Sébastien Nouchet's immolation that evokes Amal's care and concern—Suzanne's recourse to an affective register and Nawel's notion of nonsovereignty seem to offer possible alternatives to secular tolerance. They enable not only an ethos but also a practice of critical responsiveness, agonistic respect, and democratic politics, a pluralism not only in theory but in practice.

Introduction

1. *Les territoires perdus de la république* (The lost territories of the republic; 2002), a politically influential collection of essays on the *banlieues* edited by Emmanuel Brenner, describes rampant and unpunished anti-Semitism, physical violence, and sexism among teenagers of immigrant origin.

2. French and American academics and journalists today routinely refer to five or six million Muslims in France, but only after 1989 did these people, called Arabs or Maghrebis in the postcolonial period, come to be called Muslims.

3. French troops under Napoleon crushed Russian and Austrian forces at the Battle of Austerlitz in 1805. Napoleon and the French forces were defeated at the Battle of Waterloo in 1815, ending the First Empire.

4. As Soares and Osella (2009) have argued, the term *revival* remains problematic: it elides the long history of active engagement with the Islamic tradition by ordinary practitioners (see also T. Asad 1986) as well as the history of transnational link-ages that have produced the *umma* as an imagined community, and it reproduces a secular notion of religion's so-called return (as if religiosity somehow went away). Nonetheless, my interlocutors understand their engagement as part of a novel return to the sources of Islam (namely the *Quran* and *Sunna*) in order to produce a future closer to God's will. Also new is ordinary practitioners' familiarity with exegetical arguments once restricted to scholars.

5. I employ the term *second generation* with caution, using it to mark these Muslims' relationship to the Maghreb rather than to France, and to distinguish them from first-generation immigrants rather than from native French. In contrast to public discourse, my use of the term fully recognizes these Muslims are French.

6. Christian Joppke (2009), a respected political scientist, has provided one of the most explicit recent accounts of Islam in Europe as a clash of civilizations. He does so in part by willfully misinterpreting the work of anthropologists of Islam like Saba Mahmood and Lila Abu-Lughod.

7. I rely on Talal Asad's conceptualization of Islam as a discursive tradition (1986)—that is, a historically extended, socially embedded argument about the good, with a shared body of texts (the *Quran* and the *Hadith*) that gives it a particular coherence, even though contestation has been and remains vital to the evolution of the tradition. For Asad and those who draw on his work (D. Scott 1999; Mahmood 2005; Hirschkind 2006), religion is not always simply a truth proposition to which the believer assents. Rather, many ethical traditions—what we nonetheless call *religions*—are authoritative and normative systems of discourses and practices that discipline the individual practitioner, direct her toward a particular *telos*, and regulate her activity in the world.

8. The major exception is Trica Keaton (2006).

9. I focus on Kymlicka because he has thought carefully over the last two decades about the place of minorities in liberal societies.

10. For earlier examinations of what was called "new racism" or "cultural racism," see Balibar 1991a; Gilroy 1991; Stolcke 1995.

11. Though many West Africans are also Muslim, Islam and North Africa have always been tightly related in the French imagination. In the colonial era, Maghrebis were identified as Muslims, and West Africans were simply *les noirs* (blacks). French officials acknowledged that many West Africans were also Muslim, but they were not considered real Muslims in the way that North Africans were (Davidson 2012). These racial-religious configurations persevere.

12. Naomi Davidson (2012), Abdellali Hajjat (2012), and Todd Shepard (2006) examine these historical figurations for a French context; Gil Anidjar (2003) and Tomaz Mastnak (2002) do so for the West more generally.

13. Despite this nexus, secularism and racialization have largely been understood, with two major exceptions (Masuzawa 2005; Anidjar 2007), as analytically and historically unconnected. Scholars focus either on the ethno-racial dimensions of minority and national identity in colonial and postcolonial France (Balibar 1991a; Silverstein 2004; D. Fassin and E. Fassin 2006; Shepard 2006) or on secularism and religious transformation in postrevolutionary France (Boussinesq 1994; Hyman 1998; Baubérot 2000; Benbassa 2001; T. Asad 2006). Even Davidson, who meticulously examines the colonial state's efforts to create an *islam français*, nonetheless contends that "laïcité, or secularism, is not the most useful way to think about the place of Islam and Muslims in metropolitan France" (2012, 206).

14. My argument here parallels Agrama's (2012) that secularism's power lies in the underlying question it continually provokes and obliges us to answer—namely, where to draw the line between religion and politics. Although Agrama writes of secular sovereignty's indeterminacies related to the question of religion and politics,

similar indeterminacies exist in other arenas, hence my attention to the relationship between religion and race and between religion and culture.

15. The notion that French *laïcité* is more neutral than American secularism is patently false: *laïcité* privileges Catholicism and draws on a notion of religion modeled on Christianity. Where others take up secularity's relationship to Christianity (see, for example, Anidjar 2003 and 2009; T. Asad 2003; Keane 2007; Barber 2011), I examine here how that relationship affects non-Christian communities.

16. My fieldwork consisted of interviews with individuals (ordinary practitioners and Muslim French activists, non-Muslim or nonpracticing feminists and antiracist activists, Muslim community leaders, public school teachers, and state officials and bureaucrats) and participant observation in a number of civic and civil associations both large and small (the Young Muslims of France, Muslim Students of France, Union of Islamic Organizations of France, One School for All Collective, and Feminists for Equality Collective), one major state-sponsored Muslim institution (the Institute for the Cultures of Islam in Paris), and one high school.

17. Audra Simpson (2007) has also written about the ethical and political stakes of ethnographic refusal, though in the specific context of indigeneity. Sherry Ortner's eponymous essay (1995) reflects on the epistemological rather than ethical basis of ethnographic refusal.

FIELD NOTES I. "Vive la République Plurielle"

1. Aïd el Kébir, also known as Eid al-Adha or the Feast of the Sacrifice, honors Abraham's willingness to sacrifice his son to God. It falls on the tenth day of Dhu al-Hijjah, the twelfth and final month of the Islamic calendar.

Chapter One. "The Republic Is Mine"

1. *Engagement* means, in this context, civic, social, and political engagement. Both Muslim and non-Muslim civic activists use the term frequently.

2. Despite Sayad's framing, it is important to note that many first-generation immigrants were not politically silent; however, their political activism concerned their countries of origin (Aissaoui 2009).

3. For more on this tension between universal and particular, see J. Scott 1996; Blanchard, Bancel, and Lemaire 2005; Wilder 2005; Dubois 2006; Laborde 2008.

4. The term *Beur* is a play on the word *Arabe* (Arab) using *verlan*, an urban slang in which French words are reversed. The term *Beur* has itself now been *verlan*-ized to become *Rebeu*. Although *Beur* has become shorthand for people of North African descent, I use it only in reference to the specific sociohistorical moment in which it was coined and to those who identify as Beurs.

5. The UOIF, for example, was founded in 1983 by foreign doctoral students close to the Nahda movement. Banned in Tunisia as a political party during the

presidency of Zine el Abidine Ben Ali, the Nahda emerged as a leader in the country's postrevolution parliament.

6. For other accounts of public Muslim associational life, see Cesari 1998; Bouzar 2004.

7. Héla has some cause for concern. In May 2010 near Nantes, one female shopper attacked another who was wearing the niqab, likening her to the demon Belphegor and ripping off her veil (P. Allen 2010). In a second incident in October 2010 in Paris, a female French pensioner first demanded that an Emirati woman remove her niqab and then attacked her, ripping off her veil, scratching her face, and biting her hand (Samuel 2010).

8. The ministry was eliminated in November 2010, and immigration matters again became part of the portfolio of the Ministry of the Interior.

9. "Débat sur l'identité nationale avec la participation de Nadine Morano," YouTube.com (uploaded December 15, 2009). Accessed December 23, 2013. https://www.youtube.com/watch?v=BgPdqhfiTQI.

10. A similar process occurred in the 1990s, when the headscarf was routinely called a chador, a specifically Iranian term for a specifically Iranian practice.

11. Silverstein and Tetreault (2005) provide a short overview of the general marginalization of immigrant-origin citizens and residents. For more on discrimination within the criminal justice system, see Jobard 2005; de Rudder and Vourc'h 2006; Terrio 2009; D. Fassin 2011. For more on educational inequalities, see Keaton 2006; van Zanten 2006.

12. The notion that Islam is a political ideology rather than a true or universal religion has a very long history. See Anidjar 2003; Masuzawa 2005, especially chapter 6.

13. "Aux conditions permettant l'expulsion des personnes [On conditions for the expulsion of persons]," 2004, ACT No. 2004-735, official journal no. 173, page 13418 (Fr.). http://www.legifrance.gouv.fr/affichTexte.do?cidTexte=JORFTEXT000000253398&dateTexte=&categorieLien=id.

14. This antipathy is exemplified in statements like the following 2003 comment by Claude Imbert, editor of the weekly magazine Le Point and a former member of the state-appointed High Council on Integration: "I'm a little bit Islamophobic, and it doesn't bother me to say it. I have the right to say . . . that Islam—and I mean Islam, I'm not just talking about Islamists—carries within it the idiocy of multiple archaisms . . . that, in effect, makes me Islamophobic" (quoted in Collectif contre l'Islamophobie en France 2005, 28). In February 2013 the journalist Robert Ménard declared that Islam "is not a likable religion! I'm sorry, but Mohammed is not a likable prophet. I'm more drawn to Christ, who pleads for love, than to a guy who makes war and who, in the second part of his life, killed a bunch of people. . . . This Islam, it's suffocating us" ("L'islam est-il soluble dans la république?" 2013).

15. A criminal court fined the vacation-home owner €8,400 and gave her a four-month suspended sentence. See Calinon 2007.

16. Banania is a breakfast drink first marketed in 1917. It came in a yellow box with an African infantryman on the front, drinking his Banania and saying "Y a bon Banania," a white French copywriter's idea of how an African says *C'est bon, Banania* (It's good, Banania) (Macey 2001, 29).

17. For an enlightening discussion of the term *Salafi* and its evolving meanings, see Salomon 2011. For more on a range of modern Salafi movements, see Meijer 2009.

18. For more on the development of *fiqh al-aqaliyyaat* (minority *fiqh*), see Bowen 2009, especially chapters 4 and 5; Caeiro 2010. See also Ramadan 1998 and 2004.

19. Ramadan upends Olivier Roy's (1999, 2007) vacuous arguments that Ramadan and like-minded revivalists turn Islam into ethnicized culture by way of multiculturalist politics and that Salafis have no culture at all because they render Islam an acultural abstraction.

20. See chapter 3 for more on the French Council on the Muslim Religion.

21. Ramadan (1998, 1999, and 2004) is particularly invested in the idea of Europe as the site of Islamic renewal.

22. For comprehensive accounts of conservative pietist movements—called Salafism in France—see Mahmood 2005; Hirschkind 2006; Salomon 2009. Very little work in France treats the logic of Salafi engagements with the Islamic tradition in a robust, emic way.

23. One could argue that any recourse to the national as the major axis of belonging will resurrect the exclusionary distinction between citizen and foreigner (see Balibar 1991b).

24. The Natives of the Republic Party (Parti des Indigènes de la République, or PIR), a radical antiracist collective, makes the link between the colonial past and postcolonial present explicit. The PIR is also much more critical of the nation-state form than are many other Muslim French. See Bouteldja and Khiari 2012.

25. France, of course, remains an imperial nation-state, with nonsovereign colonies (called overseas departments and territories) in the Caribbean, Indian Ocean, and South Pacific. For more on the concept of nonsovereign spaces, see Bonilla 2010.

26. See Wright 1991; Rabinow 1995; Stoler 1995; Silverstein 2004. What is more, the colonial project was sustained by exceedingly violent measures that official accounts have sought to forget or make exceptional, even though they were integral to colonial governance (Stora 1998 and 2004; Cole 2005).

27. The notion that Islam and Muslims are a new presence in France, leading to new crises within the otherwise constant tradition of *laïcité*, is certainly dominant in media and political discourse. It is also present in scholarly work as well, both in France (see, for example, Boyer 1998; Kaltenbach and Tribalat 2002) and in the American academy (Kymlicka 1995; Benhabib 2002).

28. Though he specifies the year of publication for the epigraphs by Bloch and de Gaulle, for some reason, Gallo only lists the century for Char's poem "France-des-cavernes."

29. See Ramadan 1998; Roy 1999; Venel 2004; Bowen 2006. This is certainly one element of the Islamic revival, central to the UOIF's mission, for example. My point is that a number of Muslim French go much further than this.

30. This move is similar to that made by Lebanese shi'a activists (Deeb 2006), who do not claim simply that Islam and modernity can coexist but that Islam is modern.

31. Particularly interesting in French politics is Sarkozy's evolution from the multiculturalist who organized the French Council on the Muslim Religion, favored affirmative action (*discrimination positive*), and opposed the 2004 headscarf ban to the proponent of Catholic identitarian *laïcité* (*laïcité positive*) who created the Ministry of Immigration, Integration, and National Identity.

Chapter Two. Indifference, or the Right to Citizenship

1. See, for example, Finkielkraut 1987; Jelen 1997; Boutih 2001.

2. As a number of scholars have demonstrated, as part and parcel of its republican commitments, the French state has nonetheless practiced differentialist policies that target specific ethno-racial populations (see Kastoryano 2002; Lebovics 1992; Schain 1999).

3. The second theme does not apply to Göle's more nuanced analysis of Islam in Europe.

4. Touraine continues: cultural rights "compel the recognition, against the abstract universalism of Enlightenment thinkers and against political democracy, that each person, individually and collectively, can construct the conditions of life and transform social life by combining the general principles of modernization with particular 'identities'" (2005, 271). What remains pertinent is how he imagines Muslim and queer identities as particular, and therefore understands the claim to a universal civic right—the right to celebrate holy days or the right to marry—as a demand to maintain one's otherness.

5. I take up this question in chapter 6.

6. Interestingly, the CMF's position corresponds to the "critical republicanism" advocated by the political philosopher Cécile Laborde (2008), which she distinguishes from both official republicanism and the politics of recognition through its basis in the republican principle of nondomination. Laborde's is a particularly productive engagement with the republican tradition from within.

7. See chapter 4 for more on the collective.

8. The exceptions are Nancy Venel (2004) and Laborde (2008), the latter drawing on Venel's earlier sociology.

9. For scholarly versions of this accusation, see Kaltenbach and Tribalat 2002; Bouzar 2004; Fourest 2005; Taguieff 2005; Roy 2007.

10. Bouzar's conclusions, drawn in an ethnography titled *"Monsieur Islam" n'existe pas* ("Mr. Islam" does not exist; 2004), came as a shock to members of JMF-Nantes,

who had considered Bouzar an ally and with whom she had done substantial field-work for her book. Bouzar now offers her consulting services on French Islam to the government and private businesses.

11. Dominique Schnapper's *La commnunauté des citoyens* (The community of citizens; 1994) explicitly links contemporary French republicanism to Rousseau's political philosophy.

12. For more on republican citizenship, see Nicolet 1982; Rosenvallon 1992; Schnapper 1994; Wilder 2005.

13. I explore the contractual-cultural tension in chapter 5. See also Wilder 2005; Fernando 2009.

14. Hannah Arendt made a similar point, writing: "For many years I considered the only adequate reply to the question, Who are you? to be: A Jew." In using the word Jew, she continued, she was "only acknowledging a political fact," since "one can resist only in terms of the identity that is under attack" (1968, 17–18).

15. In her seminal book *Only Paradoxes to Offer* (1996), Joan Scott identifies a similar dilemma for French feminists in the eighteenth and nineteenth centuries. How feminists have attempted to resolve this dilemma by sexing the abstract universal subject as male and female is explored in Scott's *Parité!* (2005).

16. For a history and analysis of the concept of diversity candidates, see Geisser 1997.

17. The PIR, a less Islamically oriented decolonial organization, also strongly eschews a politics of recognition.

18. Taylor draws on Hegel's master-slave dialectic in *Phenomenology of Spirit*, while Honneth draws on Hegel's earlier Jena writings.

19. Most of my interlocutors cited the *Surat al-Hujurat* (49:13) of the *Quran*, which states: "O men! Behold, We have created you all out of a male and a female, and have made you into nations and tribes, so that you might come to know one another" (from the translation by Muhammad Asad [2008]).

20. Their capacious political imagination answers William Connolly's plea to "*imagine* a world in which a given field of identities might hope to recognize differences without being . . . compelled to define some of them as forms of otherness to be conquered, assimilated, or defiled" (2002, 48 [emphasis in original]).

FIELD NOTES II. Friday Prayers

1. Paris comprises twenty arrondissements, or municipal boroughs, arranged in the form of a clockwise spiral that begins in the middle of the city. The Paris municipal hall (the Mairie de Paris) governs Paris as a whole, but each arrondissement also has its own municipal government.

1. Terms like *revitalization* and *renewal* are official and should be read with scare quotes around them. The notion of revitalization implies that these neighborhoods, full of nonnormative ways of living, were somehow dead or dying.

2. For a detailed analysis of the distribution of social housing and the resulting gentrification of Paris, see Clerval and Fleury 2009.

3. The ICI's governing board is more diverse, and its president and vice president are both of Maghrebi descent, though the governing board seems to have little impact on the day-to-day running of the ICI. When I spoke to Véronique Rieffel, its director until 2013, about the symbolic politics of the ICI's administration, she argued that hiring staff on the basis of ethnic or religious background rather than professional competence would be a form of essentialist racism.

4. To make this claim is not to impugn the sincerity of staff members who seek to include Muslims in the larger *vivre ensemble*, and who see the ICI as a space of openness rather than regulation. My point is not to unmask their intentions as nefarious—they are not—but to critically examine the structural parameters and limits of inclusion itself.

5. The term *culte* is distinct from the French term *religion* and refers to the outward manifestation of spiritual life. John Bowen defines *culte* as "organized religion" (2006, 16), but I would argue that it means more than that. Though Bowen distinguishes *culte* from religion, *culte* constitutes an aspect of the broader concept of religion and therefore depends on a prior notion of religion as comprising interior spirituality (or belief) and outward manifestation (ritual practice). As Vianney Sevaistre, head of the Bureau of Religions, observed in an interview with Bowen, *culte* "is the outward expression of [the relationship of the individual to God]" (quoted in Bowen 2006, 17). The *culte-culture* distinction that is central to French secularity and that I discuss in this chapter refers to a notion of religion beyond its organized form. I therefore translate *culte* as religion. I take up the particular relationship between belief and practice in the next chapter.

6. The 1951 Barangé and Marie laws provided state financial aid to students in the private sector and subsidized the construction and repair of confessional schools. The 1959 Debré law established a contract system: in exchange for the state's paying staff salaries and maintenance costs, private confessional schools would adopt the national curriculum and accept students without regard to their religion.

7. Emile Durkheim (2002) and Jules Ferry (1996) are good examples of the new investment in teaching secular morality. The aforementioned education laws were part of a larger effort to secularize the public and political spheres. In 1884 divorce was relegalized, and religious discrimination in the allocation of cemetery space was outlawed. This meant that cemeteries could no longer designate unholy ground for suicides, freethinkers, and Catholics who had converted to Protestantism.

8. This is not to argue that law and politics in France did not remain underpinned by Catholic concepts. What I aim to show here is how the notion of religion emerged as a discrete entity that was separable from politics, but only through massive state intervention.

9. Clermont-Tonnerre went on to proclaim his confidence that Jews would agree to these terms of citizenship, and that if they did not, they would be expelled from France. In other words, Jews faced what was presented as a choice between dissolution and expulsion.

10. The Assembly of Notables drew on the rabbinic concept of *dina d'malkhuta dina* (the law of the land is the law). However, this concept had long been applied only to laws dealing with monetary issues. The assembly extended it to the domain of personal status, which had previously been regulated solely according to the norms of Talmudic law (Hyman 1998, 41–42).

11. For a more comprehensive account of this transformation in Algeria, see Christelow 1985; Le Pautremat 2003. For a similar account of the modernization of Islamic law in Yemen, see Messick 1996.

12. This process of transformation occurred in stages (Christelow 1985) and strikingly parallels the regulation of Judaism in France. In 1854, for example, the French established the Council of Muslim Jurisprudence, which met annually under the supervision of the governor-general to issue opinions on questions—and only those questions—posed by him. The minister of war then reviewed the council's opinions; without his approval, they had no force. The council had two roles: "to provide the French with well-informed advice about particular legal problems, and to give a seal of legitimacy to reforms introduced by the French" (111). The CFCM currently serves a similar purpose.

13. For more on the transformation of *shari'a*, see Messick 1996; T. Asad 2003; Hallaq 2009a and 2009b; Surkis 2010.

14. The colonial effort to transform and define Islam, and the dual imperatives to separate public and private and to scrutinize that which became private, operated in metropolitan France as well, mostly notably in the construction of the Great Mosque of Paris (see Boyer 1998; Bayoumi 2000; Davidson 2012).

15. For a more comprehensive history of this process, see Terrel 2004.

16. See footnote 12 for more on the Council on Muslim Jurisprudence.

17. To qualify as a delegate, one had to be an adult Muslim holding either French nationality or a residence permit (Kaltenbach and Tribalat 2002).

18. Ironically, these attempts to make Islam French have been undermined by the state's own practices (Fernando 2005). The composition of the CFCM, for example, demonstrates that government officials continue to prefer working with mosques and associations affiliated with the consulates of Morocco, Tunisia, Algeria, and Turkey, rather than unaffiliated or explicitly French associations. Thus, the state continues to manage Islam as a foreign phenomenon even as it tries to institutionalize an *islam de France*.

19. Government officials who supported the construction of the Great Mosque of Paris between the two world wars framed the problem of state financing in the same way (Bayoumi 2000; Davidson 2012).

20. As Naomi Davidson (2012) demonstrates, the French state has attempted to create an *islam de France* since the colonization of Algeria.

21. Again, this is not new; it undergirded the construction and architecture of the Great Mosque of Paris and what Davidson calls the "strangely public privacy" of the mosque (2012, 50).

22. After all, few secular French think to contest the similar demand that women cover their shoulders and arms before entering a Catholic church.

23. Saba Mahmood (2005) has examined the circumscribed temporality in secular conceptions of religious ritual, but conventional notions of religion and ritual also rely on a circumscribed spatiality. Space and time work together to produce the boundedness common to conventional understandings of ritual practice.

24. Gil Anidjar provides a more indepth analysis of the ambiguities pertaining to the term *partager* (2003, 115).

25. Since the census cannot inquire about religious affiliations, the number of Muslims is extrapolated from the number of foreign residents from North Africa, Turkey, and West Africa, most of whom are presumed to be Muslim. Once again, religion, ethno-racial identity, and nationality are collapsed.

26. Anidjar reminds us that the invention of religion as a distinct epistemological category occurs at the same time as the invention of race and ethnicity. He therefore cautions against turning the race-religion relationship into a temporal one (2007, 27–28).

27. As Todd Shepard (2006) painstakingly demonstrates, even though legal categories kept shifting across the ontological terrains of race, religion, and culture in colonial Algeria, the target population of this legal differentiation from white French remained the same. That differentiation continued after decolonization, though once again nomenclature changed.

28. Anidjar contends that "religion . . . is the result of a tradition and of a name, which Christianity gave itself" (2009, 373). He is not making a genealogical argument about the history of a concept but making the case for a more robust examination of Christianity as a continuing political, legal, and institutional formation.

29. On Christianity and colonialism, see Bhabha 1994; Van der Veer 2001; Fessenden 2007. On the Christian genealogies of secular law, see Jakobsen and Pellegrini 2004; Sullivan 2007 and 2009; Fernando 2010. On Europe and/as whiteness, see D. Fassin and E. Fassin 2006; El-Tayeb 2011. Anidjar (2014) considers all these various strands, in addition to that of economy, in his opus on Christianity.

30. There are, of course, plenty of politicians who believe that Islam is inherently violent, misogynistic, and intolerant. But most center Right and center Left politicians and intellectuals attempt to distinguish, at least in public discourse, between Islam and Islamism or Salafism, presented as a distortion of the real religion.

Chapter Four. Reconfiguring Freedom

1. Practicing Sikhs wear the Kakaars, or five Ks: *kesh* (uncut hair), *kanga* (small comb), *kara* (heavy silver bracelet), *kirpan* (small dagger), and *kacha* (long undergarments).

2. Though in other chapters I tend to use the terms *hijab* and *headscarf*, I use the terms *veil* (*voile*) and *to veil* (*voiler*) in this chapter, following the usage of the majority of my Muslim interlocutors and most non-Muslim French commentators.

3. For more on the evolution of legal and political argumentation concerning the headscarf from 1989 to 2004, see Bowen 2006. For a longer history of French attitudes toward the veil, see Selby 2012.

4. In fact, the previous two justifications hinge on the third. The first emphasizes a secularism defined as that which protects sexual liberty and sexual equality; similarly, in the second justification, Islamism is problematic because it ostensibly forces women to submit to religious patriarchy.

5. This modern religious sensibility is best exemplified by Marcel Gauchet (1997) in the French context and William James (1999 [1902]) and Charles Taylor (2002) in the Anglo-American context.

6. They were quoting from the *Surat-al-Baqarah* (2:256): "There shall be no coercion in matters of faith" (from the translation by Muhammad Asad [2008]).

7. They thereby reaffirm a central feature of modern religiosity (James 1999 [1902]; Smith 1962) and of modernist trends within the contemporary Islamic revival (Eickelman and Piscatori 1996; Starrett 1998; Mahmood 2005; Deeb 2006).

8. The "why" question has been comprehensively answered (Gaspard and Khosrokhavar 1995; Göle 2005; Bowen 2006), and just as the headscarf is polysemic, the reasons for putting it on vary. I am interested here in a group of women who veil as part of a broader program of piety; my analysis obviously does not hold for every veil wearer in France.

9. Traditional *'ulama'* have also retained their authoritative status. In studying the scholarly position on veiling, Amira read Ramadan and translations of works by classically trained thinkers like Yusuf Qaradawi and Ali Shariati.

10. Most Muslims who consider veiling a divine prescription point to two *suras* (chapters) of the *Quran*, Sura 24 (*Surat an-Nur*) and Sura 33 (*Surat al-Ahzab*). Sura 24:31 states: "And say to the believing women that they should lower their gaze and guard their modesty; . . . that they should draw their veils over their bosoms and not display their beauty except to their husbands, their fathers . . ." (the *Quran* then lists all those before whom a woman may remain unveiled). Sura 33:59 states: "Oh Prophet! Tell your wives and daughters, and the believing women, that they should cast their outer garments over their persons . . . so that they shall be known and not molested" (from the translation by Muhammad Asad [2008]).

11. Mahmood writes: "The women I worked with did not regard trying to emulate authorized models of behavior as an external social imposition that constrained individual freedom. Rather, they treated socially authorized forms of performance as the potentialities—the ground if you will—through which the self is realized" (2005, 31). As I noted earlier, Muslim French women valorize freedom in a way that Mahmood's Egyptian interlocutors do not, and therefore imagine the relationship between freedom, authority, and the self differently.

12. I am not claiming that headscarves are never worn intentionally to signal one's Islamic identity to others, which has been the predominant analytical frame for interpreting the headscarf both in France and elsewhere in the Muslim world (see, for example, Göle 1996; Moallem 2005; Moore 2007). I do, however, want to examine the headscarf as something more than a sign, particularly since the majority of my informants understand it primarily as an ethical practice. For another critique of the veil as a sign, see T. Asad 2006.

13. Peter Danchin observes that the United Nations' Human Rights Committee "has commented that the terms 'worship, observance, practice and teaching' should not be narrowly construed and that the freedom to manifest religion or belief 'encompasses a broad range of acts'" (2008, 258). I am nevertheless interested in the distinction between religion (or belief) and its manifestation.

14. This division "between belief and practice (the first being inviolable and the second open to limitation) has become part of the orthodoxy of First Amendment case law" in the United States as well (Evans 2001, 74). See also Sullivan 2007.

15. For more on Christian genealogies of the secular, see T. Asad 2003; Anidjar 2006 and 2014; Keane 2007; Barber 2011.

16. The "necessity test" first appears in the European Commission's 1978 *Arrowsmith v. the United Kingdom* decision, when it upheld the arrest of a committed pacifist detained for distributing leaflets to British soldiers. The Commission "held that not all actions which are motivated by religion or belief are covered by the protection in Article 9 [and] . . . the Commission suggested that a very direct link is needed between the belief and the action if the action is to be considered a 'practice' under Article 9" (Evans 2001, 115). In order to appeal for protection under Article 9, applicants must "show that they were required to act in a certain way because of their religion or belief" (115).

17. Like the Stasi Commission report itself, Weil never names or elaborates on these groups.

18. The conception of agency that underpins the discourse of social pressure is highly gendered: although Franco-Maghrebi and Franco-African girls are thought to be particularly susceptible to the outside influences of a social milieu that impinge on their agency and desires, Susan Terrio (2009) has demonstrated how Franco-Maghrebi and Franco-African male juvenile delinquents are increasingly held to be fully responsible for their criminal actions. A parallel infantilization of Muslim-

Maghrebi women, often referred to as *filles* (girls) rather than *femmes* (women), occurs in media, political, and academic discourse. Hence the use of *filles voilées* (veiled girls) and *filles de cité* (girls from the projects) to refer even to adult women.

19. Sandel cites the 1985 case of *Thornton v. Caldor, Inc.*, in which the U.S. Supreme Court struck down a Connecticut law giving all workers the right to one day off each week but guaranteeing only Sabbath observers the right to not work on their Sabbath. The Court found that "other employees who have strong and legitimate, but nonreligious reasons for wanting a weekend day off have no rights under the statute" (quoted in Sandel 1998, 88). As Sandel argues, the Court "confuses the right to perform a duty with the right to make a choice. Sabbath observers, by definition, do not *select* the day of the week they rest; they rest on the day their religion enjoins" (88 [emphasis in the original]).

20. In *Les filles voilées parlent* (Chouder, Latrèche, and Tevanian 2008) and *Des filles comme les autres* (Ordinary girls; A. Levy et al. 2004), young women forced to unveil in schools speak of feeling humiliated, exposed, and physically and psychically violated; such feelings of psychic violence were reiterated in personal conversations during my fieldwork.

21. Bowen implies, perhaps unintentionally, that the multivocality of obligation hinges on different audiences, Muslim or non-Muslim. My point is that the language of choice and obligation is always already combined in Muslim French conceptualizations of the headscarf, rather than dependent on audience.

22. For Rousseau, too, the naturally free subject is the person whose will has been curbed through education so as to decrease the difference between desire and the capacity to fulfill that desire (1993, 153). The free subject learns to desire only what he has the power to obtain.

23. Durkheim's explicit investment in the collectivity distinguishes him from Locke and other liberals.

24. The most influential remain Louis Althusser (1972), Michel Foucault (1978 and 1991), and Judith Butler (1993).

25. Here is Amara on her civics professor: "He dressed like a teacher of the Third Republic and he would walk into the class with his rod, which he put on his desk, just to say, 'watch out for punishment,' the threat stronger than the execution. . . . The Republic, the history of the Republic, the founding principles of the Republic, the values of the Republic—he shoved it down our throats, our noses, our mouths, our ears. I hated this teacher . . . but I tip my hat to him, because he is the one who taught me to love the Republic, the values of the Republic, he's the one who taught me to love democracy" (Amara and Abdi 2006, 31).

26. Even more ironically, the others who insist on the importance of authority are often conservative republican critics of Islam like Alain Finkielkraut (1987 and 2013) and Régis Debray (2004).

FIELD NOTES III. A Tale of Two Manifestos

1. For a different reading of the petition, see Mas 2006.

2. The essays in *Féminismes islamiques* (Islamic feminisms; Ali 2012) elaborate this position.

3. For more on these divisions, see Winter 2008; Kemp 2010. In contrast to Bronwyn Winter, Anna Kemp conceives of feminism more capaciously and takes Muslim French activists seriously as feminists.

Chapter Five. Of Mimicry and Woman

1. I take the term *secular Muslim* (*musulman laïque*) from a number of associations formed in recent years, including the Conseil Français des Musulmans Laïques (the French Council of Secular Muslims) and the Mouvement des Musulmans Laïques de France (the Movement of Secular Muslims of France). Hirsi Ali often refers to herself as an ex- or former Muslim.

2. As Étienne Balibar (1991b) has argued, racism is immanent to nationalism, not a perversion of it.

3. This is so much the case that in a recently published book Caroline Fourest and Fiammetta Venner (2011), who see themselves as staunch defenders of republican secularism, vigorously try to distinguish their positions from those of Marine Le Pen, leader of the National Front.

4. Kristeva moves between national (French) and supranational (European) registers in her book, positing France as the best embodiment of Enlightenment Europe.

5. Kristeva unwittingly reveals here the republican demand for recognition—one that can never be explicitly articulated—that I discuss in chapter 2.

6. This is not to argue that integralists like Jean-Marie Le Pen and his daughter Marine do not find some Muslims capable of becoming French, only that the possibility remains ancillary to their political ideology.

7. One could even argue that Amara herself is a secular Muslim woman like Amara—thus she is easily replaced. Habchi emerged as the new incarnation of the secular Muslim woman after a minor scandal tarnished the real Amara's reputation, but not the reputation of secular Muslim women like Amara. Habchi herself has now been replaced.

8. Quotations are mostly from the English translation.

9. This trope of Muslim woman as victim and Muslim man as aggressor extends beyond France. See, for example, Katherine Ewing's (2008) important work on Germany.

10. These statistics are from a 2005 report by the Ministry for Social Cohesion and Parity (Ministère Délégué à la Cohésion Sociale et à la Parité 2005), a July 2008 monthly report from the National Observatory for Delinquency (Bonvoisin and Rizik 2008), and the website SOS Femmes ("La violence conjugale: Les chiffres [11/14]").

11. The murder occurred in Vilnius, Lithuania. In March 2004 Cantat received a sentence of eight years in prison for manslaughter from a Lithuanian court. Despite Cantat's history of assaulting her, many people in France were quick to defend Trintignant's murder as an unintentional crime of passion. At Cantat's request, he was moved to a French prison in September 2004; he was released in October 2007 for good behavior after having served less than half his sentence. In contrast, Jamel Derrar, Benziane's killer, was sentenced to twenty-five years in prison for murder.

12. This parallels a global discourse. See Saba Mahmood's excellent analysis of "honor killings" (2009, 203–4).

13. The narrative of the republic that emancipates was reiterated by the republican feminist philosopher Elizabeth Badinter, who demanded: "Listen to Ni Putes ni Soumises. They are saying: 'Liberate us from this familial, religious, and cultural stranglehold'" (quoted in Kemp 2009, 23). It was also repeated in the National Assembly's introductory text to the Mariannes exhibit: "At the moment when integration is sometimes put into question, when women's rights—their freedom, their dignity, their physical integrity and even their life [sic] . . . —are threatened, [the women of NPNS] have repeated patiently but fiercely that . . . the republic is their best protection" ("l'Assemblée Nationale" 2003).

14. As Susan Terrio (2009) demonstrates, the criminal justice system confers far more agency, and responsibility, on young men and boys than on girls. Like society at large, judges see nonwhite males as intractably pathological and nonwhite women as more malleable; judges are therefore more lenient with girls than boys and see girls' delinquency as contextually produced. This notion of female potential drove many politicians' and public intellectuals' investment in the Beurettes, the Beurs' female counterparts (Guénif-Souilamas 2000; Raissiguier 2008). As I discuss below, this contemporary gendered distinction is a significant departure from the colonial logic of potential citizenship, which privileged indigenous men as possible citizens.

15. I refer to the title of a collection of essays (Brenner 2002) that describes rampant and unpunished anti-Semitism, physical violence, and sexism among immigrant-origin teenagers in banlieues schools. Cited by President Jacques Chirac in his December 2002 speech calling for a ban on headscarves in public schools, the book had a massive impact on public discourse about insecurity and Islamic communalism in the banlieues.

16. Take, for example, Dominique Strauss-Kahn, the Socialist minister of finance between 1997 and 1999, who oversaw the privatization of France Télécom and other industries. He became the managing director of the International Monetary Fund in 2007 and was predicted to be the next president of France until his arrest on rape charges in May 2011. Christine Lagarde, then minister of finance under Sarkozy, became head of the Fund.

17. These figures are from Wacquant (2009, 244). The socioeconomic devastation in the banlieues was compounded by other post-Fordist changes as well, since most

immigrant laborers were concentrated in precisely those sectors (the automotive, steel, and coal industries) that were hardest hit by economic and industrial restructuring.

18. This occurred, for instance, in episodes of *Mots croisés* (France 2; April 14, 2003); *Ripostes* (France 5; October 19, 2003); and *Revu et corrigé* (France 5; December 19, 2009).

19. For more on how this notion of femininity as sexual availability pervades mainstream republicanism, see J. Scott 2007, especially chapter 5.

20. The glamorization of Marianne began well before the exhibit, and since the 1970s Marianne has been semi-officially incarnated by a number of film stars and supermodels. See Winter 2009 for more on the origins and evolution of the figure of Marianne.

21. The exchange between Joan Scott (2011b) and Claude Habib, Mona Ozouf, Philippe Raynaud, and Irène Théry (Habib et al. 2011) outlines the major disagreements between mainstream republican feminism and American poststructuralist feminism.

22. I examine this relationship in more detail elsewhere (Fernando 2014).

23. Note the parallel reversal in the other direction as well, with Arab and African men becoming the indistinguishable and irredeemable mass against which, and through which, individual Arab-Muslim women make their claims to exceptional citizenship.

Chapter Six. Asymmetries of Tolerance

1. Most Muslim scholars hold that the fetus becomes a living soul after four months of gestation and consider necessary abortion permissible before that point (though they use various definitions of *necessity*). A minority of jurists considers abortion forbidden in any circumstances except when the mother's life is in danger. Nabila's point was that abortion is a complex matter, and there is no blanket rule either permitting or forbidding it. For more on Muslim views of abortion, see Brockopp 2003.

2. I do not have space to discuss this topic here, but another chapter could certainly be dedicated to analyzing the ascription of anti-Semitism to Muslims, for the structure of denial, deferral, and projection I trace in this and the previous chapter applies to that phenomenon, too. For some important work on this issue, see Anidjar 2003 and 2007; Marelli 2006; Badiou and Hazan 2011.

3. "Débat sur l'identité nationale avec la participation de Nadine Morano," YouTube.com (uploaded December 15, 2009). Accessed December 23, 2013. https://www.youtube.com/watch?v=BgPdqhfiTQI. I discuss Morano's statement in more detail in chapter 1.

4. The first part of this chapter treats tolerance and *respect de l'autre* as coextensive; I later explore the nuances dividing the two.

5. Queer Muslims and others would beg to differ, of course. A number of Muslim LGBTQ associations like Al-Fatiha, Imaan, and the Safra Project have emerged worldwide in recent years, and traditionally trained ʿalim like the South African Farid Esack, the American Scott Siraj al-Haqq Kugle, and the Mauritanian Mohamed El-Moctar El-Shinqiti use Quranic exegesis to take a different position on homosexuality than the orthodox one Amira cites. Amanullah De Sondy (2014) explores the diversity of Islamic masculinities in the *Quran* and throughout Islamic history.

6. Younès was introduced in chapter 1.

7. Some quoted directly from the *Quran's Surat al-Hujurat* (49:13): "O men! Behold, We have created you all out of a male and a female, and have made you into nations and tribes, so that you might come to know one another" (from the translation by Muhammad Asad [2008]).

8. Ramadan's use of negative and positive liberty differs from common usage. See, for example, Berlin 1969.

9. As Povinelli notes, neither critical reason nor moral sense are presocial facts; both have historical and social foundations.

10. I use female genital cutting to explicate a liberal discursive structure; I have no interest in discussing the practice itself or in taking a position on it. Nor, obviously, do I equate it to queer sex.

11. The asymmetrical power relations inherent to tolerance are outlined in the *Oxford English Dictionary*, which defines tolerance as "the ability or willingness to tolerate the existence of opinions or behavior that one dislikes or disagrees with." To tolerate means "to allow to exist or to be done or practised without authoritative interference or molestation."

12. As chapter 4 argues, this understanding of social pressure, and concomitant notions of agency, undergirded debates about the 2004 law banning headscarves in public schools. See also T. Asad 2006.

13. Not all Muslim French feel this way. Some of my interlocutors—though not the women of al-Houda—spoke out publicly and demonstrated against the recent legalization of same-sex marriage.

14. Bawer is the author of, among other books, *While Europe Slept: How Radical Islam Is Destroying the West from Within* and *Stealing Jesus: How Fundamentalism Betrays Christianity*.

15. Unsuprisingly, more than 50 percent of *Tirs croisés* (Crossfire; Fourest and Venner 2003), an examination of Christian, Jewish, and Islamic fundamentalisms, concerns Muslim misogyny and homophobia.

16. It is patently untrue that all images and words are allowed in the French public sphere; various laws censor libel, Holocaust denial, pornography, and the Church of Scientology.

17. Civil unions (*pacte civil de solidarité*, or PaCS) were legalized in 1999 and are available to two same-sex or opposite-sex individuals. The PaCS confers fewer rights than marriage, and the Socialist Party, which at the time opposed extending full marriage rights to gays and lesbians, framed the PaCS explicitly as not a marriage.

18. Mamère received more than 4,000 pieces of hate mail as well as death threats, collected and published in *Homophobie France 2004* (Simon 2004). The interior minister temporarily stripped Mamère of his mayoral duties, and mainstream politicians from both parties condemned him.

19. Barjot, born Virginie Merle, is the author of *Confessions of a Trendy Catholic*.

20. Secularist philosophers like Jean-Luc Nancy (2008) and Slavoj Žižek (2006) attribute secular principles to the evolution of Christianity. See also Gauchet 1997.

21. Structural reasoning is also commonly used to explain white Europeans' racism, thought to be caused by socioeconomic frustrations (Stolcke 1995; Blommaert and Verschueren 1998). My point is not that these Europeans are essentially racist, only that structural explanations apply asymmetrically, to white Europeans and not to Muslims.

22. For a more in-depth discussion of this point, see J. Scott 2005; E. Fassin 2008; Robcis 2013.

References

Agrama, Hussein Ali. 2010. "Secularism, Sovereignty, Indeterminacy: Is Egypt a Secular or Religious State?" *Contemporary Studies in Society and History* 52 (3): 495–523.

Agrama, Hussein Ali. 2012. *Questioning Secularism: Islam, Sovereignty, and the Rule of Law in Modern Egypt*. Chicago: University of Chicago Press.

Aissaoui, Rabah. 2009. *Immigration and National Identity: North African Political Movements in Colonial and Postcolonial France*. London: Tauris Academic Studies.

Ali, Zahra, ed. 2012. *Féminismes islamiques*. Paris: La Fabrique.

Allen, Danielle S. 2006. *Talking to Strangers: Anxieties of Citizenship since Brown v. Board of Education*. Chicago: University of Chicago Press.

Allen, Peter. 2010. "Burka Rage as Female Lawyer Rips Veil Off Muslim Woman in French Clothes Shop." *Daily Mail Online*, October 14. Accessed October 22, 2013. http://www.dailymail.co.uk/news/article-1279349/Burka-rage-female-lawyer-rips-veil-Muslim-woman-French-clothes-store.html.

Althusser, Louis. 1972. *Lenin and Philosophy and Other Essays*. Translated by Ben Brewster. New York: Monthly Review.

Amara, Fadela. 2003. *Ni putes ni soumises*. In collaboration with Sylvia Zappi. Paris: La Découverte.

Amara, Fadela, and Mohammed Abdi. 2006. *La racaille de la république*. Paris: Seuil.

Amara, Fadela, with Sylvia Zappi. 2006. *Breaking the Silence: French Women's Voices from the Ghetto*. Translated by Helen Chenut. Berkeley: University of California Press.

Anidjar, Gil. 2003. *The Jew, the Arab: A History of the Enemy*. Stanford, CA: Stanford University Press.

Anidjar, Gil. 2006. "Secularism." *Critical Inquiry* 33 (1): 52–77.

Anidjar, Gil. 2007. *Semites: Race, Religion, Literature.* Stanford, CA: Stanford University Press.

Anidjar, Gil. 2009. "The Idea of an Anthropology of Christianity." *Interventions* 11 (3): 367–93.

Anidjar, Gil. 2014. *Blood: A Critique of Christianity.* New York: Columbia University Press.

Appiah, K. Anthony. 1994. "Identity, Authenticity, Survival: Multicultural Societies and Social Reproduction." In *Multiculturalism: Examining the Politics of Recognition*, edited by Amy Gutmann, 149–63. Princeton, NJ: Princeton University Press.

Arendt, Hannah. 1968. *Men in Dark Times.* San Diego, CA: Harcourt Brace.

Arondekar, Anjali. 2005. "Border/Line Sex: Queer Postcolonialities, or How Race Matters Outside the United States." *Interventions* 7 (2): 236–50.

Asad, Muhammad. 2008. *The Message of the Qur'an: The Full Account of the Revealed Arabic Text Accompanied by Parallel Transliteration*, 6th edition. London: Book Foundation.

Asad, Talal. 1986. *The Idea of an Anthropology of Islam.* Occasional Paper Series. Washington: Georgetown University Center for Contemporary Arab Studies.

Asad, Talal. 1993. *Genealogies of Religion: Discipline and Reasons of Power in Christianity and Islam.* Baltimore, MD: Johns Hopkins University Press.

Asad, Talal. 2003. *Formations of the Secular: Christianity, Islam, Modernity.* Stanford, CA: Stanford University Press.

Asad, Talal. 2006. "Trying to Understand French Secularism." In *Political Theologies: Public Religions in a Post-Secular World*, edited by Hent de Vries and Lawrence Sullivan, 494–526. New York: Fordham University Press.

Asad, Talal. 2012. "Thinking about Religion, Belief, and Politics." In *The Cambridge Companion to Religious Studies*, edited by Robert Orsi, 36–57. New York: Cambridge University Press.

Augé, Marc. 2004. "Entendre les voix de la laïcité." In *La laïcité dévoilée: Quinze années de débat en quarante "Rebonds,"* edited by Jean-Michel Helvig, 212–16. Paris: Libération.

Auslander, Leora. 2000. "Bavarian Crucifixes and French Headscarves." *Cultural Dynamics* 12 (3): 283–309.

Badiou, Alain, and Eric Hazan. 2011. *L'antisémitisme partout: Aujourd'hui en France.* Paris: La Fabrique.

Balibar, Étienne. 1991a. "Is There a 'Neo-Racism'?" In *Race, Nation, Class: Ambiguous Identities*, edited by Étienne Balibar and Immanuel Wallerstein, 17–28. London: Verso.

Balibar, Étienne. 1991b. "Racism and Nationalism." In *Race, Nation, Class: Ambiguous Identities*, edited by Étienne Balibar and Immanuel Wallerstein, 37–67. London: Verso.

Balibar, Étienne. 2002. "Algerie, France: Une ou deux nations?" In *Droit de cité*, 73–87. Paris: L'Aube.

Balibar, Étienne. 2004. *We, the People of Europe?* Princeton, NJ: Princeton University Press.

Balibar, Étienne. 2007. "Uprising in the Banlieues." *Constellations* 14 (1): 47–71.

Bangstad, Sindre. 2011. "Saba Mahmood and Anthropological Feminism after Virtue." *Theory, Culture and Society* 28 (3): 28–54.

Barber, Daniel. 2011. *On Diaspora: Christianity, Religion, and Secularity*. Eugene, OR: Cascade.

Barbier, Christophe. 2004. "Enquête sur les ennemis de la république." *L'Express*, January 26. Accessed December 23, 2013. http://www.lexpress.fr/actualite/politique/enquete-sur-les-ennemis-de-la-republique_491105.html.

Baubérot, Jean. 1997. *La morale laïque contre l'ordre moral*. Paris: Seuil.

Baubérot, Jean. 2000. *Histoire de la laïcité en France*. Paris: Presses Universitaires de France.

Baubérot, Jean, and Micheline Milot. 2011. *Laïcités sans frontières*. Paris: Seuil.

Bawer, Bruce. 2004. "Tolerant Dutch Wrestle with Tolerating Intolerance." *New York Times*, November 14.

Bayoumi, Moustafa. 2000. "Shadows and Light: Colonial Modernity and the Grande Mosquée de Paris." *Yale Journal of Criticism* 13 (2): 267–92.

Béguin, François. 2013. "'Mariage pour tous': Bertinotti estime 'qu'il faut que revienne le temps de l'apaisement.'" *Le Monde*, April 23.

Bellil, Samira. 2003. *Dans l'enfer des tournantes*. Paris: Gallimard.

Benabdessadok, Chérifa. 2004. "Ni putes ni soumises: De la marche à l'université d'automne." *Hommes et Migrations* no. 1245: 64–74.

Benbassa, Esther. 2001. *The Jews of France: A History from Antiquity to the Present*. Translated by M. B. DeBevoise. Princeton, NJ: Princeton University Press.

Benhabib, Seyla. 2002. *The Claims of Culture: Equality and Diversity in the Global Era*. Princeton, NJ: Princeton University Press.

Berlin, Isaiah. 1969. *Four Essays on Liberty*. Oxford: Oxford University Press.

Bernstein, Elizabeth. 2007. "The Sexual Politics of the 'New Abolitionism.'" *Journal of Feminist Cultural Studies* 18 (3): 128–51.

Berthe, Vincent. 2013. "Eric Fassin: 'L'homophobie est sortie du placard.'" *Newsring*, April 26. Accessed October 27, 2013. http://www.newsring.fr/societe/3791-etre-contre-le-mariage-gay-est-ce-etre-homophobe/49565-eric-fassin-lhomophobie-est-sortie-du-placard.

Besson, Eric. 2009. "Organisation du grand débat sur l'identité nationale." Decree No. IMIK0900089C. November 2. http://circulaire.legifrance.gouv.fr/pdf/2009/11/cir_29805.pdf.

Bhabha, Homi K. 1994. *The Location of Culture*. London: Routledge.

Blanchard, Pascal, Nicolas Bancel, and Sandrine Lemaire. 2005. *La fracture colonial: La société française au prisme de l'héritage colonial*. Paris: La Découverte.

Blatt, David. 1997. "Immigrant Politics in a Republican Nation." In *Post-Colonial Cultures in France*, edited by Alec G. Hargreaves and Mark McKinney, 40–55. London: Routledge.

Blommaert, Jan, and Jef Verschueren. 1998. *Debating Diversity: Analysing the Discourse of Tolerance.* London: Routledge.

Bonilla, Yarimar. 2010. "Guadeloupe Is Ours: The Prefigurative Politics of the Mass Strike in the French Antilles." *Interventions* 12 (1): 125–37.

Bonnefoy, Laurent. 2003. "La stigmatisation de l'islam et ses limites dans les discours et pratiques des institutions publiques en France et en Grande-Bretagne après le 11 septembre 2001." Master's thesis. Mémoire de DEA, Cycle Supérieur de Relations Internationales. Paris: Institut d'Etudes Politiques de Paris.

Bonvoisin, Valérie, and Cyril Rizik. 2008. "Plus de 47,500 faits de violences volontaires sur femmes majeures par conjoint ou ex-conjoint ont été enrégistrés par la police et la gendarmerie en 2007, soit 31% de plus qu'en 2004." *Grand Angle (bulletin statistique de l'observatoire nationale de la délinquance)* No. 14 (July). http://www.inhesj .fr/sites/default/files/ga_14.pdf.

Boussinesq, Jean. 1994. *La laïcité française.* Paris: Seuil.

Bouteldja, Houria, and Sadri Khiari, eds. 2012. *Nous sommes les indigènes de la république.* Paris: Editions Amsterdam.

Boutih, Malek. 2001. *La France aux français? Chiche!* Paris: Mille et Une Nuits.

Boutin, Christine. 2013. "Si nous adoptons le mariage homosexuel, nous ne serons plus la patrie des Droits de l'Homme." *Atlantico,* February 3. Accessed May 15, 2013. http://www.atlantico.fr/decryptage/adoptons-mariage-homosexuel-ne -serons-plus-patrie-droits-homme-christine-boutin-626864.html.

Bouzar, Dounia. 2001. *L'islam des banlieues.* Paris: Syros/La Découverte.

Bouzar, Dounia. 2004. *"Monsieur Islam" n'existe pas: Pour une désislamisation des débats.* Paris: Hachette Littératures.

Bouzar, Dounia, and Saida Kada. 2003. *L'une voilée, l'autre pas: Le témoignage de deux musulmanes françaises.* Paris: Albin Michel.

Bowen, John. 2004. "Does French Islam Have Borders? Dilemmas of Domestication in a Global Religious Field." *American Anthropologist* 106 (1): 43–55.

Bowen, John. 2006. *Why the French Don't Like Headscarves: Islam, the State, and Public Space.* Princeton, NJ: Princeton University Press.

Bowen, John. 2009. *Can Islam Be French? Pluralism and Pragmatism in a Secular State.* Princeton, NJ: Princeton University Press.

Boyer, Alain. 1998. *L'islam en France.* Paris: Presses Universitaires de France.

Brenner, Emmanuel, ed. 2002. *Les territoires perdus de la république: Antisémitisme, racisme, et sexisme en milieu scolaire.* Paris: Mille et Une Nuits.

Brockopp, Jonathan E., ed. 2003. *Islamic Ethics of Life: Abortion, War, and Euthanasia.* Columbia: University of South Carolina Press.

Brown, Daniel. 1996. *Rethinking Tradition in Modern Islamic Thought.* Cambridge: Cambridge University Press.

Brown, Wendy. 2008. *Regulating Aversion: Tolerance in the Age of Identity.* Princeton, NJ: Princeton University Press.

Brown, Wendy. 2010. *Walled States, Waning Sovereignty.* New York: Zone.

Brubaker, Rogers. 1992. *Citizenship and Nationhood in France and Germany*. Cambridge, MA: Harvard University Press.

Butler, Judith. 1993. *Bodies That Matter: On the Discursive Limits of "Sex."* New York: Routledge.

Butler, Judith. 2008. "Sexual Politics, Torture, and Secular Time." *British Journal of Sociology* 59 (1): 1–23.

Caeiro, Alexandre. 2010. "Transnational Ulama, European Fatwas, and Islamic Authority: A Case Study of the European Council of Fatwa and Research." In *Producing Islamic Knowledge: Transmission and Dissemination in Western Europe*, edited by Martin van Bruinessen and Stefano Allievi, 121–41. London: I. B. Tauris.

Calinon, Thomas. 2007. "A Epinal, Fanny jugeait le voile 'pas convivial.'" *Libération*, October 3.

Cesari, Jocelyne. 1994. *Être musulman en France: Associations, militants, et mosquées*. Paris: Karthala.

Cesari, Jocelyne. 1998. *Musulmans et républicains: Les jeunes, l'islam et la France*. Paris: Complexe.

Cesari, Jocelyne. 2004. *When Islam and Democracy Meet: Muslims in Europe and in the United States*. New York: Palgrave Macmillan.

Chakrabarty, Dipesh. 2000. *Provincializing Europe: Postcolonial Thought and Historical Difference*. Princeton, NJ: Princeton University Press.

Chombeau, Christiane. 2005. "Le Pen dans le texte . . . des autres." *Le Monde*, December 27.

Chouder, Ismahane, Malika Latrèche, and Pierre Tevanian. 2008. *Les filles voilées parlent*. Paris: La Fabrique.

Christelow, Allan. 1985. *Muslim Law Courts and the French Colonial State in Algeria*. Princeton, NJ: Princeton University Press.

Clément, Pascal. 2004. "Rapport fait au nom de la Commission des Lois Consti-tutionnelles, de la Législature et de l'Administration Générale de la République sur le projet de loi (N° 1378) relatif à l'application du principe de laïcité dans les écoles, collèges et lycées publics." Report No. 1381. Assemblée Nationale.

Clerval, Anne, and Antoine Fleury. 2009. "Politiques urbaines et gentrification: Une analyse critique à partir du cas de Paris." *L'Espace Politique* 8 (2): 1–17.

Clifford, James, and George E. Marcus, eds. 1986. *Writing Culture: The Poetics and Politics of Ethnography*. Berkeley: University of California Press.

Clift, Ben. 2003. "The Changing Political Economy of France: *Dirigisme* under Duress." In *A Ruined Fortress? Neoliberal Hegemony and Transformation in Europe*, edited by Alan W. Cafruny and Magnus Ryner, 173–200. Lanham, MD: Rowman and Littlefield.

Cole, Joshua H. 2005. "Intimate Acts and Unspeakable Relations: Remembering Torture and the War for Algerian Independence." In *Memory, Empire, and Post-colonialism: Legacies of French Colonialism*, edited by Alec G. Hargreaves, 125–41. Lanham, MD: Lexington.

Collectif contre l'Islamophobie en France. 2005. "Rapport d'étape du CCIF sur l'islamophobie en France 2003/2004."

Collectif Féministes pour l'Égalité. 2005. "Inch'Allah l'égalité." Inch'Allah l'égalité 1: 1.

Coller, Ian. 2010. Arab France: Islam and the Making of Modern Europe, 1798–1831. Berkeley: University of California Press.

Commission de Réflexion. 2004. Laïcité et république: Rapport de la Commission de Réflexion sur l'Application du Principe de Laïcité dans la République. Paris: La Documentation Française.

Conklin, Alice L. 1997. A Mission to Civilize: The Republican Idea of Empire in France and West Africa, 1895–1930. Stanford, CA: Stanford University Press.

Connolly, William. 1999. Why I Am Not a Secularist. Minneapolis: University of Minnesota Press.

Connolly, William. 2002. Identity/Difference: Democratic Negotiations of Political Paradox. Minneapolis: University of Minnesota Press.

Connolly, William. 2005. Pluralism. Durham, NC: Duke University Press.

Coq, Guy. 1995. Laïcité et république: Le lien cécessaire. Paris: Félin.

Coroller, Catherine. 2003. "Les sages disent oui à une loi sur le voile." Libération, December 12.

Courtois, Gérard. 2013. "Le 'peuple veto': 50 ans de manifs en France." Le Monde, April 26.

Danchin, Peter G. 2008. "Of Prophets and Proselytes: Freedom of Religion and the Conflict of Rights in International Law." Harvard International Law Journal 49 (2): 249–324.

Davidson, Naomi. 2012. Only Muslim: Embodying Islam in Twentieth-Century France. Ithaca, NY: Cornell University Press.

De Rudder, Véronique, and François Vourc'h. 2006. "Les discriminations racistes dans le monde du travail." In De la question sociale à la question raciale? Representer la société française, edited by Didier Fassin and Eric Fassin, 175–94. Paris: La Découverte.

De Sondy, Amanullah. 2014. The Crisis of Islamic Masculinities. London: Bloomsbury.

Debray, Régis. 2004. Ce que nous voile le voile: La république et le sacré. Paris: Gallimard.

Deeb, Lara. 2006. An Enchanted Modern: Gender and Public Piety in Shi'i Lebanon. Princeton, NJ: Princeton University Press.

Deltombe, Thomas. 2005. L'islam imaginaire: La construction médiatique de l'islamophobie. Paris: La Découverte.

Deram, Bruno. 2012. "Christian Vanneste persiste et signe." La Voix du Nord, February 15.

"Dieu et la république." 2004. 100 Minutes pour Comprendre. France 2, January 19.

Dif, Malika. 1999. Être musulmane aujourd'hui: Statut juridique de la femme musulmane selon l'Islam. Lyon: Tawhid.

Djavann, Chahdortt. 2003. Bas les voiles! Paris: Gallimard.

Djavann, Chahdortt. 2004. "La laïcité, garante de l'unité nationale." *Le Figaro*, January 6.

Djavann, Chahdortt. 2007. *Comment peut-on être français?* Paris: J'ai lu.

Dubois, Laurent. 2006. *A Colony of Citizens: Revolution and Slave Emancipation in the French Caribbean, 1787–1804*. Chapel Hill: University of North Carolina Press.

Duggan, Lisa. 2004. *The Twilight of Equality? Neoliberalism, Cultural Politics, and the Attack on Democracy*. Boston: Beacon.

Durkheim, Emile. 2002. *Moral Education: A Study in the Theory and Application of the Sociology of Education*. Translated by Everett K. Wilson and Herman Schnurer. Mineola, NY: Dover.

Edge, Peter W. 2000. *Law and Religion in Contemporary Society: Communities, Individualism and the State*. Burlington, VT: Aldershot.

Eickelman, Dale, and Jon Anderson. 1997. "Print, Islam, and the Prospects for Civic Pluralism: New Religious Writings and Their Audiences." *Journal of Islamic Studies* 8 (1): 43–62.

Eickelman, Dale, and James Piscatori. 1996. *Muslim Politics*. Princeton, NJ: Princeton University Press.

El-Tayeb, Fatima. 2011. *European Others: Queering Ethnicity in Postnational Europe*. Minneapolis: University of Minnesota Press.

Erlanger, Steve. 2013. "At Once Catholic and Secular, France Debates Gay Marriage." *New York Times*, January 9.

Esber, Nina. 2006. "L'islam peut-il changer?" *Le nouvel observateur*, March 9.

Evans, Carolyn. 2001. *Freedom of Religion under the European Convention on Human Rights*. Oxford: Oxford University Press.

Ewing, Katherine. 2008. *Stolen Honor: Stigmatizing Muslim Men in Berlin*. Stanford, CA: Stanford University Press.

Fadil, Nadia. 2011. "Not/Un-Veiling as an Ethical Practice." *Feminist Review* no. 98: 83–109.

Fanon, Frantz. 2008. *Black Skin, White Masks*. Translated by Richard Philcox. New York: Grove/Atlantic.

Fassin, Didier. 2006. "Nommer, interpréter: Le sens commun de la question raciale." In *De la question sociale à la question raciale? Représenter la société française*, edited by Didier Fassin and Eric Fassin, 19–36. Paris: La Découverte.

Fassin, Didier. 2011. *La force de l'ordre: Une anthropologie de la police des quartiers*. Paris: Seuil.

Fassin, Didier, and Eric Fassin, eds. 2006. *De la question sociale à la question raciale? Représenter la société française*. Paris: La Découverte.

Fassin, Eric. 2006. "Aveugles à la race ou au racisme? Une approche stratégique." In *De la question sociale à la question raciale? Représenter la société française*, edited by Didier Fassin and Eric Fassin, 106–30. Paris: La Découverte.

Fassin, Eric. 2008. *L'inversion de la question homosexuelle*. Paris: Amsterdam.

Fassin, Eric. 2010. "National Identities and Transnational Intimacies: Sexual Democracy and the Politics of Immigration in Europe." *Public Culture* 22 (3): 507–29.

Fassin, Eric. 2013. "L'homophobie est sortie du placard" (interview with Vincent Berthe). *Newsring*. April 26. Accessed May 2, 2013. http://www.newsring.fr/societe /3791-etre-contre-le-mariage-gay-est-ce-etre-homophobe/49565-eric-fassin-lho mophobie-est-sortie-du-placard.

Favell, Adrian. 2001. *Philosophies of Integration: Immigration and the Idea of Citizenship.* London: Palgrave Macmillan.

Feldblum, Miriam. 1999. *Reconstructing Citizenship: The Politics of Nationality Reform and Immigration in Contemporary France.* Albany: State University of New York Press.

Fernando, Mayanthi L. 2005. "The Republic's 'Second Religion': Recognizing Islam in France." *Middle East Report* 35 (2): 12–17.

Fernando, Mayanthi L. 2009. "Exceptional Citizens: Secular Muslim Women and the Politics of Difference in France." *Social Anthropology* 17 (4): 379–92.

Fernando, Mayanthi L. 2010. "Reconfiguring Freedom: Muslim Piety and the Limits of Secular Law and Public Discourse in France." *American Ethnologist* 37 (1): 19–35.

Fernando, Mayanthi L. 2012. "Belief and/in the Law." *Method & Theory in the Study of Religion* 24(1): 71–80.

Fernando, Mayanthi L. 2013. "Save the Muslim Woman, Save the Republic: Ni Putes Ni Soumises and the Ruse of Neo-Liberal Sovereignty." *Modern & Contemporary France*. 21(2): 147–65.

Fernando, Mayanthi L. 2014. "Intimacy Surveilled: Religion, Sex, and Secular Cunning." *Signs: Journal of Women in Culture and Society* 39(3): 685–708.

Ferry, Jules. 1996. *La république des citoyens.* Edited by Odile Rudelle. Paris: Imprimerie Nationale.

Fessenden, Tracy. 2007. *Culture and Redemption: Religion, the Secular, and American Literature.* Princeton, NJ: Princeton University Press.

Finkielkraut, Alain. 1987. *La défaite de la pensée.* Paris: Gallimard.

Finkielkraut, Alain, ed. 2008. *Qu'est ce que la France?* Paris: Folio.

Finkielkraut, Alain. 2013. *L'identité malheureuse.* Paris: Stock.

Fisher, Ian. 2005. "Vatican Document Said to Ban Gay Priests." *New York Times,* November 12.

Foucault, Michel. 1978. *History of Sexuality, Volume 1: An Introduction.* Translated by Robert Hurley. New York: Pantheon.

Foucault, Michel. 1991. "Governmentality." In *The Foucault Effect: Studies in Governmentality,* edited by Graham Burchell, Colin Gordon, and Peter Miller, 87–104. Chicago: University of Chicago Press.

Fourest, Caroline. 2005. *La tentation obscurantiste.* Paris: Grasset.

Fourest, Caroline, Corinne Lepage, and Pierre Cassen. 2006. "Contre un nouvel obscurantisme." *Libération,* April 28.

Fourest, Caroline, and Fiammetta Venner. 2003. *Tirs croisés: La laïcité à l'épreuve des intégrismes juif, chrétien et musulman*. Paris: Callman-Lévy.

Fourest, Caroline, and Fiammetta Venner. 2011. *Marine Le Pen*. Paris: Grasset.

Freud, Sigmund. 1919. "The 'Uncanny.'" *The Standard Edition of the Complete Psychological Works of Sigmund Freud: Volume XVII (1917–1919): An Infantile Neurosis and Other Works*, 217–56. Edited and translated by James Strachey. London: Hogarth Press, 1955.

Gallo, Max. 2006. *Fier d'être français*. Paris: Fayard.

Gaspard, Françoise, and Farhad Khosrokhavar. 1995. *Le foulard et la république*. Paris: Seuil.

Gauchet, Marcel. 1997. *The Disenchantment of the World: A Political History of Religion*. Translated by Oscar Burge. Princeton, NJ: Princeton University Press.

Geisser, Vincent. 1997. *Ethnicité républicaine: Les élites d'origine maghrébine dans le système politique français*. Paris: Presses de Sciences Po.

Geisser, Vincent. 2003. *La nouvelle islamophobie*. Paris: La Découverte.

Gellner, Ernest. 1981. *Muslim Society*. Cambridge: Cambridge University Press.

Gill, Stephen. 2003. "A Neo-Gramscian Approach to European Integration." In *A Ruined Fortress? Neoliberal Hegemony and Transformation in Europe*, edited by Alan W. Cafruny and Magnus Ryner, 47–70. Lanham, MD: Rowman and Littlefield.

Gilroy, Paul. 1991. *There Ain't No Black in the Union Jack: The Cultural Politics of Race and Nation*. Chicago: University of Chicago Press.

Giordan, Henri. 1982. *Démocratie culturelle et droit à la différence*. Paris: Commission des Cultures Régionales et Minoritaires.

Göle, Nilufer. 1996. *The Forbidden Modern: Civilization and Veiling*. Ann Arbor: University of Michigan Press.

Göle, Nilufer. 2005. *Interpénétrations*. Paris: Galaade.

Gresh, Alain. 2013. "La commission Stasi et la loi contre le foulard: Retour sur une manipulation." *Les blogs du Diplo (Le Monde Diplomatique)*. April 15. Accessed December 23, 2013. http://blog.mondediplo.net/2013-04-05-La-commission-Stasi-et-la-loi-contre-le-foulard.

Guénif-Souilamas, Nacira. 2000. *Des "Beurettes" aux descendantes d'immigrants nord-africains*. Paris: Grasset.

Guénif-Souilamas, Nacira, and Eric Macé. 2004. *Les féministes et le garçon arabe*. Paris: L'Aube.

Guiral, Antoine, and Vanessa Schneider. 2003. "Une loi pour se draper dans la défense de la république." *Libération*, November 6.

Habchi, Sihem, and Roland Castro. 2011. *Ni voilée, ni violée: Libérons-nous!* Paris: David Reinharc.

Habib, Claude, Mona Ozouf, Philippe Raynaud, and Irène Théry. 2011. "Féminisme à la française: La parole est à la défense." *Libération*, June 17.

Hage, Ghassan. 2000. *White Nation: Fantasies of White Supremacy in a Multicultural Society*. London: Routledge.

Hajjat, Abdellali. 2012. *Les frontières de "l'identité nationale": L'injonction à l'assimilation en France métropolitaine et coloniale.* Paris: La Découverte.

Hajjat, Abdellali, and Marwan Mohammed. 2013. *Islamophobie: Comment les élites françaises fabriquent le "problème musulman."* Paris: La Découverte.

Halimi, Gisèle. 2003. "Légiférer, pour que gagne le droit." *Le Monde* 2 (November): 66.

Hallaq, Wael B. 2009a. *An Introduction to Islamic Law.* Cambridge: Cambridge University Press.

Hallaq, Wael B. 2009b. *Shari'a: Theory, Practice, Transformations.* Cambridge: Cambridge University Press.

Hamel, Christelle. 2003. " 'Faire tourner les meufs.' Le viol collectif: Discours des médias et des agresseurs." *Gradhiva* 33: 85–92.

Harvey, David. 2005. *The New Imperialism.* Oxford: Oxford University Press.

Harvey, David. 2007. *A Brief History of Neoliberalism.* Oxford: Oxford University Press.

Hazareesingh, Sudhir. 1994. *Political Traditions in Modern France.* Oxford: Oxford University Press.

Hazareesingh, Sudhir. 1998. *From Subject to Citizen: The Second Empire and the Emergence of Modern French Democracy.* Princeton, NJ: Princeton University Press.

Hegel, Georg W. F. 1977. *Phenomenology of Spirit.* Translated by A. V. Miller. Oxford: Oxford University Press.

Hirschkind, Charles. 2006. *The Ethical Soundscape: Cassette Sermons and Islamic Counterpublics.* New York: Columbia University Press.

Hirsi Ali, Ayaan. 2007. *Infidel.* New York: Free Press.

Holmes, Douglas R. 2000. *Integral Europe: Fast-Capitalism, Multiculturalism, Neofascism.* Princeton, NJ: Princeton University Press.

Holt, Thomas C. 1995. "Marking: Race, Race-Making, and the Writing of History (Presidential Address before the American Historical Association, 1994)." *American Historical Review* 100 (1): 1–17.

"Homos: Le marriage et l'adoption interdits!" 2006. *Ripostes.* France 5, January 29.

Honneth, Axel. 1995. *The Stuggle for Recognition: The Moral Grammar of Social Conflicts.* Translated by Joel Anderson. Cambridge, MA: MIT Press.

Hostalier, Françoise. 2003. "Le port du voile, un acte politique redoutable." *Le Figaro,* April 24.

Hunt, Lynn, ed. and trans. 1996. *The French Revolution and Human Rights: A Brief Documentary History.* Boston: Bedford Books.

Huntington, Samuel P. 1993. "The Clash of Civilizations?" *Foreign Affairs* 72(3): 22–49.

Hurd, Elizabeth Shakman. 2008. *The Politics of Secularism in International Relations.* Princeton, NJ: Princeton University Press.

Hurd, Elizabeth Shakman, and Linell Cady, eds. 2010. *Comparative Secularisms in a Global Age.* New York: Palgrave Macmillan.

Hyman, Paula. 1998. *The Jews of Modern France.* Berkeley: University of California Press.

"Islam radical: Que faire?" 2005. *Le forum des Européens.* ARTE, January 22.

Jakobsen, Janet R., and Ann Pellegrini. 2004. *Love the Sin: Sexual Regulation and the Limits of Religious Tolerance*. Boston: Beacon.

Jakobsen, Janet R., and Ann Pellegrini, eds. 2008. *Secularisms*. Durham, NC: Duke University Press.

James, William. 1999 [1902]. *The Varieties of Religious Experience*. New York: Random House.

Jelen, Christian. 1997. *Les casseurs de la république*. Paris: Plon.

Jobard, Fabien. 2005. "Le nouveau mandat policier: Faire la police dans les zones dites 'de non-droit.'" *Criminologie* 38 (2): 103–21.

Joppke, Christian. 2009. *Veil: Mirror of Identity*. Cambridge: Polity.

Kaltenbach, Jeanne-Hélène, and Michèle Tribalat. 2002. *La République et l'islam*. Paris: Gallimard.

Kastoryano, Riva. 2002. *Negotiating Identities: States and Immigrants in France and Germany*. Translated by Barbara Harshav. Princeton, NJ: Princeton University Press.

Keane, Webb. 2007. *Christian Moderns: Freedom and Fetish in the Mission Encounter*. Berkeley: University of California Press.

Keaton, Trica Danielle. 2006. *Muslim Girls and the Other France: Race, Identity Politics, and Social Exclusion*. Bloomington: Indiana University Press.

Kemp, Anna. 2009. "Marianne d'Aujourd'hui?: The Figure of the Beurette in Contemporary French Feminist Discourse." *Modern and Contemporary France* 17 (1): 19–33.

Kemp, Anna. 2010. *Voices and Veils: Feminism and Islam in French Women's Writing and Activism*. Oxford: Legenda.

Khosrokhavar, Farhad. 1997a. *L'islam des jeunes*. Paris: Flammarion.

Khosrokhavar, Farhad. 1997b. "L'universel abstrait, le politique et la construction de l'islamisme comme forme d'alterité." In *Une société fragmentée? Le multiculturalisme en débat*, edited by Michel Wieviorka, 113–51. Paris: La Découverte.

Kintzler, Catherine. 1998. *Tolérance et laïcité*. Paris: Pleins Feux.

Kintzler, Catherine, Pierre-André Taguieff, Bernard Tepe, and Michèle Tribalat. 2004. "Contre tout signe religieux à l'école." In *La laïcité dévoilée: Quinze années de débat en quarante "Rebonds,"* edited by Jean-Michel Helvig, 36–39. Paris: Libération.

Kristeva, Julia. 1993. *Nations without Nationalism*. Translated by Leon S. Roudiez. New York: Columbia University Press.

Kymlicka, Will. 1989. *Liberalism, Community and Culture*. Oxford: Oxford University Press.

Kymlicka, Will. 1995. *Multicultural Citizenship: A Liberal Theory of Minority Rights*. Oxford: Oxford University Press.

"l'Assemblée Nationale, ultime étape de la Marche des femmes des quartiers contre les ghettos et pour l'égalité." 2003. Assemblée Nationale. Accessed December 23, 2013. http://www.assemblee-nationale.fr/evenements/mariannes.asp.

"La journaliste Caroline Fourest 'traquée' par des anti-mariage gay." 2013. France 24, April 14. Accessed October 27, 2013. http://www.france24.com/fr/print/4685442?.

"La violence conjugale: Les chiffres (11/14)." SOS Femmes. Accessed December 23, 2013. http://www.sosfemmes.com/violences/violences_chiffres.htm.

Laborde, Cécile. 2008. Critical Republicanism: The Hijab Controversy and Political Philosophy. Oxford: Oxford University Press.

Lagrange, Hugues. 2010. Le déni des cultures. Paris: Le Seuil.

Laïdi, Zaki. 2004. "Laïcité: Le bon choix de Chirac." In La laïcité dévoilée: Quinze années de débat en quarante "Rebonds," edited by Jean-Michel Helvig, 156–62. Paris: Libération.

Laurence, Jonathan, and Justin Vaisse. 2006. Integrating Islam: Political and Religious Challenges in Contemporary France. Washington: Brookings Institution Press.

Le Cour Grandmaison, Olivier. 2005. Coloniser, exterminer: sur la guerre et l'etat colonial. Paris: Fayard.

Le Pautremat, Pascal. 2003. La politique musulmane de la France au XXè siècle. Paris: Maisonneuve and Larose.

LeBaron, Genevieve, and Adrienne Roberts. 2010. "Toward a Feminist Political Economy of Capitalism and Carcerality." Signs 36 (1): 19–44.

Lebovics, Herman. 1992. True France: The Wars over Cultural Identity, 1900–1945. Chicago: University of Chicago Press.

Lebovics, Herman. 2004. Bringing the Empire back Home: France in the Global Age. Durham, NC: Duke University Press.

Leclerc, Jean-Marc, Christophe Cornevin, and Arnauld Dingreville. 2011. "Guéant: 'Les prières dans la rue doivent cesser.'" Le Figaro, September 14.

Lemonde.fr avec AFP et Reuters. 2011. "Marine Le Pen compare les 'prières de rue' des musulmans à une 'occupation.'" Le Monde, December 13. Accessed October 22, 2013. http://www.lemonde.fr/politique/article/2010/12/11/marine-le-pen-compare -les-prieres-de-rue-des-musulmans-a-une-occupation_1452359_823448.html.

Lepoutre, David. 2001. Coeur de banlieue. Paris: Odile Jacob.

Levy, Alma, Lila Levy, Yves Sintomer, and Véronique Giraud. 2004. Des filles comme les autres: Au-delà du foulard. Paris: La Découverte.

Levy, Laurent. 2010. "La Gauche," les noirs, et les arabes. Paris: La Fabrique.

"L'islam est-il soluble dans la république?" 2013. Hondelatte Dimanche. Numéro 23, February 17.

Locke, John. 1968. Some Thoughts Concerning Education. Edited by James Axtell. Cambridge: Cambridge University Press.

Locke, John. 1975. An Essay Concerning Human Understanding. Edited by Peter H. Niddith. Oxford: Oxford University Press.

Locke, John. 2003. Two Treatises of Government and A Letter Concerning Toleration. Edited by Ian Shapiro. New Haven, CT: Yale University Press.

Long, Marceau, and Patrick Weil. 2004. "La laicité en voie d'adaptation." Libération, January 6.

Lorcin, Patricia M. E. 1999. Imperial Identities: Stereotyping, Prejudice and Race in Colonial Algeria. London: I. B. Tauris.

Macey, David. 2001. *Frantz Fanon: A Biography*. New York: Picador.

Mahmood, Saba. 2005. *Politics of Piety: The Islamic Revival and the Feminist Subject*. Princeton, NJ: Princeton University Press.

Mahmood, Saba. 2009. "Feminism, Democracy, and Empire: Islam and the War on Terror." In *Gendering Religion and Politics: Untangling Modernities*, edited by Hanna Herzog and Ann Braude, 193–215. London: Palgrave Macmillan.

Mamdani, Mahmood. 2005. *Good Muslim, Bad Muslim: America, the Cold War, and the Roots of Terror*. New York: Three Leaves.

Mandel, Ruth. 2008. *Cosmopolitan Anxieties: Turkish Challenges to Citizenship and Belonging*. Durham, NC: Duke University Press.

"Manifeste des libertés: Être de culture musulmane et contre la misogynie, l'homophobie, l'antisémitisme et l'islam politique." 2004. *Libération*, February 16.

Manji, Irshad. 2003. *The Trouble with Islam Today*. New York: St. Martin's Griffin.

Manji, Irshad. 2005. "Why Tolerate the Hate?" *New York Times*, August 9.

Marelli, Joelle. 2006. "Usages et maléfices du thème de l'antisémitisme en France." In *La République mise à nu par son immigration*, edited by Nacira Guénif-Souilamas, 133–59. Paris: La Fabrique.

"Mariage homosexuel: Simple évolution des moeurs ou changement civilisationnel profond?" 2013. *Atlantico*, January 13. Accessed October 22, 2013. http://www .atlantico.fr/decryptage/mariage-homosexuel-simple-evolution-moeurs-ou -changement-civilisationnel-profond-eric-fassin-jean-rene-binet-daoud-boughe zala-603850.html.

Markell, Patchen. 2003. *Bound by Recognition*. Princeton, NJ: Princeton University Press.

Mas, Ruth. 2006. "Compelling the Muslim Subject: Memory as Post-Colonial Violence and the Public Performativity of 'Secular and Cultural Islam.'" *Muslim World* 96 (4): 585–616.

Massad, Joseph. 2002. "Re-Orienting Desire: The Gay International and the Arab World." *Public Culture* 14 (2): 361–86.

Mastnak, Tomaz. 2002. *Crusading Peace: Christendom, the Muslim World, and Western Political Order*. Berkeley: University of California Press.

Masuzawa, Tomoko. 2005. *The Invention of World Religions: Or, How European Universalism Was Preserved in the Language of Pluralism*. Chicago: University of Chicago Press.

Mehta, Uday Singh. 1992. *The Anxiety of Freedom: Imagination and Individuality in Locke's Political Thought*. Ithaca, NY: Cornell University Press.

Meijer, Roel, ed. 2009. *Global Salafism: Islam's New Religious Movement*. New York: Columbia University Press.

Méliane, Loubna. 2003a. "Foulard à l'école: Laïcité en danger?" Interview with "Ripostes." *Chat le Monde.fr*, October 21.

Méliane, Loubna. 2003b. *Vivre libre*. In collaboration with Marie-Thérèse Cuny. Paris: Oh!

Mendus, Susan. 1989. *Toleration and the Limits of Liberalism*. Atlantic Highlands, NJ: Humanities Press International.

Messick, Brinkley. 1996. *The Calligraphic State: Textual Domination and History in a Muslim Society*. Berkeley: University of California Press.

Metcalf, Barbara Daly. 1996. "Introduction: Sacred Words, Sanctioned Practice, New Communities." In *Making Muslim Space in North America and Europe*, edited by Barbara Daly Metcalf, 1–27. Berkeley: University of California Press.

Mill, John Stuart. 1978. *On Liberty*. Edited by Elizabeth Rapaport. Indianapolis, IN: Hackett.

Ministère Délégué à la Cohésion Sociale et à la Parité. 2005. "En France, tous les quatres jours, une femme meurt victime de violences conjugales . . ." November 23. Accessed December 23, 2013. http://www.sosfemmes.com/infos/pdf/dossier -presse_violences-conjugales_20051123%5B1%5D.pdf.

Moallem, Minoo. 2005. *Between Warrior Brother and Veiled Sister: Islamic Fundamentalism and the Politics of Patriarchy in Iran*. Berkeley: University of California Press.

Modood, Tariq. 2005. *Multicultural Politics: Racism, Ethnicity, and Muslims in Britain*. Minneapolis: University of Minnesota Press.

Moore, Kathleen M. 2007. "Visible through the Veil: The Regulation of Islam in American Law." *Sociology of Religion* 68 (3): 237–51.

Mucchielli, Laurent. 2005. *Le scandale des "tournantes": Dérives médiatiques, contre-enquête sociologique*. Paris: La Découverte.

"Musulmans: La parole de modérés." 2006. *Le forum des Européens*. ARTE, March 18.

Nafisi, Azar. 2004. *Reading Lolita in Tehran*. New York: Random House.

Nancy, Jean-Luc. 2008. *Dis-Enclosure: The Deconstruction of Christianity*. Translated by Bettina Bergo, Gabriel Malenfant, and Michael B. Smith. New York: Fordham University Press.

Naseef, Fatima. 1999. *Droits et devoirs de la femme en islam: A la lumière du Coran et de la Sunna*. Lyon: Tawhid.

Nicholson, Peter P. 1985. "Toleration as a Moral Ideal." In *Aspects of Toleration*, edited by John Horton and Susan Mendus, 158–73. London: Methuen.

Nicolet, Claude. 1982. *L'idée républicaine en France (1789–1924)*. Paris: Gallimard.

Noiriel, Gérard. 1988. *Le creuset français: Histoire de l'immigration XIXè-XXè siècle*. Paris: Seuil.

Nord, Philip G. 1998. *The Republican Moment: Struggles for Democracy in Nineteenth-Century France*. Cambridge, MA: Harvard University Press.

Olender, Maurice. 2008. *The Languages of Paradise: Race, Religion, and Philology in the Nineteenth Century*. Translated by Arthur Goldhammer. Cambridge, MA: Harvard University Press.

Ortner, Sherry B. 1995. "Resistance and the Problem of Ethnographic Refusal." *Comparative Studies in Society and History* 37 (1): 173–93.

Portelli, Serge, and Clélia Richard. 2012. *Désirs de familles: Homosexualité et parentalité*. Paris: Les Éditions de l'Atelier.

Poulat, Emile. 2003. *Notre laïcité publique*. Paris: Berg.

Povinelli, Elizabeth A. 2002. *The Cunning of Recognition: Indigenous Alterities and the Making of Australian Multiculturalism*. Durham, NC: Duke University Press.

Puar, Jasbir K. 2007. *Terrorist Assemblages: Homonationalism in Queer Times*. Durham, NC: Duke University Press.

Qureshi, Regula Burckhardt. 1996. "Transcending Space: Recitation and Community among South Asian Muslims in Canada." In *Making Muslim Space in North America and Europe*, edited by Barbara Daly Metcalf, 46–64. Berkeley: University of California Press.

Rabinow, Paul. 1995. *French Modern: Norms and Forms of the Social Environment*. Chicago: University of Chicago Press.

Raissiguier, Catherine. 2008. "Muslim Women in France: Impossible Subjects?" *Dark Matter*, May 2. Accessed October 26, 2013. http://www.darkmatter101.org/site/2008/05/02/muslim-women-in-france-impossible-subjects/.

Ramadan, Tariq. 1998. *Les musulmans dans la laïcité: Responsabilités et droits des musulmans dans les sociétés occidentales*. Lyon: Tawhid.

Ramadan, Tariq. 1999. *Être musulman européen*. Paris: Tawhid.

Ramadan, Tariq. 2004. *Western Muslims and the Future of Islam*. Oxford: Oxford University Press.

Rawls, John. 1971. *A Theory of Justice*. Cambridge, MA: Belknap Press of Harvard University Press.

Renan, Ernest. 1990. "What Is a Nation?" Translated by Martin Thom. In *Nation and Narration*, edited by Homi K. Bhabha, 8–22. London: Routledge.

Rieff, David. 2005. "An Islamic Alienation." *New York Times Magazine*, August 14.

Robb, Graham. 2007. *The Discovery of France*. New York: W. W. Norton.

Robcis, Camille. 2013. *The Law of Kinship: Anthropology, Psychoanalysis, and the Family*. Ithaca, NY: Cornell University Press.

Robert, Philippe, and Marie-Lys Pottier. 2004. "Les préoccupations sécuritaires: Une mutation?" *Revue française de sociologie* 45 (2): 211–41.

Rojtman, Suzy, Maya Surduts, and Josette Trat. 2004. "Contre le racisme et pour les femmes." *Libération*, January 27.

Rosenvallon, Pierre. 1992. *Le sacre du citoyen: Histoire du suffrage universel en France*. Paris: Gallimard.

Rousseau, Jean-Jacques. 1972. *The Government of Poland*. Translated by Willmoore Kendall. Indianapolis, IN: Bobbs-Merrill.

Rousseau, Jean-Jacques. 1988. "Discourse on Political Economy." In *Rousseau's Political Writing*, edited by Alan Ritter, 58–83. Translated by Julia Conaway Bondanella. New York: W. W. Norton.

Rousseau, Jean-Jacques. 1993. *Emile*. Translated by Barbara Foxley. London: J. M. Dent.

Roy, Olivier. 1994. *The Failure of Political Islam*. Translated by Carol Volk. Cambridge, MA: Harvard University Press.

Roy, Olivier. 1999. *Vers un islam européen*. Paris: Esprit.

Roy, Olivier. 2007. *Secularism Confronts Islam*. Translated by George Holoch Jr. New York: Columbia University Press.

Saada, Emmanuelle. 2006. "Un racisme de l'expansion: Les discriminations raciales au regard des situations coloniales." In *De la question sociale à la question raciale? Représenter la société française*, edited by Didier Fassin and Eric Fassin, 55–71. Paris: La Découverte.

Said, Edward W. 1979. *Orientalism*. New York: Vintage Books.

Salomon, Noah. 2009. "The Salafi Critique of Islamism: Doctrine, Difference and the Problem of Islamic Political Action in Contemporary Sudan." In *Global Salafism: Islam's New Religious Movement*, edited by Roel Meijer, 143–68. New York: Columbia University Press.

Salomon, Noah. 2011. "The Ruse of Law: Legal Equality and the Problem of Citizenship in a Multireligious Sudan." In *After Secular Law*, edited by Winnifred Fallers Sullivan, Robert Yelle, and Mateo Taussig-Rubbo, 200–220. Stanford, CA: Stanford University Press.

Samuel, Henry. 2010. "Retired French Schoolteacher in 'Niqab Rage' Case." *Telegraph*, October 14.

Sandel, Michael J. 1998. "Religious Liberty: Freedom of Choice or Freedom of Conscience?" In *Secularism and Its Critics*, edited by Rajeev Bhargava, 73–93. Delhi: Oxford University Press.

Sarkozy, Nicolas. 2002. "Discours du ministre de l'intérieure, de la sécurité intérieure et des libertés locales devant la COMOR." Ministry of the Interior. Report. October 21.

Sarkozy, Nicolas. 2003. Interview by Jean-Pierre Elkabbach. *Europe 1*, April 15.

Sarr, Felwine. 2003. "Le port du voile: Un rapport à sa propre corporalité." *Oumma .com*. December 18. Accessed October 25, 2013. http://oumma.com/Le-port-du -voile-un-rapport-a-sa.

Sayad, Abdelmalek. 2004. *The Suffering of the Immigrant*. Translated by David Macey. Cambridge: Polity.

Schain, Martin. 1999. "Minorities and Immigrant Incorporation in France." In *Multicultural Questions*, edited by Christian Joppke and Steven Lukes, 199–223. Oxford: Oxford University Press.

Schielke, Samuli. 2009. "Being Good in Ramadan: Ambivalence, Fragmentation, and the Moral Self in the Lives of Young Egyptians." *Journal of the Royal Anthropological Institute* 15 (Special Issue): S24–40.

Schnapper, Dominique. 1994. *La communauté des citoyens*. Paris: Gallimard.

Schneider, Peter. 2005. "The New Berlin Wall." *New York Times Magazine*, December 4.

Schneiderman, Daniel. 2004. "Van Gogh, un meurtre en travers de la gorge." *Libération*, November 19.

Sciolino, Elaine. 2005. "Immigrants' Dreams Mix with Fury in a Gray Place Near Paris." *New York Times*, December 12.

Sciolino, Elaine. 2011. *La Seduction: How the French Play the Game of Life*. New York: Times.

Scott, David. 1999. *Refashioning Futures: Criticism after Postcoloniality*. Princeton, NJ: Princeton University Press.

Scott, David. 2006. "The Trouble of Thinking: An Interview with Talal Asad." In *Powers of the Secular Modern: Talal Asad and His Interlocutors*, edited by David Scott and Charles Hirschkind, 243–303. Stanford, CA: Stanford University Press.

Scott, Joan W. 1996. *Only Paradoxes to Offer: French Feminists and the Rights of Man*. Cambridge, MA: Harvard University Press.

Scott, Joan W. 1999. "The Conundrum of Equality." Princeton, NJ: Institute for Advanced Study. Unpublished paper.

Scott, Joan W. 2005. *Parité: Sexual Equality and the Crisis of French Universalism*. Chicago: University of Chicago Press.

Scott, Joan W. 2007. *The Politics of the Veil*. Princeton, NJ: Princeton University Press.

Scott, Joan W. 2011a. *The Fantasy of Feminist History*. Durham, NC: Duke University Press.

Scott, Joan W. 2011b. "'Féminisme à la française.'" *Libération*, June 9.

Selby, Jennifer. 2012. *Questioning French Secularism: Gender Politics and Islam in a Parisian Suburb*. New York: Palgrave Macmillan.

Sellami, Stéphane, and Frédéric Vézard. 2003. "'Ils deviennent enfin des citoyens à part entière' (entretien avec Nicolas Sarkozy)." *Le Parisien*, April 15.

Shepard, Todd. 2006. *The Invention of Decolonization: The Algerian War and the Remaking of France*. Ithaca, NY: Cornell University Press.

Shore, Cris. 2000. *Building Europe: The Cultural Politics of European Integration*. London: Routledge.

Sicard, Mathieu. 2013. "MARIAGE GAY. Barjot et Boutin du 'sang' à la 'guerre civile': Salutaire ou dérapage?" *Le nouvel observateur*, April 14. Accessed October 27, 2013. http://leplus.nouvelobs.com/contribution/817133-mariage-gay-barjot-et-boutin-entre-sang-et-guerre-civile-salutaire-ou-derapage.html.

Silverman, Maxim. 1992. *Deconstructing the Nation: Immigration, Racism and Citizenship in Modern France*. London: Routledge.

Silverstein, Paul. 2004. *Algeria in France: Transpolitics, Race, Nation*. Bloomington: Indiana University Press.

Silverstein, Paul, and Chantal Tetreault. 2005. "Urban Violence in France." *Middle East Report Online*, November. Accessed October 22, 2013. http://www.merip.org/mero/interventions/urban-violence-france.

Simon, Serge. 2004. *Homophobie France 2004*. Lormont, France: Le Bord de l'Eau.

Simpson, Audra. 2007. "On Ethnographic Refusal: Indigeneity, 'Voice' and Colonial Citizenship." *Junctures* 9 (December): 67–80.

Smith, Wilfred Cantwell. 1962. *The Meaning and End of Religion: A New Approach to the Religious Traditions of Mankind*. New York: Macmillan.

Soares, Benjamin, and Filippo Osella. 2009. "Islam, Politics, Anthropology." *Journal of the Royal Anthropological Institute* 15 (Special Issue): S1–23.

Song, Sarah. 2007. *Justice, Gender, and the Politics of Multiculturalism*. Cambridge: Cambridge University Press.

Spivak, Gayatri Chakravorty. 1988. "Can the Subaltern Speak?" In *Marxism and the Interpretation of Culture*, edited by Cary Nelson and Lawrence Grossberg, 271–313. Urbana: University of Illinois Press.

Starrett, Gregory. 1998. *Putting Islam to Work: Education, Politics, and Religious Transformation in Egypt*. Berkeley: University of California Press.

Stolcke, Verena. 1995. "Talking Culture: New Boundaries, New Rhetorics of Exclusion in Europe." *Cultural Anthropology* 36 (1): 1–24.

Stoler, Ann Laura. 1995. *Race and the Education of Desire: Foucault's History of Sexuality and the Colonial Order of Things*. Durham, NC: Duke University Press.

Stora, Benjamin. 1998. *La gangrène et l'oubli: La mémoire de la guerre d'Algérie*. Paris: La Découverte.

Stora, Benjamin. 2004. *Histoire de l'Algérie coloniale (1830–1954)*. Paris: La Découverte.

Sullivan, Winnifred Fallers. 2007. *The Impossibility of Religious Freedom*. Princeton, NJ: Princeton University Press.

Sullivan, Winnifred Fallers. 2009. *Prison Religion: Faith-Based Reform and the Constitution*. Princeton, NJ: Princeton University Press.

Surkis, Judith. 2006. *Sexing the Citizen: Morality and Masculinity in France, 1870–1920*. Ithaca, NY: Cornell University Press.

Surkis, Judith. 2010. "Hymenal Politics: Marriage, Secularism, and French Sovereignty." *Public Culture* 22 (3): 531–56.

Taguieff, Pierre-André. 2005. *La république enlisée: Pluralisme, communautarisme, et citoyenneté*. Paris: Editions des Syrtes.

Taubes, Jacob. 2010. *From Cult to Culture: Fragments toward a Critique of Historical Reason*. Stanford, CA: Stanford University Press.

Taylor, Charles. 1994. "The Politics of Recognition." In *Multiculturalism: Examining the Politics of Recognition*, edited by Amy Gutmann, 25–73. Princeton, NJ: Princeton University Press.

Taylor, Charles. 2002. *Varieties of Religion Today*. Cambridge, MA: Harvard University Press.

Terrel, Hervé. 2004. "L'état et la création du Conseil Français du Culte Musulman (CFCM)." In *L'islam en France*, edited by Yves Charles Zarka, 67–92. Paris: Presses Universitaires de France.

Terrio, Susan. 2009. *Judging Mohammed: Juvenile Delinquency, Immigration, and Exclusion at the Paris Palace of Justice*. Stanford, CA: Stanford University Press.

Tevanian, Pierre. 2007. *La république du mépris: Métamorphoses du racisme dans la France des années Sarkozy*. Paris: La Découverte.

Ticktin, Miriam. 2008. "Sexual Violence as the Language of Border Control: Where French Feminists and Anti-Immigrant Rhetoric Meet." *Signs* 33 (4): 863–89.

Tietze, Nikola. 2002. *Jeunes musulmans de France et d'Allemagne*. Paris: L'Harmattan.

Touraine, Alain. 2000. *Can We Live Together?* Translated by David Macey. Stanford, CA: Stanford University Press.

Touraine, Alain. 2005. *Un nouveau paradigme: Pour comprendre le monde aujourd'hui*. Paris: Fayard.

Trouillot, Michel-Rolph. 2003. *Global Transformations: Anthropology and the Modern World*. New York: Palgrave Macmillan.

"Un 'apéro saucisson et pinard' à Paris contre 'l'islamisation.' " 2010. *L'Express.fr*, June 14. Accessed December 29, 2013. http://www.lexpress.fr/actualite/societe/un -apero-saucisson-et-pinard-a-paris-contre-l-islamisation_899122.html.

Unis Face à l'Islamophobie. 2010. "Stop au Grenelle de l'Islamophobie!" January 27. Unpublished manifesto. Audio reading of manifesto available online at http://www.dailymotion.com/video/xcopb2_stop-au-grenelle-de-l-islamophobie _news.

Van der Veer, Peter. 2001. *Imperial Encounters: Religion and Modernity in India and Britain*. Princeton, NJ: Princeton University Press.

Van Zanten, Agnès. 2006. "Une discrimination banalisée? L'évitement de la mixité sociale et raciale dans les établissements scolaires." In *De la question sociale à la question raciale? Representer la société française*, edited by Didier Fassin and Eric Fassin, 195–210. Paris: La Découverte.

Venel, Nancy. 2004. *Musulmans et citoyens*. Paris: Presses Universitaires de France.

Wacquant, Loïc. 2009. *Punishing the Poor: The Neoliberal Government of Social Insecurity*. Durham, NC: Duke University Press.

Walzer, Michael. 1997. *On Toleration*. New Haven, CT: Yale University Press.

Warner, Michael. 1999. *The Trouble with Normal: Sex, Politics, and the Ethics of Queer Life*. Cambridge, MA: Harvard University Press.

Weale, Albert. 1985. "Toleration, Individual Differences and Respect for Persons." In *Aspects of Toleration*, edited by John Horton and Susan Mendus, 16–35. London: Methuen.

Weber, Eugen. 1976. *Peasants into Frenchmen: The Modernization of Rural France, 1870–1914*. Stanford, CA: Stanford University Press.

Weil, Patrick. 1991. *La France et ses étrangers*. Paris: Calmann-Lévy.

Weil, Patrick. 2004. "Lifting the Veil." *French Politics, Culture and Society* 22 (3): 142–49.

Wieviorka, Michel. 1997. "Culture, société, démocratie." In *Une société fragmentée? Le multiculturalisme en débat*, edited by Michel Wieviorka, 11–60. Paris: La Découverte.

Wikan, Uni. 2002. *Generous Betrayal: Politics of Culture in the New Europe*. Chicago: University of Chicago Press.

Wilder, Gary. 2005. *The French Imperial Nation-State: Negritude and Colonial Humanism between the Two World Wars*. Chicago: University of Chicago Press.

Wilder, Gary. 2007. "Thinking through Race, Confronting Republican Racism." Unpublished paper. Racing the Republic Conference, University of California, Berkeley, September 7–8.

Winter, Bronwyn. 2008. *Hijab and the Republic: Uncovering the French Headscarf Debate*. Syracuse, NY: Syracuse University Press.

Winter, Bronwyn. 2009. "Marianne Goes Multicultural: Ni Putes ni Soumises and the Republicanisation of Ethnic Minority Women in France." *French History and Civilization: Papers from the George Rudé Seminar* 2: 228–40.

Wright, Gwendolyn. 1991. *The Politics of Design in French Colonial Urbanism*. Chicago: University of Chicago Press.

Young, Iris Marion. 2009. "Structural Injustice and the Politics of Difference." In *Contemporary Debates in Political Philosophy*, edited by Thomas Christiano and John Christman, 362–84. Chichester, UK: Wiley-Blackwell.

Younge, Gary. 2004. "Convert or Be Damned." *Guardian*, November 15.

Zemouri, Aziz. 2005. "Faut-il faire taire Tariq Ramadan." *Oumma.com*. January 25. Accessed October 22, 2013. http://oumma.com/Faut-il-faire-taire-Tariq-Ramadan.

Žižek, Slavoj. 2006. "Defenders of the Faith." *New York Times*, March 12.

associational life: and Beur generation, 38–39, 71; history of, 37–38, 71, 82, 85–86; Islamic revivalism and, 5, 13, 34, 37–40, 69, 77–80, 83, 85–86, 90, 145, 150, 159, 221–22, 225, 243. *See also* cultural associations (law of 1901); religious associations (law of 1905)

Association of Muslims of Openness (AMO), 125, 129, 134

authority. *See* religious authority; republican authority

Balibar, Étienne, 14, 16–17, 60, 63–64, 204–5, 280n2

Baubérot, Jean, 8, 31, 110

belief: as basis for religion, 20, 38, 90, 109, 132–33, 138, 140, 164–66; freedom of religion and, 146, 164–66, 170, 278nn13–14, 278n16; practice and, 83, 133, 146, 164, 166, 274n5; privatization of, 90, 109, 138–40

belief/practice: ethical self-cultivation and, 146–47, 149–50, 154–62, 166–67, 172; Muslim French conception of, 83, 146, 166; secular-republican conception of, 164–67

Beur generation, 37–41, 46–47, 50, 59, 70–71, 95, 139, 269n4, 281n14

bled, 35, 49, 58–59, 66

Bouteldja, Houria, 79–80. *See also* Natives of the Republic Party (PIR)

Boutin, Christine, 246–48

Bouzar, Dounia, 85, 90, 152, 175, 179, 273n10

Catholicism, 81, 87, 110–11, 177, 179, 274n7, 275n8; Council of Bishops and, 118, 137; homosexuality and, 79, 243, 246–50, 254, 258; laïcité and, 4, 9, 11,

19, 30, 54, 108, 118, 269n15; national identity and, 37, 43, 72, 86. *See also* Christianity

Chirac, Jacques, 7–8, 281n15

Christianity: colonialism and, 218; Europe and, 191, 249, 254, 256; Islam and, 127, 131, 139, 143, 230; as model for religion, 112, 117, 124, 132–34, 140, 166; secularism and, 23, 75, 110–11, 140–41, 216, 284n20. *See also* Catholicism

citizenship. *See* republican citizenship

"clash of civilizations," 14, 19, 121, 244, 268n6; sexual freedom and, 193, 223, 245

Collective Against Islamophobia in France (CCIF), 42, 46, 53–54, 69

Collective of French Muslims (CMF), 39, 55, 80–82, 86, 90, 92, 97–98, 146, 152, 209, 272n6

communalism (*communautarisme*), 36, 228, 61, 81; accusation of Jewish, 111, 113; accusations of Muslim, 69–70, 72, 85, 87, 89–90, 120, 127, 129–30, 229, 281n15; interpretation of Islamic revival as, 14, 82, 72; as threat to laïcité, 30–31, 147, 203

colonialism: citizenship and, 58, 115, 192–93, 216, 218, 281n14; and decolonization, 9, 276n27; legal variegation during, 10; Muslim alterity and, 7, 18, 36, 61, 189, 268n11, 276n27; and postcolonial continuities, 7, 18, 26, 58–61, 118, 196, 268n11; republicanism and, 60, 188–89, 218; transformation of Islam during, 114–16, 268n13, 275n14

Concordat system, 9, 11, 109–11, 118. *See also* Alsace-Moselle

Connolly, William, 71, 261–62, 265, 273n20

Conseil d'Etat, 7–8, 113, 163

Great Mosque of Paris, 119, 123, 134, 275n14, 276n21, 276n19
Green Party, 84, 145, 183, 231–32, 246

headscarf ban. *See* Law of March 15, 2004
headscarves. *See* veiling
Hegel, Georg W. F., 93–96, 273n18
history: Muslim French sense of, 58, 60–61, 93, 96; scholarly approaches to, 7, 60
homosexuality: Muslim French attitudes toward, 79–80, 223, 227, 231–33, 241–43, 264–65; non-Muslim attitudes toward, 246–48, 253–54, 256–57; theological defense of, 283n5

immigration, 3, 9, 17, 43, 57, 190, 207, 248; as analytic framework, 15, 63–64; first generation and, 2, 33, 35; Ministry of Immigration, Integration, and National Identity and, 9, 43, 272n31; postcolonial history of, 33, 60, 105, 195. *See also* integration; Sayad, Abdelmalek
inequality. *See* discrimination
Institute for the Cultures of Islam (ICI), 101–2, 107–9, 116–17, 119–34, 137–39, 141, 143–44, 274n4. *See also* religion: and culture
integration, 36–37, 73, 111–12, 138, 188, 191, 210, 217, 219, 281n13; as analytic framework, 15, 27, 63, 72; Ministry of Immigration, Integration, and National Identity and, 9, 43, 272n31; Muslim French and, 35, 41, 49–50, 79; republican model of, 72, 80, 90, 191, 210, 218; sex norms of, 210
interpretation (ijtihad), 50, 55, 155, 162, 167, 264

Islam: as authoritative tradition, 40, 56, 132, 268n7; in Christian theology, 139–40; evolution in Europe of, 51, 271n18, 271n21; and personal status in Algeria, 115, 275n10; secularization of, 21, 108–9, 114–16, 119, 125–26, 133, 135, 138, 143–44, 275nn11–12, 275n14; as universal, 51, 58, 83, 86, 230, 263. *See also* French Islamic revival; *islam de France*; Muslim French
islam de France, 118–19, 121–22, 133, 135, 143, 275n18, 276n20
Islamophobia, 14, 18, 24, 42, 45–46, 69, 240. *See also* Muslims: as Other

Jewish emancipation, 111–14, 119, 122; and Grand Sanhedrin, 113, 118

Kristeva, Julia, 189–91, 217
Kymlicka, Will, 16, 268n9

laïcité, 5–6, 10–11, 43, 120, 135, 163–64, 175, 190, 209, 269n15, 271n27; Alsace-Moselle and, 9, 11, 21, 30; defense of, 7–9, 102, 203–4, 209–11; definition of, 19–20, 31; history of, 109–16; Islam and, 20, 30, 120–21, 182, 203; Muslim appeals for equality via, 11, 72, 81, 117–18; national identity and, 20, 141; non-application in Algeria of, 11; public debate about, 7, 29–31, 88; recognition of religion via, 117–19; as regulation of religion, 11, 109–16, 121, 124, 126, 133, 143–44, 179. *See also* 1905 law of separation; secularism
Law of March 15, 2004, 1, 3, 24, 45, 87, 163, 174, 232; contestation of, 53, 81, 145, 183, 229; justifications for, 8, 147,

of, 46–47, 92, 273n17; of religion, 110–14; politics of, 47, 55, 65–67, 71, 75, 80, 90–91, 95–96, 121, 138, 272n6; subjectivation via, 47–48; 93–94. *See also* Hegel, Georg W. F.; religious representatives

regionalism. *See* decentralization

religion: as belief, 20, 38, 90, 109, 132–33, 138, 140, 164–66; and culture, 15, 22, 38, 107, 109, 116, 120–26, 129, 132, 135, 164, 269n14; in liberalism, 15–16; regulation of, 11, 20–21, 108–17, 121, 125–26, 133, 135, 143–44, 275nn11–12, 275n14; secular conception of, 17, 109, 112, 124–25, 132–34, 140, 142, 148, 167. *See also* race/religion

religious associations (law of 1905), 110, 122, 125, 129, 134, 137

religious authority: Muslim French conception of, 151–57, 159–62, 167; secular-republican conception of, 117, 133, 135, 147–49, 167, 172, 175, 179–80; secular transformation of, 111–15, 119, 133, 135, 139, 275n12, 275n14

religious freedom, 23, 111, 165, 169, 278n14, 278n16; as freedom of choice, 169–71; *forum internum* and, 165–66; *laïcité* and, 20, 109–10, 117, 120, 126; headscarf ban and, 145, 163–64, 170, 172, 229; secular conception of, 147, 164, 169–70, 172; street prayer and, 121

religious representatives, 108, 113, 117–19, 133, 136–37. *See also* French Council on the Muslim Religion (CFCM)

Renan, Ernest, 140, 188–89

representational burden, 48, 57, 67, 222–23, 250–52, 254–56

republican authority, 61, 147–48, 174, 176–80, 204, 279n26; neoliberal sovereignty and, 199, 202–7

republican citizenship, 11, 37, 57, 61, 64, 71–72, 74, 82, 85, 111, 175, 177–78, 240; colonialism and, 58, 115, 192–93, 216, 281n14; as cultural and contractual, 36, 86, 188–92; exclusion of Muslims from, 43, 45, 65–67, 69, 76, 85; Jews and, 111–13, 275n9; Muslim French engagement with, 13, 17, 39, 41, 52–53, 58–59, 62, 65, 70–71, 75–76, 78–79, 81–85, 90–91; nationality law and, 190; sex/gender and, 210–14, 282n23

republicanism: abstract universalism and, 36, 51, 62, 70, 85–86, 89, 179, 188–89, 191–93, 214, 217; feminism and, 26; general will in, 72, 85–87, 89, 91; Islam and, 45, 57, 192, 244–45; sexual difference and, 214–16; tensions and contradictions in, 6, 37, 62, 73, 89–90, 188, 193, 217. *See also* republican authority; republican citizenship

republican model of integration, 72, 80, 90, 191, 210. *See also* republican citizenship

respect de l'autre, 224–25; limits and impasses of, 231–37, 259; Muslim French discourse of, 229–32, 237, 241–43; state power and, 239–40, 243–44, 257

right to difference, 37, 70–74, 79, 82, 190

right to indifference, 25, 27, 70–71, 79–80, 82, 91

Rousseau, Jean-Jacques, 85, 176, 180, 273n11, 279n22

Rue Myrha mosque, 101–3, 107, 116, 129, 134, 141

Salafi Islam, 13, 50, 56–57, 271n17, 271n19, 271n22, 276n30

same-sex adoption, 246–48

Union of Islamic Organizations of France (UOIF), 4, 29, 34–35, 37–38, 50–52, 54–55, 57, 65, 81, 90–95, 119, 121, 135, 137, 153, 157–59, 175, 269n5, 272n29

Union of Young Muslims (UJM), 38–40, 55, 82, 85, 90

United Against Islamophobia (UFI), 69–70, 76, 86, 90, 92

urban renewal, 106–7, 274nn1–2

veiling: forced unveiling and, 171, 279; laws against, 5, 7, 45, 87, 186; Muslim French conception of, 146–47, 149–53, 155, 157–58, 160, 167–68, 170–73, 230; by Muslim women, 41, 50, 149–52, 155–56; public debate about, 44, 88–89, 147, 162, 193, 209; secular-republican criticism of, 142, 147–48, 168–70, 181, 183. *See also* 1989 headscarves affair; Law of March 15, 2004

virginity tests, 56–57

visibility/invisibility, 6, 36, 62–63, 70, 73–74, 79, 210, 252; Beur generation and, 38, 40; mosques and, 124

vivre ensemble, 29, 107–9, 127, 129–31, 138, 274n4; Muslim French practice of, 97–98

Weil, Patrick, 169–70, 172, 278n17

welcome contract (*contrat d'acceuil*), 43, 48, 66

Walzer, Michael, 234–39, 242, 244

Wieviorka, Michel, 72–74, 76

Wikan, Uni, 254–56

Young Muslims of France (JMF), 34, 38, 40, 50, 52, 55, 77–80, 82–86, 272n10, 269n16

CPSIA information can be obtained
at www.ICGtesting.com
Printed in the USA
FSHW020159101121